CAMBRIDGE
ILLUSTRATED
ATLAS

WARFARE

The Middle Ages
768–1487

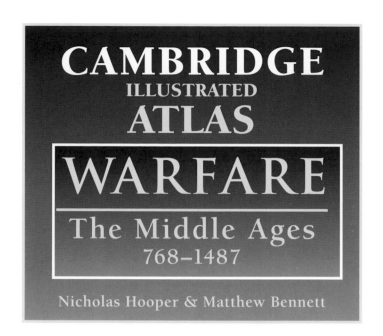

CAMBRIDGE
ILLUSTRATED
ATLAS

WARFARE

The Middle Ages
768–1487

Nicholas Hooper & Matthew Bennett

CAMBRIDGE
UNIVERSITY PRESS

Published by the Press Syndicate of the University of Cambridge
The Pitt Building, Trumpington Street, Cambridge CB2 1RP
40 West 20th Street, New York, NY 10011-4211, USA
10 Stamford Road, Oakleigh, Melbourne 3166, Australia

First published 1996
This book was designed and produced by
CALMANN & KING LTD
71 Great Russell Street
London WC1B 3BN

Project editor: Ailsa Heritage
Picture research: Anne-Marie Ehrlich
Layout design: Alastair Wardle
Cartography by European Map Graphics Ltd, Finchampstead, Berkshire
Battle plans by Advanced Illustration, Congleton, Cheshire

Printed in Great Britain at the University Press, Cambridge

A catalogue record for this book is available from the British Library

Library of Congress cataloguing-in-publication data
The Cambridge illustrated atlas of warfare : the Middle Ages/
Nicholas Hooper & Matthew Bennett.
p. cm.
ISBN 0-521-44049-1 (hardcover)
1. Military history, Medieval—Maps.
2. Military art and science-History—Medieval, 500-1500—Maps.
3. Middle Ages—Maps.
4. War and society—Maps.
I. Bennett, Matthew, 1954-
II. Title.
G1034.H6 1995 <G&M>
355'. 009' 02—dc20
95-36851
CIP
MAP

ISBN 0 521 44049 1 hardback

I wish to thank my parents for all their support through my education, but above all my gratitude goes
to my wife Jennie and our daughters Kate and Elizabeth for their love and uncomplaining understanding during all
the hours I spent, especially during school holidays, at the word-processor and not being a good husband and father.

NAH

I would also like to record my thanks to my wife, Gerda, and sons Thomas and Henry for putting up with the
endless hours I spent in this atlas's creation. I dedicate this book to them, and to my parents also.

MB

CONTENTS

INTRODUCTION

This book is based on three premises. First, that warfare is a worthwhile subject of study, since it has been one of the primary focuses of human endeavour. All aspects of human society have been shaped for better or worse by warfare. All states owe their shape and a good deal of their political and economic structure to war; to give a specific example from the Middle Ages, the English parliament owed much of its early development to the monarchy's need to pay for war in the fourteenth century. Second, that the great deal of valuable academic research on the warfare of the Middle Ages in the past forty years has been slow to filter through to the public. One of our main objectives is to make that work available to a wider audience. Third, history is about time and space, but historians are often remiss in ensuring their works are provided with adequate and informative maps. Although there are honourable exceptions, these observations are especially true of medieval warfare. So, having seen a gap in the market, the authors set out to fill it with the aim of combining academic respectability with accessibility to general readers. We hope that this atlas will function both as an attractive, well-illustrated book and a valuable work of reference.

The most influential modern writer on war, Karl von Clausewitz (1780-1831), described war as 'simply the continuation of policy with the admixture of other means'. He also advanced the theory of two types of war, 'either to totally destroy the enemy…or else to prescribe peace terms to him'. The main tool of his strategy was the decisive engagement. Although he recognized that 'campaigns whose outcomes have been determined by a single battle have been fairly common only in recent times, and those cases in which they have settled an entire war are very rare exceptions', he stated, 'we are not interested in generals who win victories without bloodshed' (from Michael Howard, *Clausewitz*, 1983). His outlook was very influential on successive generations of historians, who looked at battles as representative of the warfare of a given period. In English this trend is represented by Sir Charles Oman in his *History of the Art of War in the Middle Ages*, published in 1924. This book is a readable introduction to the subject (and is still in print at the time of writing), but it has many flaws and has simply been overtaken by modern research.

The most influential work on the conduct of war during the Middle Ages was by the late Roman author Flavius Vegetius Renatus. Vegetius's *De Rei Militari* was widely read, and one of his dictums was to avoid battle: 'Every plan therefore is to be considered, every expedient tried and every method taken before matters are brought to this last extremity' (cited from John Gillingham, *Richard Coeur de Lion*, 1994). Since medieval commanders frequently followed this advice, 'great battles' military history is in danger of ignoring the daily reality of campaigning in the Middle Ages. There were occasions when campaigns did end in battles which, if not decisive in themselves, had a major political impact. There were occasions, too, when medieval commanders did adopt battle-seeking strategies, often in civil wars or large-scale 'one-off' expeditions, as in 1066 at the battle of Hastings. But most of the time they did not, for battle was risky. The control of territory could often be achieved by a combination of ravaging and sieges. Broadly speaking, this book sets out to analyze strategy, defined as all matters relating to generalship. Our building blocks will not be battles, for they were relatively rare in this period. In fact, the exact course of battles can rarely be established, and frequently their very site is unknown or is disputable.

Moreover, Clausewitz's dictum on the relationship between war and policy does not fully hold true for the Middle Ages. Many campaigns, of course, do fit his bill, and were designed to put a policy into effect. Karl Leyser reminded us, though, that 'war…was a primary and perennial preoccupation of Carolingian and post-Carolingian society from the eighth to the early eleventh century…[and] in the early Middle Ages, one is tempted to say, policy was a continuation of war by other means – like gift-giving, bribery, and suborning loyalties – rather than his [Clausewitz's] way round' ('Early Medieval Warfare', *The Battle of Maldon: Fiction and Fact*, ed. J. Cooper, 1993). On frontiers, low-intensity warfare was almost continuous; feuds were endemic, and fundamental to much medieval warfare was a quest for wealth and resources. Successful war also increased a man's standing, and this was not simply true of early medieval rulers – the first three English kings to be deposed (Edward II, Richard II, and Henry VI) exhibited no interest in warfare, and the immediate predecessor of each had a great military reputation.

We have been extremely selective in deciding the scope of this book, and have restricted the subject material to western Europe and Latin Christendom. The reason for this narrow geographical scope is threefold. First, we did not wish to write about areas in which we do not have some degree of expertise as historians, or possess relevant language skills. The Middle Ages is a concept of western European history, not Islamic or Byzantine history, and to include these regions would have necessitated too superficial a survey. Consequently, the Byzantine and Muslim worlds are discussed in this work only when western Europeans came into contact with them. Secondly, the reader will not find every single skirmish or low-intensity war analyzed here. Selection was based on availability of source material, and a (no doubt subjective) judgement as to how much analysis of warfare in a particular time and place could contribute to our overall analysis. Finally, there is a rationale behind the chronological period we have chosen. There was much warfare before c.750, but a great deal of it was low-intensity and poorly recorded, and a serious problem was where to draw the dividing line earlier. The end of the Western Roman Empire in the fifth century seemed particularly arbitrary. In England, little detailed analysis of warfare before the mid-ninth century is feasible, and in Germany none before the late eighth century. Consequently, starting with the process of reassembling the Frankish dominion in the eighth century seemed a logical choice, especially in view of its significance for the very concept of Europe. The closing date of the late fifteenth century was chosen because it is conventionally viewed as the end of the Middle Ages. In the final chapter, considerable reservation is expressed as to the reality of a sixteenth-century military revolution.

There is a great deal in this book on crusading warfare. This is largely because the sources are so rich on this subject, but also it enables the reader to see how the military structures of western Europe adapted and developed in the many different environments of crusading. Indeed, it was the impetus of the crusade which produced, for the first time since the end of the Roman Empire, a universal taxation system in Christendom, soon to be exploited by national rulers. It used to be thought that there was significant influence in narrower areas, such as the design of castles. While this view has been seriously modified, there can be no doubt that contact with the more technologically advanced civilizations of Islam and the Byzantine Empire had a broader influence, especially in the area of medicine. It was from the West, though, that technological innovation began to have an impact in war. This was notably so in the area of naval architecture, for although the Mediterranean did not give up the galley for centuries, bigger and bigger warships gave the Europeans a significant advantage, strategically, in battle and in sieges. This was matched by the development of gunpowder weapons from the mid-fourteenth century onwards, which although slow at first, soon began to set western civilization apart from more ancient societies further east which proved slower to adopt such innovations.

In modern journalistic usage, 'medieval' is frequently employed as an insult, having acquired pejorative qualities in much the same way as has the word 'peasant'. Medieval is simply an adjective meaning 'of the Middle Ages', a period in western European history which had no unity. The Middle Ages is a handy label for the centuries between the end of the Roman Empire in the West, conventionally 476 (in the East it continued in one form or another until the fall of Constantinople to the Turks in 1453), until the end of the fifteenth century (in English history the change of dynasty in 1485 is for some questionable reason said to represent a new age). Historical change rarely falls neatly into brackets such as these, and many of the intellectual and economic trends which characterized early medieval Europe were present before 476. In the same way there was no late fifteenth-century turning point, although 'Renaissance' men believed that there was, and that they were returning to the values of Rome. Since they had access to the printing press, their prejudices have been influential. In fact, what we hope will emerge from this book is that the timeless 'essentials' of warfare were not neglected between 750-1500 AD. The romanticized idea of knights rushing to battle is so simplified as to be ludicrous. Medieval commanders were as concerned with logistics and fortress warfare as those of any other age. True there were heroes, whose image and activities could play a vital role in motivating their troops. But the fame acquired by such 'front-line' generals as Rommel in this century show that such personalities still have a role in modern warfare.

Two books deserve especial mention in relation to this project. The first is David Chandler's *Atlas of Military Strategy* (1980) which suggested the format, and the second, *The Atlas of the Crusades* (ed. Jonathan Riley-Smith, 1991), and by extension The Times series in general. The creation of maps for this atlas has been a complex project, especially in relation to those areas outside the British Isles. Many of the areas mapped (especially the Holy Land) have two or three names for one site, owing to the ebb-and-flow of the rulers of those regions and their different languages. In some cases, it is still politically offensive to use one name in preference to another. We suspect that it has been impossible to avoid all these pitfalls, and that some errors or infelicities may remain. For these we take responsibility.

The authors have referred to the works of many recent medieval historians, which are listed at the back of this book, taking inspiration from their research and writings. We both wish to acknowledge a particular debt of gratitude and friendship to two of our former teachers in the University of London, the late Professor R. Allen Brown and Professor John Gillingham, with whom we have spent many pleasurable hours in the classroom and pub discussing medieval warfare. Professor Gillingham gave us great help in launching this project, which has become one of the atlases of warfare published by Cambridge University Press. He has also read the text and made invaluable suggestions. In addition, we owe especial thanks to Ailsa Heritage, the atlas editor, for bringing this project to fruition. Without her expertise and dedication it could not have been achieved. We also wish to thank our editor at Calmann and King, Mary Scott. Finally, there are our friends in the study of medieval warfare, who have helped us with this volume wittingly or unwittingly: Roy Boss, Jim Bradbury, Christopher Duffy, Paddy Griffith, Gary Sheffield, Anne Curry, Ian Roy, and David Morris.

I

THE CRUCIBLE OF EUROPE

The linguistic and ethnic map of Europe took shape during the great migrations of the fifth to the tenth centuries. The eighth and ninth centuries were of particular importance. The Carolingian Charles Martel reunited northern Gaul, and after defeating Arab raiders from Spain at the battle of Poitiers (732-3), he began a series of campaigns to bring southern Gaul under Frankish rule again. The Arabs were not driven out of Provence until the 750s, while the conquest of Aquitaine was completed only by his grandson, Charles the Great (Charlemagne), in the late 760s. Charlemagne completed his ancestors' expansion, and changed the political face of Europe. In three decades of energetic campaigning he conquered Saxony and crushed the Avar kingdom in Hungary; he subjected Bavaria, several Slav tribes, and conquered Lombardy; and began the reconquest of Spain from the Muslims. His empire was a military creation: it may not have lasted long, but it was important for the future Europe. The balance of power shifted from the Mediterranean to north of the Alps, and Charles left the powerful legacy of a Christian empire.

Civil wars between Charlemagne's grandsons led to the partition of the empire in 843 (treaty of Verdun); their continuing rivalry, and the Frankish practice of dividing kingdoms between heirs, resulted in its dissolution. In England, also, there was fighting between kingdoms and, in Northumbria and Mercia at least, dynastic feuds. The Vikings, who had been raiding the North Sea and Irish Sea coasts since the 790s, took advantage of such dissensions to raid deep inland. They hastened the collapse of West Frankia, although Charles the Bald had considerable success in the 860s, and ravaged Middle Frankia in the 880s. Tenth-century West Frankia fragmented into dozens of political units. A number of strong regional principalities emerged, such as Flanders, Anjou, and Normandy. In England, Vikings conquered three of the four ninth-century kingdoms, but Alfred of Wessex preserved his kingdom's independence, and in the first half of the tenth century his descendants conquered the Viking kingdoms to create the first united kingdom of England. In the ninth century, Muslim raiders attacked the coasts of Provence and Italy, and conquered Sicily and the Balearic Islands. The Magyars (Hungarians) appeared in the plains north of the Danube at the end of the century, and until the 930s launched devastating raids westwards. The East Frankish king, Henry I, reshaped his army in the 920s, and defeated the Magyars in the 930s. His son, Otto I, completed their defeat in 955. The East Frankish (German) kingdom remained one of strong regional identities, and the pursuit of resources to maintain their overlordship led Otto and his successors into Italy, while the Saxon nobility expanded east at the expense of the Slavs.

Around the year 1000, the dominant state in the British Isles was England, a unified and wealthy country although vulnerable to external take-over, as happened in 1016 (after which it became part of Cnut's North Sea empire) and in 1066. In France, royal authority had decayed almost to nothing and the king was one of many princes. The German monarchy needed to pursue the resources of Italy to compensate for the weaknesses of central government institutions in Germany. Spain remained largely under Muslim control, and the Christian reconquest had yet to gather momentum.

THE WARS OF CHARLEMAGNE

T HE FRANKS WERE THE MOST SUCCESSFUL of the barbarian groups which overran the western Roman empire in the fifth century. At their peak in the sixth century, the Frankish Merovingian dynasty held sway over all the land north of the Pyrenees and Alps and west of the Rhine and had extensive overlordship across the Rhine. In the later seventh century, the kingdom broke up. The reconstruction of the kingdom by the Carolingians was begun by Charles Martel, 'mayor of the palace' to the Merovingian king. He reunited northern Gaul, began to reassert Frankish rule in Burgundy and Aquitaine, and turned the Arabs back at Poitiers (732). His son, Pippin III, campaigned in southern Gaul and across the Rhine. It was Pippin III's son who became known as Charles the Great, or Charlemagne.

No helmets survive from the time of Charlemagne, since the Franks ceased to bury goods with the dead after about 700. Surviving helmets, like this sixth-century one, bear no resemblance to those depicted in ninth-century manuscripts. The materials used in their construction were probably the same, iron, bronze, and leather. Only the very wealthy possessed helmets and body armour.

THE FOUNDATIONS OF CAROLINGIAN EXPANSION

Charles the Great (742-814) succeeded to an already vast inheritance (map 1) after a brief period of shared rule with his brother Carloman (768-71). He continued the family tradition of expansion because it was expected of him, but also because he possessed the resources and the vocation. His motives for expansion were the rights he claimed over neighbours and the search for plunder to underpin his power. By 814, his authority stretched beyond the Elbe, to Hungary, south of Rome, and almost as far as the Ebro in Spain, an authority achieved by military success.

Before 800 there was scarcely a year in which Charles, like his father and grandfather, did not campaign. Later he was less active, although in his late sixties he led an army against a Danish threat and organized naval defences on the North Sea coast (810-11). The dominant theatre was Saxony (maps 2-4), but what Charles' biographer Einhard (c.770-840) called a thirty-three year war was in fact a series of intermittent campaigns against different groups of Saxons, beginning with raids and turning to conquest and conversion in 776. Saxony's lack of centralized authority and difficult terrain made subjugation extremely difficult, whereas by contrast the established Lombard kingdom of Italy was taken in a single campaign. In the Saxon wars Charles employed almost the full range of Carolingian military methods: plundering raids, establishing garrisons in forts, use of multiple columns, over-wintering in Saxony, massacres and, from 795, deportations. There were pitched battles, including a Frankish defeat in 782, but they achieved little of permanence. The subjugation of south Saxony seemed complete by 785, although Charles had also been involved in Lombardy (autumn 773-June 774) and northern Spain (778), where the establishment of a Spanish March in Catalonia was overshadowed by the disaster at Roncesvalles in 778 (page 16).

For nearly a decade Charles' attention turned eastwards. Bavaria was quickly annexed (787), followed by campaigns along the Danube against the Avars in 790-91 (page 17). Preparations for another expedition in 792 were aborted by new trouble in Saxony, and the final elimination of the

Avar threat was left to subordinates. The southern Saxons were crushed in two campaigns (794, 795), followed by the subjugation of northern Saxony (796-99), climaxing in the winter campaign of 797-98 (map 4). Charles had now almost finished with campaigning. He had always relied on subordinates, such as duke Eric of Friuli, to lead campaigns, a tendency which now became more marked. At the end of 800, Charles took an army to Italy, but while he was crowned emperor in Rome, military operations were left to his son Pippin. In 802, an army was sent into Saxony while he spent the late summer hunting, and his final Saxon campaign took place in 804. With the exception of 810, Charles left the direction of military operations against the Slavs, against the Moors in Spain, and his wars in Italy and the Mediterranean to his sons and subordinates.

The cause of Carolingian success was long held to be the creation of an effective force of heavy cavalry by Charles Martel in the 730s, to which has been added the adoption of the stirrup which made mounted shock combat possible. This interpretation had the advantage of explaining both eighth-century Carolingian expansion and the emergence of feudalism, but its grounds have been successfully challenged. The stirrup appears not to have been known in the Frankish lands until the late eighth century, and there

Horses were used extensively by Frankish armies. Although not important in siege warfare, a central part of Carolingian strategy, they did provide great mobility. Artists did not begin to depict stirrups until the later ninth century.

MAP 1

Charles 'the Great' completed the reunification of Gaul by conquering Aquitaine. He led an army almost every year up to 800, when he retired from active command. The resources of his empire were so great that he could field more than one well-equipped army in a year, and frequently used converging columns. One driving force behind his campaigns was the search for plunder.

was certainly no military revolution which resulted in new cavalry tactics. The Franks did fight on horseback in the late eighth century, but with swords and lances used as striking and throwing weapons, rather than employing the cavalry charge with lances held at rest. An equally significant function of horses in eighth-century Frankish armies was as a means of transport, and it was the death of most of the horses during the 791 expedition (*page 17*) which prevented renewed invasion of Pannonia for two years. The sole advantage of a heavy cavalry force was to win battles, yet Charles himself fought very few. The real advantages of his armies were their size and mobility.

In many years, often around Easter, Charles held an assembly of his great men. This was in effect the Frankish army muster, for assembly was often followed by campaign. The reason for timing the assembly in May in 782 (*map 3*) is made clear: 'At the beginning of summer, when fodder was at last plentiful enough to enable an army to march, he [Charles] decided to enter Saxony and to hold the general assembly there' (*Revised Annals of the Kingdom of the Franks*).

However, campaigning was not restricted to any fixed season. When rapid response or semi-permanent forces were required, small, mobile units (*scarae*), often drawn from the royal escort of vassals, could be sent on specific tasks. In 776, for example, *scarae* were left in Saxony to garrison two fortresses, and another *scara* was sent after Saxon raiders in 778. Such forces probably numbered only a few hundred men.

For major campaigns, Charles mobilized thousands of warriors from different regions. Modern estimates of well-equipped horsemen raised by royal vassals alone vary from 5,000 to 35,000, excluding attendants. The extent of Charles' domains provided a vast reservoir of potential manpower, and Charles made regulations for the military equipment to be owned and brought to his campaigns by all ranks, from the wealthy vassals who served as armoured cavalry, to the mass of poor free men armed with shield and spear, and cart-drivers with a bow and a dozen arrows. He showed deep concern for the armament of his warriors, issuing regulations in 792-93 requiring vassals to have horse, lance

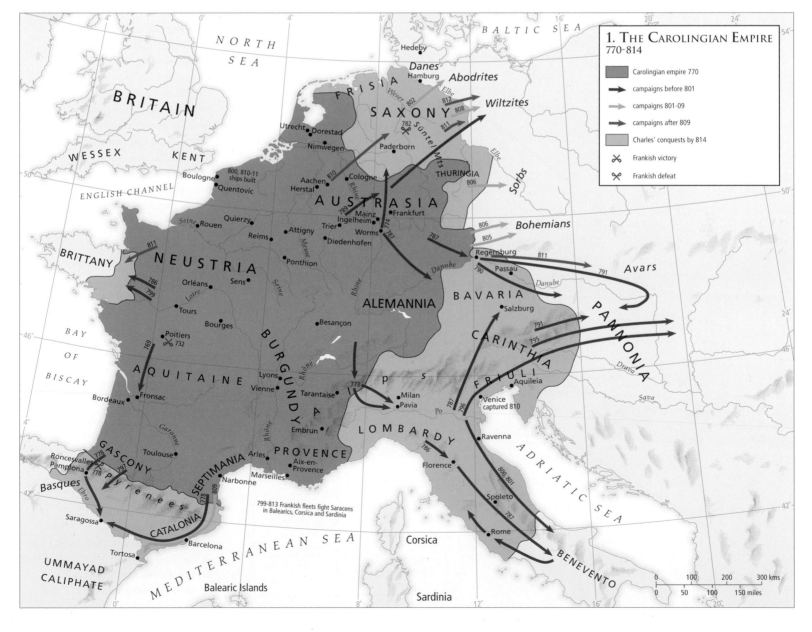

and shield, long and short swords. In 802-03, wealthy men had to possess body-armour, and counts were to inspect lesser men to ensure each had spear, shield, bow, and twelve arrows. Staves, the simplest weapons, presumably carried by attendants and carters, were prohibited in favour of bows. Throughout his reign Charles banned the export of armour and swords.

The most effective forces were the soldier-followers of kings and magnates, lay and ecclesiastical, who had the most complete equipment and were virtually professional warriors. Probably only a fraction of the available warriors were actually assembled for a single campaign. In frontier regions, such as the Breton march, a prefect or duke was appointed over several counties with responsibility for defence. By 802 at the latest, the populations of marches had special obligations of guard duty (*wacta*, *warda*) and a high state of readiness to campaign. Such burdens, and the great distances which some contingents had to travel to join armies, created many problems. In Saxony, a royal

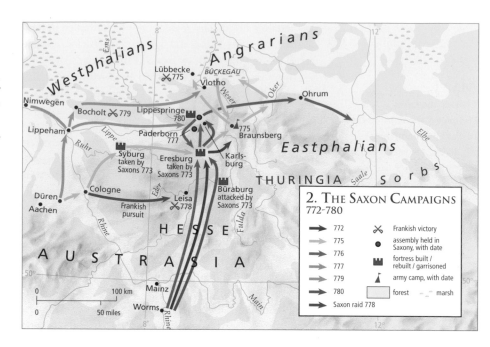

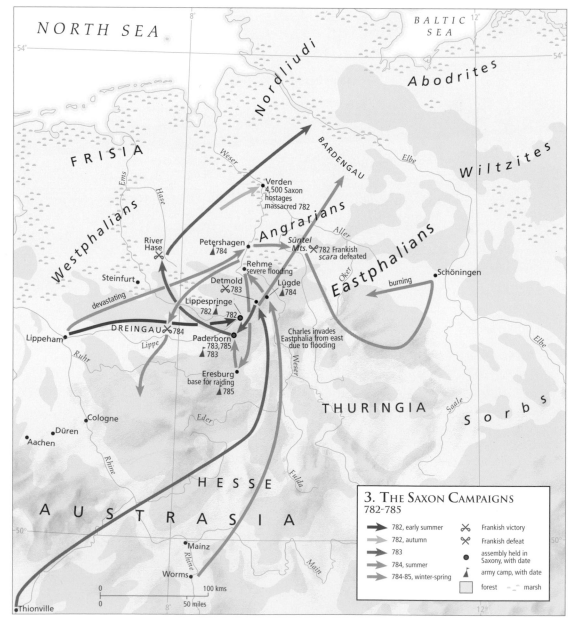

MAP 2

The primitive political organization and difficult terrain made Saxony hard to control. Early clashes arose from border disputes, and only from 776-77 did Frankish strategy turn to conquest and conversion. The south Saxons submitted when Charles led large armies to Lippespringe, but rebelled and threw off the new Christian religion when the Franks withdrew.

MAP 3

Saxon rebellion and defeat of a Frankish host in the Süntel mountains prompted a massive retaliation by Charles: a massacre in 782, extensive ravaging in 783 and 784, culminating in Charles wintering in Saxony (784-85). According to the *Revised Frankish Annals* 'he gave the Saxons there a winter of discontent… he inflicted immense destruction on well-nigh all the regions of the Saxons'. Finally, the Saxon leader Widukind submitted and was baptized.

MAP 4

The Saxon rebellion in 793 made Charles abandon his Avar campaign. In the next three years he again ravaged the territory of the Westphalians, and beyond to the river Elbe. In 797-98, he determined to winter in Saxony again 'in order to bring the Saxon war to its conclusion'. Despite this, and mass deportations intended to cut Saxony off from Danish support, some resistance continued until 803-04.

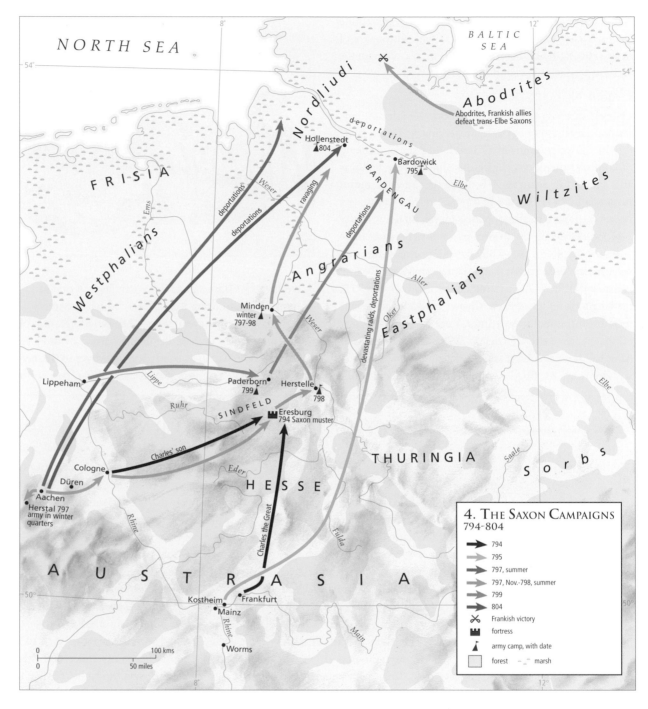

memorandum of 806 laid down a sliding scale of military contributions: five Saxons were to equip a sixth to campaign in Spain, two were to equip a third for Bohemia, but against the nearest enemy, the Sorbs, all were to attend. Similar concessions probably existed earlier for the Spanish and Italian marches. It was thus possible to raise several forces, as in 811, when there were operations on the Elbe, the Danube, the Breton border, and the Ebro.

The key to Carolingian military success was elaborate organization which allowed systematic conquests to replace raids. Success depended not on winning battles, but on capturing fortresses, the establishment of permanent garrisons, and keeping comparatively large numbers of well-equipped soldiers in the field for longer than their opponents. Eighth-century Frankish armies consisted largely

of the king's vassals and great men with their followers. Their greatest incentive to serve was the profitability of Carolingian warfare: plundering and conquest produced a steady flow of slaves, treasure, and land. In 796, Charles distributed among his vassals part of the Avar treasure, sent to him by duke Eric of Friuli. The great cost and range of Carolingian expeditions probably excluded many free men, despite their liability for military service, but after 800, when profitable expansionist wars were replaced by defensive burdens, Charles demanded military service from free men with small estates, requiring the poorest to form small groups to equip one warrior. However, it proved difficult to mobilize large numbers of men for defence against the Danes and Arabs since there was no profit motive to make defensive duties attractive. After 800, Charles was active in organizing defence of the North Sea coastline against Viking attacks (*page 19*) and in the construction of fleets (800, 810-11); Frankish fleets were also active in the western Mediterranean and the Adriatic.

CAROLINGIAN STRATEGY

Charles' campaigns demonstrate considerable strategic insight. Large resources made converging attacks possible: the use of two columns in 773 permitted the outflanking of Lombard attempts to block the Alpine passes and was also adopted in Spain in 778, in Bavaria in 787, and in Pannonia in 791. The use of a pincer movement in 794 caused the Saxons to abandon their muster. In Saxony (*maps 2-4*), Charles frequently divided his forces to devastate more widely (774, 775, 784, 785, 799). Great resources and determination also meant that he could campaign whatever the season. When Charles invaded Lombardy in late 773, the king took refuge in Pavia. Charles blockaded it for nine months, throughout the winter, until June 774. Winter campaigns were also effective in Saxony, where the Saxon habit had been to submit and rebel again when the Franks withdrew. In 784, Charles established his court and family

The helmets and shields in this late ninth-century manuscript probably represent Frankish equipment, but the armour may be based on Roman illustrations. Shield and lance were standard weapons for rich and poor. Skill in capturing fortified places made possible the Carolingian conquest of southern France and north Italy, for which plentiful infantry was necessary.

at Eresburg for Christmas and Easter, sending out devastating columns and capturing Saxon forts, which broke south Saxon resistance for several years. The second invasion of 797 was mounted because 'he then resolved, in order to bring the Saxon war to its conclusion, to winter in Saxony' (*Revised Annals of the Kingdom of the Franks*). When the north

TWO CAROLINGIAN BATTLES

Although there were many campaigns during Charles' reign, there were few battles. Charles fought only three, all against the Saxons (775 and 783), and his lieutenants add few to the number. All were against the Saxons or Avars; in 'civilized' lands where there were fortified towns, sieges and devastation, rather than battles, were the normal way to wage war. For most battles which were fought no details were recorded, but when the royal annals were revised after Charles' death, two defeats were elaborated, although the actions had originally been presented as victories.

Roncesvalles entered legend as an epic struggle between Christian Franks and Muslim Arabs. The reality was much more prosaic. As Charles' army left Spain through the pass of Roncesvalles in 778, the baggage train, laden with plunder, and its escort bringing up the army's rear, was ambushed by Christian Basques hiding in the forests, taking advantage of the fact that the main army was far ahead. When help came, the Basques had disappeared. The annals express the anger felt against guerrilla fighters: 'Although the Franks were manifestly superior to the Basques in both weapons and courage, yet they were rendered their inferiors by the steepness of the terrain and the character of the battle, which was not fought fairly' (*Revised Annals of the Kingdom of the Franks*).

The battle fought in Saxony near the Süntel mountains in 782 revealed what resulted when jealousy and lack of discipline clouded military judgement. Charles sent a punitive column of Franks and Saxons under three household officials against the Sorbs, a Slav tribe. En route they learned of a Saxon revolt. Leaving behind the Saxon contingent, the Franks advanced, joining another band of

Franks under count Theodoric, a relative of the king. Sensibly, he sent out patrols to locate the rebels and proposed to the other commanders that they mount a pincer attack. The two hosts established separate camps, but then jealousy took over. The household officers, fearing that the credit for victory, and the plunder, would be Theodoric's, engaged the Saxons without him: 'Each individual seized his weapons and charged with as much speed as he could muster, just as fast as his horse would carry him, upon the place where the Saxons were drawn up in battle-array in front of their camp; they acted as if their task was to pursue a fleeing foe and seize booty rather than to take on an enemy standing marshalled to face them. Since the approach had gone badly, badly also went the battle' (*Revised Annals of the Kingdom of the Franks*). They were surrounded by the Saxons and suffered very heavy losses, including the chamberlain, the count of the stables, four counts, and twenty other nobles, together with those followers who chose to die with them rather than to survive through flight. Defeat was here ascribed to an intemperate approach and undisciplined charge, perhaps through over-eagerness at finding the Saxons for once drawn up in the open, rather than behind a river or in their camp.

There is a marked contrast in the sources between detailed descriptions of particular campaigns (captured fortresses, winter expeditions, logistical planning) and the lack of interest the annals show in battles, indicating the minor role battles played in Frankish military successes. Victory or defeat in battle was transient and contributed little to successful conquests which were achieved by grinding down the enemy.

CAROLINGIAN STRATEGY – THE 791 CAMPAIGN

The acquisition of Bavaria in 787 brought Charles into contact with the Avars, a race of Hunnish nomads who held subject the Slavs of the middle Danube. This problem preoccupied him for much of the next five years. Charles visited Regensburg in 788 to organize border defence, and sent the greater part of his army against the Avars the following year. His 791 campaign reveals meticulous planning and organization. The army and its provisions were concentrated from May that year at Regensburg, where the assembly endorsed the decision to proceed. They moved to the border, on the Enns, where three days of prayer were held (5-7 September). Charles had also ordered an army from Lombardy against the Avar rear, and before he crossed the Enns he knew that this column, which entered Pannonia on 23 August, had defeated an Avar host and captured an unidentified fortress. This probably had an effect on the morale of both sides. Charles commanded a Frankish corps on the south

bank of the Danube, while another corps of Franks, Saxons, Thuringians, and Frisians advanced along the north bank. This tactic outflanked the Avar positions and reduced congestion on the advance. A Bavarian flotilla carried supplies on the Danube and linked the two wings. Avar resistance collapsed and they were driven out of the defences on the Kamp and in the Weinerwald. Each of the columns plundered and ravaged as it advanced, and Charles was able to pillage Avar territory for two months. A well-executed concentric assault reduced the Avars to civil war. Charles planned a second invasion, for which a portable pontoon bridge was prepared in 792, but famine, shortage of horses, and conspiracy prevented its execution. Unable to mount the final assault in person, it was carried out instead by armies from Italy in 795-96, which captured the Avar 'ring' (situated between Carinthia and the Danube) and removed the treasure of centuries of Avar plundering.

Saxons subsequently rebelled in 798, while the army was dispersed in winter quarters, the force was at hand to crush them and effectively complete the conquest of Saxony.

Large armies, travelling over long distances, and the mounting of winter campaigns were made possible by careful organization, especially of supply. Armies marching to assembly had access to pasture, wood, and water, but were instructed not to consume their provisions until specified points were reached. They were accompanied by herds of cattle (mentioned only in 810, when plague devastated the herd). Charles laid down that food for three months and weapons and clothing for six months should be carried in carts with the tools needed for military works, and on campaign Sunday prohibitions were relaxed. In 791, supplies were carried along the Danube.

Attention was also paid to military communications. Within Frankia, counts were required to ensure bridges were passable, and in Saxony more were constructed; in 789, two bridges were thrown over the Elbe, one with a fort at either end, and in 792, a portable pontoon bridge was prepared for use against the Avars. In 809, collapsible boats were used in order to cross the Ebro. An unsuccessful attempt to link the Rhine and Danube (793) by canal was intended to facilitate communications between the two main theatres of war at the time, Saxony and Hungary.

The significance of fortifications in eighth-century

Carolingian expansion is often underrated. In Aquitaine, Italy, and Spain, capturing towns with stone walls was the vital element in conquest as, for example, in Pavia in 773-74. The less redoubtable Saxon and Avar fortifications were no obstacle to the Franks. Frankish strongpoints were garrisoned with vassals, and the royal annals emphasize the building of camps and permanent fortresses during the conquest of Saxony, and the establishment of a border against Danes and Slavs after 800 (map 1). They were not impregnable, in fact the Saxons captured Eresburg several times, but control of fortified places was the essential element in converting raiding into conquest.

Eighth-century Carolingian expansion was not founded on a revolution in tactics which made Frankish heavy cavalry masters of the battlefield, not least because battles played a very small role in their success. Charlemagne's armies were able to grind down their opponents by bringing superior force to bear. Several Frankish armies could be raised at once, to operate in the same theatre or in different parts of the empire, and without detracting from the simultaneous defence of the marches. Although there was concern that defensive measures were being evaded in the last years of his reign, this was not a period of decomposition, but rather one of stabilization under a new generation of commanders, who had been trained and inspired by Charles after years of spectacular success.

THE VIKINGS
IN THE NINTH CENTURY

ALTHOUGH THERE WAS a constructive side to ninth-century Scandinavian activity, their primary impact on western Europe was military. Ninth-century sources used several terms for the Scandinavian raiders – Rus, Northmen, Danes, pagans, heathens, shipmen – but the Anglo-Saxon word 'viking' (meaning pirate or sea-borne raider) is in general use today. The Swedes went east across the Baltic, penetrating as far as the Byzantine empire and the Muslim east. The Norwegians operated mostly in the north and west of the British Isles until about 850. The Danes sailed along the North Sea and Channel coasts, only reaching Ireland in 851. In Russia, the Vikings formed the first states, but in western Europe they were mainly destructive, despite their colonization of Iceland and Greenland and their settlements in Britain and Normandy.

The Gokstad ship, a 76ft (23m) Norwegian oak vessel, carried sixty-four warriors. Although its shallow draught made it suitable for rivers, a replica was sailed across the Atlantic in 1893.

THE VIKING EXPLOSION

The Vikings' exploits were made possible by their ships. It is difficult to know from surviving ninth- to eleventh-century ships if there was a 'typical' longship, but with thirty to fifty men on board they could cross the North Sea and sail into the Atlantic, while their shallow draught made it possible to follow rivers far inland. It is impossible to calculate the size of Viking hosts, but it has been argued that even the largest armies of the 860s to the 890s numbered hundreds rather than thousands, on the grounds that contemporary sources exaggerated numbers of ships and casualties, vessels differed in size, and that fleets carried captives, wives, children, even horses, as well as warriors. However, there are grounds for believing that some hosts did contain thousands of warriors. From about 840, chronicles in different parts of western Europe refer to fleets

of fifty or more ships campaigning for several years. In the 850s, warbands combined and large fleets in excess of 100 ships are believable. The achievements of the 'Great Army' after 865 are inconceivable if it comprised only a few hundred warriors.

Most Viking leaders are unknown. Some were nobles seeking to reward their warbands, others were royal exiles. Harald, his son Godefrid, and his nephew Roric are found at different times as allies of emperor Lothar (ruler of Middle Frankia), as raiders, and bidding for power in Denmark. Seven kings commanded the Great Army in the 870s to 880s, up to four at a time. They were not territorial rulers, but their royal blood enabled them to assemble substantial warbands. The prime objective was plunder: Vikings struck at soft targets, monasteries and trading settlements, where

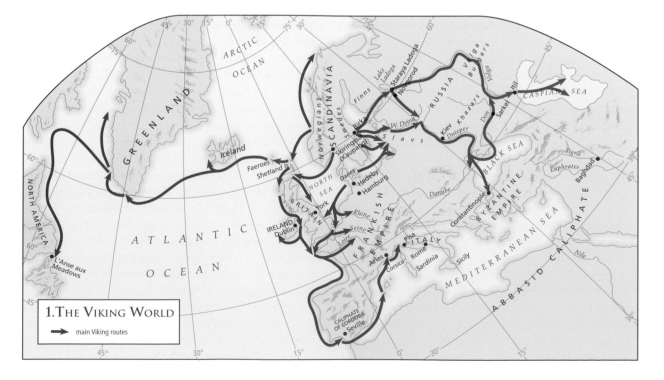

1. THE VIKING WORLD

→ main Viking routes

MAP 1

Although the Scandinavian peoples first appear in written sources as raiders, they were also involved in trade, supplying furs, amber, walrus ivory, and slaves to the east and west. They founded trading settlements deep within Russia, in Ireland, and northern England, and colonized Iceland from c.870, subsequently reaching Greenland and Newfoundland.

MAP 2

The first Viking raids in northern England, Scotland, and Ireland were probably by Norwegians. Early raids involved small numbers of ships and were mainly coastal; larger Danish fleets in the 830s, attracted by political turmoil in Frankia, turned to England when Louis the Pious reorganized his defences. The Vikings were drawn to Frankia again by the civil wars following his death. The first recorded wintering was in Ireland in 840-41. This map is certainly incomplete. Knowledge of raids depends on surviving monastic annals: their destruction for Northumbria and Mercia means few raids there are known.

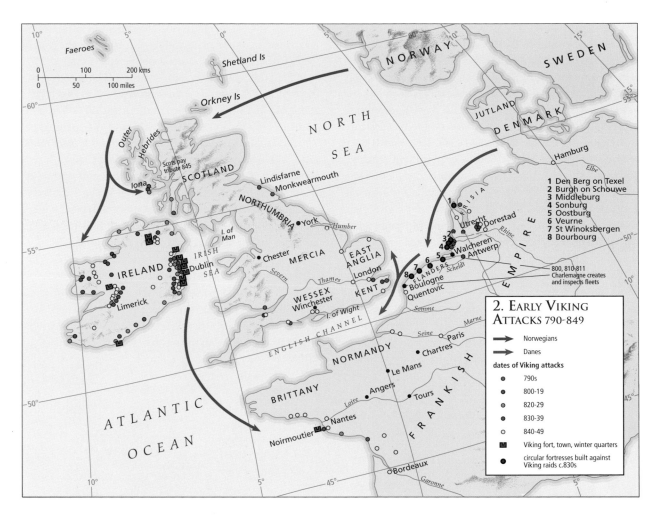

1 Den Berg on Texel
2 Burgh on Schouwe
3 Middleburg
4 Sonburg
5 Oostburg
6 Veurne
7 St Winoksbergen
8 Bourbourg

800, 810-811 Charlemagne creates and inspects fleets

2. EARLY VIKING ATTACKS 790-849

→ Norwegians
→ Danes

dates of Viking attacks
- 790s
- 800-19
- 820-29
- 830-39
- ○ 840-49

▣ Viking fort, town, winter quarters
● circular fortresses built against Viking raids c.830s

---

movable wealth was concentrated. Captives were taken for slavery, or ransom if well-born: the West Frankish king Charles the Bald paid an enormous sum for abbot Louis, a grandson of Charlemagne, and in 841 sixty-eight monks of St Wandrille were ransomed. Vikings ransomed whole towns, single buildings and churches, even books: an English Gospel Book records that it was ransomed 'from the heathen army with pure gold'. Some leaders acquired land. From the 840s, Harald, Godefrid, and Roric intermittently held Frisia from Lothar; in the 870s the Great Army took over parts of England, and in the early tenth century there were settlements in Normandy, which derived its name from the Northmen. Some Viking leaders entered the fabric of their victims' society, accepting baptism, serving kings, and joining in noble feuds.

The earliest attacks (map 2) in the 790s, probably by Norwegians, were on coastal monasteries such as Lindisfarne and Iona, reaching as far south as Aquitaine. Until the 840s, Ireland was the main target. Kings reacted rapidly: in 792, Offa of Mercia required the church's military service in Kent against 'pagan seamen' ; a few years later Charlemagne prepared ships to defend the Channel 'since it was infested with pirates'. In the 830s, political turmoil in the Frankish empire attracted the Vikings, who were ever ready to exploit dissension. The crisis of the deposition of emperor Louis, Charlemagne's son, in 833-34, was exploited by consecutive attacks from 834-37 on the important port of Dorestad, 50

miles (80 km) up the Rhine. After his restoration, Louis strengthened the Frisian coastal defences as a deterrent. For a time the raiders turned to England. The raids on Ireland abated in 848 after several Norwegian defeats.

THE FRANKISH KINGDOMS 840-865

The death of Louis in 840 resulted in war between his three sons and in the division of the empire in 843: Louis the German (840-76) took East Frankia; Charles the Bald (840-77) West Frankia; and Lothar I (840-55) Middle Frankia (Lotharingia). Their rivalry attracted the Vikings (map 3), who penetrated deeper into Frankia, in greater numbers, and for ever longer periods as the wealth and vulnerability of the Frankish interior was revealed. East Frankia, apart from its coast, was free of serious raids for more than thirty years after the sack of Hamburg in 845, reflecting Louis the German's military reputation. Middle Frankia also largely escaped until the 880s, as Lothar I established warbands at the mouth of the Rhine at Walcheren in 841 and at Dorestad in 851. While not entirely reliable, as a raid up the Rhine in 863 shows, they were a buffer against other Vikings. West Frankia was systematically exploited by Vikings for twenty-five years, taking advantage of Charles the Bald's weak position. He was threatened by Lothar I, then by Louis the German, by rebellious nobles, by Breton and Aquitainian separatism, and then by his own sons. All distracted him from effectively dealing with the Viking raids.

The Vikings' new tactic of wintering on a small island, first used in Ireland in 840, was developed to great effect in the raids on West Frankia. In 843 a Norwegian fleet set up 'something like a permanent settlement', probably on Noirmoutier in the mouth of the Loire, which became a Viking haunt for decades. In the Seine they chose Jeufosse (852-53, 856-57) and Oissel (858-61); the first instance in England was the Isle of Thanet (851). Such islands were secure bases where ships could be beached and repaired, and plunder, supplies and captives accumulated. In one case 'they made a base for their ships…on an island near the monastery of Fleury. They put up their huts…and there they kept their herds of prisoners bound in chains while they themselves rested…they made unexpected forays from this base, sometimes in their ships, sometimes on horses, and laid waste the whole province' (Adrevald of Fleury). Movement up meandering river-courses was slow and lacked surprise, so the Vikings quickly acquired horses to increase their range; some bands even carried them by ship. It was this mobility which made the Vikings so difficult to

suppress without an enormous investment of time, men, and resources, for Frankish and English armies were geared to profitable raids, not burdensome defensive duties.

In 856, the Seine became the focus for Viking activity in the west. A fleet based on Jeufosse sacked Paris in December, and again in 857. Charles the Bald bought off Sidroc and Bjorn in 857-58, but could not dislodge the main force which launched widespread raids overland from Oissel (858-59). They were finally shifted when Charles hired Weland's fleet from the Somme; if the figure of 260 ships attributed to him is reliable, the Vikings in the west were massing in the Seine. In 862, most left for the Loire, where the raids resumed. Apart from a fleet at Oissel (865-66), no more Vikings are recorded in the Seine until 876.

Viking methods can be traced in Frankish sources. The trading emporium Quentovic was surprised by a dawn attack (842), and Bordeaux was taken at night (848) after it was thought the raiders had been driven off. Tours was attacked in 853 during a religious festival when the town would be crowded, but there was warning of this attack as

MAP 3

West Frankia suffered most from Viking depradations, its great rivers giving Viking fleets access deep into the heart of the kingdom. In the 860s, Charles developed an effective strategy of building fortified bridges and forts to deter the Vikings; he also hired Viking leaders. In the mid-860s, most Viking bands moved to England, aware that there were easier pickings to be had there.

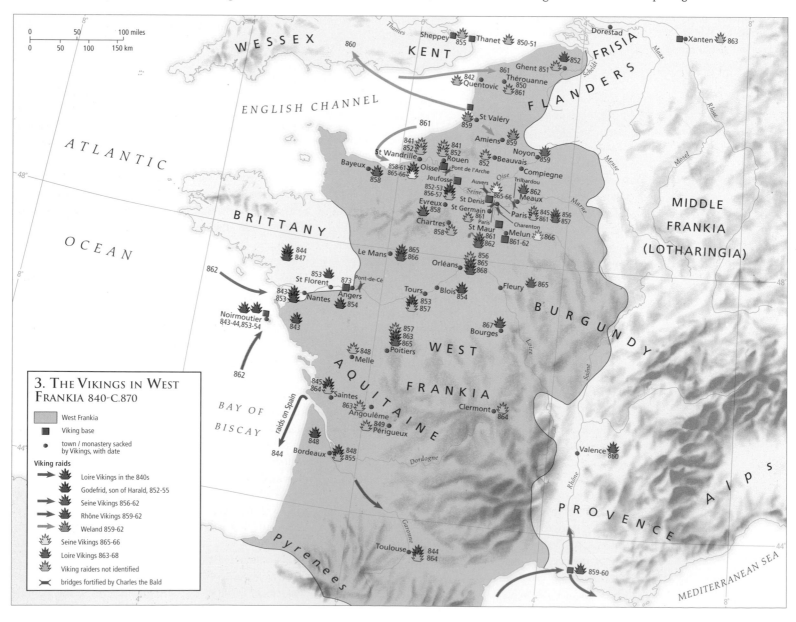

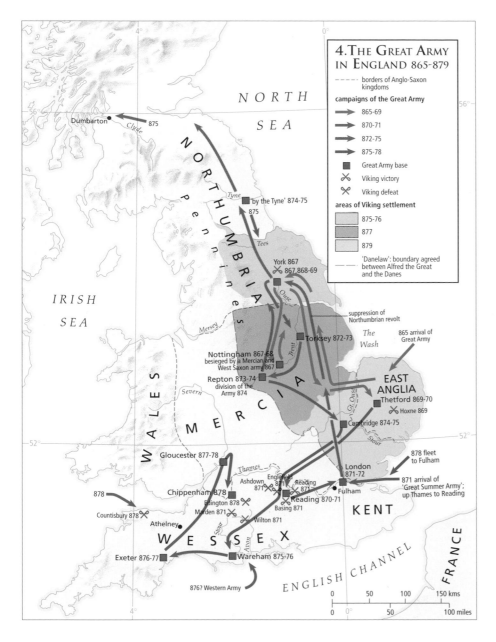

4. THE GREAT ARMY IN ENGLAND 865-879

— — — borders of Anglo-Saxon kingdoms

campaigns of the Great Army

→ 865-69

→ 870-71

→ 872-75

→ 875-78

■ Great Army base

✕ Viking victory

✕ Viking defeat

areas of Viking settlement

875-76

877

879

'Danelaw': boundary agreed between Alfred the Great and the Danes

MAP 4

Within ten years of their arrival in England, only Wessex remained fully independent of the Vikings, and parts of the Great Army began to settle in Northumbria and Mercia. They failed to overcome Alfred of Wessex, but agreed to a frontier which nevertheless left half England to the Vikings. Part of the army then settled in East Anglia. The remainder crossed to Frankia.

the Vikings approached by river. One trick was to create a false sense of security by putting out that they had no intention of moving. In 857, on Easter morning at dawn, they attacked the monastery of St Denis near Paris, after a night approach by horse, to maximize the chance of taking noble prisoners.

As Viking fleets moved along rivers, they destroyed bridges and boats to disrupt pursuit, sending out parties on either bank. Raids from base camps covered considerable distances, to Poitiers from the Loire on foot, for example, in 865, a distance of more than 50 miles (80 km). But overland raids were vulnerable to interception, which led to Viking defeat, although defeating raiding parties did not suffice to dislodge the main force from its base. This required time and manpower when kings and local leaders had other priorities. Moreover, the severity of the raids must be kept in proportion: for much of West Frankia the Vikings were an intermittent nuisance rather than a constant threat. It was often easier to pay them off. As king of West Frankia, Charles

the Bald had many pressing concerns, chiefly rebels and his brothers. Thus his raising of the Viking siege of Bordeaux in 848 was part of Aquitainian politics rather than a serious attempt to combat raids in the south-west. He was not seriously concerned until Viking armies encamped in the Seine basin and threatened the centre of his power. Here, the monarchy's economic resources provided one method of dealing with the Vikings. Fleets were paid to quit the Seine (845, 857, 866), and Viking leaders such as Bjorn and Weland were hired for money and provisions.

The military solution Charles adopted was to contain the Vikings closely in their camp and deny them supplies, but this was difficult to achieve. The blockade of Jeufosse by Charles and Lothar I at the end of 852 failed when Charles' army refused to spend Christmas in the field: motivating men for such defensive duties with little prospect of plunder was a constant problem. In 857-58 Charles weakened the Seine fleet by the 'seduction' of Sidroc and Bjorn, then when it moved to Oissel in 858 he blockaded it in July to protect the harvest and prevent foraging for the winter. Again he failed. In the autumn, Louis the German invaded, allied with West Frankish nobles unwilling to pay for defence against the Vikings, forcing Charles to raise the blockade. He came close to losing his throne.

After his recovery, Charles found an effective strategy to clear the Seine valley. Hiring Weland's fleet in 861 made possible the blockade of Oissel: 'the besieged were forced by starvation, filth and general misery to pay the besiegers...and to make an alliance with them.' (*Annals of St Bertin*). For the winter, Charles quartered them all along the Seine, but early in 862 one warband attacked up the Marne. Charles pursued but, unable to overtake them, he rebuilt the bridge over the Marne at Trilbardou and stationed troops on the banks to prevent foraging. This was decisive. The Vikings quickly made terms which brought about the withdrawal of the whole fleet. Most went to the Loire, although Weland remained with Charles and was baptized. Charles followed this action by ordering the construction of a fortified bridge to close the Seine, but this was not completed in 865-66 when a new fleet encamped on Oissel, and containment of the raiders had mixed success. Guards for the river-banks were slow to assemble. A sortie against Chartres was prevented, but the monastery of St Denis was sacked and the Frankish troops on one bank driven off. It proved easier in the end for Charles to buy them off again. Nevertheless, he continued to organize defences. As recently as 858 he had permitted the Roman walls of Melun to be quarried for building stone. Now new walls were ordered at several exposed sites.

In 873, Charles finally acted against the Loire Vikings who had occupied Angers for some years, and forced them to withdraw. For the next nine years this area too enjoyed some freedom from raids, and a fortified bridge was built across the Loire above Angers. Much of the burden of defence fell on local forces, with mixed results. In 854, ships and men assembled on the Loire by the bishops of Orléans and Chartres saved Orléans, but it was sacked only

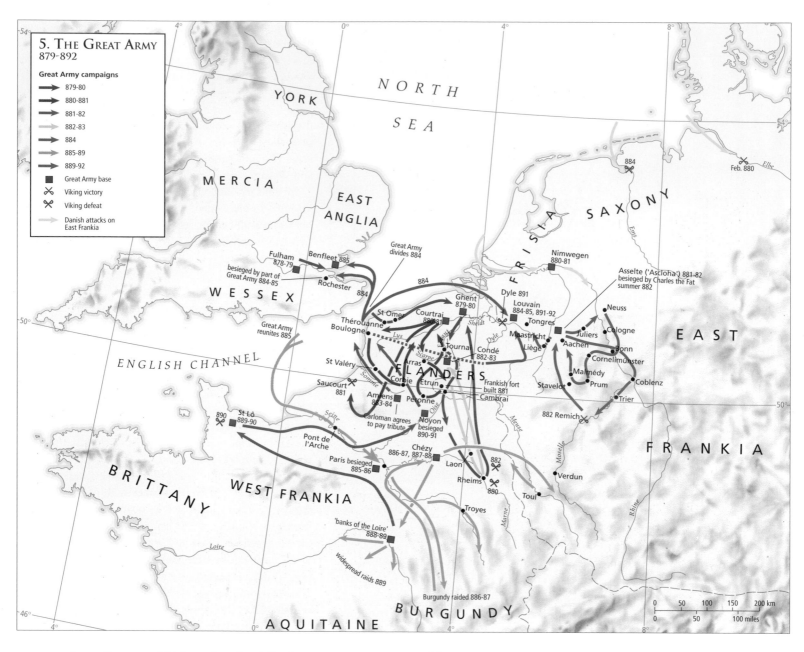

5. THE GREAT ARMY
879-892

Great Army campaigns
→ 879-80
→ 880-881
→ 881-82
→ 882-83
→ 884
→ 885-89
→ 889-92

■ Great Army base
⚔ Viking victory
⚔ Viking defeat
→ Danish attacks on East Frankia

two years later. Counts and bishops found it difficult to assemble forces at the right time and place – it was easier to pay ransom, or for the wealthy (especially monasteries) to move inland. In the 860s, count Robert of Angers scored several successes against the Loire Vikings, but he was killed in 866 by raiders returning from Le Mans. In 859 the common people rose up against the Seine Vikings, but were put down by their own lords for their affront to social order. Indeed, Vikings made useful allies in feuds between noble families.

THE GREAT ARMY

From 865, Viking activity in the west was concentrated in a 'great army'. From 882-92 the Viking Great Army (*magnus exercitus*) – 'everyone called it that on account of its numbers' (*Miracles of St Bertin*) – operated on the continent. When it crossed to England it was also called the Great Army (*se micle here*). It began its activities in England (*map 4*), and whilst there the raids in Ireland and Frankia abated.

It was made up of fleets led by several kings. Squadrons departed and new ones arrived, resulting in continuous activity over three decades.

The Great Army introduced a new tactic in 865: each autumn it seized a significant inland centre from which to plunder a fresh district. Most of these sites already possessed Roman walls or later earthworks; if not, defences were improvised, as at Reading where a ditch and bank fortified a promontory between two rivers. The Army relied on horses for mobility – it was 'horsed' as soon as it arrived in 865 – and although its bases were mostly on navigable rivers, little use was made of the fleet. Its leaders were ambitious. Puppet regimes were established in Northumbria, East Anglia, and Mercia, then parts of the army shared out the land. They were replaced by new contingents in 871 – a 'great summer fleet' (*Anglo-Saxon Chronicle*) – at Reading, and in 876, and 879.

The Anglo-Saxon Chronicle (in fact a West Saxon source) gives the impression that for a decade the Anglo-Saxon kingdoms

MAP 5

The failure of the Great Army's attack on Wessex in 878 coincided with renewed confusion in the Frankish kingdoms. After reinforcements arrived in 878, the Great Army crossed to Frankia, devastating new areas in Flanders, raiding deep into the Rhine valley in 882, and in 885 moving on to the Seine valley. Although they failed to capture Paris in the winter of 885-86, the Vikings did go on to plunder Champagne and Burgundy, which had hitherto escaped.

put up ineffectual resistance before paying tribute, and only Wessex led by Alfred resisted effectively. During the invasion of 870-71, the West Saxons fought nine battles against the Great Army, winning two, and many skirmishes against raiding parties. Despite killing one Scandinavian king and nine earls, in the end king Alfred (871-99) made peace and doubtless paid tribute too, as his neighbours had done.

From 875 to 878, Wessex, the only kingdom not in the Great Army's power, endured a sustained assault. How king Alfred survived is not clear. Like Charles the Bald, he used a containing strategy against the Great Army in Wareham (875-76) and Exeter (876-77), forcing it to move on. When the Vikings then made a surprise attack in January 878 and Alfred was temporarily deserted, he had the tenacity to keep up the struggle. He defeated the Great Army at Edington (June 878), then blockaded it in Chippenham until king Guthrum made peace. Alfred was fortunate. By 878 the Great Army was weakened by departures; the fleet which arrived in 876 lost many ships in a storm; and in 878 another fleet only arrived after his victory over Guthrum.

It was renewed discord in Frankia that beckoned the Great Army: after the deaths of the experienced rulers Louis the German and Charles the Bald (876, 877), six kings shared the kingdom in a decade – Louis the Stammerer (877-79), Louis III (879-82), and Carloman (879-84) in West Frankia, Carloman (876-80), Louis the Younger (876-82), and Charles the Fat (876-87) in East Frankia. From 879 the Great Army systematically scoured Middle Frankia (map 5), which had experienced few raids in the 850s and 860s and whose towns and monasteries lacked defences. In 880,

BRIDGES AND BURHS

The most successful way to thwart the Vikings was to build fortifications; even the Great Army was incapable of taking strongly held defences. However, this required the mobilization of manpower and the overcoming of local apathy. Charles the Bald concentrated on blocking the Seine, which led to the heart of his kingdom. In 862, he began work on a fortified bridge at Pont de l'Arche near Pîtres, consisting of a wooden superstructure and bridgehead forts of wood and stone. In 865, Vikings were still able to reach Paris, so Charles went to Pîtres with workmen 'to complete the fortifications, so that the Northmen might never again be able to sail up the Seine'. Yet in 868 'he measured out the fort into sections…and assigned responsibility for them to various men of his realm', and the next year men were detailed 'to complete and then guard the fort' (*Annals of St Bertin*). The work seems finally to have been completed by 873. This was part of a campaign of fortification. In 864, Charles ordered that men too poor to campaign were to work on and garrison fortifications, and in 865 bridges were rebuilt to block access to the Oise and Marne. The monastery of St Denis near Paris was walled in 869, and a fortified bridge was built at Paris. He also ordered the restoration of walls at Tours, Le Mans, and Orléans in 869, and a bridge was built at Pont-de-Cé to block the Loire. Before Charles went to Italy in 877 he showed continuing concern by issuing instructions for garrisons and the inspection of defences. However, in 885 the Great Army sailed up the Seine to Paris. Since the death of Charles in 877, royal power had declined, and Pont de l'Arche was probably no longer garrisoned. At Paris, effective resistance was led by the local commanders abbot Gauzlin and count Odo. During the 880s, defences were constructed throughout the area between the Seine and Rhine, but now it was on local rather than royal initiative.

In England, Alfred's contemporary biographer Asser wrote of 'the cities and towns he restored, and the others he constructed where there had been none before'. *The Burghal Hidage*, an early tenth-century document, lists thirty West Saxon *burhs* (fortresses) and the number of *hides* (a measure of land for assessing taxes and dues) attached to each to provide manpower. Each *hide* was to send one man with responsibility for four feet of rampart, and where the walls survive their length often corresponds closely to the allotted garrison. Although changes had occurred by the early tenth century, there is little doubt that the system originated in the 880s. The *burhs* had several functions. They were refuges for the local population, their garrisons ensured the Vikings could not seize them, and men from the *burhs* were a mobile reserve which could be used against raiders, as in 893. They had various origins: reused Roman walls, earthworks from the Iron Age and later, and new foundations. Some were small forts close to existing sites, but others like Wallingford were founded as new towns with planned layouts. *The Burghal Hidage* arrangements required the mobilization of 27,000 men – perhaps one-fifth of the adult male population of Wessex. Unsurprisingly, there was some apathy in face of such a demand: in 892, the Great Army overran a half-made *burh* (probably the lost Eorpeburnan in East Sussex) which contained an incomplete garrison. Yet generally the system worked. Whereas in the 870s the Great Army seized existing forts at will, from 884, when it vainly besieged Rochester, it was unable to penetrate the heart of Wessex.

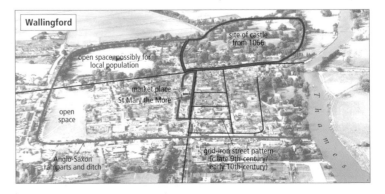

Wallingford — site of castle from 1066 — open space, possibly for local population — market place St Mary the More — open space — Anglo-Saxon ramparts and ditch — grid-iron street pattern (late 9th-century/early 10th-century) — Thames

armies from West and East Frankia failed to trap the Great Army on the Scheldt, but Louis III defeated a raiding force at Saucourt in August 881. The construction of a fort at Etrun to block the Scheldt persuaded the army to move to the Meuse. Charles the Fat besieged their camp at Ascloha (Asselt?) in July 882, but after only two weeks he bribed the army to return to West Frankia, to Condé. The West Frankish ruler Carloman defeated a party near Rheims, recovering its plunder, but could not prevent further raids and finally paid the Army to depart in 884. Now the Great Army divided: part crossed to England to besiege Rochester unsuccessfully; part was defeated at Louvain in 885 and besieged by East and West Frankish forces, finally escaping by night.

In Flanders and Lotharingia, little impeded Viking pillaging before 885. Local forces (led by counts, bishops, and abbots) were generally beaten, and while larger royal armies could defeat raiding parties, victories like Louis III's at Saucourt had little permanent effect. The Viking raiders' mobility made interception difficult as they were willing to use terrain like forests to escape. By 885, however, the area had been thoroughly ravaged and Carloman's death without an heir in December 884 made the Seine valley, after a twenty-year break from serious raids, an inviting target. In July 885, the Great Army reunited in the Seine. The bridge at Pont de l'Arche failed to stop them, but that at Paris was strongly held, even though the defences were incomplete when the army arrived. The town stood on an island connected to the banks by bridges defended by two forts. The Vikings failed to storm the northern fort (26 November), so they fortified winter quarters from which to maintain the siege and pillage the surrounding region for the next year. The siege was the subject of a long poem written by Abbo, an eye-witness; although prone to exaggeration – he estimated the Great Army as 40,000 men and 700 ships, resisted by a mere 200 Franks – he gave valuable details, such as descriptions of the siege weapons built for the Vikings by renegade Franks, and the use of a fire ship against the bridge. Paris resisted all the Viking attacks, but nor could the Franks dislodge the Vikings from their camp.

Charles the Fat ended the deadlock by making another humiliating treaty: the Great Army was paid tribute and allowed up-river to winter in Burgundy, the very thing the bridge at Paris had been intended to prevent. For three years it pillaged in the upper Seine basin, ravaging towns and monasteries hitherto untouched, such as Verdun, Toul, and Troyes. Charles' failure led to his deposition. In 889 the new West Frankish king, Odo, checked the Vikings near Paris and bribed them to move on. Defeated by the Bretons at St Lô (890), they made again for Flanders. There the respite from Viking attack had been put to good use: in the 880s town walls had been restored, monasteries fortified, and forts built for the population. In the winter of 890-91, the Great Army had to besiege Noyon, and a force which assaulted an earth and timber fort near St Omer, one of the 'forts that had been recently built' (*Miracles of St Bertin*),

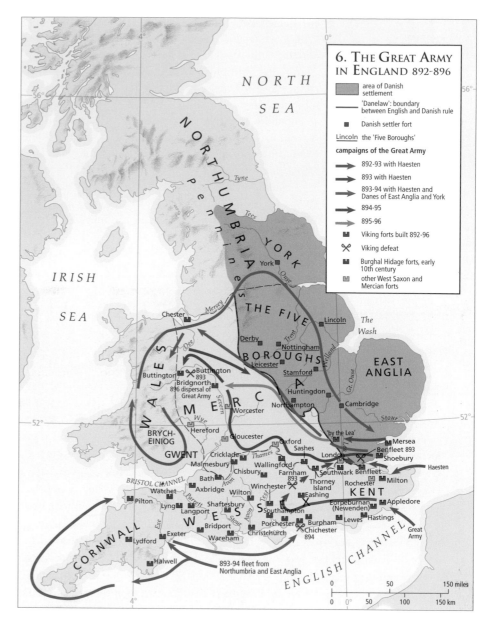

was repulsed. Haesten's army from Amiens likewise found Arras held against it. In spring, the Great Army moved to Louvain and dug in between the river Dyle and a marsh, and the East Frankish king Arnulf stormed the camp (the battle of the Dyle). East Frankish writers duly claimed a decisive victory, yet the Great Army soon reoccupied the camp. The campaigns in Frankia had followed the familiar pattern of fortifying winter quarters and raiding by horse all year round. The ships seem to have followed from camp to camp; 200 are said to have left Ascloha on the Meuse in 882. Sometimes they had a separate base, but were readily available when required. Godefrid, one of two kings leading the Great Army, left in 882 when Charles the Fat granted him land in Frisia. When Haesten's fleet arrived from the Loire, forced out by Louis III in 882, it kept its identity and in 890-92 had a separate base. What finally made the Great Army quit Frankia was not resistance but a famine.

In autumn 892, the Vikings crossed to Kent (*map 6*) – the Great Army 'in one journey, horse and all' (*Anglo-Saxon Chronicle*), in an estimated 200 or 250 ships, Haesten's fleet

MAP 6

When the Great Army left England in 879, the Danes in East Anglia, east Mercia, and at York remained a potential threat to Wessex. This added urgency to Alfred's reform of West Saxon defences. When the Great Army returned in 892 it met a vigorous response. In 896, the Great Army recognized that Wessex could not be conquered, nor even plundered, and it finally broke up.

Charles the Bald's succession to West Frankia was troubled by his half-brothers' resentment of his share of their father's inheritance. The Vikings exploited the ensuing political confusion from the mid-840s. Charles only found a way of removing the Vikings from the Seine valley in the 860s; a mixture of fortification, restricting the opportunity for plunder, and setting one Viking band against another. However, it was difficult to persuade his kingdom to pay for these measures.

in 80 — and established winter bases. For four years these Vikings, with the Danes already settled in England, raided into Wessex and the rump of Mercia (now close allies). However, Alfred had used the 880s to reorganize the defences of Wessex. He had divided the available warriors so that while some were on garrison duty, of the remainder 'always half its men were at home, half on service' (*Anglo-Saxon Chronicle*). He had created a network of fortresses, *burhs* in Old English. These were refuges, but their garrisons formed rapid reaction forces against Viking raids. The result was that the Vikings were hotly pursued wherever they went.

During the winter of 892-93, Alfred kept a close watch on the two Viking bases. When the Great Army moved into Wessex, in the spring of 893, his son Edward defeated it at Farnham and besieged the Vikings on an island in the Thames. Then, while Alfred led an army to Exeter, besieged by a fleet from the Danish settlements, Edward's army stormed Haesten's new base at Benfleet in Essex. A third raid by the Great Army in 893, up the Thames and Severn,

was pursued by troops from West Saxon and Mercian *burhs* and Welsh princes. They besieged the Vikings at Buttington, where allegedly they were forced to eat their horses, and defeated them, although this did not prevent the Vikings from returning to Essex. Alfred's division of his forces had proved equal to the challenge in 893, but nonetheless the Great Army regrouped and mounted another raid in the autumn, after the Vikings 'had placed their women and ships and treasure in safety' (*Anglo-Saxon Chronicle*). The pursuing English could not prevent them from occupying the Roman fortress of Chester, but by clearing the grain and cattle from the surrounding area they forced the army to winter in Wales instead.

After the hectic campaigning of 893, the next two years appear calmer in the *Anglo-Saxon Chronicle*. In autumn 894, the Great Army rowed up the Thames and Lea to Hertford and established new winter quarters, remaining there until August 895 when Alfred positioned an army to deny the harvest to the Vikings. In a move reminiscent of Charles the Bald in 862, he built a fortified bridge to block the Lea. This forced the Great Army to abandon its ships. It moved to Bridgnorth on the Severn for the winter of 895-96, a safe distance from Wessex.

The following summer the Great Army broke up, some settling in eastern England, the remainder crossing to West Frankia. That summer Danish settlers raided the West Saxon coast and tested the ships Alfred had designed, 'built neither on the Frisian nor the Danish pattern, but as it seemed to him they could be most useful' (*Anglo-Saxon Chronicle*). They were not an unqualified success. In contrast to the 870s, Wessex itself had hardly been touched by the Great Army raids of 892-96. Part of the explanation must lie in the network of defended forts Alfred had established. Tight marking by forces from Wessex and Mercia, matching the Vikings' mobility, had been able to prevent the Great Army from operating profitably. After thirty years of pillaging it finally dispersed. Those who had capital joined the settlers in eastern England; those without returned to the Seine where they established the nucleus of the future Normandy.

This whale's bone box made in Northumbria, England, depicts a mixture of Romano-Christian and Germanic traditions. Its vivid scenes portray English warriors in the eighth century. The helmet resembles one of similar date found in York and others worn by Northumbrian warriors on a carved stone at Aberlemno, Scotland. One warrior is depicted in mail, the others seem to wear no armour, but all the attackers carry swords and shields.

TENTH-CENTURY KINGDOMS: THE GROWTH OF ENGLAND, GERMANY, AND FRANCE

WARFARE WAS A FORMATIVE INFLUENCE in the tenth-century development of Europe. In England, the kings of Wessex used fortress-building to conquer the Viking states and create a unified kingdom. In East Frankia (Germany), the disintegration of the Carolingian world was reversed by the Ottonian kings who asserted primacy over the German duchies, crushed the Magyars, and conquered Italy. A strategy of penetrative fortification permitted their exploitation of Slav lands across the Elbe. In West Frankia (France), the collapse of royal power accompanied the struggles between Charles the Bald's successors. The dispersal of many royal estates allowed castle-building aristocrats to create principalities, the so-called 'feudal anarchy' from which a new form of French royal power would emerge.

This stone cross from Middleton, near Pickering in Yorkshire, is dated to the ninth or tenth century. It depicts a well-armed warrior wearing a conical helmet with nose-guard, and a tunic, although there is no indication of mail. He is surrounded by a shield, spear, sword, and axe.

ENGLAND: THE CREATION OF ONE KINGDOM 899-954

By the time he died in 899, Alfred had ensured the survival of Wessex under English rule and was acknowledged as overlord by Aethelred, ruler of English Mercia. The Vikings remained a formidable threat, however. The Danes who settled in England established two kingdoms, East Anglia and York, and five earldoms based on the fortified bases in east Mercia (the Five Boroughs). The Norwegian kings of Dublin were a further threat to north-west England and to York, which they claimed. Clearly the first priority of Alfred's son, king Edward 'the Elder' (899-924) and of his son-in-law, Aethelred, was consolidation, to secure their lands against both the Danish settlers and further Viking bands. Even Edward's succession was disputed by his cousin Aethelwold, who joined the Danes and raided across west Mercia in 902. He was killed in battle during Edward's retaliatory raid on East Anglia.

Edward did not take the offensive until 909, when he sent a West Saxon and Mercian army against the Danes of York. He was preparing a fleet to attack East Anglia in 910, when the York Danes raided across Mercia into Wessex at the same time as a Viking fleet from Brittany was in the Severn (map 1). The army was overtaken and defeated at Tettenhall, which decisively weakened Danish York and limited the support it could give the southern colonies in the following years. Edward annexed London and Oxford in 911 after Aethelred's death, which gave him a common border with the Danes.

The establishment of fortresses at Hertford and Witham (911-12) secured the frontier, but was also the first tentative step in the conquest of the Danish colonies south of the Humber. The Danes retaliated by raiding from Leicester and Northampton in 913. Despite the intervention of a Viking fleet from Brittany, Edward and his sister Aethelfled (Aethelred's widow) began an offensive in November 914, which continued until all the Danish colonies south of the Humber submitted in 920. Although Aethelfled's

campaigns were mainly against the Welsh and Norse settlers in north-west England, she played a vital role in Edward's success by dividing the Vikings so that they could not present a united front.

The founding of two fortresses at Buckingham (914) secured Bedford's submission, where an English fortress kept watch on the Danes. The construction of Maldon (916) was a prelude to the crisis year of the conquest in 917 (page 28). Concerted Danish assaults on Towcester and 'Wigingamere' (unidentified) failed, and were followed by the submission of East Anglia, Northampton, Essex, and Cambridge. While the northern armies were engaged against West Saxon forces, Aethelfled captured Derby. These setbacks broke the will of the remaining Danish armies: in 918, Leicester submitted to Aethelfled, and York sought her aid against the Dublin Norwegians; Stamford and Nottingham submitted to Edward, who also took over Mercia when Aethelfled died in June 918. The English triumph was sealed

A mid-eleventh-century Biblical scene from Canterbury reflects English and Viking usage. Armies used horses for transport, but generally dismounted to fight. Unlike the Franks, they do not seem to have developed cavalry tactics.

when, following a Norse raid on north-west Mercia in 920, Edward took an army to Bakewell which resulted in the submission of the Scottish king, of Strathclyde, English Bamburgh, and king Raegnald of York.

Fortresses played a vital role in Edward and Aethelfled's advance. The earthwork defences took about a month to construct, and captured Danish works were also used. They were garrisoned by king's thegns (landowners owing direct allegiance to the king) with their retainers. The complex fighting of 917 illustrates the use of fortresses as an offensive weapon. So long as their garrisons were able to resist attack until relieved, the establishment of frontier fortresses threatened the Danes nearby. In addition, groups of garrisons could combine to attack Danish centres or deal with raiders

(913, 914). The English ability to capture Danish fortresses during this period, in marked contrast to Danish failures, cannot be explained on the available evidence. Each successful stage of the conquest was completed by garrisoning captured Danish fortresses or planting an English fort nearby. The construction of these fortresses required the mobilization of labour and soldiers for field armies and garrisons, an achievement which is rarely recognized. Edward's genius was to harness fortresses to expansion, a new type of warfare in Anglo-Saxon England (although familiar in eighth-century Frankia), to create permanent conquest rather than the temporary overlordships which had gone before. None of this would have been possible without Alfred's military reforms (*pages 23-25*).

MAP 1

Although the last Viking 'Great Army' dispersed in 896, English Wessex and Mercia still had to guard against the Danish settlers. From 911, Edward of Wessex and his sister Aethelfled conquered the southern Viking colonies using a method new to English warfare, planting fortified garrisons to secure and then to advance their frontiers. While Edward advanced from the south, Aethelfled applied pressure from the west. By 924, all England south of the Humber was subject to a single king for the first time.

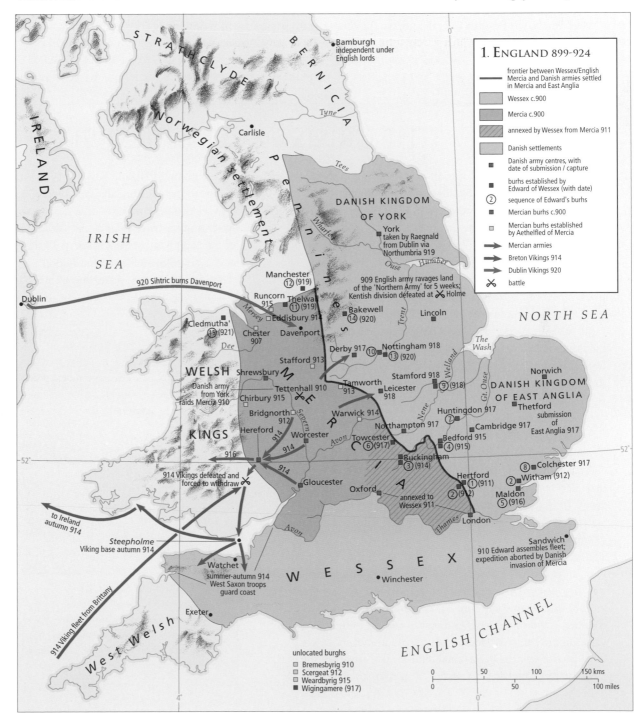

By his death in 924, Edward had transformed the kingdom of Wessex into a kingdom of England. His sons Athelstan, Edmund, and Eadred consolidated the lands south of the Humber but only intermittently controlled York. Their campaigns north of the Humber reverted to long-distance raids reminiscent of seventh- to ninth-century warfare because Northumbria was so distant from Wessex. It lacked fortified centres to facilitate conquest, resented southern overlordship, and from 910 the Dublin Norwegians also sought to control it. Analysis of the campaigns of these years is hindered by the brevity of the *Anglo-Saxon Chronicle* after its detailed account of Edward's campaigns.

Athelstan's control of Northumbria (927-34) created new military problems. An agreement with the kings of the Scots and Strathclyde Britons (927) did not last. In 934, he invaded Scotland in an impressive display of the reach of West Saxon power (*map 2*). The leaders assembled at Winchester in late May, and a week later they were at Nottingham. The army, including Welsh kings, English ealdormen, and Danish earls, harried nearly to Aberdeen, while a fleet reached Caithness. This provoked the invasion of England by a coalition of Dublin Norwegians, Scots, and Strathclyde Britons in 937. They were defeated at Brunanburh (site unknown), a famous battle of which little is known. However, when Athelstan died in 939, Olaf of Dublin seized York and attacked north Mercia. The fortresses built by Edward the Elder were doubtless in disrepair, their garrisons long since removed after years of peace. Athelstan's successor, Edmund, had to make peace at the cost of ceding the Five Boroughs, but just as Athelstan's death presented Olaf's opportunity, so Olaf's death benefited Edmund. He reconquered the Five Boroughs (942), subjected York (944), and invaded Strathclyde (945) in campaigns of which nothing is known. Still the southern hold on Northumbria remained tenuous. Scandinavian kings again ruled in York between 948 and 954. King Eadred's punitive raid in 948 secured the temporary submission

THE CRISIS OF CONQUEST 917

There follows a simplified version of the account in the *Anglo-Saxon Chronicle* for the year 917. Numbers refer to the map.

'In this year before Easter [13 April] (1) King Edward ordered the burh at Towcester to be occupied and built, and…at the Rogation days [19-21 May] (2) he ordered the burh at Wigingamere [unidentified] to be built…(3) [July] The Danish army from Northampton and Leicester and north of these places…went to Towcester, and fought all day against the burh…yet the people who were inside defended it until more help came to them…(4) [July: Aethelfled stormed Derby] (5) [August: the Danes raided Buckinghamshire] (6) At the same time the Danish army came from Huntingdon and East Anglia and made the fortress at Tempsford…thinking that from Tempsford they would reach more of the land with strife and hostility. (7) And they went until they reached Bedford, and the men who were inside…put them to flight…(8) After that a great Danish army assembled from East Anglia and Mercia, and went to the burh at Wigingamere… and attacked it long into the day…yet the men who were inside defended the burh. And then the enemy left the borough and went away. Then after that during the same summer a great folk assembled in King Edward's dominions from the nearest burhs… (9) and went to Tempsford and…took it by storm…Very soon after that a great English folk assembled in autumn, both from Kent, from Surrey, from Essex and from the nearest burhs…(10) and they went to Colchester and…attacked it until they took it…Still in the same autumn, a great Danish army from East Anglia collected…and of the Vikings they had enticed to their assistance… (11) They went to Maldon…and attacked it until more troops came out to help the garrison; and the Danish army left the burh [and were pursued and defeated]…Very soon afterwards in the same autumn (12) King Edward went with the army of the West Saxons to Passenham and stayed there (13) while the burh of Towcester was provided with a stone wall (14) [submission of the Northampton army as far as the Welland] And when that division of the English army went home (15) the other [division] came out and captured the burh at Huntingdon…and restored it [submission of the Danish armies of East Anglia and Cambridge].

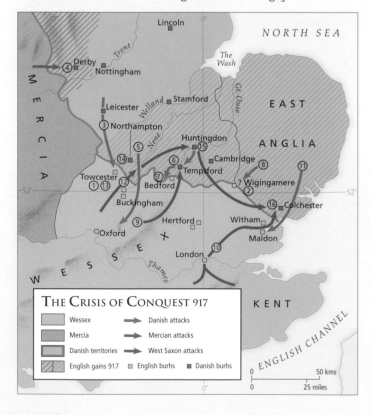

THE CRISIS OF CONQUEST 917

Wessex	→	Danish attacks
Mercia	→	Mercian attacks
Danish territories	→	West Saxon attacks
English gains 917	□ English burhs	■ Danish burhs

0 — 50 kms
0 — 25 miles

MAP 2

Attempts to control the Viking kingdom of York were hindered by its distance from Wessex, although Athelstan's 934 raid into Scotland, and his defeat of a Viking-Celtic coalition at 'Brunanburh', indicate the extent of West Saxon power. Control of York was also disrupted by the Vikings of Dublin, and it took frequent raids from the south before York's independence was broken and a united English kingdom was created in 954. Even then, West Saxon royal power was strictly limited north of the Humber.

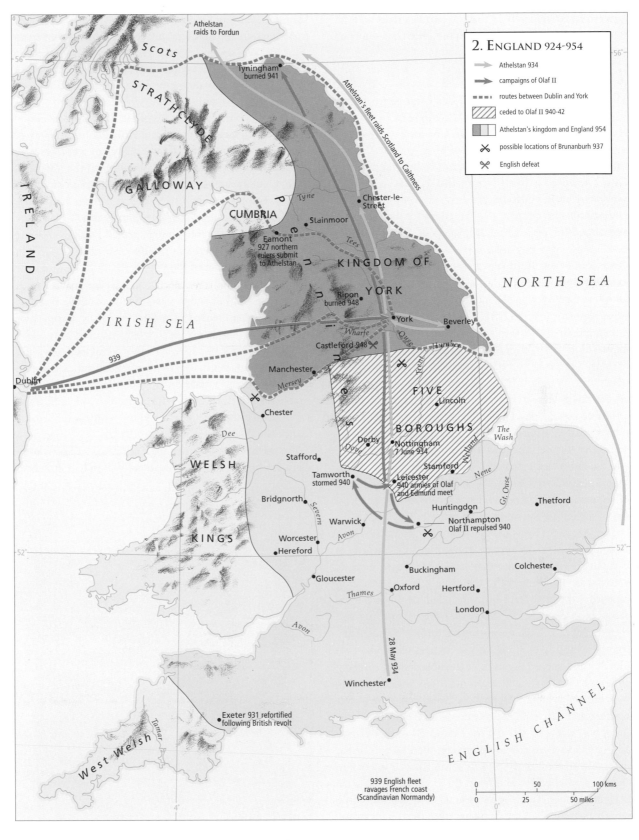

2. ENGLAND 924-954

→ Athelstan 934
→ campaigns of Olaf II
┅ routes between Dublin and York
▨ ceded to Olaf II 940-42
▦ Athelstan's kingdom and England 954
✕ possible locations of Brunanburh 937
✖ English defeat

of York, despite the defeat of his rearguard at Castleford, but there was an element of fortune in the final submission of Northumbria following its rejection of king Eric Bloodaxe, who was killed on Stainmoor in 954. Northumbria was not strong enough to assert its independence for long against the kingdom south of the Humber.

The kingdom of England was thus a military creation of the first half of the tenth century. Its emergence was not inevitable, and it faced a severe setback in 940. The step-by-step conquest of east Mercia and East Anglia proved lasting because it was tied down by fortresses, and was followed by conversion to Christianity and political integration. Many fortresses developed into towns, although they must have lost some military effectiveness. Pitched battles played little part in making permanent conquests: what was crucial was the ability to plant, defend, and support fortified sites.

TENTH-CENTURY GERMANY

The East Frankish kingdom was one of three to emerge from the division of Charlemagne's empire in 843. When Henry, duke of Saxony, became king in 919, many of the royal powers and resources had been taken over by the rulers of the ethnic duchies. Henry I (919-36) and his son Otto I (936-73), from whom the dynasty is named, prevented further devolution of power. They welded the German duchies into a unified kingdom for the first time, and ended the devastating Magyar raids (map 3). Under both kings, large Slav areas were laid under tribute, and Otto conquered northern and central Italy. Ottonian expansion was halted by the Arabs of Sicily, who defeated Otto II at Cap Colonna in southern Italy in 982, and by the great Slav revolt of 982-83. The Ottonian achievement depended in the first place on the development and exploitation of Saxony's military resources.

Henry I possessed sufficient power to secure acceptance of his rule by the other dukes, but little more. His main achievements were to contain the Danes and the Magyars. On his accession, Otto I faced internal rebellions, overcome with a good measure of fortune, and external attacks (937-41). After this he strengthened his grip over the duchies, and the last major rebellion (953-55) was a family affair. In 955, he defeated both Magyars and Slavs (at the battles of Lechfeld and Recknitz), and was secure enough to spend ten of the last twelve years of his reign in Italy.

The Magyars (Hungarians), a mixed group in which Turkic peoples predominated, moved into the Carpathian basin in the 890s, whence they launched devastating raids westwards – some thirty in the years 898-955 – seizing captives and booty. Their hosts included contingents from Slav subject-peoples. The Magyars were fast-moving and elusive, but lacked the means to take fortified places. They fought as lightly equipped horse archers who relied on mobility and feigned flights in pitched encounters, disliking close combat for which many of them lacked suitable weapons and armour. Magyar bows were ineffective in wet weather and they suffered several defeats, but battle with them was risky: in 907-10 they defeated three German armies and so were able to raid freely, yet a Magyar defeat in 913 brought little respite to south Germany. For the Germans, pitched battle offered the opportunity to seize Magyar plunder. The Magyars sought slaves and movable wealth and, like the Vikings, were quick to take advantage of internal dissension. Saxony and Bavaria were hit hardest. Both paid tribute in the 920s, but hit back hard in the 930s and 940s. The Magyar raids were already in decline when they suffered a crushing defeat in 955 at the battle of Lechfeld (page 32).

Tributes imposed on the Slav tribes across the Elbe underpinned the Saxon military successes until the 970s, and Saxon slave-raiding was every bit as brutal as the Magyars'. Much of Saxony's strength was committed to the massive eastward advances in German overlordship from the 940s. When Otto I became preoccupied with Italy after 961, further advances were mainly the work of margraves (counts who commanded the eastern marches), such as Hermann Billung and Gero.

The tenth-century Saxon historian, Widukind, credited Henry I with creating in the late 920s the twin pillars of Saxon military success: an effective field army and a network of forts. The process took much longer than the few years he says, but the improvement in Saxon military organization is unquestionable. The ninth-century Saxons had a low military reputation, lacking the equipment to fight in the battle line beside the more heavily armed Franks, but some at least were employed as mounted skirmishers. When Henry became duke of the Saxons (911) he realized the need for a core of armoured cavalry (*milites armati, loricati*) to fight the Magyars and the Slavs, and to compete on equal terms with the Franks of the duchies of Lotharingia and Franconia. In the late 920s, a truce with the Magyars – bought at the cost of paying tribute – permitted Henry and the Saxon magnates to improve the training and equipment of their followings, paid for by Slav tribute which Henry restored at this time. In 932, he stopped tribute, and at the subsequent battle of Riade the lightly equipped Magyars fled rather than engage the Saxon cavalry.

The *milites armati*, the strike force of the Saxon hosts, were recruited from the nobility, many of whom had little land

This tenth-century German depiction of the martyrdom of St Boniface (754) shows the Ottonian *milites armati*. They were never numerous, owing to their expensive equipment, but their mailcoats, swords, and shields were a major advantage against poorly armed neighbours. They were the instruments of Ottonian unification of the German duchies, and of expansion against the Slavs and into Italy.

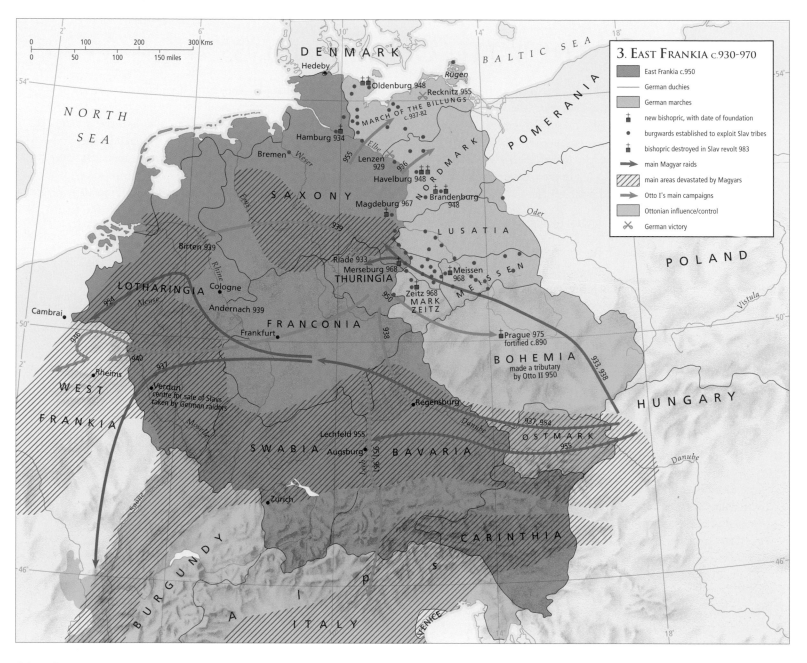

MAP 3

Henry I of Saxony prevented the German duchies from becoming independent, and created a force of armoured cavalry. His son, Otto I, used these foundations to crush the Magyars, assert his rule over Germany, and to gain imperial title and the precious resources of the Italian kingdom.

due to the Saxon practice of dividing inheritances. Armour and horses were frequently provided by the king or ecclesiastical and lay landowners. They were armed and trained to fight at close quarters with spears and swords. Equipment was worth more than numbers: fifty men were decisive at Lenzen (929) against Slavs possessing few horsemen; one hundred defeated a rebel Saxon and Lotharingian host at Birten (939). Success over Slavs and Magyars, and greater control of the duchies, increased the numbers available. Widukind employs the term 'legion' loosely to describe the units in German hosts, none numbering more than a few hundred cavalry. The Merseburg 'legion' consisted of pardoned criminals, both horse and foot, guarding the border on a permanent war footing; other 'legions' were provided by the dukes. At Lechfeld, Otto's eight 'legions' possibly numbered 3,000 to 4,000 armoured horsemen – the only Saxons present were Otto's following, the Slav threat tying down most

of the Saxon forces in the north. In 946, Otto I was able to lead a host from all the duchies into West Frankia. Widukind puts its strength at thirty-two 'legions', which should be taken to mean a very large army. The only precise figure available is the 2,090 *loricati* (armoured cavalry) sent by ecclesiastical and lay princes of south and west Germany to Otto II in 981. This was only a fraction of the kingdom's strength, for Otto II already had a host containing a large Saxon contingent with him in Italy, while more warriors remained in Germany. For local defence, the free peasantry provided unarmoured cavalry and infantry, who were of little value for long-distance warfare.

Widukind also describes Henry ordering the building of forts garrisoned by the free peasantry: one out of every nine performed garrison duty, while the remainder worked the fields of all and sheltered in the forts. This represents an idealized picture, but while archaeological remains of the forts are elusive, there is full documentary evidence for the

THE BATTLE OF LECHFELD 955

By the early 950s, the Magyars had ceased to be a serious threat to western Europe. In 950, they were raided by the Bavarians, while German control of north Italy (951) restricted their access to its wealth. The renewal of dissension within Germany (953-55) offered the Magyars the opportunity to restore their fortunes. In 954, they crossed the Rhine as allies of the rebel duke Conrad of Lotharingia, but by raiding into northern France they showed their

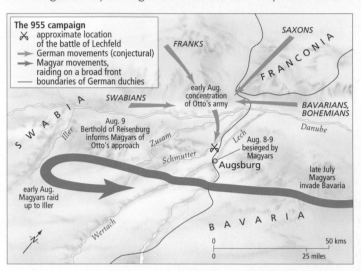

The 955 campaign
⚔ approximate location of the battle of Lechfeld
→ German movements (conjectural)
→ Magyar movements, raiding on a broad front
— boundaries of German duchies

true intentions. In July 955, they invaded Bavaria again, but by remaining in the vicinity of Augsburg they invited a pitched battle, instead of using their mobility to evade Otto I as they had in 954. For Otto, a victory would crown the restoration of his authority following the 953-54 rebellion.

Otto's rapid move to the Danube in July sacrificed numbers for surprise. He had with him his Saxon household troop, but the bulk of the Saxon forces were left to deal with the Slavs. His main strength came from the other duchies, although many Lotharingians were unable to muster in time, and a Bohemian contingent, perhaps 4,000 armoured horsemen in all. They were outnumbered by the Magyars who were besieging Augsburg when a Bavarian rebel informed them of Otto's approach from the north-west. On 9 August, both sides prepared for battle. The next morning, as the Germans approached in column (1), the Magyars launched an encircling movement along the east bank of the Lech

to take them in the rear (2). They must have hoped to destroy Otto's host by this stratagem without risking close combat, for which many of them lacked swords, spears, and defensive armour. The Bohemians, escorting the baggage, were scattered by the Magyar archery and the rout spread to the Swabian uints (3). Otto sent back the Franks of duke Conrad, who had returned to his allegiance, to restore the situation (4). They drove off the Magyars, who had started to plunder, before returning to Otto for the final stage of the engagement, a frontal charge by the leading German contingents (5). The best equipped Magyars, the leaders and their followings, held fast and were cut down as the rest fled (6). Many more were killed or captured during the pursuit that day, and subsequently as they retreated across Bavaria (7). Instead of being ransomed, the captured Magyar princes were hanged at Regensburg. This departure from normal policy destroyed the Magyar leadership and accelerated the end of their nomadic way of life. Lechfeld was thus a decisive victory which finally freed western Europe from the threat of Magyar raids, consummated Otto I's kingship, and permitted him to concentrate on exploiting the resources of the Slavs and later of Italy.

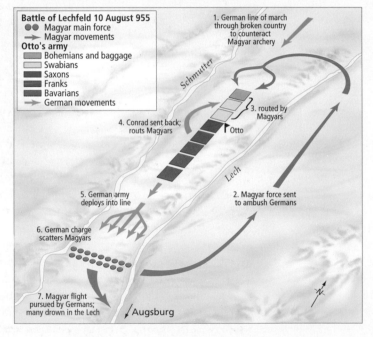

Battle of Lechfeld 10 August 955
●● Magyar main force
→ Magyar movements
Otto's army
▮ Bohemians and baggage
▮ Swabians
▮ Saxons
▮ Franks
▮ Bavarians
→ German movements

1. German line of march through broken country to counteract Magyar archery
2. Magyar force sent to ambush Germans
3. routed by Magyars
4. Conrad sent back; routs Magyars
5. German army deploys into line
6. German charge scatters Magyars
7. Magyar flight pursued by Germans; many drown in the Lech

development of a network of fortresses in the East Saxon and Thuringian marches, where the German and Slav peasantry owed labour and watch services. Ten or twenty settlements (forming a ward) were allocated to a fortress (burg). Frontier forts were garrisoned by the followers of bishops and counts in monthly shifts, although reliefs did not always take place so regularly. The fortresses were more than places of refuge: in 938, Magyar invaders were harassed by their garrisons, and they served as centres to exploit the

Slav peasantry whose tributes in silver and in kind maintained the Saxon nobility on a war footing. Although the tributes were lost in the great Slav revolt (982-83), they were already being replaced by silver from the Harz mountain mines, and by land grants to warriors. After 961, Italy provided further resources for the crown.

Saxon expansion slowed after Otto I's death, and was ended by Otto II's defeat by the Sicilian Arabs at Cap Colonna in 982, and by the Slav revolt. By that time, Henry I's

Doué-la-Fontaine stands 20 miles (32 km) south-east of Angers. Built c.900, possibly as a Carolingian royal hall, it was later partially destroyed in a fire. The present stone keep, built by the count of Blois, was taken by Fulk Nerra of Anjou c.1025. This transformation from royal residence into grim blockhouse symbolizes the militarization of tenth-century Gaul.

military reforms had laid the foundation for the German kingdom, whose rulers were also emperors after 962, and which dominated central and western Europe for the next two and a half centuries.

TENTH-CENTURY FRANCE

During the tenth century, the western part of the Carolingian empire dissolved into a number of principalities (map 4). A succession of short reigns and child kings led to a decline of royal power, and the counts of Anjou, Aquitaine, Champagne, and Flanders rose to prominence. Normandy also began to make its presence felt, while Brittany and Burgundy became detached. The growth of local fortifications changed the nature of warfare, or rather it forced potential rulers to engage in a multiplicity of small campaigns – of raid, siege, and (occasionally) battle – in order to establish their authority. Lords of all ranks constructed fortifications and collected bodies of armed men about them. Siege warfare became increasingly significant, the castle a chesspiece on the political map. Some, like Fulk Nerra, count of Anjou, were masters of the new game.

Carolingian palaces had been sprawling, undefended building complexes. Town walls seem to have been non-existent in the earlier ninth century, the old Roman walls having been used as quarries (pages 22-23). Paris, besieged by Vikings in 885-86, was an exception. In 882, Rheims was still unfortified; Laon was burnt by the Vikings in the same year, either because it was defenceless, or because it may have had wooden walls like those built at Le Mans and Tours in 869. In contrast, small, local fortifications were springing up in the face of external raiders: Vikings from the north and west, Muslims from the south and, later, Magyars from the east. Internal warfare also encouraged their development. Already, in the Edict of Pîtres of 864, Charles the Bald was forbidding unlicensed fortifications, such as the 'strong house' of Egfrid, burnt down in 868.

The situation had changed dramatically by the tenth century. Laon was well enough defended to stand siege in 931, 938, and 939. Châlons had a citadel in 963, and, by 985, Verdun possessed both ramparts and a citadel. In 990, the Angevin garrison of Nantes retired into the citadel and held out until relieved. As local notables fortified their residences, supposedly against 'pagan persecution', they had their eyes upon expropriating public authority. When Raymond III of Rouergue built his castle on the rock at Conques, the monks there complained that he 'proposed to force his yoke and domination on those who would not freely accept his lordship'. Rights to tax, justice, and military service fell into the hands of local castellans. As these new political units became heritable, greater lords had to enforce their vassalage upon castellans if they wished to employ their military resources.

As fortifications developed, their builders began increasingly to use stone. Doué-la-Fontaine, in Anjou, is a model of how a one-storey Carolingian stone hall was heightened to form a two-storey 'donjon' or keep. Fulk Nerra built in stone at Loches and Langeais in the 990s. That towns were also walled in stone is proved by the increasing number of references to siege weaponry. The Vikings had already learnt to employ siege techniques at Paris in 885-86. These included contravallation, mining, and battering rams. They also attacked the bridge from their boats, the defenders replying with catapults, mangonels, and ballistas.

Besiegers also employed mobile siege towers and sheds for rams. In 938, at Laon, Louis IV used a battering ram on wheels. In 988, at Verdun, Hugh the Great had a huge engine of the same type. King Lothar's siege tower, also at Verdun (985), was oxen-drawn, and so overtopped the walls that the defenders had to build a wooden tower on top of them to oppose it. Nevertheless, the most frequent action taken by the besiegers was the seeming inaction of blockade: mounted troops ravaged the countryside and prevented supplies from reaching the defenders. Starvation was a much surer and more economical way of taking a castle or town than dangerous and costly assaults. Also, this might encourage the besieged's lord to make an attempt at relief and so be brought to battle on ground of the besiegers' choosing.

Most campaigns involved raiding expeditions (chevauchées) to ravage enemy territory, rather than battles. For these to take place required mutual intent. In 990, Charles of Lorraine decided to fight Hugh Capet's forces only if they attacked. Battles usually resulted from sieges or attempts to relieve besieged fortifications. In 994, Louis IV fell into an ambush while attempting to relieve Laon. In 925, king Rodolf's men refused to attack a Viking encampment on the Seine. The wisdom of this attitude would seem to have been born out by Fulk Nerra's experience in 992, whilst besieging the citadel at Nantes. He attacked the Bretons' fortified camp, but was repulsed with heavy loss. Fortunately for Fulk, Conan, the Breton leader, was killed whilst pursuing the Angevin troops, reversing the result. Encounter battles were rare, although in 923 the battle at Soissons was brought about by the unintended clash of the Carolingian and Capetian forces after a campaign of manoeuvre.

Writing c.1000, the chronicler Richer makes much of the 'royal cavalry' (*regii equitatus*), which he says struck fear into its enemies. Apparently they played an important role in defeating count Ricouin in 921, the Vikings in 930, 936, and 943, and the Aquitanians in 955. Whether cavalry generally enjoyed a clear-cut superiority is open to doubt. Much may have depended upon the tactical situation. For his attack on Langres, Louis IV deployed footmen against the town, while his 'royal cavalry' won the battle. Although Richer depicts Louis' victory over Viking forces in 943 as that of cavalry over infantry, encounters are usually described in such a way as to make it impossible to identify the respective roles of horse and foot. For example, in 990, when Hugh Capet fought Charles of Lorraine, the former deployed in three lines: the first to attack (possibly cavalry); the second to support (infantry?); and the third to gather booty (mounted reserve?).

Military resources are also difficult to determine. In Flanders and Champagne there were *milites casati* (stipendiary soldiers). Bruno, bishop of Langres, apparently possessed a well-disciplined force of such men, which he used to attack Burgundy. A late tenth-century charter for Vendôme describes how the town was guarded. Its count was responsible for the five months from April to August, then seven vassals took one month each. Five men served per night, three guarding the gates while two more patrolled the walls. Some served as vassals, others were paid. Two types of campaign service were distinguished: *ost* for short expeditions, and *chevauchée* for longer ones (up to two months at most). Numbers were probably small. Richer's '40,000' cavalry attributed to Robert, count of Paris, is mere rhetoric. Even an agreement between William V of Aquitaine and Hugh de Lusignan, which speaks of *chiliarchs* ('commanders of 1,000') is suspect. An Angevin source ascribes 200 cavalry and 1,000 foot to the castellan of Amboise, but this was more likely the order of magnitude for the forces of kings and great lords.

The foot were equipped with bows or spears and served either for pay or under the 'ban', an obligation that was in origin public, but was increasingly in the hands of counts and castellans. A 'new' infantry weapon was the crossbow. This had been known in the later Roman empire, then apparently fell out of use until it reappeared at Senlis in 949 and Verdun in 985. The crossbow played an important part in sieges and, from the middle of the eleventh century, on the battlefield too.

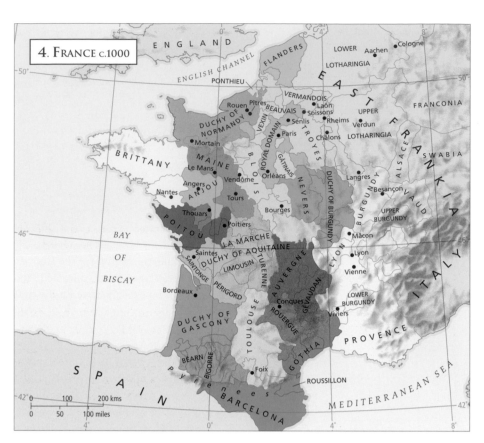

FULK NERRA AND THE CREATION OF ANJOU

For over half a century, from 980 to around 1030, Fulk Nerra dominated his county by means of a fortress strategy (*map 5*). At first this was defensive. His greatest competitor was Odo I, count of Blois, and ruler of the important city of Tours. Odo also controlled Saumur, so cutting off Angevin contact with the Touraine. In 992-94, Fulk constructed Langeais to secure a route south from Angers. He also drew upon his father's alliance with Bouchard of Vendôme to outflank Tours. His prime aim was to establish lines of communication with his southern fortresses of Loudun, Loches, and the Vienne valley. There was a risk that Fulk's vassals might transfer their allegiance to the count of Blois to preserve their lands; their defenders could submit to a besieger without penalty – only if they held out would they suffer massacre. So, Fulk's fortifications acted as staging posts, both defensible refuges and bases for supporting advances. They needed to be within a day's march of one another; no more than 20 miles (32 km) apart.

The sudden death of Odo in 996 allowed Fulk to take the initiative. He seized control of the Loire valley from Montsoreau to Amboise; but he had overreached himself. The new king of France, Robert, married Bertha of Blois and recaptured the city. Fulk learnt his lesson and was a most scrupulous vassal thereafter. He worked instead on developing a secure route through the northern Touraine to Amboise, constructing and rebuilding castles a day's march apart at Semblançay, Château-la-Vallière, and Baugé. Once again this was defensive, while the fortification of a *domus* (house) at Morand to harass communications between Tours and Château Renault was aggressive.

MAP 4

Around 1000, France (still called 'Gaul' by contemporaries) was not as unified as the name suggests. The king of France was just one of many princes, exercising his authority through balance-of-power politics. Authority became localized under castellans, controlling castles garrisoned by troops of horsemen. Effective rulers, like those of Anjou, used these fortifications in slow campaigns of military conquest.

South of the Loire, Fulk was strong in the valleys of the Indre and Vienne, but lacked a good link from Angers to Vihiers above the Layon. The situation was worsened by the defection of his previous ally, viscount Aimeri of Thouars, in 994. Needing a link to Loudun, Fulk began by fortifying Passavant and Montglan, a little further east. Montreuil-Bellay was only constructed c.1030, after the fall of Saumur. Its castellan, Berlaius, and his garrison of *caballarii* (mounted warriors) were tasked with protecting the area from attacks by the men of Thouars.

Meanwhile, following the loss of Tours in 997, Fulk began to encircle the city, building Montbazon in the same year. The castle also operated against the Blésois communications between Tours and Ile-Bouchard and, in co-ordination with the garrison of Langeais, against Chinon. Soon after 1000, Fulk established a castle south-east of Tours at Montrésor. Montrichard was constructed c.1005 to increase the pressure on St Aignan, a castle captured later and used as a base for further penetration of the Cher valley. Odo II's campaigns to recover St Aignan led to his defeat by Fulk at the battle of Pontlevoy in 1016.

In the west, Fulk used his vassals effectively, with Renaud controlling Champtoceaux c.998, and Drogo in Château-panne c.1006. Montjean was constructed shortly afterwards. St Florent-le-Vieil completed the defence of the Loire in the 1030s. Pushing south, Montrevault was established at the same time and later, in the 1020s, Montfaucon and La Tour Landry stood against hostile Thouars. Mirebeau, built c.1000, protected the southern march from attack from Poitiers. Fulk's influence may have spread even further south, supporting the lord of Parthenay in constructing that castle (c.1012) and later an outpost at Germond (1026). The strength of William V, count of Aquitaine, meant that it was advisable to use a less direct strategy than that employed against the count of Blois.

In the north, Fulk built upon the position established by his father at Sablé. Château-Gontier, on the Mayenne, and Château du Loir were constructed after 1005 against Le Mans. Most of the castles were built in the 1010s and 1020s, establishing a deep frontier, or *limes*, along the river Loir. It is possible to identify several strategic groupings of castles in a similar fashion, defending Fulk's territories. Of course, these did not form a rigid defensive line, rather a flexible defence-in-depth against the *chevauchée*. In 1026 and 1027, Odo II of Blois penetrated as far as Saumur, which had fallen to Fulk in the former year – but to no avail.

Castle garrisons were not intended to challenge an invading force, rather to harass it. Unless the attacker wished to commit his forces to siege, and risk being surprised by a relief force, he could achieve little. Fulk avoided battle and preferred to develop a strategic stranglehold through his fortifications. The final result, although not in his lifetime, was the conquest of Tours in 1044, after a half-century of pressure.

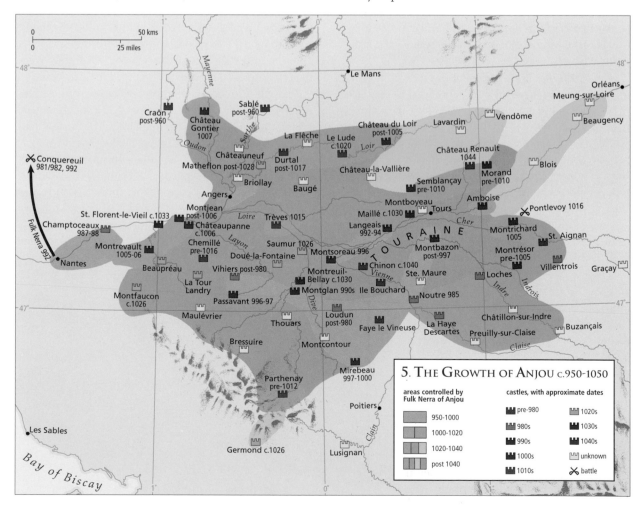

MAP 5

Fulk Nerra's fortress strategy greatly expanded Anjou. He constructed a network of castles, fortified houses, and towns no more than a day's march apart, to surround and isolate his enemies. The map shows the defensive beginnings and later offensive momentum which this strategy of conquest generated.

THE DANISH CONQUEST OF ENGLAND 980-1016

AFTER THE ENGLISH VICTORY at Brunanburh in 937, no Viking raids on England are recorded for nearly half a century. The raids resumed in 980, coinciding with the accession of Edgar's son Aethelred 'the Unready' (978-1016) at the age of eleven, and grew in intensity until England was conquered by Danish kings in 1016. From 991, the assaults were carried out by substantial forces consisting of several warbands rather than by hit-and-run raiders. The Danish king, Swein, was involved from an early date (991), as were the would-be kings Olaf Tryggvason and Olaf Haraldsson of Norway, and largely independent warlords like the earls Thorkell and Eric. The fleets were recruited not only from Denmark, but also from Norway and southern Sweden. Most of the raiders were attracted by plunder and English silver.

This coin was probably minted as part of a broad attempt by Aethelred to improve the military equipment of his forces in response to the Danish threat, and was part of the government's efforts to collect armour in 1008-09. It represents a helmet type possibly current in the early eleventh century, although this bust was copied from a fourth-century Roman coin.

VIKING RAIDS 980-1015

Viking activity in the Irish Sea never ceased in the tenth century, but healthy respect for Edgar's fleet brought immunity for England. The *Anglo-Saxon Chronicle* records 'nor was there fleet so proud nor Viking host so strong that got itself prey in England as long as the noble king held the throne'. In the 980s, the Irish Sea Vikings attacked Cheshire and south-west England; minor raids on southern England (980-81) may have been overspill from the Irish Sea or the work of pirates from Denmark or Normandy. Other raids may not have been recorded. However, Scandinavian activity in the 980s was spasmodic and isolated (map 1).

In the 990s, the raids became more serious. A fleet of ninety-three ships arrived in 991, possibly led by king Swein of Denmark and Olaf, future king of Norway. If the *Chronicle's* figure is accurate, this was a force of up to 7,000 warriors. From this account, it is impossible to be sure whether the raids up to 1005 were the work of a single host, as in the 860s to 890s. There is a strong impression that this was the case, even though bases are rarely specified.

Ealdorman Brihtnoth intercepted the first raid with an army from Essex at Maldon, where he was defeated and killed (991). The battle was immortalized in an Old English poem, and its literary fame has led to an exaggeration of its military significance: although it was followed by the first English payment of tribute, it would be many years before resistance collapsed. The Viking host seems to have remained in English waters, operating along the east coast (992-93), before a failed assault on London (994) was followed by pillaging along the south coast. In Hampshire, they seized horses and raided inland before being bought off with money, provisions, and winter quarters at Southampton. In the short term this worked: Olaf and Swein then departed and no raids are recorded for two years.

Across the Channel, the Normans, of Scandinavian descent, offered a ready market for the disposal of Viking plunder, which caused friction with Aethelred. The papacy had brokered a peace between England and Normandy in 991, but at some later date, probably the 990s, Aethelred sent a fleet to harry the Norman coast. A Viking fleet raided the south coast of England from 997 to 1000 (map 2) before withdrawing to Normandy. Aethelred used the respite to attack Strathclyde, for a reason now unknown. When the

In the peaceful years after about 950, Alfred and Edward's system of garrisoned fortresses decayed. Stone walls were added at certain sites, like Wallingford. Further, 'emergency' defensive boroughs were built to shelter local communities, as here at South Cadbury. But, after 1000, the Danes had the ability to capture them, and only London resisted successfully.

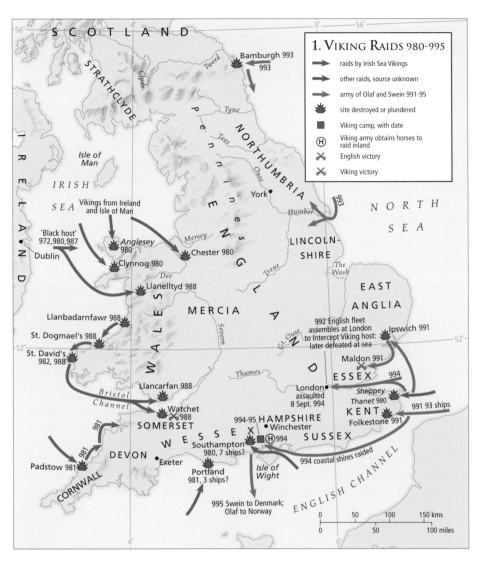

Map key:

1. VIKING RAIDS 980-995

→ raids by Irish Sea Vikings
→ other raids, source unknown
→ army of Olaf and Swein 991-95
🔥 site destroyed or plundered
■ Viking camp, with date
Ⓗ Viking army obtains horses to raid inland
✕ English victory
✕ Viking victory

MAP 1

Irish Viking raids in the west in the 980s, encouraged by Edgar's death, were a nuisance, but the east coast raids of 991-95 were more serious. They seem to have been the work of a large fleet based in English waters, which defeated an English army and was bold enough to attack London and raid inland before being bought off.

Vikings returned in 1001, they resumed coastal raiding until they were bought off early in 1002. In that year Aethelred married the count of Normandy's daughter, presumably hoping to close Norman ports to the Vikings.

Swein's return in 1003, either with a new host or to join Vikings already in England, marked a significant increase in the scale of Viking activity. The raiders penetrated farther inland and for the first time captured important towns: Exeter, which had held out in 1001, was captured in 1003, as was Wilton; Norwich and Thetford fell in 1004. It was at Thetford that Ulfcetel, a local noble, with an East Anglian host, fought them to a standstill. The 1006 raid was even bolder. During the summer and autumn, the Vikings harassed the south coast, despite the presence of an army from Wessex and Mercia. When it went home, the Viking army took winter quarters on the Isle of Wight before raiding deep inland to Wallingford, defeating an English army at the river Kennet, and marching back past the walls of Winchester (November-December 1006). Once again, they were finally bought off with tribute and provisions.

The host led by the great Danish chieftain Thorkell in 1009 comprised two fleets, and included the future Norwegian king, Olaf Haraldsson. It used ships to move to new coastal bases and penetrated far inland, although its

movements cannot be mapped with complete accuracy. In the autumn, southern England was plundered from the Isle of Wight, then in the winter it was the turn of the Thames valley from a base in the estuary. In 1010, the host pillaged East Anglia for three months after defeating Ulfcetel at Ringmere (unidentified), then the Thames valley again and the south Midlands. By the end of the year, English resistance was paralyzed and early in 1011 it was decided to offer tribute again, although peace was not concluded until April 1012. The army dispersed while Thorkell went into Aethelred's pay with forty-five ships and their crews.

The traumatic years from 1009 to 1012 brought England to its knees. In 1013, Swein returned with a new fleet intent on conquest. Northumbria and the Midlands north of Watling Street (the late ninth-century boundary between English and Danes) submitted and, as Swein advanced, Oxford and Winchester surrendered. London, where Aethelred was stationed with Thorkell's forces, held out, but in the autumn Wessex submitted. By the end of the year, Swein was accepted as king of England, while Aethelred fled to his father-in-law in Normandy. Swein's death in February 1014 saved him. He returned and drove Swein's son Cnut out of Lincolnshire.

THE ENGLISH DEFENCES

The *Anglo-Saxon Chronicle* creates the false impression that from 991 onwards the English were beaten. Before 1009, the raiders met some stout resistance, and if they were not defeated, at least they moved on or accepted tribute. Only after 1009 did creeping paralysis set in, the widespread ravaging of 1010 breaking the will to resist in many regions.

The first line of defence was the local forces of individual shires (counties). Historians refer to these forces as the 'fyrd', the Old English word for an army. While it is possible that most free men turned out for local defence, it was the landowners of the shires who formed the backbone of the English army. Service was due from all who held a certain amount of land (five hides, a quantity associated with the noble rank of thegn); owners of less were expected to join together to equip one of their number. The great landowners, ealdormen, wealthy thegns, bishops, and abbots, led their tenants in proportion to their landholding, influence, and political pretensions.

The *Chronicle* has many references to the forces of one or more neighbouring counties taking on the raiders: Essex (991), Hampshire (1001), Devon and Somerset (1001), East Anglia (1004), all led by royal officials, ealdormen, or royal reeves. None were victorious, but they put up effective resistance at Dean (1001) and Thetford (1004). The local forces may well have been outnumbered and were probably outclassed by the invaders.

Coastal raids were unpredictable and inevitably provoked local responses, but Aethelred and his advisers can be criticized for failure to co-ordinate the defence. The problem was not lack of resources. Aethelred inherited from his father Edgar the machinery for raising a fleet – one warship (*scegth*) and its crew of sixty from each 300 hides. As early as 992 'all the ships that were any use' were assembled at London to intercept the Vikings. A fleet was again assembled in 999, and in 1008, during a respite from attack, 'the king ordered that ships be built unremittingly all over England'. At the same time, he ordered the owners of every eight hides to produce a helmet and mailshirt, part of an effort to improve the equipment of the English forces which is echoed in other contemporary documents.

The national forces were not put to effective use, however. The 992 fleet was defeated, that of 999 did nothing, while the new fleet assembled at Sandwich in 1009 broke up in dissension before Thorkell's fleet arrived (*map* 3). In 1006, 'the king ordered the whole nation from Wessex and Mercia to be called out, and they were out on service against the Danish host the whole autumn…[but] in spite of it all, the Danish host went about as it pleased'. Aethelred probably first campaigned in person against the raiders in 1009. He summoned a large army but failed to engage Swein. This ineffectiveness was caused by divided, irresolute, and incompetent leadership, for his son Edmund later used the same demoralized forces effectively.

According to the *Chronicle*, during Aethelred's reign the English agreed to pay the Scandinavian raiders tributes of at least £137,000, in addition to provisions and the pillage they took. This was resorted to only after the failure of military methods. Paying tribute has a bad reputation and had its critics then, but was sometimes advantageous: in 994 and 1007 it brought relief – in the latter case, two years which were devoted to defensive preparations. It was combined with a policy of dividing the raiders. The Norwegian Olaf Tryggvason was party to the 994 treaty. He kept his vow not to return and became a nuisance to Swein in Norway, which they both claimed. Pallig, Swein's brother-in-law, who defected to him in 1001, entered Aethelred's service at an earlier date, and Thorkell was in Aethelred's pay from 1012 until the end of 1015.

Fighting could be as expensive, if not more so, than tribute-paying when the costs of campaigning and plundering are taken into account, and English forces were not above 'foraging' for provisions either. Moreover, there was little 'national' feeling. The inhabitants of Wessex and East Anglia bore the brunt of the raids for much of the reign, and Mercians and Northumbrians may have been more willing to lay down their money than their lives for them. In 1013, the leaders of Northumbria and north Mercia, where there had been Scandinavian settlements in the late ninth century, submitted to Swein.

In fact, there was no clear division between English and Danes: Scandinavians fought for Aethelred, while ealdorman Eadric Streona, who enjoyed great favour from 1006, defected to Cnut in 1015. An isolated instance of collaboration with the raiders is recorded as early as 991. The author of the *Anglo-Saxon Chronicle*, writing in Cnut's reign, was free with allegations of treachery. He accused ealdorman Aelfric of Hampshire of informing the Vikings of the plan to entrap them at sea in 992. If this was true, it is difficult to explain how Aelfric retained his position.

He would eventually die in 1016 fighting for Edmund. Certainly, serious aristocratic rivalries existed in the later years of the reign, when political murders and the rise of Eadric Streona cannot have encouraged unity. But above all, Aethelred failed to offer effective leadership. He is remembered as 'the Unready' (meaning 'ill-advised' or 'without counsel'), but the greatest indictment of his kingship is the English recovery under his son Edmund.

THE DANISH CONQUEST 1015-1016

The final campaigns were of an intensity unmatched in England since the late ninth century (*map* 4). Aethelred, by now suffering from ill health, took little part, and his son Edmund emerged as a more forceful leader. He was in the north, in revolt against Aethelred, when Cnut invaded Wessex in late summer 1015. After several weeks of ravaging, Wessex submitted, and Cnut was joined by Eadric of Mercia and Thorkell's force. This was not simply a war of conquest: Cnut had support within England.

In late December, Cnut and his allies ravaged across the Thames into Mercia. Edmund made two unsuccessful attempts to raise armies in Mercia before joining earl Uhtred

MAP 2

After 997, Viking raids on southern England penetrated deeper inland, favouring the Isle of Wight as a base. Aethelred's government was far from supine. Punitive expeditions went against the north-west and Normandy to discourage support or raiders, and in 1008 there was a major effort to collect military equipment and build warships.

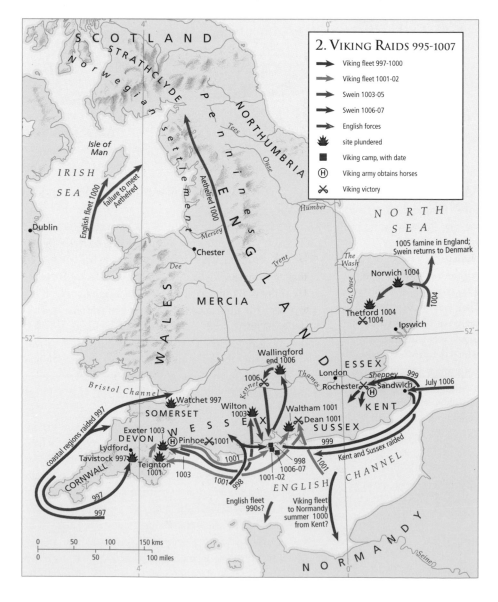

of Northumbria. Instead of fighting Cnut they attacked the north-west Midlands, presumably to draw off Eadric. However, Cnut's threat to march to York caused Uhtred's submission. He was murdered and replaced by one of Cnut's men. Northumbria played no further part in the fighting.

The most intense fighting followed Aethelred's death in London (23 April 1016). Cnut's siege of London in May demonstrates the sophistication of his forces. For the first time, Vikings moved their ships upstream of London Bridge (built since Alfred's time) by making a canal around its southern end, to Brentford, 'and then afterwards surrounded the borough with a ditch, so that no man could go in or out'. London continued to resist while Edmund raised troops in Wessex, and Cnut followed with part of his army. They fought two indecisive battles at Penselwood and Sherston in late June but, for the first time since 1004, the invaders were not victorious. Edmund returned to raise the siege of London, and then defeated Cnut near Brentford.

Edmund was unable to follow up this victory and had to return to Wessex to raise more troops. After attacking London again, Cnut reverted to raiding, employing the mobility of his fleet. A foray through East Anglia into Mercia may have been necessary to restore the morale of his men and to secure supplies. Edmund's tactics were to harass the invaders: when Cnut moved his forces into the Medway, Edmund followed by land and chased him into the Isle of Sheppey. Ealdorman Eadric defected to Edmund at this point, perhaps hedging his bets. When Cnut crossed into Essex, Edmund followed again and intercepted him at Assandun (Ashingdon or Ashdon in Essex). But now the danger of a battle-seeking strategy became clear: on 18 October, Edmund suffered a heavy defeat, which the Chronicle blames on Eadric's treachery. A peace was made by which Cnut gained Mercia (he already held Northumbria) and London, which he had never been able to take by force. Shortly afterwards, Edmund died. The fierce resistance he made in his brief reign suggests that more resolute leadership a quarter of a century earlier might have prevented the Danish conquest altogether. As it was, Cnut was left to rule over England, which formed part of his North Sea empire.

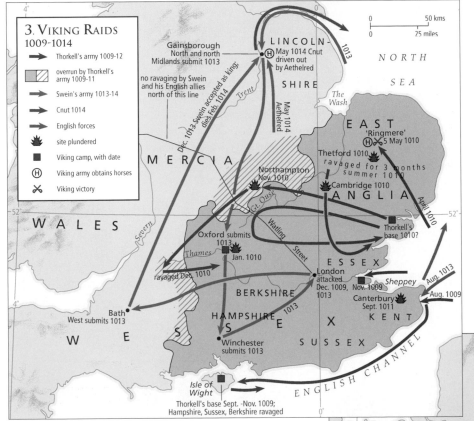

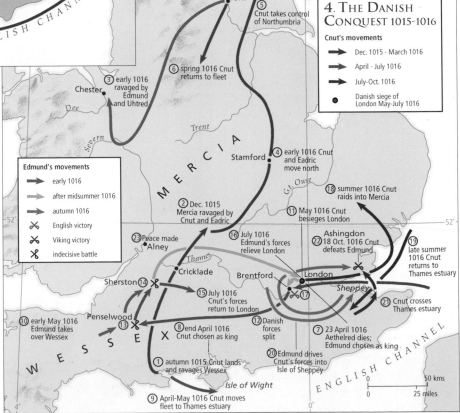

MAP 3

English military and naval preparations proved useless in 1009. The Danish noble, Thorkell, ravaged across the south-eastern quarter of England. After he was bought off in 1012, the Danish king Swein arrived. His ravaging, and Aethelred's ineffectiveness, induced the English nobles to submit to Swein. His death in February 1014 robbed him of his prize, and Aethelred was restored.

MAP 4

In the campaigns of 1016, Edmund showed a determination lacking in his father, mustering five armies as king, and hotly pursuing Cnut's forces. London resisted elaborate sieges, but while Edmund was able to check and defeat the Danes, he could not shatter them. It was Cnut who inflicted such heavy losses on Edmund at Ashingdon that he was forced to partition England.

II
WESTERN EUROPE IN THE ELEVENTH TO THE THIRTEENTH CENTURIES

Around AD 1000, the invasion era was coming to an end in western Europe. England was conquered twice in fifty years, by Scandinavians in 1013-1016, and by a northern French alliance led by the duke of Normandy in 1066-71. These were established states within a recognized Christian power structure, though, and not raiders. The Norman Conquest brought the British Isles more closely in touch with French social and military structures. Although not yet a nation, France was beginning to dominate Europe culturally. In military terms this meant exporting the combination of armoured cavalry, castles, crossbows, and siege techniques.

Politically, the conquest of the rich kingdom of England made the Norman, and later Angevin, dynasties more powerful than any king of France. Henry II (1154-89) created and Richard I (1189-99) exploited the military potential of their empire. In Germany, the actual western emperor, Frederick Barbarossa (1152-90), was drawn to campaign across the Alps in Italy for the wealth its cities generated. Meanwhile, on his eastern frontiers, German magnates and Danish kings expanded into the pagan territories south of the Baltic under the guise of crusading. Here too, technological advantages in armour, weapons, fortification, siege engines, and shipping gave the westerners the upper hand.

The growth of German military orders provided a cutting edge to this expansion, although it received a check from Alexander Nevsky's north Russian state of Novgorod (1242). The pagan Prussians and Lithuanians also acquired western military technology along with conversion to Christianity. But the Mongol armies which appeared in Russia and Eastern Europe (1237-42) completely overwhelmed any opposition. In one devastating campaign (1241), they penetrated as far as Vienna before withdrawing to choose a new ruler for their world empire. It is not certain that Europe could have escaped domination had they stayed, but the threat lessened as the Mongol state broke up into several regional powers.

The loss of the Angevin empire by king John (1199-1216) led to civil war in England, which was resumed under different terms in the reign of his ineffectual son Henry III (1216-70). But this was also the period of great military expansion within the British Isles. Ireland had fallen prey to private expeditions in the reign of Henry II, before the king himself took a hand, while never coming firmly under English rule. Edward I (1270-1307) proved himself a great warrior king. His conquest of Wales (1277-83) was assured by the construction of some of the finest castles ever built. The financial burden was heavy, however, and Edward I's attempt to conquer Scotland stretched his resources too far. Determined resistance and incompetent generalship by Edward II ensured Scotland its independence under the inspired leadership of Robert Bruce (1306-27).

THE NORMAN CONQUEST OF ENGLAND

THE DEATH IN 1066 of Edward the Confessor, without an adult male heir, made a war of succession to the throne of England inevitable. Harold Godwineson, earl of Wessex, immediately assumed the throne, but there were other contenders. Duke William of Normandy was a formidable commander who understood the importance of reconnaissance, rapid movement, supply in defence and attack, and made calculated use of brutality. King Harold had less experience of command, but had enjoyed military successes against the Welsh. But neither had commanded in a pitched battle before 1066. Harold's exiled brother Tostig, a nuisance rather than a serious rival for the kingdom, aimed to regain favour. The third claimant, king Harald of Norway, had long experience of warfare in Norway, Russia, and in the service of the Byzantine emperors.

THE CAMPAIGNS OF 1066

Tostig moved first, in late April 1066, raiding along the south coast where he owned land and attracted some support (map 1). He left Sandwich upon Harold's approach but was defeated in Lindsey by the northern earls Edwin and Morcar, and deserted by most of his force. His fortunes now depended upon the actions of others, but he may have forced Harold to accelerate his mobilization.

Harold was caught in the dilemma of needing to defend against two widely separated threats. He left the defence of the north to the brothers Edwin and Morcar, and concentrated on the Norman threat to the south. The military resources of southern England provided a fleet and land forces. Harold took command of the fleet at the Isle of Wight; this was his strike force positioned on the flank of a Norman invasion of Sussex or Kent. The coast was watched by further detachments of the shire levies. There is no sign that Harold attempted to disrupt the Norman preparations. These forces waited all summer until 8 September when, their provisions consumed, they were demobilized. The levies consisted of a proportion of the manpower of each county and were required to serve for two months, for which they were provided with money for provisions. Harold's success in defending the coast for four months shows that he called them out in two relays. It was a considerable achievement to keep them at their stations throughout the summer, in idleness and without prospect of plunder. In the end, however, English resources were insufficient for a 'phoney war' of such length.

The delay in the Norman invasion was due in part to the magnitude of the task confronting William. He had to secure the support of the Norman nobility for an invasion, assemble an army, train and supply it during the weeks of enforced inactivity, and construct a fleet to transport it and its horses across the Channel. The logistical and sanitary challenges posed by large bodies of men and animals in one place for many weeks were overcome by both William and Harold. William's army, of mounted knights and infantry, was recruited from the Norman nobles and from neighbouring territories. All were attracted by the prospect of plunder and by William's reputation. That the invasion was possible

at all was due to the favourable political situation in northern France, which meant Normandy was no longer threatened by hostile neighbours.

By early September, the doubtless deliberate delay in invading had successfully stretched Harold's resources to the limit. On 8 September, Harold rode to London, leaving the Channel undefended. About 12 September, William embarked his army, which moved to the mouth of the river Somme. Although the crossing from there would be shorter, he must have known of Harold's difficulties by then, and it is likely that this was an invasion attempt which was aborted by the same storms that scattered Harold's fleet as it returned to London. Contrary winds then delayed the crossing until late September. But by this time, William's chance of success had been increased by the actions of king Harald of Norway.

In September 1066, Harald Hardrada ('Ruthless') of Norway reached the estuary of the Tyne with a fleet which chroniclers put at 300 ships or more, to be joined by Tostig, before disembarking at Ricall near York on 18 September. Harold Godwineson's decision to ride north was proved

To invade England, William had to build a fleet, a major achievement which demonstrated the co-operation of his leading subjects in his great enterprise.

The size of William's fleet is unknown. As well as requisitioned and hired vessels, the Bayeux Tapestry shows that it contained ships built for the invasion. This involved a major mobilization of craftsmen and resources, and manpower for the crews. The ships shown represent Viking-style cargo vessels rather than longships, since they had to transport horses.

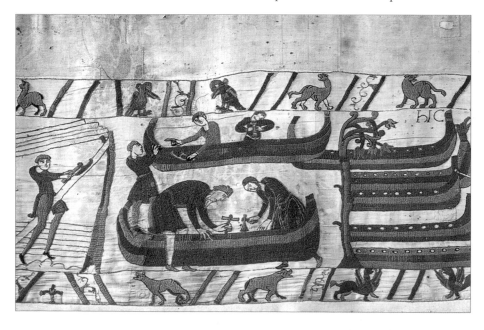

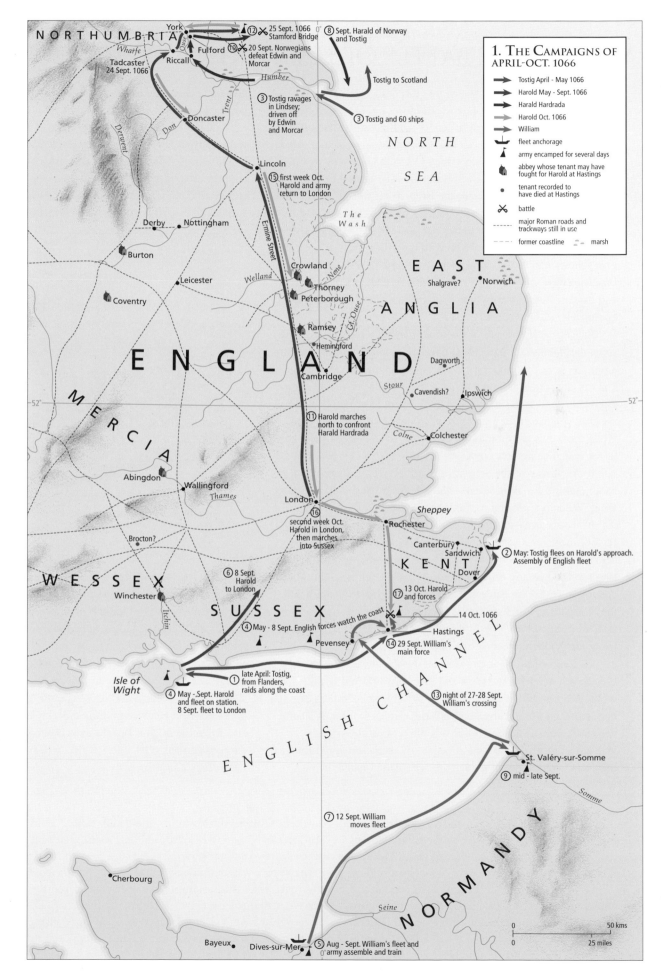

MAP 1

King Harold faced widely separated threats, and Tostig's raids made him deploy too early. The Norwegian landing drew him north, leaving William an unopposed landing. Harald Hardrada successfully brought a large fleet across the North Sea, but found no support in Yorkshire. Duke William had the greatest task, for the Normans had long ceased to be Vikings. Constructing a fleet and moulding a disciplined force were great achievements, but he was aided by Harold's rashness.

---

1. THE CAMPAIGNS OF APRIL–OCT. 1066

- Tostig April – May 1066
- Harold May – Sept. 1066
- Harald Hardrada
- Harold Oct. 1066
- William
- fleet anchorage
- army encamped for several days
- abbey whose tenant may have fought for Harold at Hastings
- tenant recorded to have died at Hastings
- battle
- major Roman roads and trackways still in use
- former coastline
- marsh

NORTHUMBRIA

York
12 25 Sept. 1066 Stamford Bridge
8 Sept. Harald of Norway and Tostig
Fulford
10 20 Sept. Norwegians defeat Edwin and Morcar
Wharfe
Ouse
Tadcaster 24 Sept. 1066
Riccall
Tostig to Scotland
Humber
Trent
Doncaster
Don
Derwent
3 Tostig ravages in Lindsey; driven off by Edwin and Morcar
3 Tostig and 60 ships

NORTH SEA

Lincoln
15 first week Oct. Harold and army return to London

Derby
Nottingham

The Wash

Burton
Ermine Street
Crowland
Nene
EAST

Leicester
Welland
Thorney
Peterborough
Shalgrave?
Norwich

Coventry
Ramsey
ANGLIA
Hemingford

ENGLAND
Dagworth

Cambridge
Stour
Cavendish?
Ipswich

52°
52°

MERCIA
11 Harold marches north to confront Harald Hardrada
Colne
Colchester

Abingdon
Wallingford
Thames
London
16 second week Oct. Harold in London, then marches into Sussex
Sheppey
Rochester

Brocton?
Canterbury
2 May: Tostig flees on Harold's approach. Assembly of English fleet

WESSEX
KENT
Sandwich
Dover

Winchester
Itchin
SUSSEX
17 13 Oct. Harold and forces

6 8 Sept. Harold to London
14 Oct. 1066
Hastings

4 May – 8 Sept. English forces watch the coast
14 29 Sept. William's main force

Isle of Wight
Pevensey
ENGLISH CHANNEL

1 late April: Tostig, from Flanders, raids along the coast
13 night of 27-28 Sept. William's crossing

4 May – Sept. Harold and fleet on station. 8 Sept. fleet to London

St. Valéry-sur-Somme
9 mid – late Sept.
Somme

7 12 Sept. William moves fleet

NORMANDY

Cherbourg
Seine

Bayeux
Dives-sur-Mer
5 Aug – Sept. William's fleet and army assemble and train

0   50 kms
0   25 miles

THE BATTLE OF HASTINGS 14 OCTOBER 1066

The strength of the armies which met 7 miles (11 km) north of Hastings cannot be even approximately assessed. Modern estimates which put the Norman army at 6,000-7,000, and the English slightly higher, are only guesses. Both armies may well have been smaller. William's army included knights with lance and sword, and infantry armed with bows and spears. The tactical flexibility of this combination would decide the battle in his favour. The English used horses for mobility, but were not trained to fight as cavalry. They fought on foot in the traditional shieldwall, the better-armed probably forming the front rank, with the others arrayed behind to give solidity and to throw missiles. Great lords, like Harold and his brothers, were surrounded by their military retainers, housecarls, and thegns. Harold's army was deficient in archers, although not completely without them.

The course and details of the battle may be reconstructed with some confidence. Of particular importance are the Bayeux Tapestry, a unique, near contemporary, pictorial depiction, and William of Poitiers' account – although an admirer of William, he had been a knight and had access to eye-witnesses. Harold's army occupied a position of great natural strength: in front the ground fell gently, while the flanks were protected by marshy valleys and a steep bank to the east. The highest point, left of his centre, was where Harold raised his banner of the dragon standard. However, there was not room enough for all his men. Although the battle would take place when William wanted it to, the ground favoured the English.

William's army formed three divisions in the valley below, each of three lines: in the front, archers, next heavy cavalry, last cavalry. In the centre stood William and the Normans, his Breton allies on the left, and other French contingents on the right. The circumstances of the battle committed the English to defend, and the Normans to attack, but it is also true that William had more options open to him. The battle started around 9 a.m. and began badly for William. His first two lines were repulsed and even the cavalry could make no impression on the shieldwall. The English had the advantage of the slope and their axes inflicted terrible wounds. Some of the attackers began to fall back – Poitiers cites the Bretons – and a rout threatened as a rumour spread that William was dead. For the Normans this was the crisis of the battle. William's personal intervention rallied the army which returned to the attack, cutting down the English who had pursued them. A

general English advance at this point might have been decisive, but the shieldwall was unmanoeuvrable.

As the main body of the English army stood firm, another tactic was required. The archers harassed the shieldwall, while groups of knights attacked breaches in it and employed feigned flights to tempt more of the English down from the ridge. These units were contingents of individual lords which trained and fought together. Such co-ordinated assaults ground down the English. During the

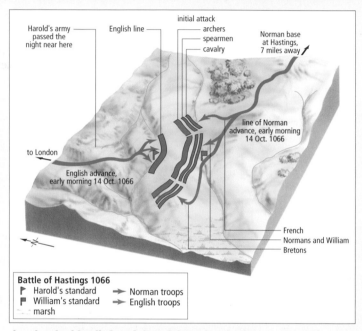

Battle of Hastings 1066
- Harold's standard
- William's standard
- marsh
- → Norman troops
- → English troops

day the shieldwall shrank but did not break, though Harold's brothers Gyrth and Leofwine fell. The only hope now was nightfall and escape. Towards dusk, Harold was shot in the face and then cut down by a party of knights who had broken away from the shieldwall. When the king's banner fell, the survivors melted away into the Weald. Victory had gone to the more mobile and adaptable army, but it was not a foregone conclusion: the Normans recognized the magnificent English resistance, and it had required all the skill of William and his soldiers to win. In the end, the difference between victory and defeat lay in the fate of the two leaders. In the small-scale, close encounters of medieval warfare, the commanders were often at risk, which is why pitched battles were often a last resort.

correct by Hardrada's defeat of Edwin and Morcar at Gate Fulford (20 September), followed by the submission of York to the invaders. Astonishingly, Harold was at Tadcaster by 24 September; having heard of the Norwegian landing he had covered the 190 miles (304 km) from London and assembled a new army. Next day, he caught the Norwegians by surprise at their camp at Stamford Bridge. The English victory was complete, in a battle of which little concrete is known. It was the last battle fought in England in the

northern fashion, shieldwall to shieldwall. Both Harald Hardrada and Tostig were killed, and only a small remnant of the Norwegian fleet survived.

The victory was an immense achievement, but the cost was high. The casualties must have been severe, and the survivors drained by their exertions. In the Channel, moreover, the wind changed direction, allowing William to sail from St Valéry-sur-Somme to land unopposed in Pevensey Bay on 28 September. Here a garrison was left in a castle constructed within the Roman walls, while William transferred the bulk of his forces to Hastings (where the clifftop hillfort furnished another ready-made camp). For the next two weeks the Norman army foraged from this base without venturing far inland. William has been accused of being at a loss for what to do at this stage; in fact, for the first time in his military career William was adopting a battle-seeking strategy. Operating near his fortified base and line of communications was a sensible precaution, while foraging both supplied his army and provoked Harold to fight soon, and on William's terms.

Harold cannot have learned of the Norman landing before early October; in less than fourteen days he confronted William in Sussex. What this involved has excited both admiration and criticism. For the second time in a month he rode the 190 miles (306 km) from York to London, pausing there for less than a week to assemble another army and to order a fleet into the Channel, before covering the 50 miles (80 km) to the place of battle. His reliance on speed is understandable: he had used it against the Welsh in the winter of 1063, and it had also led to a great victory days earlier. He perhaps hoped he might be able to destroy parts of the Norman host while it was dispersed to forage, and then blockade William within his defences until starvation resulted in submission, a strategy previously used by king Alfred (*pages* 24–25). Alternatively, it is possible that Harold, buoyed up by one victory, eagerly sought another to end the threats to his security once and for all. Whatever his strategy, the reliance on speed was flawed; his host had suffered heavy casualties at Stamford Bridge, the men who rode with him were tired, and he did not wait long enough for significant reinforcements to come in before he left London. The army he took to Hastings was probably recruited mainly from the south-east. The reasons for speed may have seemed compelling to Harold, but he may have acted precipitately. Time, after all, must have been on his side: how long could William wait on the Sussex coast

before he exhausted the provisions available and the patience of his men?

Had Harold faced a commander of lesser skills, he might still have achieved surprise. But William placed heavy emphasis on reconnaissance, and customarily patrolled in person. He became aware, late on 13 October, of the approach of Harold, and ordered his army to stand to all night, fearing an attack. This is how close Harold did come to achieving surprise. The next morning, William skilfully seized the opportunity he needed to fight a pitched battle and to submit the justice of his claim to the judgement of God. His army marched out and confronted Harold's around the hill where Battle Abbey was later erected, either the place where the English passed the night or where they first caught sight of the Normans. The battle which followed was long and hard fought, and it did not all go the way of the Normans (*page* 44). At the end of the day, however, William had won a decisive victory. Harold and his brothers lay dead, and the following weeks would reveal that even if the remaining English leaders were still not ready to give up, nor were they capable of organizing effective opposition.

The last phase of the 1066 campaign was the march on London, during which the Norman army followed a large, inverted S-shaped march of 350 miles (560 km). While William rested his army at Hastings, some reinforcements joined him from Normandy. In late October, he secured Dover, already recognized as a significant fortress, and Canterbury. It proved impossible to enter London from the south. Although a sortie from London was defeated, the bridge was held against the Normans. Within the city, Edwin and Morcar, with the two archbishops, were planning to make the young Edgar Aetheling king; they were not yet ready to submit, although their efforts lacked conviction. William responded by mounting a threatening circuit around London, ravaging heavily all the way (*map* 2). He crossed the Thames at Wallingford (where another castle was built and archbishop Stigand submitted) before marching around

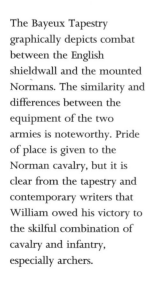

The Bayeux Tapestry graphically depicts combat between the English shieldwall and the mounted Normans. The similarity and differences between the equipment of the two armies is noteworthy. Pride of place is given to the Norman cavalry, but it is clear from the tapestry and contemporary writers that William owed his victory to the skilful combination of cavalry and infantry, especially archers.

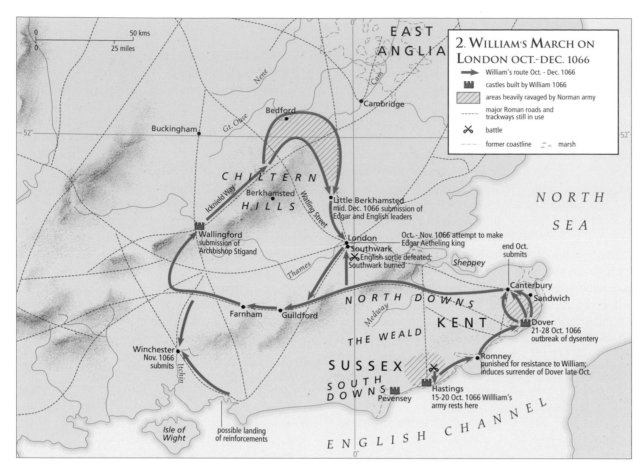

MAP 2

After Hastings, the surviving English leaders tried to rally support in London for the legitimate heir, Edgar, but he was a boy. William skirted the thinly populated Weald, but the English held London Bridge, forcing him to cross the Thames at Wallingford and then march around the Chilterns. His army ravaged all the way. The result was an intimidating circuit which induced London to submit, dictated by the need to supply his army and so avoid sparsely populated areas.

the Chilterns, effectively cutting London off. In December, Edgar and his sponsors surrendered to William, who was crowned on Christmas Day 1066.

THE DEFENCE OF THE CONQUEST

Despite the submissions in December 1066, only south-east England was directly under William's control. In the following years, he faced risings in the west and north (map 3), whose fighting strength had not been dissipated in 1066. Scotland, Wales, and Ireland provided refuges and freebooters for raids, while a large Danish fleet operated on the east coast. William's success in suppressing the risings again owed much to his skilful generalship, which displayed great energy, rapid movement (like Harold), and the use of calculated brutality. He was aided by the competence of his subordinates, and the construction of castles anchored the conquest firmly to the soil of England. He continued, however, to enjoy good fortune: he never had to face a united English uprising, while the political situation in northern France allowed him to concentrate his resources on England until conquest was complete. Although resistance was national, it was unco-ordinated. Its leaders were opportunists, concerned with personal as much as national interests, while the English heir to the throne, Edgar Aetheling, was young and wanted powerful backers. The rebels took to the fens, uplands, and forests (whence they derived the nickname silvatici) to fight as guerrillas, but were no match for the Normans in the field. Meanwhile, intervention from Ireland and Denmark was not welcomed

by all Englishmen. After 1066, a significant proportion of the native population was prepared to acquiesce in the conquest and fight for the new regime.

The early revolts were small-scale. In 1067, the garrison of Dover saw off an attack led by Eustace of Boulogne, who had fought for William in 1066, while the Shropshire landowner Edric the Wild harried Herefordshire with Welsh support. At the beginning of 1068, William besieged Exeter for eighteen days, which submitted on terms. Harold's illegitimate sons were repelled by local forces in the south-west (1068 and 1069), and the inhabitants of Exeter resisted a revolt in Devon and Cornwall. In the summer of 1068, northern resistance dissolved when William marched north and built several castles to tighten his grip on the north-east Midlands. The submission of king Malcolm of Scotland brought the campaign to a satisfactory conclusion.

However, the problem of the north was far from solved, and the next two years were decisive in the completion of the Norman conquest of England. In January 1069, the Norman earl, Robert, was slain in Durham, and York castle was besieged. Like Harold in 1066, William reacted decisively. A rapid march enabled him to surprise and rout the rebels, led by Edgar Aetheling, in the streets of York. William raised a second castle there and by Easter he was back at Winchester, the north apparently subdued. In August, a large Danish fleet arrived off the coast of Kent. It raided north along the coast to the Humber, although their landings were driven off at all points by castle garrisons and natives. In Yorkshire, Edgar joined them at the head of

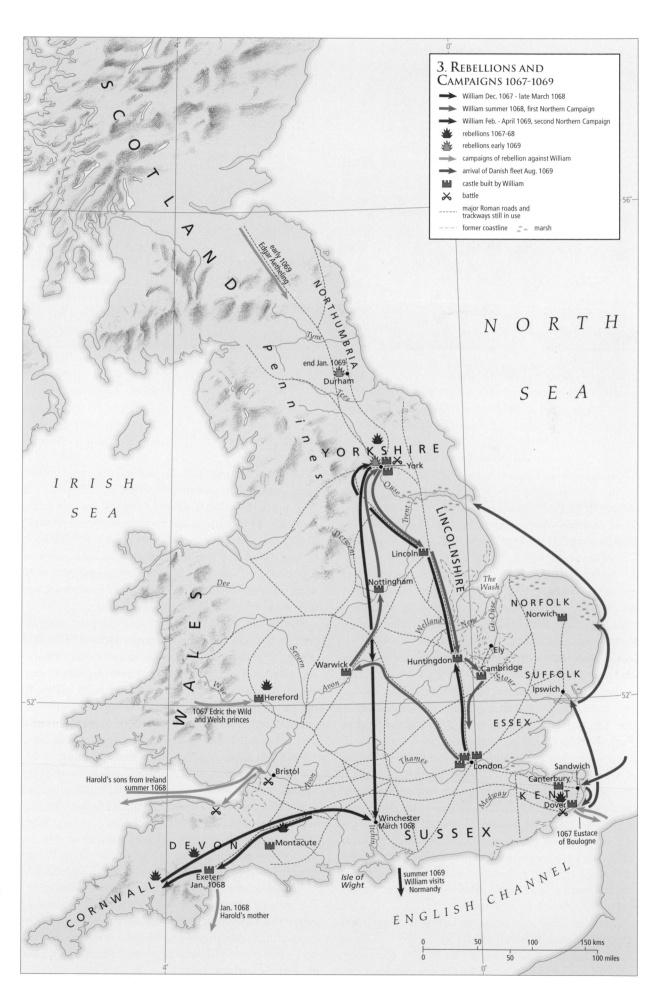

3. REBELLIONS AND CAMPAIGNS 1067-1069

→ William Dec. 1067 - late March 1068

→ William summer 1068, first Northern Campaign

→ William Feb. - April 1069, second Northern Campaign

rebellions 1067-68

rebellions early 1069

campaigns of rebellion against William

arrival of Danish fleet Aug. 1069

castle built by William

✕ battle

- - - major Roman roads and trackways still in use

- - - former coastline   marsh

SCOTLAND

early 1069 Edgar Aetheling

NORTHUMBRIA

Tyne

end Jan. 1069
Durham

Tees

NORTH SEA

Pennines

YORKSHIRE ✕ York

Ouse

IRISH SEA

Trent

LINCOLNSHIRE

Derwent

Lincoln

The Wash

Nottingham

NORFOLK
Norwich

Dee

Welland

Nene

Gt. Ouse

WALES

Severn

Warwick

Huntingdon

Ely

Cambridge

SUFFOLK

Ipswich — 52°

Avon

Stour

Wye

Hereford

1067 Edric the Wild and Welsh princes

ESSEX

Thames

London

Sandwich

Canterbury

Harold's sons from Ireland summer 1068

Bristol

Avon

KENT

Dover ✕

Medway

Itchen

Winchester
March 1068

SUSSEX

1067 Eustace of Boulogne

DEVON

Montacute

Isle of Wight

summer 1069
William visits Normandy

Exeter
Jan. 1068

CORNWALL

Jan. 1068
Harold's mother

ENGLISH CHANNEL

0   50   100   150 kms

0   50   100 miles

MAP 3

Initially, William faced little resistance, perhaps because Norman rule had little impact outside the south-east. The early revolts, occasioned by the impositions of Norman lords collecting money and provisions, were easily defeated. Suppression was accompanied by the building of castles, firstly in earth and timber. However, up to the middle of 1069, William was faced only by sporadic outbreaks of rebellion.

Castles were a vital tool of the conquest. The first castles were quickly constructed from earth and timber, and often located in English towns – London was overawed by three, York by two. The great stone keep, the White Tower, at London, both a palace and a fortress, was started before 1087. Originally whitewashed, it was an architectural symbol of Norman domination.

a large rebel army. In York, the castles were captured after a failed sortie by their Norman garrisons (21 September). Other risings flared up in Devon and Cornwall, Shropshire and Staffordshire, and rebels from Cheshire joined Edric the Wild and his Welsh allies.

Leaving his lieutenants to deal with the troubles in the Welsh marches and the south-west, William identified the northern revolt as the most serious, and marched to deal with it, collecting troops on the way. As he approached York, the rebels withdrew again, while the Danes used their fleet to put the Humber between William and themselves – none dared face William in battle. He left part of his force to contain the Danes, and led the rest to crush the rebels at Stafford. He returned to York in time to prevent a renewed occupation by the Danes, who agreed to withdraw the next spring. William held the Christmas feast in the ruins of York, before dealing with the problem of the north.

It is likely that twelfth-century writers exaggerated the degree of systematic destruction of stores of seed, corn, animals, and agricultural implements which caused widespread famine and created many refugees. However, the 'harrying of the north' (map 4) did put an end to northern resistance. It created a dead zone, incapable of further rebellion and unattractive to Scottish and Danish invaders. Early in 1070, William's columns reached the Tees before returning to York where the castles were rebuilt. Still he had not finished, although part of his army came close to mutiny at the prospect of crossing the Pennines in mid-winter. Now Cheshire and Staffordshire were devastated and castles were erected at the county towns, while a threat to Shrewsbury was crushed. Returning south, his troops were paid and at last demobilized at Salisbury. By early April 1070, William was at Winchester.

There remained two postscripts. In May, king Swein joined his Danish fleet in the Humber and led it to Ely to join the English rebel Hereward ('the Wake'); there were still Englishmen who preferred the Danes to the Normans.

However, after plundering the Fenlands, the Danes came to terms with William and departed. With characteristic thoroughness, William invested the isle of Ely by land and sea, constructing a 2-mile (3-km) causeway across the Fens. Finally, in the summer of 1071, this last centre of resistance was snuffed out.

The sequel was a campaign by land and sea, in the manner of an Anglo-Saxon monarch, to secure the submission of Scotland in 1072. The conquest of England was complete. Rapid and decisive action, striking at the centres of rebellion undeterred by the season, enabled William to finish the job he had started in 1066. Completion came not a moment too soon, for from 1070 Normandy's neighbours were again becoming hostile and William found all his resources were required in the defence of his duchy.

The key to securing the Norman conquest was the possession of effective means of holding each part of England as it came under their control. The army of conquest was kept substantially in being, William's Norman vassals being augmented by paid soldiers from elsewhere in France. In the early years, Norman rule was essentially predatory. Certain lords were assigned spheres of influence, where they built castles and collected taxes to support their men, especially in the strategic regions of Sussex, the south-west, the Welsh marches, and East Anglia, while the military households of William and his chief men provided permanent troops. Not until the early 1070s were knights granted land, and this process was still not complete when William died in 1087 whilst campaigning in France. Castles were built in corners of English town walls and in open country, a type of small-scale fastness practically unknown in pre-conquest England. These rudimentary defences of earth and timber, while not invulnerable, overawed many potential rebels and were not easy to capture. In a crisis, their garrisons could withdraw to them and await relief. They featured prominently among the reasons for Norman success.

Map 4

The crisis of conquest was 1069-70. Edgar, the legitimate heir, headed a general insurrection in the north, coinciding with the arrival of a Danish fleet and revolts in the west and south-west. William's reaction gives the measure of his generalship, spending winter 1069-70 crushing the northern revolt. The 'harrying of the north' was a ruthless punishment and destroyed the supplies invaders needed. After the arrival of king Swein, William paid the Danish fleet to depart, leaving the rebels in the lurch. William was then free to subdue the rebels in the Fens, then to chastise the Scottish king.

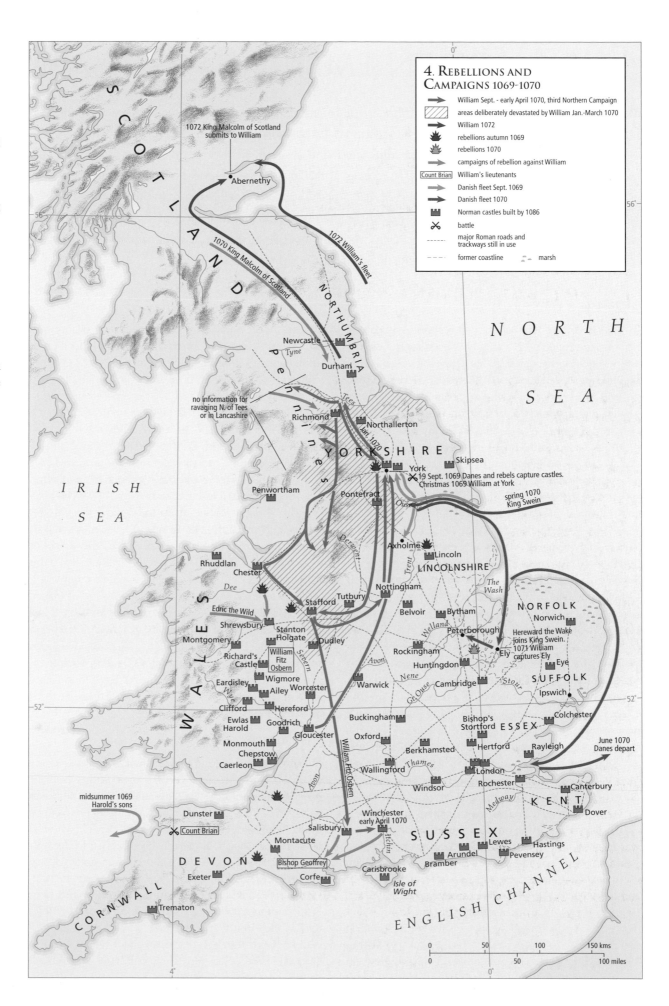

4. REBELLIONS AND CAMPAIGNS 1069-1070

→ William Sept. - early April 1070, third Northern Campaign
▨ areas deliberately devastated by William Jan.-March 1070
➤ William 1072
🌿 rebellions autumn 1069
🌿 rebellions 1070
→ campaigns of rebellion against William
[Count Brian] William's lieutenants
➤ Danish fleet Sept. 1069
➤ Danish fleet 1070
🏰 Norman castles built by 1086
✂ battle
···· major Roman roads and trackways still in use
— — former coastline   marsh

1072 King Malcolm of Scotland submits to William

Abernethy

1070 King Malcolm of Scotland

1072 William's fleet

SCOTLAND

NORTHUMBRIA

Newcastle
Tyne
Durham

no information for ravaging N. of Tees or in Lancashire

Richmond
Tees
Northallerton

PENNINES

Penwortham

YORKSHIRE
Skipsea

York
✂ 19 Sept. 1069 Danes and rebels capture castles.
Christmas 1069 William at York

Pontefract
Ouse

spring 1070 King Swein

Derwent

Axholme
Lincoln

LINCOLNSHIRE

Rhuddlan
Chester
Dee

Nottingham
Trent

The Wash

NORFOLK
Norwich

WALES

Stafford   Tutbury
Belvoir   Bytham

Welland
Peterborough

Hereward the Wake joins King Swein.
1071 William captures Ely

Edric the Wild
Shrewsbury
Stanton Holgate   Dudley
Severn

Rockingham

Ely
Eye

Montgomery

Richard's Castle   William Fitz Osbern

Nene
Avon

Huntingdon

SUFFOLK

Eardisley   Wigmore
Ailey   Worcester
Wye

Warwick

Gt. Ouse
Cambridge
Stour

Ipswich

Clifford   Hereford

Buckingham

Bishop's Stortford

ESSEX
Colchester

Ewlas Harold   Goodrich
Gloucester

Oxford

Hertford
Rayleigh

June 1070 Danes depart

Monmouth
Chepstow

Berkhamsted

London
Rochester

Caerleon

Avon

William Fitz Osbern

Wallingford
Thames

Windsor

Canterbury

KENT
Dover

midsummer 1069 Harold's sons

Dunster
✂ Count Brian

Salisbury

Winchester early April 1070
Itchin

Medway

SUSSEX
Lewes
Arundel   Hastings
Bramber   Pevensey

Montacute

DEVON

Bishop Geoffrey

Carisbrooke

Exeter
Corfe
Isle of Wight

CORNWALL

Trematon

IRISH SEA

NORTH SEA

ENGLISH CHANNEL

0   50   100   150 kms
0   50   100 miles

56°

52°

0°

THE ANGEVIN EMPIRE 1154-1217

THE ANGEVIN EMPIRE, which stretched from the Scottish borders to the Pyrenees, was built up as much by marriage as by conquest. It was created and defended by three warrior kings: Henry II, Richard I, and John. Their warfare was characterized by speed of movement, the building and intelligent use of castles, and the avoidance of battle. The revenues of the English crown provided a secure base for expansionist activities. Ireland was invaded, Wales suppressed, and Scotland neutralized, while widespread revolt in 1173-74 was put down in England. The French kings posed the greatest military threat in the Seine and Loire valleys, but were kept in check by a system of alliances. Only when this broke down was the Angevin position weak. John could not sustain Richard's successful fortress strategy in the Vexin, nor win battles.

The seal of Henry II, showing him seated in majesty. His energy and shrewd political sense created an Angevin 'empire', which he defended successfully in 1173-74, when his sons rebelled with French support. After his death in 1189, the military skills of Richard I maintained his inheritance for a decade; but king John lacked them, and presided over the loss of the continental dominions from 1204.

EXPANSION OF THE EMPIRE

In 1128, Geoffrey V le Bel married empress Matilda, the heiress to England and Normandy. When Henry I died in 1135 she did not succeed, as his nephew Stephen, count of Boulogne, seized the throne. There followed almost two decades of intermittent civil war in England pursued by Matilda and, from 1152, by her son Henry. Meanwhile, Geoffrey operated against the old enemy – Normandy. Although unsuccessful at first, Stephen's preoccupations enabled an Angevin conquest by 1145.

Geoffrey died in September 1151, aged only 40, which precipitated a crisis for duke Henry. But his feats of political and military daring turned the situation around. In May 1152, Henry married Eleanor of Aquitaine. She was Louis VII's recently divorced queen and the outraged king drew together a dangerous military alliance: in England, king Stephen and his son Eustace; in France, count Henry of Champagne, Louis' brother Robert of Dreux, count of Perche (strategically placed between Maine and Normandy), and Henry's own brother Geoffrey. Henry struck at him first, rushing back from Barfleur (map 1), where he was about to embark for England, to besiege and take Montsoreau and force Geoffrey to sue for peace. Then Louis fell ill, which halted the alliance's plans, but Henry's next move was still a piece of calculated daring. Abandoning his continental possessions, he set sail for England in January 1153 to oppose Stephen. The ensuing campaign led to a stand-off at Wallingford and a 'Magnates' Peace'. Following the death of Eustace (August 1153) Henry became Stephen's heir (November 1153), and after the king's own death (October 1154), was crowned in December 1154.

Threatened as he was on all frontiers, Henry's energy was essential to consolidate and expand his realms. The Norman Vexin, the Seine valley between Paris and Rouen, was central to his concerns, especially as the castles of Vernon and Neufmarché had been taken by Louis in 1152-53. But Henry was now rich; he bought them back in 1154 and secured the Vexin through a marriage alliance in 1158. He also recovered important castles from Perche and Blois in the same year to secure his position in Anjou. This heartland was also threatened through the Berry, making Lusignan

support crucial. Aquitaine was defended by an alliance with the ruler of Aragon and Barcelona. A costly expedition to Toulouse in 1159 brought the acquisition of the Quercy.

Henry was also on the attack in the British Isles (map 1). Admittedly, in 1149, he had been compelled to agree to the king of Scots holding all the lands north of Newcastle and the Tyne; but in 1157 he recovered them and imposed homage upon Malcolm IV. The Welsh presented a more difficult problem. It took invasions of Gwynedd in 1157, and Deheubarth in 1158 and 1163, to bring them to terms, but this only resulted in a massive revolt in 1164. The 1165 expedition drew soldiers from throughout the empire: England, Normandy, Anjou and Gascony, as well as mercenaries from Flanders and Scotland, and a fleet of Norsemen from Dublin. However, the Welsh survived this formidable concentration owing to torrential rain.

Henry received papal support for an invasion of Ireland in 1155, but he was forced to postpone his invasion. It was left to the initiative of the Welsh Marcher barons to begin the assault in 1169, followed by a royal expedition in 1171. In 1175, the Irish high king, Rory O'Connor, became his vassal and Ireland became a province of England as Henry distributed those lands already conquered or yet to be acquired.

THE REVOLT OF 1173-1174

In creating the Angevin empire Henry had made many enemies, not least Louis VII of France, with whom he had disputed control of Toulouse since 1159, in what was to become a 'forty years war'. The French king played upon the restlessness of Henry's sons: 'Young Henry' (who had been crowned king of England in 1170), Richard, effectively ruler of Aquitaine since 1172, and Geoffrey, duke of Brittany. In alliance with William the Lion, king of Scots; Philip, count of Flanders; Philip's younger brother and heir, Matthew, count of Boulogne; and Theobald, count of Blois, they assailed Henry on all sides.

In England, four great earls revolted: Hugh Bigod of Norfolk, Robert of Leicester, Hugh of Chester, and William de Ferrers of Derby. Their alliance created a swathe of rebel fortresses across the Midlands. In response, Henry put forty-four royal castles on a war-footing throughout the country and deployed his fleet at Sandwich against seaborne invasion. He concentrated his efforts in England at first. Leicester, in the absence of its lord (who was with Louis), was besieged and taken in a month (3-28 July 1173), although the castle held out until Michaelmas (22 September).

Meanwhile, in Normandy, with a diversionary attack against Avranches from Brittany, Louis launched a pincer movement against his real goal, Rouen, by besieging Drincourt and Verneuil. Matthew of Boulogne took Drincourt (25 July) but he was mortally wounded in the

MAP 1

Campaigns in 1152-54 established a military status quo in England and with Louis VII of France. This freed Henry to make inroads into Wales and follow up Strongbow's invasion of Ireland. In 1173, he was challenged by a dangerous alliance of France, Scotland, and internal rebels. Royalist castle garrisons held firm, while their field forces defeated an invasion of East Anglia, allowing Henry to attack in Normandy and Brittany. In 1174, royalist troops captured the king of Scots and Henry defeated Louis outside Rouen.

1. THE CAMPAIGNS OF HENRY II

borders of England 1154

French royal domain and dependencies 1180

• conquests of Count Geoffrey, with date

Henry II's campaigns

→ 1152-54

→ 1157-71

→ 1173-74

campaigns of Henry II's opponents

→ Louis VII of France 1152

→ Louis VII of France 1174

→ William, king of Scots 1174

→ rebels 1173-74

border of Angevin empire 1189

process, and his death caused Philip to withdraw from the campaign. Henry gathered his forces and rushed across from England, arriving at Verneuil on the day it had agreed to surrender if not relieved (9 August). Louis' forces fled in disorder, firing the town to cover their retreat, but losing their rearguard nonetheless. Henry continued his lightning campaign by driving the Breton forces into Dol, and forcing the surrender of their leaders Ralph of Fougères and Hugh of Chester (26 August).

Attempts at peace negotiations broke down, and Robert, earl of Leicester, took the war back to England by landing in Suffolk with Flemish mercenaries. At the end of September, he joined forces with Hugh Bigod of Norfolk at Framlingham, and together they took Haughley castle from the king. But on their way to relieve the garrison of Leicester castle they were attacked at Fornham St Mary (near Bury St Edmunds) by royalist forces under the justiciar, Richard de Lucy. The rebels were routed; Robert of Leicester and many knights were captured, while the Flemings were hunted down and massacred by the local population.

In the autumn, Henry restored the situation in the Touraine, a zone crucial to his links with fortresses further south, and recovered Vendôme. A rebel surprise attack on Séez, in southern Normandy, in January 1174, was beaten off by the citizens. When Henry's enemies moved again it was against his northern borders where king William and Roger de Mowbray attacked Carlisle and Wark. Several Northumberland castles fell, and William's brother David led a relief force to Leicester. Threat of seaborne invasion from Flanders forced Henry to return to England, but when he did, count Philip and king Louis joined up to besiege Rouen (22 July). The English king needed a stroke of luck, which was delivered to him by the initiative of Yorkshire royalists. Approaching in a thick fog, they surprised the king of Scots outside Alnwick, which he was besieging, and captured him, so ending the threat in the north (13 July). Henry cleared up the Midlands following the fall of Huntingdon, and at Northampton there was a general surrender. Sailing back to Normandy (8 August) he marched to relieve Rouen. Despite an attempt by king Louis to seize the city on a holy day, he was repelled. When Henry arrived (10 September), his light troops cut the French lines of communication and forced their withdrawal.

The campaigns of 1173-74 epitomize with what skill warfare could be conducted in the twelfth century. Henry knew when to wait and when to act; when to defend and when to attack. His control of royal fortifications in England, combined with intelligent action on the part of his subordinates, restored the situation there and freed Henry to act as a 'fire brigade'. His continental possessions he defended and regained by swift, ferocious action in the face of attacks on all fronts. It was consummate strategy and generalship. Henry II is usually represented as a peacemaker and lawgiver; he was, but he also conducted widespread and aggressive campaigning. He extended his rule to Ireland, beat down the Scots and Welsh, and forged a new dominion in France greater than the French king's.

The castle at Gisors, one of the most important fortresses in the Vexin, was originally built for William II of England in the 1090s. The keep is twelfth-century, attributed to Philip Augustus. Its curtain walls contained an area large enough to hold an encampment of 1,000 men.

RICHARD OF ENGLAND VERSUS PHILIP OF FRANCE

Henry's successor, Richard I (the Lionheart), won a longlasting reputation as a warrior. His crusading exploits are well known (*pages 96-101*), but his defence of the Angevin dominions is at least as significant a measure of his ability. In contrast, his brother John, merely a competent commander, failed miserably. Whilst Richard was a prisoner in Germany in the spring of 1193, Philip Augustus of France seized control of castles on the Norman border, notably Gisors and Neaufles, and laid siege to Rouen, but fruitlessly. Richard returned to England in March 1194, and only two months later took a 100-ship fleet across the Channel from Portsmouth (10 May).

Richard moved with speed, receiving the submission of his rebellious brother John along the way, to raise the siege of Verneuil. Throwing a relief force into the castle he sent more troops around the French rear. Philip of France retired abruptly, abandoning his siege engines (28 May). While Richard led a force into Normandy to recover Beaumont-le-Roger from its rebel lord, his Angevin forces stormed Montmirail (*map 2*). Advancing swiftly on the important castle of Loches, already besieged by his Navarrese allies without success, he took it in a day by prolonged assault (13 June). He then took up position outside Vendôme where Philip made as if to attack him, but then fled. Richard caught up with the French rearguard at Fréteval, capturing Philip's wagon train, including all his siege equipment, treasure, and government documents. Philip recovered quickly, surprising prince John who was besieging Vaudreuil, and driving off his forces. It was at this castle in 1195 that the two kings met to arrange peace terms. By then Philip's position was so insecure that he was content to destroy the walls of castles which he knew he could not hold. Meanwhile, Richard extended the defences of Pont de l'Arche just to the north. In this war of fortresses, this

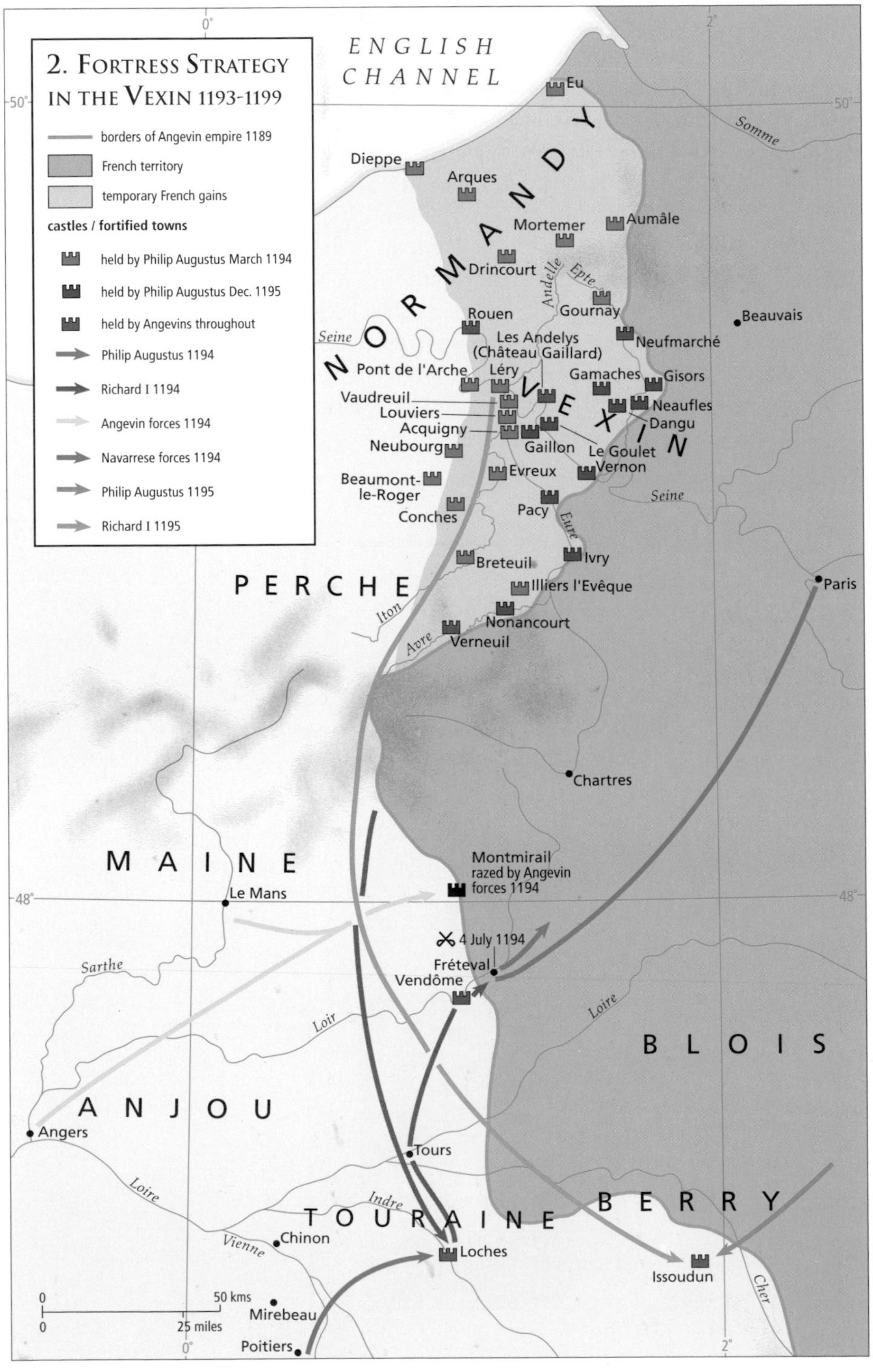

MAP 2

When Philip II seized the Vexin, a heavily fortified zone lying between Angevin, Rouen, and Paris, Normandy lay exposed to French attack. Richard's reconquest was based upon rapid movement, defeat of French field armies, determined sieges, and the construction of Château Gaillard.

war of attrition, Richard was gaining the upper hand.

Thwarted in the Vexin, Philip attacked in the Berry. He besieged Issoudun, taking the town and pressing the castle, but Richard led a relief force which trapped the French and forced their king to sue for peace. The Peace of Louviers (January 1196) recovered almost all of Richard's losses in the Vexin and elsewhere, although 1196 was a less successful year for Richard. Philip's diplomacy brought Arthur of Brittany, and the three northern French counts of Ponthieu, Boulogne, and Flanders into his camp. While Richard was busy capturing Nonancourt, on the southern border, Philip besieged Aumâle. Richard dashed north, but his attack on the French camp was repulsed. Aumâle's defences were

razed by Philip, and Richard paid to ransom the garrison.

Richard then threw massive resources into constructing Château Gaillard as a base to strengthen his assault on the Vexin (*page 54*). In 1198, Richard scored significant victories at Vernon and Neufmarché as he drove back Philip's defences and forced the French king, defensively, to fortify Le Goulet. But Richard's unexpected death during the siege of the castle of Châlus, in Poitou, on 7 April 1199, shifted the balance in favour of Philip. The years 1194-99 had seen almost unchecked advance of Angevin dominion, but over the next two decades almost all of the English crown's lands in France were lost.

ANGEVIN DECLINE UNDER KING JOHN

It is perhaps ironic that John won his nickname 'Softsword' as a result of his treaty with Philip, made at Le Goulet in May 1200, which actually strengthened his position. Certainly Richard would have agreed with this assessment of his younger brother's military ability, and historians have been equally scathing. But, on occasion, John displayed skill as both a strategist and a field commander. In 1202, his nephew Arthur attacked from Brittany into Anjou with French backing (*map 3*). Marching swiftly from Le Mans to Mirebeau, John captured both his nephew and his Lusignan allies, extinguishing the revolt. His decisive speed of action matched that of his father and brother. Yet his cruel behaviour after this success, when twenty-two prisoners died and Arthur 'disappeared', undid the good work. This was to be the story of his reign.

John was unable to win the trust of his barons in England or his continental dominions. He drove the seneschal of Anjou, William des Roches, into the enemy camp, and by spring 1203 had lost control of the Loire valley. He had offended the Lusignans by marrying an important heiress, Isabel of Angoulême. When they revolted, he would not rescue her from Chinon and instead relied on a mercenary captain to do the job; this became another undesirable trait in the eyes of his nobles. In August 1203, John devised a two-pronged attack to relieve Château Gaillard, besieged by Philip. An attempt at a co-ordinated riverborne assault and land attack went awry because his commanders had failed to consider the effect of the Seine's tides. Unable to draw Philip away from the siege by diversionary tactics, John left Normandy for England in December. Château Gaillard, Richard's great masterpiece, fell on 6 March 1204; it was a symbol of how far John had let things slip.

John failed to maintain the network of alliances which Richard had used to protect his territories and balance the power of the French crown. He lost the trust of the Flemish princes in the north, and in the south the count of Toulouse turned against him. In Normandy itself there were mass desertions by its barony and castellans in the face of Philip's advance. In the spring and summer of 1204, Philip overran the western part of the duchy in a matter of weeks and its 'capital', Rouen, fell on 24 June. Gerald of Wales blamed the defections upon 'despotic' governmental practices introduced from England; while with hindsight Roger of

2. FORTRESS STRATEGY IN THE VEXIN 1193–1199

— borders of Angevin empire 1189

French territory

temporary French gains

castles / fortified towns

held by Philip Augustus March 1194

held by Philip Augustus Dec. 1195

held by Angevins throughout

→ Philip Augustus 1194

→ Richard I 1194

→ Angevin forces 1194

→ Navarrese forces 1194

→ Philip Augustus 1195

→ Richard I 1195

Wendover regarded the fall as inevitable. Modern historians have tended to agree with that chronicler, arguing that Philip's income was double that of John. But the case is far from clear-cut and may underestimate sources of revenue outside England. Even if true, it serves rather to emphasize the skill of Richard in contrast to John.

In 1205, John gathered a large fleet on the south coast intending to support the land forces in Poitou, but it never sailed, in the face of baronial opposition. A smaller expedition set out in 1206 from La Rochelle and captured the supposedly impregnable southern fortress of Montauban (1 August). But, faced by Philip, John could not get his Poitevin barons to fight their overlord, and he settled at Thouars for a two-year truce. John did not give up, and worked for an alliance with the counts of Flanders and Boulogne, who were dependent upon English trade and now feared growing French power. Otto of Brunswick, a claimant to the imperial crown, also joined him, and by 1212 John was poised to invade once more. But once more his barons refused to serve. In 1213, a French assault on Flanders was the base for a seaborne invasion of England by prince Louis, and demanded a swift response. The earl of Salisbury, Renaud of Boulogne, and the count of Holland led a combined fleet of 500 ships against the French fleet moored at Damme, the outport of Bruges, and utterly destroyed it.

Building on this success, John constructed a pincer strategy for 1214. He led a force from La Rochelle while his Low

Country allies gathered in the north-west. John was initially successful, forcing the submission of the viscount of Limoges in April and the Lusignans in May, and also capturing Nantes (13 June). Besieging La Roche-au-Moine near Angers, he drew prince Louis and 800 knights to its relief; but once more he could not get the Poitevins to fight and he had to pull back. The earl of Salisbury and the Flemish counts needed to wait for the arrival of Otto's Germans before challenging Philip. They were not ready until mid-July, giving the French time to redeploy. In a rare pitched battle at Bouvines on 27 July, Philip soundly defeated John's allies. The victory was both decisive and symbolic of the importance of effective military leadership by a king. It was a test which John signally failed.

On his tomb in Worcester Cathedral, king John is shown drawing his sword, a common piece of contemporary symbolism. The figure almost mocks his nickname 'Softsword', a product of his defeats in France which also led to him being called 'Lackland'. He was a competent commander, but an inadequate statesman who lost the trust of his barons.

CHÂTEAU GAILLARD

In 1196, on the Seine, Richard began to construct a fortified complex including the fortress island of Andely, a new walled town (Petit-Andely), and a stockade blocking the river linked by a turreted wall up to a castle on the rock: Château Gaillard. This castle presented only one line of approach to an attacker, who first faced a barbican, separated by a rock-cut ditch from the outer ward, then an inner ward built, uniquely, of a series of connected towers, and finally, a monolithic keep, which was built like a ship's prow to deflect missiles. The sophistication of the fortifications, the speed of their construction, and their enormous cost bear witness to Richard's initiative.

The entire complex was built in the two accounting years ending in September 1198, at a cost of £11,500. This sum exceeded the expenditure on almost all the rest of Richard's castles and towns. It was a huge commitment to the reconquest of the Vexin, and a challenge to Philip's fortifications at La Roche Guyon, 5 miles (8km) up the river Seine.

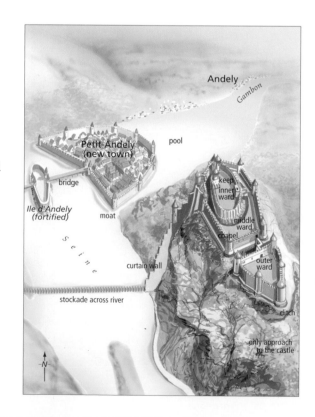

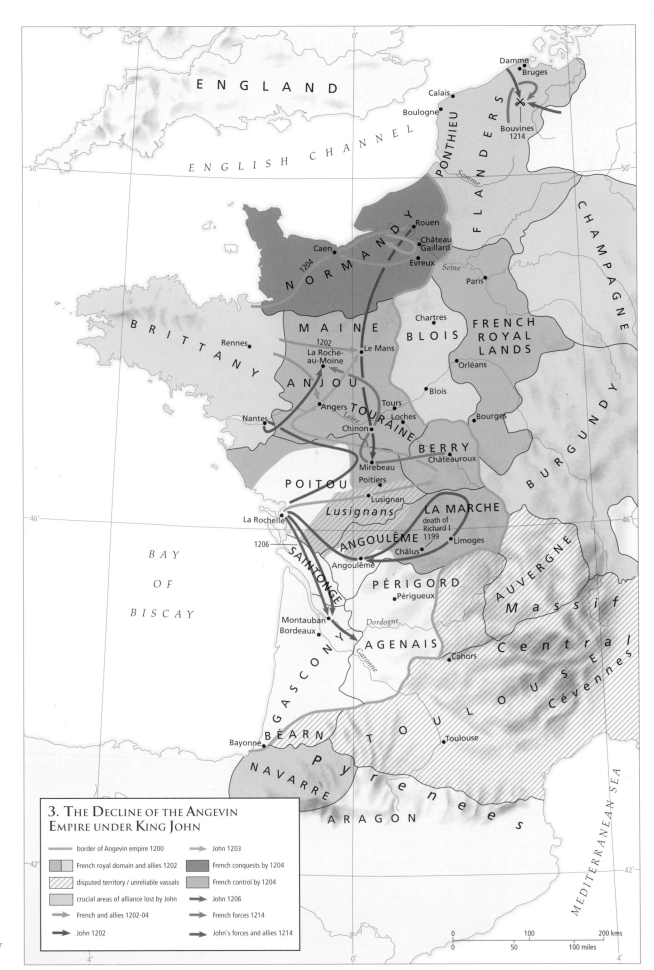

MAP 3

After Richard's death in 1199, Philip II continued his strategy of pressurizing Normandy, but John failed either to bring the French to battle or to raise the siege of Château Gaillard (1203). Unsupported, Normandy swiftly surrendered to Philip in 1204, to be followed by almost all Angevin vassals outside Aquitaine. John's subsequent campaigns were negated by the refusal of his barons to fight against their French overlord. In contrast, Philip personally led his forces to victory at Bouvines (1214), ending any hope of Angevin recovery.

3. THE DECLINE OF THE ANGEVIN EMPIRE UNDER KING JOHN

- border of Angevin empire 1200
- French royal domain and allies 1202
- disputed territory / unreliable vassals
- crucial areas of alliance lost by John
- French and allies 1202-04
- John 1202
- John 1203
- French conquests by 1204
- French control by 1204
- John 1206
- French forces 1214
- John's forces and allies 1214

| 0 | | 100 | | 200 kms |
| 0 | 50 | | 100 miles | |

THE GERMAN EMPIRE UNDER FREDERICK BARBAROSSA 1152-1190

WHEN FREDERICK HOHENSTAUFEN was elected to succeed his uncle Conrad III in 1152, he was already an experienced warrior, having fought on the ill-fated crusade of 1146-48. He was also wealthy enough, from his lands in Swabia and the Rhineland, to seek to re-establish imperial power in Italy. His election made him king of Germany, but only papal coronation in Rome would make him emperor. Italy was also wealthy and provided tax revenue and, notionally at least, the German emperor commanded the largest military forces in the Christian west. But Frederick's attempts to maintain his authority south of the Alps produced two decades of warfare. It also proved that the military resources of the Italian city-states were more than a match for his German vassals.

Frederick Barbarossa as emperor and crusader. Despite his later reputation, military operations did not always bring the success he desired. He had a heroic stature, though, and his death on crusade was the result of a typical piece of bravado. At the age of eighty he was drowned crossing, or possibly swimming in, a river in southern Asia Minor.

THE ITALIAN CAMPAIGNS

Frederick's first campaign, conducted with a small force, was intended merely to establish his authority by means of holding an Imperial Diet (council) at Roncaglia, followed by a quick coronation. That this did not work out was a result of the unwillingness of the increasingly independent Italian cities to pay the royal rights: *regalia* (taxes) and *fodrum* (provisions). They were also engaged in internal disputes and wars. Frederick's response was heavy-handed: the sacking of several cities and the ravaging of their territories, while avoiding those too strong to tackle. Tortona, an old enemy of the imperial city of Pavia, was reduced in nine weeks, largely through the efforts of the contingent of Henry the Lion, the duke of Saxony.

Frederick's main objective was Rome, where Hadrian IV eventually complied with coronation, although the Romans had to be fought in the streets. When disease broke out amongst his troops, Frederick was obliged to retreat to Germany, taking in an attack on Spoleto and the condemnation of Milan for rebellion along the way.

Milan was the most powerful of the north Italian city-states. Fearful of the emperor's intentions and unable to rely upon ancient Roman city walls, between 1156 and 1158 the citizens constructed a 3-mile (5-km) earthen rampart called the *Terraggio*, surrounded by a water-filled ditch. Milan became the centre of opposition to imperial authority and rallied other cities to its cause. Frederick, meanwhile, was securing his borders with Denmark and Hungary through diplomacy, and Poland through invasion, capturing Breslau (Wrocław) and Posen (Poznań).

After diplomatic clashes with the pope, Frederick returned to Italy to crush Milan in July 1158 (map 2). His forces were ordered not to pillage and provided with a commissariat. In addition to calling out the imperial vassals, such as the marquis of Montferrat, his ambassadors won the obedience of most of the communes (self-governing cities). By combining their forces with his own, he was able to invest the city (6 August). Bombardment, undermining, and

assaults through siege engines followed. After defeating a desperate sally, the imperial forces systematically destroyed the bridges across the ditch. Milan starved, and capitulated after a month on 7 September.

Frederick held another Diet at Roncaglia in November 1158, which defined and promulgated his regalian rights. These took away city privileges, such as the rights to self-government. Milan refused to accept this and, in 1159, supported by Brescia and Crema, revived attacks on Lodi and Como. His German forces having dispersed, Frederick was powerless to intervene. Not until 7 July was he able to besiege Crema, a small but well-defended city on the river Serio, boasting double walls with a water-filled ditch between. Siege engines were constructed, two *cats*, a tower and artillery pieces, and a bombardment began. On 12 August, empress Beatrice arrived with Henry the Lion, now also duke of Bavaria, and a powerful following. The Cremascans responded with a dangerous sally.

The first assault was delivered across a causeway constructed of 200 barrels of earth and 2,000 cartloads of gravel. A *cat* preceded the siege tower, to which were chained Cremascan prisoners. This atrocity backfired on Frederick as the assault failed and he lost the confidence of other cities. Milan began to construct an anti-imperial alliance and attacked Manerbio castle in order to draw Frederick from Crema. But he refused to be distracted and renewed his attack, the *cat* having now damaged the wall with its ram. Crema's defenders responded by building another wall behind the breach. The stalemate was only broken by the defection of Marchisio, a siege engineer who had been working for the Cremascans. Bribed by Frederick, he constructed for him an armoured siege tower, 150 feet (45m) high and with a bridge 70 feet (21m) long and 15 feet (4.5m) wide for dropping onto the wall. In January 1160, this monster was manoeuvred into position alongside the first tower; attacks from both convinced the defenders that further opposition was hopeless. They surrendered on

MAP 1

In terms of size, the German empire dominated the map of medieval Europe. Potentially, Frederick Barbarossa possessed wide military resources, especially in armoured knights. In practice, it was difficult for him to bring this force to bear. Crusades expanded German influence to the east, but it was Henry the Lion, duke of Saxony, who dominated operations. Frederick was unable to bring him to heel until 1181. Italy provided both wealth and the imperial crown, but its independently-minded city-states proved difficult to subdue. Only after the Peace of Constance in 1183 was Frederick able to contemplate a crusade to Jerusalem.

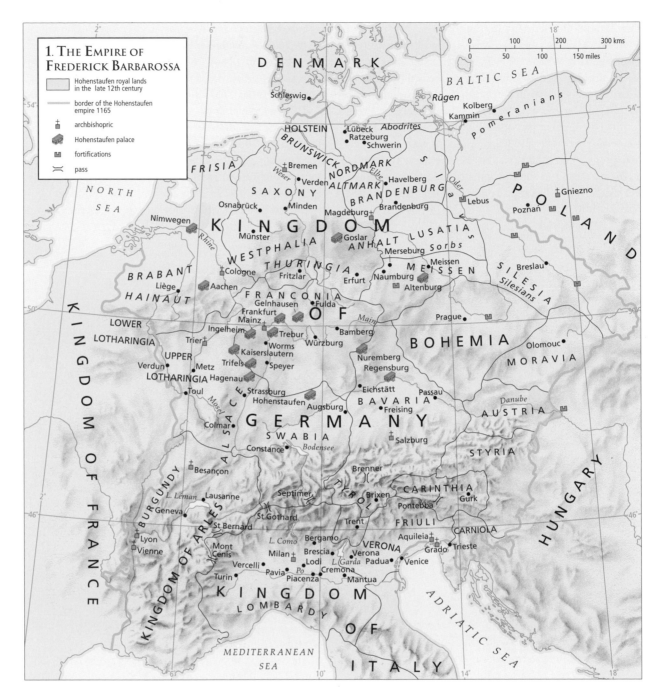

1. THE EMPIRE OF FREDERICK BARBAROSSA

- Hohenstaufen royal lands in the late 12th century
- border of the Hohenstaufen empire 1165
- ✝ archbishopric
- Hohenstaufen palace
- fortifications
- pass

27 January and the city suffered sack, burning, and the razing of its walls, buildings, and even its churches. This destruction signalled the penalty for rebellion.

The ferocity of his actions made this a hollow victory for Frederick. The example of Crema, which had held out for six months, encouraged further opposition. He also lost credibility by supporting Victor IV against Alexander III in a disputed papal election, but failing to get him recognized throughout Europe. This made little difference in Italy, but was a crucial factor in his wider diplomacy.

After receiving German reinforcements in May 1160, Frederick moved to crush Milan. In June, he refused battle at San Romano, apparently deterred by the Milanese battle formation. This comprised 100 'scythed chariots' in front, behind them the *carroccio* (an ox-drawn wagon carrying the city's standards), surrounded by archers, then the cavalry,

and finally the militias of the gates. Emboldened, in July, the Milanese advanced. When Frederick responded by moving to cut off their supplies, they attacked his camp (8 August 1160). Initially, this was successful, but a cavalry counter-attack led by the emperor seized the *carroccio* and drove them into retreat.

In May 1161, following the arrival of further German reinforcements, Frederick closed in. In an encounter battle outside the walls of Milan, the Milanese were worsted and the imperial forces invested the city. Learning from his experience at Crema, Frederick preferred blockade to assault. The Milanese starved. On 1 March 1162, they agreed to surrender terms that meant the handing-over of their consuls and 400 knights as hostages, the destruction of their churches and walls, and the filling-in of the city moats. The population was dispersed to live in villages. Frederick then returned to Germany in triumph.

Frederick's next objective was to control Rome and to challenge king William of Sicily's protectorate over Rome. When the king died in 1166, the time seemed ripe. But by then the strategic balance in northern Italy had changed. Verona and Padua, who had formed an alliance in 1164, fortified the Brenner pass against him: Frederick was forced to use another route into Italy. His troops were also fewer, and after wintering in Pavia, he spent the early months of 1167 tax-raising in the Romagna to fund his expedition. He also attempted to capture Ancona, held by Byzantine allies, before marching on Rome. On 24 July, his troops

assaulted St Peter's and after a seven-day siege during which Rome burnt, he enthroned his own pope, Paschal III (Victor having died in 1164). Disease ravaged his army, which, retreating in disorder, lost its baggage crossing the Po. On 1 December 1167, the Lombard League was formed, and Frederick withdrew across the Alps.

The Lombard League was a confederation of sixteen cities. It could put 20,000 men into the field, and also set about constructing a symbolic new city, Alessandria, surrounded by ramparts. When Frederick eventually returned to Italy in September 1174, he made this city his target, but withdrew to Pavia when relieving forces of the League

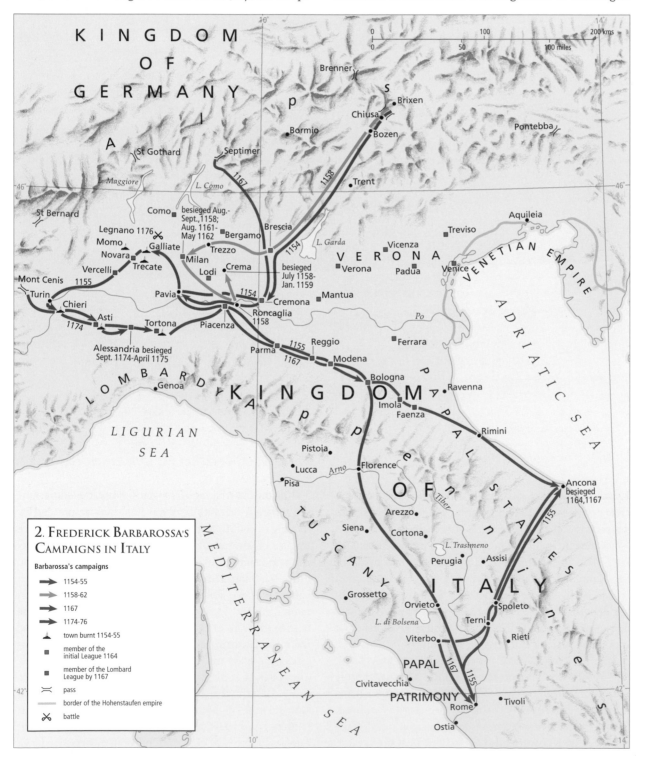

MAP 2

Frederick's military involvement in Italy lasted twenty years. Initially he had the upper hand, and was able to take Milan and force the city to raze its fortifications in 1158. Yet his heavy-handed policy failed as the city-states combined to oppose him, in what became known as the Lombard League. After his crushing defeat in battle at Legnano in 1176, he turned to diplomacy in order to achieve his political objectives.

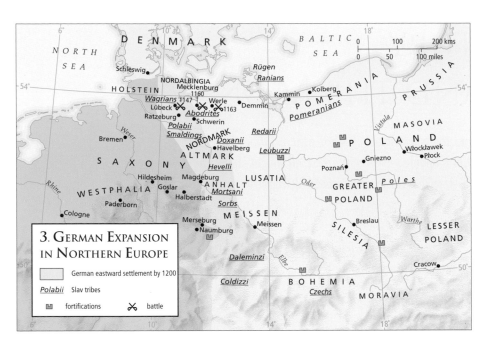

3. GERMAN EXPANSION IN NORTHERN EUROPE

☐ German eastward settlement by 1200

Polabii Slav tribes

🏰 fortifications   ⚔ battle

MAP 3

In the mid-twelfth century, the crusading impetus swept eastward into Slav lands. Henry the Lion, duke of Saxony, and Waldemar, king of Denmark, were merely the greatest of many lords seeking to expand their authority in the name of Christianity. Deploying armoured warriors and siege technology, the westerners advanced into the lands between the Elbe and Oder rivers.

Valturius' late fifteenth-century treatise on war presents an idealized representation of the ox-drawn wagon known as the *carroccio*. It was usually decorated with the city's banners and carried priests praying for victory. The *carroccio* represented the communal identity of the Italian city-state at war, boosting morale and providing a rallying point in battle.

arrived (13 April 1175). Negotiation failed, Henry the Lion refused to help Frederick, and the emperor had to rely upon largely Italian forces recruited from enemies of the sixteen. The League raised 2,760 cavalry, an additional 900 from Milan alone, supported by urban militias, and challenged battle at Legnano on 29 May 1176. The League's reconnaissance cavalry was routed and Frederick attacked the left wing, driving it back on the *carroccio* in the centre. But its defenders held, and Frederick, leading the attack, was unhorsed and believed dead, causing his troops to flee. Some 8,000 imperial troops and 2,000 Leaguers were believed dead. The emperor escaped on foot, only reaching safety at Como three days later.

The wealth that had drawn Frederick to Italy had proved his downfall. Isolated, the Italian cities were vulnerable, but in combination they possessed the fortresses and armies to defy an emperor. In the end, in the Peace of Constance of 1183, Frederick accepted this.

THE BALTIC CRUSADES

In 1146, preaching by the charismatic Cistercian monk, Bernard of Clairvaux, encouraged a crusading spirit against the pagan Slavs. Their ruler, prince Nyklot, launched a pre-emptive strike against Lübeck on 26 June 1147, destroying ships and killing 300 men. The crusaders' two armies

seemed more interested in attacking Christian armies anyway. Their larger, northern force led by Albert the Bear, margrave of Nordmark, attacked Pomerania, unsuccessfully besieged Demmin, and was only dissuaded from attacking Stettin by its bishop. The Saxon princes, led by Henry the Lion, invaded the territory of the Abodrites and besieged Dobin in conjunction with Danish crusaders. A relief force of Ranians from Rügen persuaded the besiegers to withdraw. For as they realized: 'Is not the land we are devastating our land, and the people we are fighting our people?'

In fact, German forces were generally larger and better equipped in both horses and armour than their pagan opponents. The westerners also had a technological advantage in the art of building fortifications — especially stone castles — and constructing siege engines to take Wendish (western Slav) fortifications. Between 1158 and 1166, Henry the Lion made a determined attempt to deploy these advantages and overthrow the native rulers. In 1158, he invaded Abodrite territory, capturing and temporarily imprisoning Nyklot. Much of the warfare was conducted in conjunction with the Danes, who relearnt Viking techniques to raid and land forces on the northern coasts. In 1160, Henry combined with king Waldemar in a two-pronged attack. Nyklot was forced to burn his fortresses and retreat to Werle, conducting a guerrilla warfare against the invaders. Then his sons were defeated at Mecklenburg and he was killed on a sortie, forcing them to accept Henry's overlordship. In 1163, Henry took Werle by means of a ram and siege tower, and though he suffered heavy casualties, defeated Nyklot's son, Pribislav, in battle near Demmin in 1164. The Germans suffered heavy casualties though, including several notables. When Pribislav converted in 1167, he was set up as ruler of most of the Abodrite country except Schwerin, and accompanied Henry on crusade in 1172. This was also the occasion of Henry's first refusal to fight for Frederick in Italy. After the emperor had settled internal warfare in Saxony, he turned his mind to defeating Henry, who was outlawed in 1179. Henry held out until 1181, fortifying his castles in Nordalbingia and Lübeck, but when the city fell in August, he surrendered and accepted exile.

The contrast between Frederick's military success in Germany and defeat in Italy bears further examination. His Italian expeditions required a higher level of diplomacy than he was at first able to manage. The dispute over the relative status of pope and emperor was woven into a network of alliances and feuds of wealthy cities run by ambitious oligarchies. The municipal identities which they fostered, when combined with opposition to imperial financial demands, proved too strong for Frederick to overcome. He was successful in the late 1170s and 1180s with a diplomatic offensive. He was a shrewd operator and knew how to employ law to wrong-foot his opponents in Germany. The northern campaigns, conducted largely against pagans outside the Christian power structures, were easier to manage for that very reason. Here military power translated more easily into political supremacy.

THIRTEENTH-CENTURY EASTERN EUROPE AND THE MONGOLS

A FTER 1200, CHRISTIAN EXPANSION into the pagan lands of north-eastern Europe was achieved largely through crusades and orders of military monks. Eventually, these all fought under the banner of the Teutonic Order, which established a state in Prussia and Livonia, defended by impressive castles. The Knights made no progress against the Russian principalities, however. Then, in 1238-40, these states were briefly overwhelmed by Mongol invasions. In 1241, the Mongols penetrated Germany and Hungary, scoring great victories. A conquest of Europe seemed likely, but they withdrew and never returned. In the later thirteenth century, the Teutonic Knights resumed their advance and constructed a powerful state based on an extensive network of fortifications such as Königsberg and Marienburg.

The great castle of Marienburg became the headquarters of the Teutonic Order in Prussia in 1309. It was typical of their fortifications, being built of brick, rectangular in plan, and placed in low-lying ground near a river. Its architectural style represented the Order's dual role as both ecclesiastical and military.

GERMAN MILITARY ORDERS

Concerned about the temporary nature of crusading gains, German bishops established new military orders: the Sword Brothers (at Riga, c.1202), and the Knights of Dobrin (in Prussia, c.1222), to secure the land. The Teutonic Knights' origins went back to the siege of Acre in 1190, but it only became an international order under the patronage of the crusading German emperor Frederick II between 1215 and 1230. Its base was the magnificent castle of Montfort (Starkenberg) in Syria. In 1226, *Hochmeister* Hermann of Salza was given the status of an imperial prince to enable him to organize Baltic expeditions. These proved enormously popular with eastern lords: the 1232 crusade was joined by seven Polish dukes, and in 1233, margrave Henry of Meissen alone led 500 knights. Such large forces rapidly overwhelmed western Prussia, where the Knights set up bases at Kulm and Thorn (map 1).

Further east, in Livonia, the Sword Brothers had been fighting for two decades to establish authority in the region. Their advantages lay in superior technology. Despite small numbers, around 120 knights, armour for man and horse made them near-invulnerable to the lighter Livonian cavalry. Accompanying foot soldiers with crossbows were effective in battle and sieges. In 1211, Fallin was battered by trebuchets and taken by siege towers pushed across a fascine-filled ditch. Another 'great machine' was used at Kirkholm in 1220. While the Livonians did develop siege techniques of their own in time, initially they were totally overmatched, and they were never able to compete with the crusaders' use of the cog.

These distinctively shaped ships could be built to over a 200-ton capacity, ten times that of previous Baltic vessels. After defeat by the Curonians in the Gulf of Riga in 1210, using smaller ships, the Brothers relied upon the cogs of their Hanseatic allies. Capable of carrying 500 men, they towered over longships. Filled with supplies, and used in conjunction with the *bolskip* (river boat), they provided crucial logistic support for expeditions. Newly conquered

territories were fortified, at first by wooden blockhouses, and later by stone towers, less vulnerable to fire. Just a handful of these castles, manned by small garrisons, secured the land.

By such means, Estonia was conquered (1209-18) and Curonia submitted in 1230-31. Lithuanian raids from south of the Dvina continued, and were countered both by fortifying the river line and by pouncing on an enemy on the way home and slowed by booty. However, the Sword Brothers' heterodoxy and ruthless rule lost them papal support. In 1236, their master, Folkwin, supported by the prince of Pskov, led an overambitious expedition deep into Lithuania. Floundering in the marshes around Saule, unsuitable terrain for their knights, the crusaders were massacred: Folkwin and fifty brothers were killed. In the next year, the Teutonic Order took over their possessions and commenced attacks on Novgorod. These were repelled by Alexander Nevsky in the Battle on the Ice at Lake Chud (5 April 1242), where allied Mongol archers played a vital role in his victory.

In 1237, the attack was renewed in Prussia, with crusaders taking two river boats from subject Pomeranians to push north along the Frisches Haff, establishing fortifications and settlements. Alarmed by the commercial competition these represented, in 1242, duke Swantopelk of Danzig led his Pomeranians in support of the Prussians. This began a ten-year war which nearly defeated the Order. Swantopelk deployed a river fleet of twenty ships, built forts to contain the Germans, and ravaged their territories. He also learnt to counter their heavy cavalry by using ambush and bad terrain, winning victories at Rensen (1244) and Krücken (1249). But he could not take their castles. Polish support for the Order and the threat of crusade from the papacy eventually subdued him. In 1254, king Ottocar of Bohemia founded Königsberg whilst on crusade, which supported the Order's base at Memel (1252) to push further up the river Neman.

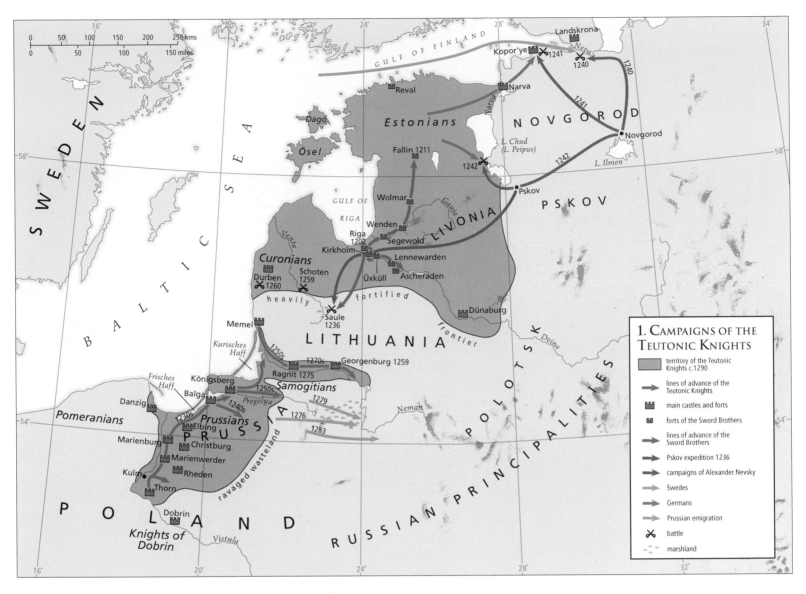

1. CAMPAIGNS OF THE TEUTONIC KNIGHTS

- territory of the Teutonic Knights c.1290
- lines of advance of the Teutonic Knights
- main castles and forts
- forts of the Sword Brothers
- lines of advance of the Sword Brothers
- Pskov expedition 1236
- campaigns of Alexander. Nevsky
- Swedes
- Germans
- Prussian emigration
- battle
- marshland

MAP 1

Military orders provided the cutting edge for Christian expansion along the southern Baltic shore. After 1237, they were all brought together under the banner of the Teutonic Knights. The crusaders possessed a technological superiority over their heathen opponents. This was expressed through heavier armour, crossbows, and siege engines, and the logistical support and mobility provided by large vessels known as cogs.

In Livonia, by 1255, the Order had recovered its lands south of the Dvina and forced Mindaugus, prince of Lithuania, to accept baptism. But in 1259, the Samogitians attacked in Curonia and defeated master Burchard von Hornhausen, killing thirty-three brothers. When he tried to escape into Prussia, his force was ambushed at Durben in 1260, killing him and 150 knight-brothers. Many Lithuanians renegaded and thirty years of warfare followed. The Order suffered defeats in 1262, 1270, 1279, and 1287 before it could re-establish a heavily fortified border between the Dvina and Neman around 1290.

In Prussia, the situation was equally dangerous in the 1260s. Duke Swantopelk and his son Mestwin organized their forces in imitation of the westerners, based around forts and deploying crossbows, siege weapons, and river fleets. Their rebellion deprived the Order of all but a few fortifications. The Prussians were only defeated by influxes of crusaders in 1265, 1266, and 1272. The Order also rebuilt its main fortresses in stone or brick: Königsberg in the 1260s, Marienwerder and Marienburg in the 1270s. By concentrating its efforts upon the destruction of the Prussians through devastation and guerrilla warfare, using native converts, the Teutonic Knights completed this phase of conquest. In 1309, following the loss of Acre (1291), the Order's headquarters was moved to Marienburg.

RUSSIA AND THE MONGOLS

By 1200, Russia consisted of several warring principalities, but these had proved able to hold back external attacks. On the steppe frontier, the nomadic Polovtsy (Pechenegs) had been contained, as had the crusaders and the pagan Livonians and Lithuanians. When reports came of new eastern invaders in 1223, a group of princes crossed the Dnieper and advanced to the Kalka river. Encountering Mongol forces for the first time, they were routed in a campaign which also ended the military power of their Polovtsy allies. The Mongols did not reappear until 1237, by which time further internecine conflict had weakened Russia still further.

At this time no-one in the Christian world could conceive the danger of the Mongol threat. It was widely believed that it foreshadowed the destruction of Islam by the legendary ruler Prester John. Nothing could have been further from the truth. The Mongols were inspired by a

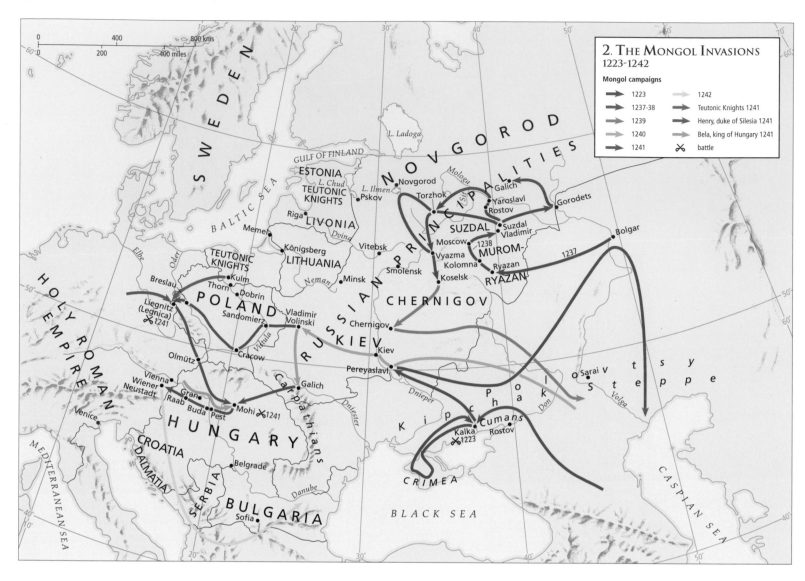

zeal for world conquest begun by their creator, Temujin, later called Chingiz Khan (1167-1227). By 1206 he had united the tribes of Mongolia under his leadership, symbolized by a *kuriltai* (acclamation). Chingiz created an army of horse-archers on the traditional steppe model, employing a decimal unit structure from 10 to 10,000, which facilitated command and control. Before the full development of gunpowder and firearms, they were almost invincible in battle against sedentary enemies.

Such nomads traditionally lacked siege techniques, but the Mongols learnt them, and in 1215 took Beijing. The conquest of China was completed, incredibly, by 1234, although it took another fifty years to subdue. Meanwhile, Chingiz had turned his attention to the empire of the Khwarizm Shah, who ruled from Samarkand. In a brilliantly organized three-pronged attack, the Khwarizmians were overwhelmed (some of their soldiers, fleeing west, ousted the last Latin troops from Jerusalem). Chingiz spent his last years securing the Asian steppe, and this is what gave his empire such durability. Ögedei, Chingiz's successor, who ruled from the Caspian to the China Sea, was said to command an army of 129,000 men.

Much larger numbers are often cited for Mongol hordes,

based on Islamic sources, but the sheer logistical problems of moving cavalry armies in which each soldier had several horses, contradicts exaggerated claims. Their invasion of Russia consisted of twelve to fourteen *tumans*, each notionally of 10,000 men. What made the Mongols so superior, though, was their strategic flexibility and rigorous discipline. When they fell upon Russia in 1237, the princes could respond with neither.

The Mongols attacked in winter, the favoured season because frozen marshlands facilitated rapid movement by their cavalry. The first place to fall was Ryazan (map 2), taken after a five-day siege (21 December). A relief force sent by grand prince Yury of Vladimir was surrounded and defeated at Kolomna. Yury fled his capital and took his main army north-west to the river Sit, placing all available Suzdalian troops in a defensive position between the Volga and Mologa rivers to the east and north. The Mongol general Batu first took Vladimir (3-7 February 1238) then swept through the rest of the principality, while a subordinate attacked on the river Sit. The Suzdalians fled, possibly even offering up their prince's head, without a fight (4 March). Meanwhile, another Mongol force besieged Torzhok, the southernmost town of Novgorod, which fell on 5 March.

MAP 2

The Mongol incursions presented Europe with insuperable military problems. An initial raid in 1223 tested the Russian states' mettle and found it wanting. Then, in a series of consecutive campaigns from 1237-41, Mongol forces overran Russia and devastated Poland and Hungary. Against their strategic speed and discipline in battle, western arms proved totally inadequate. A Mongol conquest of Christian Europe might have been possible, although logistically difficult, but it was never attempted.

But Novgorod itself was spared, the Mongol cavalry getting to within 60 miles (96 km) of the city before turning back, possibly because the spring thaw threatened to cut them off if they began a siege.

After regrouping, the next phase of the Mongol campaign began in spring 1239. Möngke's army swept through Chernigov, besieging its capital with 'a giant catapult capable of hurling stones, which could only be lifted by four men, a bowshot's distance'. A relief force from Kiev was defeated, and Chernigov fell on 18 October. The main Mongol army then withdrew to encampments on the Kipchak steppe. In autumn 1240, the third and last phase of the campaign was directed against Kiev. An army of ten *tumans* surrounded the city which was pounded by artillery in the area of the Polish Gates, before the city was stormed on 6 December. Concentrating his forces near Galich, Batu was poised to strike into Europe.

THE MONGOL INVASION OF EUROPE 1241

News of the Mongol invasions caused panic in Europe. Their unified command and purpose contrasted strongly with a divided response. German bishops and the only supranational authority – the papacy – preached crusades against the impending attack, but the Mongols were superior in both their strategy and tactics. In the spring of 1241, Batu launched a twin-pronged attack into Poland and Hungary. The Mongol advantages of discipline, manoeuvring to the direction of their horse-tail banners, flexibility, as they fled in front of an enemy charge to return when it was blown, and the arrow-storm created by their bows, gave them superiority in the field.

The northern army encountered a force led by Henry, duke of Silesia, and the Prussian master of the Teutonic Knights, supported by German town militia infantry, at Liegnitz (9 April 1241). The crusaders were lured into a trap by the classic Mongol tactic of feigned flight and

encirclement. In Hungary, it was the same story. Despite king Bela IV's attempts to block the Carpathian passes, Batu's forces swept into the Hungarian Plain, heading for Gran at a speed of 60 miles (96 km) per day. Desperately, Bela mustered his forces on the river Sajo at Mohi. The Mongols then threw a pontoon bridge over the river to outflank the defenders, forcing the crossing against the main body with firebombs. Despite withdrawing into a wagon fortress, the Hungarians were overwhelmed.

Throughout the rest of 1241, Mongol forces ravaged eastern Europe, almost reaching the walls of Vienna. Then, in early 1242, news came that Ögedei was dead and that all Mongols were recalled for the *kuriltai* to choose his successor. Batu retired to the Eurasian steppe where he established the Golden Horde, but Mongol armies never returned to Europe. In 1258-59, Möngke Khan conquered Baghdad and Persia, establishing the Il-Khanate in the region (*map 3*). But his death in 1259 meant that further advances into Syria were led by Kitbugha, in command of two weak *tumans* largely made up of subject Turks. As a result, he was defeated and killed by the Mamluk sultan Qutuz at Ain Jalut (3 September 1260). Later attacks on the Mamluks were also defeated.

It used to be thought that only chance spared Europe from Mongol domination. Certainly their troops were superior in the field, and their Chinese (and later, Persian) siege engineers could take any city they wished. Yet the Mongol army depended upon its horse-power for strategic and tactical mobility. Once away from the grasslands of the Hungarian Plain it is possible that they would not have been able to feed their horses. The Mongols' failure to conquer Syria would seem to confirm this, although the Mamluks did beat them at their own game with better-equipped horse-archer troops. But crucial to the Mongol military decline was the splitting of their empire into separate regional, sedentary dynasties.

MAP 3

The vast extent of Mongol dominion puts western military achievements into perspective. But their very success was the undoing of Mongol dreams of world domination. The empire built up by Chingiz and his heirs could not be sustained as a unified organization. After the death of the Great Khan Möngke in 1259, only the Il-Khanids possessed ambitions to expand westwards.

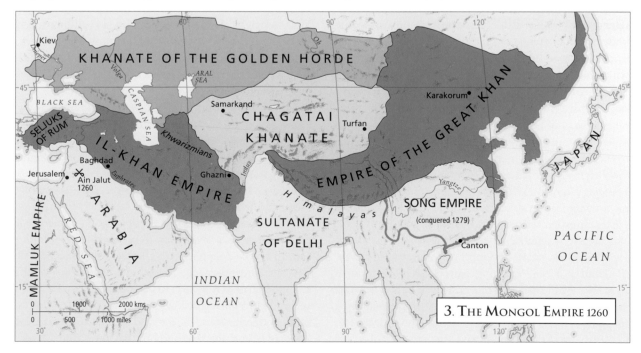

3. THE MONGOL EMPIRE 1260

THIRTEENTH-CENTURY ENGLISH CIVIL WARS

THE REBELLIONS IN ENGLAND of 1215-17 and 1264-65 had similar roots in failed attempts by groups of barons to impose reform on kings who abused their authority. Revolt threatened king John (1199-1216) from 1212, but his failure to regain Normandy and Anjou in 1214 led to open rebellion. John's promise to reform – Magna Carta, sealed 15 June 1215 – failed due to his bad faith. The rebels declared John deposed and offered the crown to Louis, son of Philip II of France (1180-1223). Half a century later, after the failure between 1258 and 1261 to impose reform on John's son Henry III (1216-72), revolt again erupted, but baronial unity was broken by personal feuds. While Henry III was naive and unwarlike, his bellicose son Edward and brother Richard were the military brains behind him.

Henry III was pious, politically naive, and unwarlike. The driving forces behind the royalist military strategy in the 1260s were his brother Richard, duke of Cornwall and titular king of Germany (whose seal this is), and Henry's son Edward. Edward's role in the civil war formed a military apprenticeship for his great campaigns as king after 1272.

KING JOHN'S WAR

The uprising against king John began when rebel barons (mainly from north and east England) seized London in May 1215. John had the great advantage of a network of stone castles across the kingdom (map 1). For months he had strengthened them while recruiting knights and crossbowmen from Poitou and hiring mercenaries (routiers) from the Low Countries. His garrisons threatened the estates of rebel barons, forcing them to disperse their forces. But John's position was flawed. Welsh princes threatened the marches, prince Louis of France and Alexander II of Scotland were poised to invade at opposite ends of the kingdom, and many apparently loyal barons were waiting upon events. The civil war was dominated by local struggles for castles: organized campaigns depended on the availability of a field army, which at first only John possessed.

John invested Rochester in mid-October: its capture would complete the isolation of London and the siege was pressed relentlessly. John's artillery made little impact, so he undermined the walls, bringing down a tower. The same method gained entry to the keep, but the defenders withdrew behind a cross-wall and held out until their food ran out. A contemporary wrote 'our age has not known a siege so hard pressed nor so strongly resisted'. The main rebel army could do little to interfere: Louis was slow to send help and John's captain, Falkes de Breauté, was operating menacingly north of London.

When Rochester fell on 30 November, Alexander II was besieging Norham (19 October-late November 1215), and the northern barons submitted to him. John led a punitive winter campaign against the north before Louis' arrival. He also needed to plunder rebel estates to reward his routiers. He left St Albans on 19 December and stormed Berwick on 15 January 1216, harrying into Scotland to punish Alexander. By the end of February, he was back at Bedford, having covered over 600 miles (965 km), then spent March mopping up rebel castles in East Anglia. John had taken an impressive list of castles and received the surrender of several

rebels. Meanwhile, Falkes and other royal captains had been harrying widely in East Anglia and the east Midlands.

However, the main rebel force remained intact in London, and John had failed to crush the rebellion in the north. Submissions there were temporary – many rebels withdrew into Scotland knowing that John would soon depart. By now, the threat from Louis was growing. John offered easy terms to rebels while gathering his mercenaries in Kent. A storm on 18 May dispersed his fleet, allowing Louis to land. John prepared to fight, but his captains, including the experienced William Marshal, persuaded him not to risk the kingdom in one battle.

As John's support in the south and east collapsed, he fell back to Corfe. The rebellion revived and many royalists defected, including four earls: two-thirds of the baronage were now in revolt. Louis' substantial force permitted him to take the offensive in June 1216 (map 2). He made for Winchester, where he thought John was to be found, seeking a quick victory while John's cause tottered. The betrayal of Marlborough threatened John's control of the south-west, and in July he even temporarily lost control of Worcester.

A quick victory eluded Louis, however, and by mid-July he turned on the castles still holding out in his rear. While a force invested Windsor, in early August Louis besieged Dover where Alexander and many northerners joined him. Artillery battered the wall and towers, while miners worked in the ditch under cover of a cat (mobile shelter). The north-west barbican was taken and the gate behind it undermined, but the assault failed. On 14 October, Louis agreed to a truce. The siege allowed John to regain his nerve. In the second week of September he harassed the besiegers of Windsor before drawing them off by a rapid march north, from the Thames at Walton to Cambridge in two days. He relieved Lincoln, and at King's Lynn arranged the supply of his northern castles. The threat to their estates so alarmed Alexander and the northerners that they quit Dover,

MAP 1

King John's control of the network of royal castles forced the barons opposed to him to remain dispersed in defence of their estates. This allowed John to take the initiative, pressing home the siege of Rochester and then conducting a winter *chevauchée* the length of England. Other royal captains raided the zone north of London. But John failed to crush the main baronial host, which remained intact in London awaiting the arrival of prince Louis from France and king Alexander from Scotland with reinforcements.

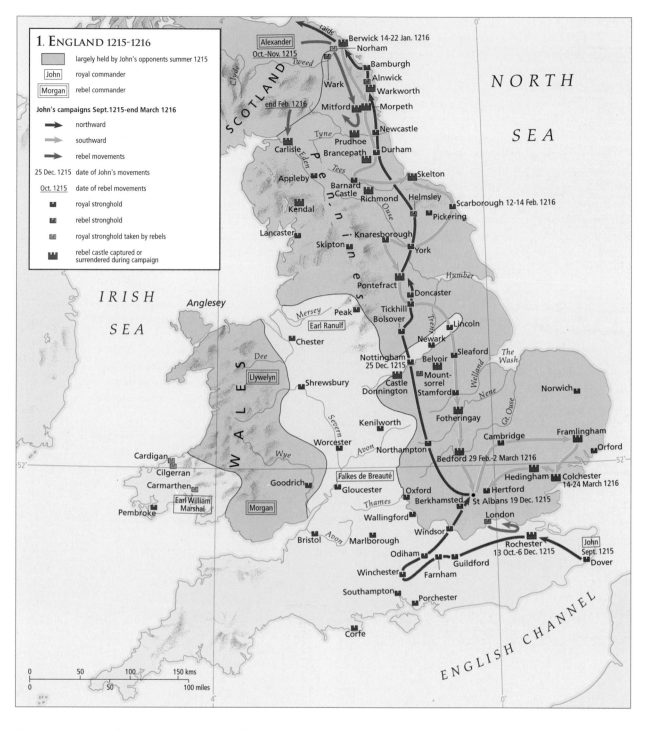

dispersing the rebel forces again. John's death from dysentery at Newark (18 October) ended an effective foray.

John's death did not cause the rebellion to collapse – the barons swore to continue the war, and Louis captured Hertford in early December. William Marshal, appointed guardian ('rector') of John's young son Henry III, was unable to take offensive action: the royal treasury was empty, there were disputes among royalist barons, and there was the Welsh threat. Consequently, William secured a truce to last over the winter at the cost of ceding the castles north of London.

The tide began to turn when Louis went to France to raise reinforcements (late February–April 1217). He was briefly trapped in Winchelsea by royalists and guerrillas

from the Weald under 'Willikin of the Weald'. Two leading rebel barons and many lesser ones defected, resenting the favour Louis showed to the French. The guardian William summoned the royalist captains and regained many of the castles lost the previous summer, if only temporarily. The hard core of rebels remained, and when Louis returned in late April with an advance party of 140 knights, he regained Farnham and Winchester.

Louis' failure to capture Dover now resulted in the division of his forces. He returned to the siege, sending strong forces to relieve Mountsorrel, and then to conclude the siege of Lincoln. This presented William Marshal at Northampton with an unmissable opportunity. The main royalist forces were already at hand, and if the army which concentrated at Newark (17-18 May) was modest – 406 knights, at least 200 sergeants, and 317 crossbowmen – it had surprise on its side. William approached Lincoln from the north, to maintain the element of surprise and gain the slope. The crossbowmen led the way in order to break up any rebel charge. But the rebels refused battle, wrongly thinking they were outnumbered, and sheltered in the city to continue the siege of the castle and await Louis.

The day was saved by the bishop of Winchester's reconnaissance. He found a blocked gate in the city walls, which was opened under cover of diversionary attacks on other gates. William burst in, and achieved such surprise that the rebels' artillery master was killed by men he thought were from his own side. After a stiff fight in the streets of Lincoln itself the rebel army broke. Only three of the heavily armed knights were killed, but the capture of 46 barons and 300 knights tore the heart from the rebellion.

The battle of Lincoln did not end the rebellion however. The royal captains dispersed with their prisoners. Louis, incapable now of taking the initiative, negotiated. But, loyal to his dwindling number of English partisans, he waited upon a final throw: in late August reinforcements sailed from Calais. On 25 August, the fleet was defeated off Sandwich. The guardian, William Marshal, by this time about seventy years of age, was persuaded not to put to sea, but he ensured his cog (ship) was lightly laden, enabling his sergeants to throw potfuls of powdered lime to blind those on the heavily laden French flagship.

Following this disaster, Louis of France sued for peace. What remains particularly striking about this civil war is the way in which both sides generally avoided battle on the grounds that it was far too risky.

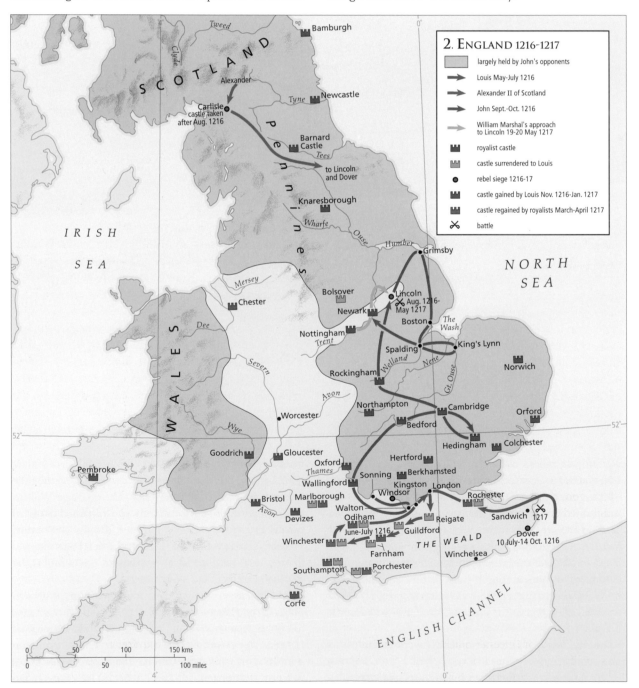

MAP 2

When Louis landed in May 1216, there were mass defections to him, but after failing to bring John to battle, he had to besiege the royal castles holding out in his rear. John's death removed a major rebel grievance. However, it required William Marshal's opportunistic victory at Lincoln in May 1217, and the interception of reinforcements from France before Louis gave up. The money spent in the twelfth century on royal castles was amply justified, since their resistance prevented the complete collapse of John's cause.

It is ironic that Henry III gave Kenilworth to earl Simon as a sign of favour in 1253. The extensive water defences (Mere) occupied the left foreground. They were probably king John's work, and enabled the castle to resist the full force of the crown for six months until its provisions were exhausted. No castle was intended to resist for ever, but to tie down and wear out attackers until their provisions were consumed or relief arrived.

KING HENRY'S WAR

In 1256, Simon de Montfort, earl of Leicester, assumed the leadership of English barons determined to halt Henry III's misrule. In 1258, at the Council of Oxford, under the additional threat from Welsh lords, they agreed to rule according to the provisions of his father's Magna Carta. By 1263, following further troubles on the Welsh borders, opposition to Henry had fragmented. This would have an important effect on the way the subsequent war of revolt was fought. De Montfort returned from France to join the earl of Derby and Gilbert of Clare (heir to the earldom of Gloucester) as the only notable nobles in opposition to the king, together with the citizens of London. Most magnates, especially the warlike lords of the Welsh marches, supported Henry III.

Feuding between rival nobles in the marches turned into civil war when Henry III unfurled the royal banner, a red silk dragon, on 3 April 1264 (map 3). His army at Oxford, summoned on the pretext of invading north Wales, held a central position between the Montfortians in the Midlands and the south-east. Their strength lay in Kenilworth castle, London, and Dover, described as the 'key to England' by a contemporary writer.

The royalists struck rapidly at Northampton. The town and castle, with a rich haul of prisoners, fell almost at once, rather than resisting long enough for de Montfort to bring relief. His town of Leicester quickly followed. Instead of pressing the advantage, prince Edward indulged himself by attacking Derby's estates and the castle of Tutbury. This

gave de Montfort the opportunity to launch the manouevre which culminated in battle at Lewes.

By assaulting Rochester, de Montfort presumably meant to remove a threat to London. He crossed the Medway although the bridge was defended, and quickly took the town and the castle bailey (18 and 19 April). However, as in 1215, the great tower held out. After moving south at a leisurely speed, part of Henry's army made a spurt to cover some 45 miles (72 km) on 26 April. If the aim was to surprise the Montfortians, it failed. News of Henry's approach (night of 25-26 April) caused de Montfort to return to the security of London. His strategy had failed to capture Rochester, but by bringing the king south it permitted the Montfortian forces to unite in London. While Henry's forces moved into Sussex prior to investing London or Dover, de Montfort marched south to seek battle. This was a risky strategy, but was the only way to seize the initiative after a run of reverses.

News of de Montfort's movement caused the royalists to cancel their advance to Canterbury. Instead, they moved cautiously to Lewes, whose castle, town walls, and priory offered a secure base. De Montfort bivouacked at one of his own manors nearby. The royalists' leaders, confident after their recent successes and outnumbering de Montfort's army, rejected compromise. The size of the armies is unknown. Henry probably had over 1,000 cavalry – heavily armed knights and lighter esquires and sergeants – and de Montfort only one-third as many. Several thousand infantry were present, archers and spearmen from London,

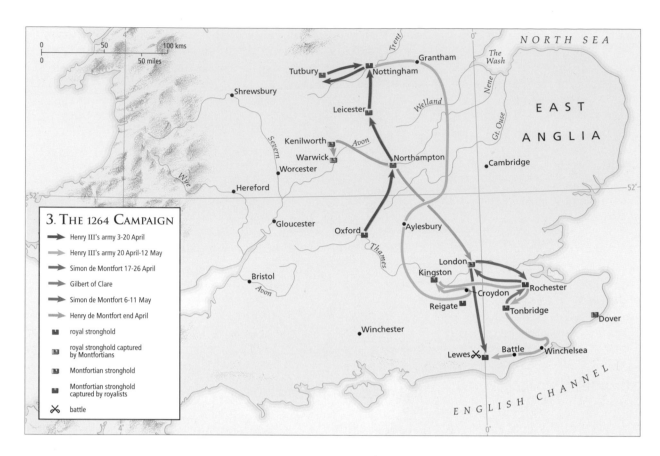

3. THE 1264 CAMPAIGN

- Henry III's army 3-20 April
- Henry III's army 20 April-12 May
- Simon de Montfort 17-26 April
- Gilbert of Clare
- Simon de Montfort 6-11 May
- Henry de Montfort end April
- royal stronghold
- royal stronghold captured by Montfortians
- Montfortian stronghold
- Montfortian stronghold captured by royalists
- battle

MAP 3

Earl Simon's threat to Rochester terminated the successful royalist *chevauchée* in the Midlands and drew Henry III's army south. Simon united his forces in London, then advanced to provoke battle before his support melted away. He won the battle at Lewes, but the royal forces escaped into Lewes priory and subsequent negotiations let the marcher barons go free to fight again.

Kent, and Sussex, but probably not of high quality.

De Montfort had nothing to gain from delay and a great deal to lose. He surprised the royal army by seizing the high ground west of Lewes early on 14 May 1264. Only a broad outline of the battle of Lewes can be given. It probably took place west of the town. De Montfort's army advanced down the slope, suffering an early setback when its left, of cavalry and the Londoners, was routed by prince Edward and the marcher barons. Edward, inflamed by a personal quarrel with the citizens, pursued them for several miles. While he was absent with the most experienced soldiers, the battle was lost: the royalist centre and left were smashed. Henry, who had two horses killed under him, sought refuge in the walled priory south of Lewes. By

midday the main battle was over. When Edward returned, he plundered de Montfort's baggage before his force was scattered. He joined his father in the priory with the remnants of his division. The bulk of dead were the lightly armed infantry. A contemporary estimate of 2,000 dead has found support in the discovery of mass graves holding over 1,000 corpses. However, de Montfort had not won an outright victory. Royal forces held the castle and priory, and a long siege would be politically risky. A compromise peace (15 May) left Henry and Edward in de Montfort's hands, but the marcher barons, including his avowed personal enemy Roger Mortimer, escaped.

By late May 1265, de Montfort's position was deteriorating as Gilbert of Clare defected and prince Edward

The death of some thirty of earl Simon's well-armed knights is evidence of the savagery of the fighting at Evesham. The mutilation of his body – his head, hands, feet, and testicles were cut off – is testimony to royalist hatred of him. De Montfort's infantry, although barely engaged, were massacred as they fled.

escaped. With the marcher barons they isolated de Montfort (at Hereford with few men) west of the Severn by seizing the bridges, planning to defeat him before he received help (map 4). De Montfort seriously underestimated the danger until late June, when he made for Newport in Wales, intending to reach England by ship. Monmouth and Usk castles delayed him, then his ships were intercepted, and finally Edward caught up with him at Newport. De Montfort burned the bridge and escaped to Hereford by crossing the inhospitable Black Mountains.

After failing to crush de Montfort, Edward was recalled to the Severn by the approach of de Montfort's son Simon, who had organized an army in London. In mid-July he sacked Winchester, then waited at Oxford, hoping to draw off Edward's army or join his father. He reached Kenilworth on 31 July, and at once his father earl Simon set off by night march (1-2 August) to unite their armies. On the same night, Edward marched on Kenilworth, making a feint towards Shrewsbury, having learned that the Montfortians had camped outside the castle. At dawn, the royalists fell on the sleeping army and captured many, before returning to Worcester to finish off de Montfort.

On learning that his son still had an army, de Montfort made a final attempt to join him. On the night of 3-4 August, he marched south-east to put the Avon between his army and pursuit. At daybreak, he paused fatefully at Evesham, while his son rested 9 miles (14 km) distant at Alcester, both on the north bank of the Avon. By a remarkable feat of anticipation, Edward trapped earl Simon in Evesham, using his great advantage in numbers. Mortimer's division, following de Montfort, blocked escape

to the south back over the bridge; Clare held the road north to Alcester; while Edward overtook de Montfort to ensure the Kenilworth road south of the Avon was clear before rejoining Clare. When de Montfort caught sight of Edward's division he at first believed it to be his son's.

Earl Simon and his followers had no choice but to fight. In the early morning, taking the captive king with them, Simon with his cavalry advanced to the flat hill-top north of Evesham. Their charge failed to pierce the royalist line of Edward and Clare, which then enveloped de Montfort's force, crushing it in a dense mass. De Montfort's cavalry, left in Evesham, escaped the ensuing massacre. The king, wearing borrowed armour, narrowly escaped. It was unusual for more than a handful of heavily protected and ransomable nobles to die in battle, but at Evesham at least thirty perished. De Montfort, unhorsed, was deliberately killed, and his body horribly mutilated.

Unlike Lewes, Evesham was decisive, even though Montfortian strongholds resisted until mid-1267. The major problem was Kenilworth. Behind its complex water defences the castle defied the resources of the kingdom for six months; bombardment of the walls and assault by barges brought from Chester both failed. Finally, starvation brought about its surrender in December 1266.

If the two battles of 1264-65 showed little tactical ingenuity, the manoeuvring which preceded them shows both de Montfort and Edward to have been skilled generals, possessing strategic oversight and capable of bold strokes. Both based their moves on sound information-gathering, a capacity with which medieval commanders have rarely been credited.

MAP 4

After earl Simon's rapid marching allowed him to escape being trapped west of the Severn, Edward occupied a central position at Worcester. After a night march and feint north he ambushed a Montfortian force at Kenilworth, then divided his army to trap Simon, whose force was overwhelmed at Evesham before he could unite with his son.

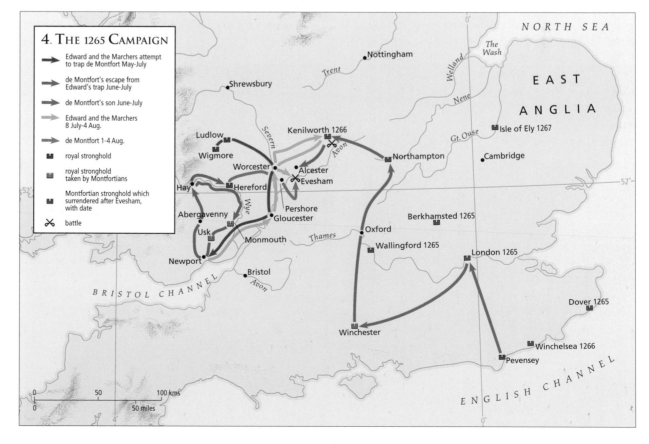

4. THE 1265 CAMPAIGN

→ Edward and the Marchers attempt to trap de Montfort May-July

→ de Montfort's escape from Edward's trap June-July

→ de Montfort's son June-July

→ Edward and the Marchers 8 July-4 Aug.

→ de Montfort 1-4 Aug.

▥ royal stronghold

▥ royal stronghold taken by Montfortians

▥ Montfortian stronghold which surrendered after Evesham, with date

⚔ battle

ENGLAND AND THE CELTIC FRINGE: COLONIAL WARFARE

T HE NORMAN CONQUEST *opened a new phase in England's expansion in the British Isles. English kings were preoccupied with their French lands. Expansion into Wales and Ireland was left to the lords of the Anglo-Welsh marches. Despite disunity and limited resources, many Welsh and Irish princes maintained their independence. Scottish kings took advantage of periodic disorder in the southern kingdom to raid and to expand, while English kings were content with punitive measures. Edward I (1272-1307) made the first royal attempts to conquer Wales and Scotland. Superior English resources overwhelmed the Welsh princes, but Edward overreached himself in Scotland, initiating three centuries of warfare. No English monarch tried to conquer Ireland before the late sixteenth century.*

An illustration of McMurrough Kavanagh attacking the English in 1399. Irish horsemen rode 'without a saddle on a cushion, each wearing a slashed cloak and armed with mail coats. They have throat-pieces of mail and round helmets of iron, swords, and very long, thin, old-fashioned lances up to twelve feet long... and they fight like Saracens'.

ENGLAND AND WALES

Wales was the one part of southern Britain which was not brought under Anglo-Saxon control and where independent Celtic principalities survived. The Anglo-Saxon kings did not attempt to conquer Wales, although they did establish intermittent overlordships. Raiding in both directions was widespread. Generally, the border in 1066 followed Offa's Dyke (a series of eighth-century earthworks) and the river Wye. Wales was poor, mountainous country, a land of petty kingdoms and short-lived overlordships like that of Gruffydd of Gwynedd, until his men killed him during an English invasion (1063). Bad communications and shortage of supplies impeded permanent conquest, so that warfare in Wales consisted mainly of guerrilla operations and harrying.

William I very early established defensive lordships along the border (marches), with licence to advance into Wales. Marcher lords were granted royal rights including free authority to build castles, an essential tool of conquest (*map* 1). At first they advanced rapidly (1067-75), then the Welsh princes rallied and recovered (1093-1100). Thereafter the initiative lay alternately with marchers such as the Braose, Mortimer, and Clare families, and Welsh princes. The marchers lacked the resources to complete the conquest, while intermittent royal expeditions, even on the scale of Henry II (1165), and John (1211), were inadequate. The Welsh were too disunited to drive out the English, and temporary overlordships, such as those of Rhys of Deheubarth's (died 1197) or Llewelyn of Gwynedd's (died

Caernarfon was Gwynedd's ancient centre, and was emperor Constantine's city in Welsh legend. Edward I chose it to ram home his conquest through a deliberately symbolic design. His other Welsh castles had whitewashed, cylindrical towers; Caernarfon's polygonal towers and banded masonry mimicked Constantinople (Constantine's city). Edward's wife was brought here to bear his heir in 1284. Its cost was double that of the other Welsh castles, and it was still unfinished fifty years later.

1240) were bitterly resented. A vivid account of late twelfth-century Wales was composed by Gerald of Barry, an ecclesiastic and royal servant, descendant of a marcher family and a Welsh princess. He described a typically 'dirty' style of war (*page 72*). The Welsh were lightly armed guerrillas who took advantage of the woods and mountains, and whose strength lay in ambushes and sudden night attacks. On home ground they could defeat the Norman heavy cavalry.

Gerald's experience made him well informed to offer advice on how to subjugate Wales. Determination, royal resources, and time – a whole year – would be necessary, he wrote. His counsel was to blockade 'free' Wales by land and sea in the autumn and to prepare castles in the marches and interior. English money should be used to exploit dissension between Welsh princes and to recruit expendable mercenaries, although Gerald also advocated using marchers experienced in Welsh warfare. Late winter, when the trees

were bare, was the time to push into the mountain and forest fastnesses, using overwhelming English manpower to wear down the Welsh. The Welsh he advised to unite under a single prince, and, more dubiously, to adopt the tactics and armour of northern France.

During the thirteenth century, the rulers of Gwynedd subjected the other princes and recovered large areas from the marchers, a supremacy crowned when Henry III of England recognized Llewelyn ap Gruffydd as 'prince of Wales' (1267). Although Edward I probably did not intend conquest when war broke out in 1276, it was achieved in three campaigns. His strategy was traditional and unspectacular, advancing along the north Wales coast while marchers attacked in the south and centre. Edward did not need to read Gerald of Barry to understand that the key to success would be mobilizing his superior resources to isolate Snowdonia. Although the marcher victories in 1282 and 1295 steal the headlines, the real damage was done by the unwieldy armies of heavy cavalry and infantry Edward cautiously led into north Wales. They threatened the heartland of Welsh independence and the Welsh were powerless to repel them.

Preparations began late in 1276. In the first weeks of 1277, forces began to press in from south and mid-Wales. Edward's army – lords and knights performing feudal service, paid royal household knights, and infantry from England and south Wales – cut a wide road through the forests to Flint, and fortified it as an advanced base (*map 2*). By late August, some 800 cavalry and 15,000 foot were at Rhuddlan. Troops sent to Anglesey harvested its grain, thereby increasing pressure on 'fortress' Snowdonia and supplying the English army. Then there was a stalemate: Edward would not risk ambush in the mountains, nor could Llewelyn fight in the open. In November, as supplies ran low on both sides, compromise was reached and Llewelyn recognized Edward's lordship.

The 1282 campaign resulted from a Welsh rising at Easter. Once again, armies of marchers operated in south and mid-Wales, while Edward assembled the magnates at Rhuddlan, his advance base. By late August, he had at least 750 cavalry and 8,000 foot, while a labour corps of 1,000 diggers and 345 carpenters was summoned from twenty-eight English counties. Columns were sent out to capture Welsh castles, and Anglesey was again occupied. Constructing a pontoon bridge to the mainland caused a long delay, then an English raid across it ended disastrously with many dead, mainly drowned (6 November). In the south and centre the marchers too were making little progress.

This time, Edward was determined not to let up. Reinforcements assembled at Carmarthen, and more infantry was summoned to north Wales, where troops arrived from Edward's duchy of Gascony. The stalemate was broken when Llewelyn, perhaps lured by treachery, raided into the central march where he was surprised and killed by marchers near Irfon Bridge (11 December). His death was a disaster for the Welsh who had no other leader of similar authority, and Edward moved in for the kill. In January

MAP 1

At first, the Normans made rapid inroads into Wales, building castles as they advanced. At the end of the eleventh century, and while there was civil war in England (1135-54), the Welsh princes successfully counter-attacked. Deheubarth and Gwynedd were consolidated and prevented further English advances.

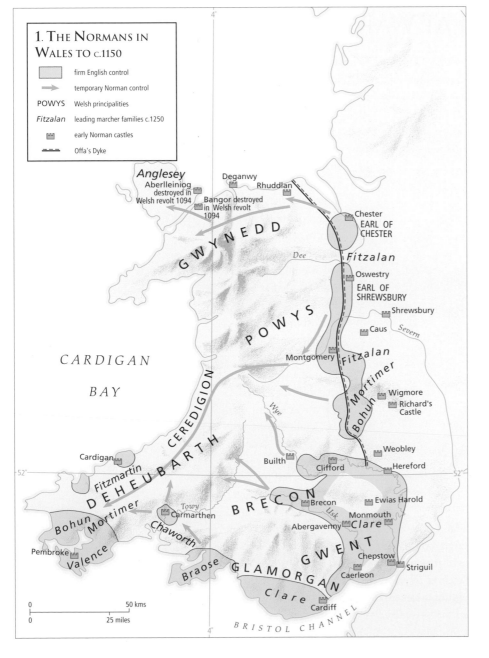

1. THE NORMANS IN WALES TO c.1150

- firm English control
- → temporary Norman control
- POWYS Welsh principalities
- *Fitzalan* leading marcher families c.1250
- early Norman castles
- Offa's Dyke

Anglesey
Aberlleiniog destroyed in Welsh revolt 1094
Deganwy
Rhuddlan
Bangor destroyed in Welsh revolt 1094
Chester EARL OF CHESTER
Dee
Fitzalan
Oswestry EARL OF SHREWSBURY
Shrewsbury
Caus
Severn
GWYNEDD
POWYS
Montgomery
Fitzalan
Mortimer
Wigmore
Richard's Castle
Bohun
CARDIGAN BAY
CEREDIGION
Wye
Cardigan
Fitzmartin
DEHEUBARTH
Mortimer
Builth
Clifford
Weobley
Hereford
BRECON
Towy
Carmarthen
Brecon
Ewias Harold
Chaworth
Abergavenny
Usk
Monmouth
Clare
Pembroke
Valence
GWENT
GLAMORGAN
Braose
Chepstow
Caerleon
Striguil
Clare
Cardiff

0 ___ 50 kms
0 ___ 25 miles

BRISTOL CHANNEL

1283, he entered Snowdonia and garrisoned Dolwyddelan, advancing to Conwy in March. The planned mid-Wales campaign proved unnecessary: Castell-y-Bere, the last of the significant Welsh strongholds, fell to marcher forces in April 1283.

The Welsh rebelled twice. The 1287 rising was easily contained, although Edward was in Gascony. The 1294-95 rebellion was more threatening: several baronial castles were lost, while Edward faced war with France and Scotland too. He was able to redeploy men, money, and materials assembled for Gascony, but spent some uncomfortable weeks in Conwy on short rations when his baggage train was captured, while the marchers defeated the most important Welsh leader, Madog, at Maes Moydog.

The logistics of the 1282-83 campaign were vital to success. The magnates brought provisions with them and merchants were encouraged to bring supplies to the armies.

Royal officials from England, Ireland, and Gascony sent victuals — wheat, oats, beans and peas, pigs, wine — to Chester to be sent on by the road made in 1277 and by ship to Rhuddlan, where there was a mill. Arrows and crossbow bolts by the hundred thousand, and prefabricated hurdles for temporary defences were shipped from Chester. The attention to detail included issuing white clothing to troops in Snowdonia for winter warfare. By these means, large armies and workforces could be maintained in a hostile environment until victory was achieved.

The Edwardian castles in their shining whitewash were a formidable symbol of conquest and a remarkable achievement. An outer ring begun in 1277 was supplemented by an inner ring after 1283. Beaumaris was added after the 1294-95 rebellion. All were designed to be supplied by sea, and were the work of the Savoyard master mason James of St George, who fully understood their

THE WELSH AT WAR

The chief weapon of south Wales was the bow. The archery of Gwent was renowned. The bows were roughly made of wych-elm, but had great penetration at short range. The marcher lord, William de Braose, told Gerald of one man who 'was struck by a Welsh arrow in the thigh. It penetrated through his padded cloth hauberk and right through his leg armour, and this same arrow then passed on through his saddle flap and deep into his horse, mortally wounding it.' Another was pinned to his saddle by both legs: 'what more could you expect, even from a crossbow?' The north Welsh preferred a long spear. A mail hauberk 'offers no resistance to one of these lances when it is thrown a short distance as a javelin.' Light armament — leather or mail body armour, helmet and small round shield — did not impede the agility, which was their chief advantage.

Gerald described the Welsh as a nation in arms who thought only of war. The chiefs rode horses, but often dismounted to fight alongside the common people 'in view of the marshy, uneven terrain'. They were fiercest in their first assault, accompanied by screeching trumpets. But 'if the enemy resists manfully and they are repulsed…they turn their backs…seeking safety in retreat', pausing to turn and shoot arrows. They were difficult to subdue for 'though they may be routed today, and shamefully put to flight with great slaughter, yet tomorrow they are quite ready for another campaign, quite undaunted by their losses and humiliation…They are deterred neither by hunger nor cold, fighting does not exhaust them, nor adversity cause them to despair…it is easy to beat them in a single battle, but very difficult indeed to win a war against them.'

Gerald depicted the Celts as noble savages against whom normal standards did not apply: 'The tactics of French troops are no use at all in Ireland or Wales. There they fight on plains, here in rough terrain; they fight in fields, we in woods; there armour is honourable, here it is a nuisance; they win by standing firm, we by agility; they capture the enemy, we cut off his head; they ransom prisoners, we slaughter them.'

MAP 2

The major problem in conquering Wales was that of supply, and Edward I's 1277 campaign ground to a halt even though he built a road as he advanced. In 1282, he was prepared for a winter campaign in Gwynedd to maintain pressure, although Llewelyn's death at Irfon Bridge hastened the end of Welsh resistance. To anchor English rule in the newly conquered lands, a network of impressive castles was built.

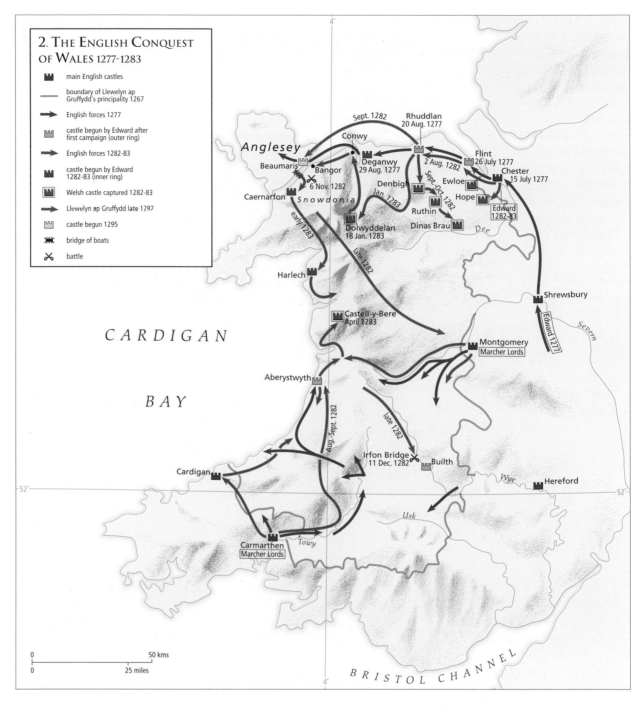

function as symbols of conquest (map 2). They represent the apogee of English medieval military architecture, yet they were also white elephants. They cost £80,000 to build in the period 1277-1304, but financial constraints meant they were never completed. Their small garrisons of thirty to forty men were unable to prevent rebellions. However, the castles with their linked new towns anchored English rule in Wales.

The last Welsh revolt began in 1400, and by the end of 1403, English rule was confined to isolated strongholds – the Edwardian castles of Conwy, Beaumaris, Harlech, and Aberystwyth were captured. Owain, acclaimed prince of Wales, allied with the powerful Percy family who rebelled against Henry IV (1403, 1405), and in 1405, a French force of some 2,000 men joined an unsuccessful Welsh

rebel march on Worcester. Owain's strength lay in ambushes and widespread Welsh sympathy. Henry IV, beset by rebellions, foreign threats, and chronically in debt, was unable to devote resources to Wales.

The defeat of the Percys and the decline of France into civil war left the Welsh isolated. The conquest of Anglesey by English forces from Dublin (1405-06) and a naval blockade cut off north Wales, and the recapture of Aberystwyth and Harlech after long sieges (1408-09) broke the back of the revolt. The future Henry V supervised this stage of the war, learning how to stretch scarce resources and motivate men in harsh and unrewarding conditions. It was also where prince Henry forged the partnership wih many English barons, which would serve him well when he invaded France.

ENGLAND AND SCOTLAND

A united Scottish kingdom emerged in the tenth century, its kings ambitious to expand into the power vacuum in northern England. The Norman kings of England, whose main interests lay in France, secured the far north by building castles (*map 3*), not in a systematic network, but piecemeal over half a century. Although the small garrisons of the border zone could not prevent invasions, the castles guaranteed English rule – without them land could not be held, as king William the Lion of Scotland knew when he refused Richard I's offer in 1194 of Northumberland without its castles. Their function in war was to buy time until relief arrived. The Scots usually lacked the resources to besiege castles, and generally withdrew when the better-armed English reinforcements arrived.

Hostilities were limited to two periods when dissension in England invited Scottish attacks. Encouraged by civil war, David I launched five invasions between 1136 and 1138. In February 1136 and 1138, king Stephen led armies north within a month, but he could not devote himself to the north. In 1138, David returned twice, and although a Yorkshire army defeated him at Northallerton (the battle of the Standard), Stephen purchased security by ceding both Northumberland and Cumbria which the Scots held until 1157.

An opportunity to regain them arose during the great revolt of 1173-74 against Henry II. While Henry was engaged in France and England, William the Lion ravaged widely before besieging the northern castles. However, sieges removed the Scots' mobility. When Henry could

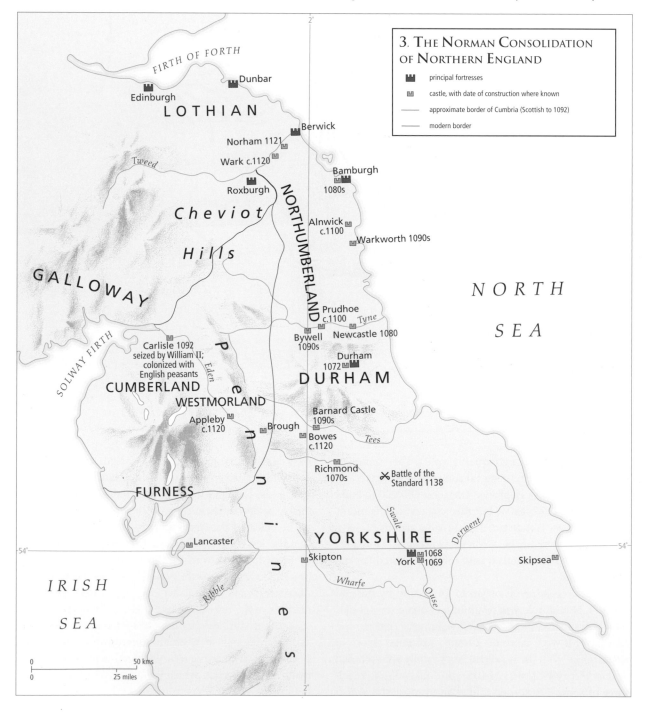

3. THE NORMAN CONSOLIDATION OF NORTHERN ENGLAND

- principal fortresses
- castle, with date of construction where known
- approximate border of Cumbria (Scottish to 1092)
- modern border

FIRTH OF FORTH

Dunbar
Edinburgh
LOTHIAN
Berwick
Norham 1121
Wark c.1120
Tweed
Bamburgh
Roxburgh
1080s
Cheviot
Alnwick c.1100
Warkworth 1090s
Hills
NORTHUMBERLAND
GALLOWAY
Prudhoe c.1100
Tyne
Bywell 1090s
Newcastle 1080
NORTH
Carlisle 1092 seized by William II; colonized with English peasants
Durham 1072
SEA
Eden
DURHAM
CUMBERLAND
WESTMORLAND
Barnard Castle 1090s
Appleby c.1120
Brough
Bowes c.1120
Tees
Richmond 1070s
Battle of the Standard 1138
SOLWAY FIRTH
P e n n i n e s
FURNESS
YORKSHIRE
Swale
Derwent
Lancaster
Skipton
York 1068 1069
Skipsea
IRISH
Wharfe
Ouse
SEA
Ribble

0 50 kms
0 25 miles

MAP 3

Between c.950 and 1018, Scottish kings acquired English Edinburgh and Lothian. In the 1070s, they naturally exploited the power vacuum the Norman Conquest created in northern England. After 1066, the Norman defence of the north was based on a combination of the piecemeal growth of a network of castles with intermittent, unrewarding punitive expeditions. The Scots usually avoided battle, and there was little to plunder in the sparsely populated uplands.

MAP 4

Large English armies kept to the eastern seaboard of Scotland in order to be supplied, while Scottish resistance could rekindle in the remote Highlands. Opposition in England to the cost of Edward's wars forced him to scale down his operations, but his persistence paid off after he spent two winters harrying in Scotland. Having won the war, Edward lost the peace by failing to give Scottish nobles a place in his new regime.

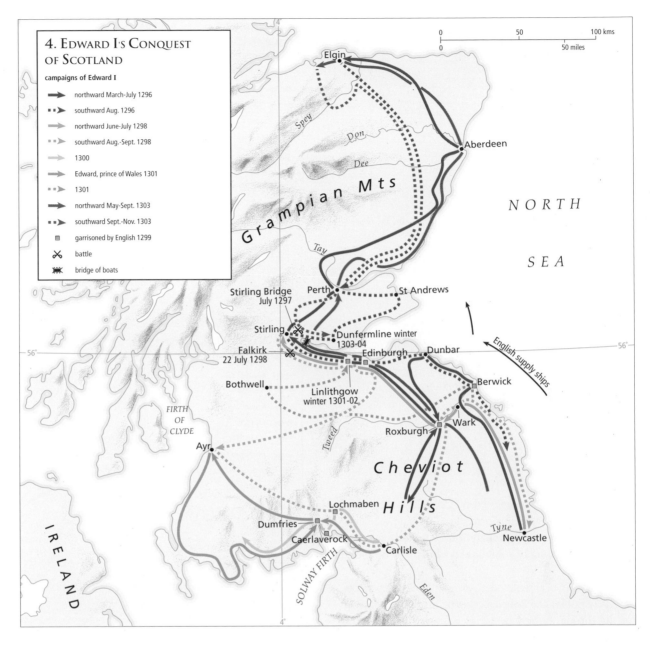

4. EDWARD I'S CONQUEST OF SCOTLAND

campaigns of Edward I

→ northward March-July 1296
∙∙▶ southward Aug. 1296
→ northward June-July 1298
∙∙▶ southward Aug.-Sept. 1298
→ 1300
→ Edward, prince of Wales 1301
∙∙▶ 1301
→ northward May-Sept. 1303
∙∙▶ southward Sept.-Nov. 1303
▪ garrisoned by English 1299
✗ battle
✖ bridge of boats

spare reinforcements, a cavalry commando struck rapidly from Newcastle, making good use of scouting to capture William at Alnwick while his army was dispersed. This effectively ended Scottish expansion to the south, and for a century there was usually peace.

When Edward I decided to take direct control of Scotland he found it a much greater challenge than Wales. With hindsight, the problems of distance, terrain, and finance seem insuperable, yet failure was not inevitable. Edward's ungenerous treatment of the Scots when he was victorious in 1296 and 1304 ruined his military achievements.

The war began well for Edward (map 4). In 1296, a military promenade followed the capture of Berwick, the massacre of whose men set the tone for the whole war. The next year, while he fought the French, the Scots led by William Wallace rebelled, defeated an English force at Stirling Bridge, and raided Northumberland. Edward retaliated with a large army of 3,000 heavy cavalry and over 20,000 foot in 1298, but they were short of supplies.

The campaign was going nowhere until the muster of a Scottish army at Falkirk gave Edward an opportunity to strike. He advanced overnight from Edinburgh and attacked without pausing. The Scottish cavalry fled while the rings of spearmen (schiltrons) were broken by combined cavalry and infantry assaults. Yet victory brought conquest no closer. Edward could not follow it up due to domestic unrest caused by the burden of war taxation. Resistance rekindled in the remote Highlands and the Scots learned to avoid battle and rely on starving out English garrisons at the end of tenuous supply lines.

From 1300, Edward was less ambitious, seeking to subdue southern Scotland. The 1300-01 campaigns, with dwindling armies, yielded only two castles and a precarious control. Shortage of money was a constant problem. Yet persistence paid off. In 1302, Robert Bruce, a leading Scottish noble, submitted. The Scots were isolated when French support was withdrawn after defeat by the Flemish. In 1303, Edward crossed the Forth by a bridge of boats towed from Norfolk,

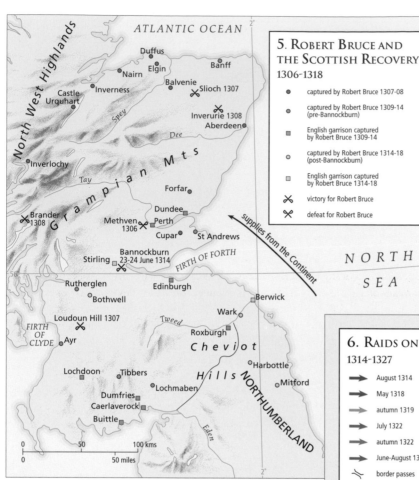

5. ROBERT BRUCE AND THE SCOTTISH RECOVERY
1306-1318

- ● captured by Robert Bruce 1307-08
- ● captured by Robert Bruce 1309-14 (pre-Bannockburn)
- ■ English garrison captured by Robert Bruce 1309-14
- ○ captured by Robert Bruce 1314-18 (post-Bannockburn)
- □ English garrison captured by Robert Bruce 1314-18
- ✗ victory for Robert Bruce
- ✗ defeat for Robert Bruce

MAP 5

Robert Bruce's rebellion began in 1306 as a feud between Scottish nobles, then developed into a war of independence. Robert conducted a strikingly successful guerrilla campaign which was aided by the new king Edward II's lack of interest in Scotland. The fight at Bannockburn, which was forced upon Robert against his policy of avoiding battle, completed the liberation of Scotland.

MAP 6

Bannockburn was followed by devastating raids on northern England. Mounted on ponies, the Scots were mobile and elusive. They attacked down both sides of the Pennines and crossed them at will. But the strategic objective of the raids failed as Edward II would rather see the north wasted than relinquish his claim to the Scottish crown.

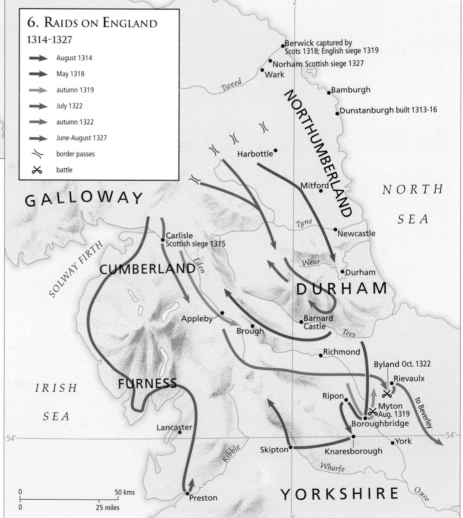

6. RAIDS ON ENGLAND
1314-1327

- → August 1314
- → May 1318
- → autumn 1319
- → July 1322
- → autumn 1322
- → June-August 1327
- ✗ border passes
- ✗ battle

and English columns raided Scotland throughout the winter. The Scots' leaders submitted early in 1304, and the fall of Stirling after thorough preparations – including use of an explosive mixture of sulphur and saltpetre – completed the conquest.

Edward's political settlement gave the Scots few benefits, especially nobles like Robert Bruce. By murdering his rival for the throne, Robert set off a civil war. At the end of 1306, he was a defeated fugitive. However, Edward's savage reprisals stoked resistance and Robert's victory at Loudoun Hill (1307) began a remarkable comeback from factional leader to king of a nation (*map 5*). He waged a guerrilla campaign, far from English bases and beyond infantry range, fighting only on ground unsuitable for heavy cavalry. By 1309, he had won the north, starving out or surprising isolated English garrisons. Captured castles were dismantled to prevent their reuse by the English.

Edward I's death in 1307 allowed Robert Bruce to defeat his Scottish rivals, as Edward II lacked the drive of his father. When he invaded Scotland in 1310, Robert avoided battle, awaiting his retreat. In 1314, Edward II tried to relieve Stirling with a substantial army – some 2,500 heavy cavalry and 15,000 infantry, English, Scots, and Irish – under experienced commanders. Robert reluctantly blocked the road near Bannockburn with a smaller army, mainly infantry, in a narrow, boggy, defensive site. Incompetent command led the English to launch frontal cavalry assaults which the Scots' schiltrons repulsed. Some English archers

tardily brought up were scattered by Bruce's small cavalry reserve. The Scots counter-attacked and Edward's army disintegrated. The English nobles, who were normally protected by their armour and rank, suffered very heavy casualties crossing the deep Bannockburn.

Despite his humiliation, Edward II refused to abandon

his claim to Scotland. The Scots, mounted on light horses, harried deep into Lancashire and Yorkshire (map 6), taking at least £20,000 ransom money over ten years. Robert sent his brother Edward to invade Ireland (1315), hoping to raise a pan-Celtic front against the English, but Edward's defeat and death in 1318 ended the threat. In England, Edward II was incapable of defending the north, nor could Robert reach politically sensitive targets. Finally, a thirteen-year truce was agreed in 1323. Robert invaded again after the deposition of Edward II in 1327. His mobile horsemen ran rings around the heavy English cavlary before slipping away. This exhausted the English defences, allowing Robert Bruce to begin the conquest of Northumberland, enough to make the English government recognize Scottish independence.

The 1327 treaty could not last after Robert Bruce's death in 1328 – his son David was only eight years old. Disinherited Scottish nobles led by Edward Balliol invaded in 1332, initially with great success. Edward III entered the war openly in 1333, defeating the Scots and capturing Berwick. Edward Balliol repaid his support by ceding the southern Scottish shires. Since Bannockburn, the English had developed standard battle tactics, placing dismounted men-at-arms (heavy cavalry) in the centre, with archers (mounted for mobility on campaign) on the wings, in a defensive position. This was used to great effect at Dupplin Moor (1332) and Halidon Hill (1333), and would be the basis of English success in France.

Edward III campaigned every year until 1337, in 1335 with one of the largest armies he had ever raised. Like Edward I he could not keep control once the Scots reverted to Robert's strategy of avoiding battle and recovering castles at the end of each campaign. English pillaging only destroyed resources needed for garrisons. French support for the Scots (under the terms of a 1326 treaty) added a new dimension to the war. As English resources were diverted to France after 1337, the Scots regained the lost territory. During one foray into England, hoping to take advantage of Edward's siege of Calais, David was defeated and captured at Neville's Cross (1346).

Nevertheless, by 1357 the English held only the border fortresses from Lochmaben to Berwick. The conflict changed to long truces punctuated by raids. The English gave up trying to control Scotland: after 1347, English armies spent no longer than three weeks in Scotland. The main English fear during the Hundred Years' War was of France using Scotland as a 'back door'. In fact, the Scottish-French invasion of 1385 achieved little, and the 1402 invasion was crushed at Homildon Hill, despite the Scots' French-supplied armour intended to cancel out the English archery. More significantly, some 6,000 Scots, mainly archers, fought in France between 1419 and 1424, playing a major role in thwarting Henry V (pages 128-135). Berwick changed hands intermittently until 1482, the only prize of Edward IV's costly war.

The outbreak of war in 1296 started a period of incessant strife on the borders which lasted until the mid-sixteenth century. Fortifications proliferated on all scales, and on both sides kings appointed wardens to defend the marches. From the late fourteenth century, the English wardenships were monopolized by the Percy and Neville families, who became bitter rivals. The government paid the wardens to recruit men for border defence, in effect private armies of some of the best natural fighting men in the kingdom. As a result, the Percys and Nevilles became very influential in national politics, not least in the Wars of the Roses (pages 140-147).

ANGLO-SCOTTISH WARFARE IN THE TWELFTH CENTURY

A major purpose of Scottish raids was slaving. An anonymous writer with first-hand knowledge of Scottish techniques in the 1130s wrote: 'It was pitiable to see what they did to the English: old men and women were either beheaded by swords or stuck with spears like pigs…babes were tossed high in the air, and caught on the spikes of spears…Young men and women, all who seemed fit for work, were bound and driven away into slavery.'

Scottish armies were ethnically a mixture of men of British, Scots, Pict, and English origins. David I's army in 1138 included tribesmen from Galloway, Cumbria, Lothian, the Isles, Aberdeenshire, and Moray, mainly poorly armed infantry bearing long spears, javelins, long knives, hide shields, and little defensive armour: to southern eyes they were 'unarmed'. They relied on agility and ferocity, delivering a wild charge.

There is no evidence in the twelfth century of the schiltron, a disciplined circle of spearmen, used to great effect in the wars of independence. David also had heavy cavalry provided by French settlers and his own household,but they were few in number.

David's third invasion of 1138 was the most ambitious, penetrating into Yorkshire. He was confronted at Northallerton by a smaller, northern army reinforced by a troop of king Stephen's knights. David took the disastrous decision to abandon the Scottish practice of non-engagement with Anglo-Norman armies. The battle of the Standard got its name from the English rallying point, a mast bearing St Peter's flag on a cart. The English host was mainly on foot: first a line of infantry (spearmen, archers, and dismounted knights), a second line of knights on foot, and a small mounted reserve. David planned to strike with his knights and best armed men, but the Galwegians insisted on a right to the front line. He also hoped to take advantage of the mist to gain surprise. Instead, the tribesmen were routed by the English archery, while a charge by the Scottish knights was repulsed. It was all over in two hours.

ENGLAND AND IRELAND

Neither the Romans nor the Anglo-Saxons reached Ireland, although the Norse established coastal towns and married into the native population. Ireland was a poor country with a pastoral economy. It was also politically anarchic: five regional kings ruled many sub-kings and fought for the empty title of High King. Irish warfare was characterized by cattle-raiding in boggy and wooded terrain. Even the greater kings of the eleventh and twelfth centuries, who campaigned widely and built fleets and fortifications, fought in the same way. The importation of knightly cavalry, archers, and castles had a great impact on the natives, but the Anglo-Norman invaders were few and fitted into the Irish pattern of war and politics. Except during infrequent royal expeditions, the English were generally on the defensive.

The king of Leinster brought in earl Richard 'Strongbow's' forces from the Welsh marches as mercenaries. The English knights and archers shattered MacGillipatric of Ossory's army at Gowran (1169), although it was McMurrough's Irish who exploited the pursuit (*map 7*). Strongbow went on to conquer Leinster in 1170-71. Small companies of English knights were able to achieve much. Ten knights and seventy archers defeated 3,000 Waterford men in 1170; a surprise sally of knights broke up the Irish-Norse siege of Dublin (1171); and 'Strongbow' stormed high king Rory O'Connor's camp at Castleknock with three 'battles', each of forty knights brigaded with archers and Irish light horse and foot (1171). Yet as the English returned to Wexford, they narrowly survived ambush in the heavily wooded Scollagh gap. They had much to learn. Significantly, Gerald of Barry reused his analysis of Welsh warfare in his account of Ireland.

English expertise in siege warfare ensured the capture of the four Scandinavian-Irish centres: Wexford surrendered to avoid being sacked (1169), while parties of young knights stormed Waterford (1170), Dublin (1171), and Limerick (1175). King Henry II was drawn to Ireland in 1171-72 to assert his lordship, with a sizable host of some 4,000, including 400 knights, but he only achieved the temporary submission of the Irish kings. King John (1199-1216) visited Ireland twice: his feckless tour in 1185 achieved nothing; the 1210 expedition reasserted royal control over the English barons. No English king returned until Richard II (1377-99). In the absence of royal expeditions, the English invaders depended on their castles for survival. Gerald of Barry credited the second governor, Hugh de Lacy, with 'making an excellent job of fortifying Leinster and Meath with castles'. But the authority of the royal governor rarely extended beyond the Pale around Dublin, while the settlers began to think of themselves as Irish and separate from the effete English and French.

The Irish called the English in their mail coats 'grey men', while the invaders considered native warriors 'naked' due to their lack of armour, which made them vulnerable to archery. The Irish techniques of 'plashing', weaving the edges of woods together for defence, and digging ditches,

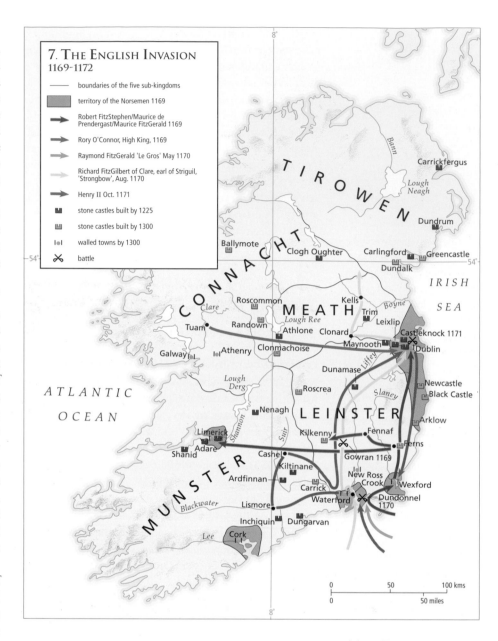

could not remedy this weakness. However, English forces depended on Irish auxiliaries: thus, in 1201, when John de Courcy with dismounted knights struck ahead of his Irish allies, he barely escaped across Lough Ree, losing his rearguard in an ambush.

The Irish armies did adapt, however. From 1247, the unarmoured *kern*, carrying sword and javelin, was supplemented by the Scottish *gallo glach*, wearing a helmet, mail cape, and mailcoat or padded jerkin, and armed with double-handed axe, sword, or lance. In principle, their function was to protect the *kerns* while they plundered. Irish cavalry did adopt armour, but their failure to employ stirrups put them at a disadvantage against the English. The Irish were powerless against stone castles, but they were few in number – only twenty had been raised by 1225 – and the timber-and-earth, motte-and-bailey castles were vulnerable. The Irish did not ransom prisoners, and the English adopted their practice of killing them. Cattle-raiding was central to warfare in Ireland: it was a major source of wealth and vital to supply. During John's 1210 expedition, 360 infantry

MAP 7

The first English invasion was a piece of private enterprise with tiny forces. By the end of 1169 there were only 50 knights, 90 other cavalry, and 400 archers in Ireland. In 1170, 'Strongbow' brought 200 knights and 1,000 other troops. The combination of armoured knights and archery proved irresistible against the unarmoured Irish. As the English settled, they built castles and fortified towns to secure their rule.

This print of 1581 illustrates traditional Irish warfare – the cattle raid. Only the chief wears contemporary dress. That of the foot soldiers, and their weapons, had not changed for hundreds of years.

MAP 8

In May 1315, Robert Bruce sent his brother Edward to 'free' Ireland. He conducted devastating raids and twice defeated the English lords in battle. Made High King in May 1316, Edward threatened to take Dublin. But the tide turned when king Robert withdrew, the Irish chiefs wavered, and the English received reinforcements. Edward's death in battle (Fochart, 1318)) was a desperate last throw.

consumed the equivalent of 166 cows in food and wages in ten days. When the alarm (*rabadh*) was raised, native chieftains moved whole communities with their cattle to safety.

Supplies and manpower from the English settlements were used by Edward I in his campaigns in Wales and Scotland. The weakness of the English settlers was amply demonstrated in 1315 when Edward Bruce, the Scottish king's brother, landed in Ulster with 6,000 men to open a second front (*map 8*). The Bruces planned a pan-Celtic alliance against the English. Edward Bruce launched a series of devastating raids, defeating the pursuing Anglo-Irish lords at Connor (September 1315) and Skerries (January 1316). His destruction was intensified by a devastating famine. The capture of Carrickfergus castle after a year's siege and the arrival of king Robert (September and December 1316) were alarming developments, and Dublin itself was threatened in February 1317. However, the Irish kings failed to provide the anticipated support, and the famine forced the Scots to withdraw. King Robert's departure (May 1317) and Edward II's appointment of a lieutenant with adequate resources turned the tide against Edward Bruce. His defeat and death at Fochart in October 1318 ended the Scottish intervention.

For much of the fourteenth and fifteenth centuries, the English nobility showed scant interest in Ireland; there were greater opportunities in France. Richard II's lack of interest in France permitted him to answer the entreaties of the English lords in Ireland to save them from extinction. His 1394 expedition enjoyed temporary success, but as the historian Froissart was informed: 'It is hard to find a way of making war effectively on the Irish for, unless they choose, there is no one there to fight and there are no towns to be found… Even Sir William of Windsor, who had longer experience of campaigning on the Irish border than any other English knight, never succeeded in learning the lie of the country or in understanding the Irish mentality.' In the fifteenth century, some Irish chiefs began to adopt English methods, living in castles and undertaking sieges. Irish troops were also employed, in France by Henry V, and on the Scottish border as light cavalry. However, no English government was seriously concerned about Ireland until it appeared to threaten the new Protestant order in the late sixteenth century.

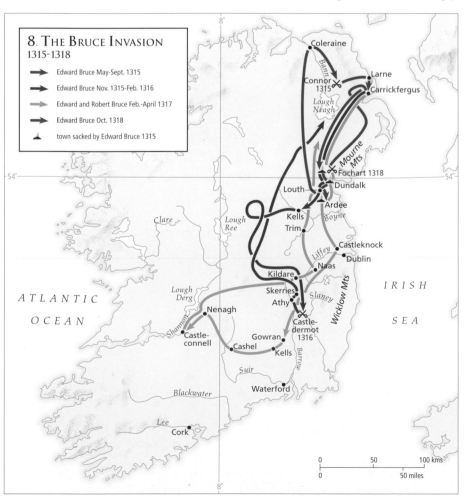

8. THE BRUCE INVASION
1315-1318

→ Edward Bruce May-Sept. 1315

→ Edward Bruce Nov. 1315-Feb. 1316

→ Edward and Robert Bruce Feb.-April 1317

→ Edward Bruce Oct. 1318

⚔ town sacked by Edward Bruce 1315

III

EXPANDING EUROPE: THE CRUSADES

On 27 November 1095, Pope Urban II preached an open-air sermon at Clermont which initiated centuries of crusading. He was responding to the request of the Byzantine emperor, Alexius Comnenus (1081-1118), who had asked for Frankish mercenaries to help replace the army lost against the Turks at Manzikert in 1071. Instead of the small, disciplined force he had expected, waves of thousands of pilgrims and warriors poured eastward.

By this date Frankish adventurers, many of them Norman, had been selling their services in Italy for a century. Robert Guiscard and his brother Roger d'Hauteville rose from mercenaries to rulers of southern Italy and Sicily respectively from the 1050s to the 1080s. Robert had even attacked the Byzantine Empire in 1081 and 1084. In Spain, too, Frankish warriors played their part, but here native rulers took the lead in the Reconquista. This reconquest of lands lost to the Muslims in the eighth century – from the conquest of Toledo in 1085 to the taking of Granada in 1492 – was fuelled by crusader ideology from early on.

The First Crusade (1095-99), despite lacking an overall leader, was incredibly successful. The great fortress cities of Edessa and Antioch fell into Christian hands and Jerusalem itself was captured. But how to defend these conquests? At the end of the eleventh century, the Muslim world had been divided, but it had its own great commanders who gradually retrieved the situation. In 1144, Zangi took Edessa, and in 1187 Saladin captured Jerusalem. Both events sparked crusades in the west, usually called the Second (1146-48) and Third (1189-92), although there were many more expeditions to the Holy Land than these bare numbers suggest.

Orders of military monks arose, dedicated to fighting non-Christians. The first were the Knights Templar, established by 1128, soon followed by the militarization of the Order of St John of the Hospital, the Teutonic Knights of Germany, the Knights of Calatrava in Spain, and many more. Growing rich from donations, these orders built castles and established garrisons of Knight Brothers on all the borders of Christendom. They were the cutting edge of military Christianity.

The crusading movement also operated within the bounds of Christian Europe. In 1202-04, crusaders being conveyed to Syria by a Venetian fleet became involved in Byzantine politics and ended up conquering Constantinople. The victors set up a Frankish empire which lasted until the Greek reconquest of 1261, and states under western rulers survived in Greece until the conquests of the Ottoman Turks in the fourteenth century. Meanwhile in France, the Albigensian crusades were preached against the heretic Cathars. This led to a northern conquest of the region.

Despite the leadership of Richard the Lionheart in 1191-92, the crusaders could not recover Jerusalem. In the thirteenth-century crusades, they turned their attention to the possessions in Syria. They almost succeeded in taking Cairo in 1218-21, but were eventually defeated by the waters of the Nile delta. Jerusalem was briefly in Christian hands after the German emperor, Frederick II, negotiated its handover in 1229, but in 1244 it fell again to a group of Khwarizmian soldiers fleeing the Mongols. In response, Louis IX of France – Saint Louis – invaded Egypt but suffered the same fate as the 'Fifth' crusaders, being captured and ransomed. His invasion caused a crisis in Egyptian government which caused the Mamluk palace guards to overthrow the sultan and take power for themselves. This brought to power sultan Qutuz (1250-60), who defeated a Mongol invasion of Syria, and the even greater general Baibars (1260-77). Under his leadership the bulk of the remaining crusader fortifications were conquered in the 1270s, leaving only the well-defended port of Acre in Christian hands. After this fell in 1291, the Latins never recovered a position in the Holy Land.

THE RECONQUISTA AND THE NORMANS IN THE MEDITERRANEAN c.1050-1150

FROM THE EARLY DECADES of the eleventh century, western Christendom went from the defensive onto the offensive. Franks, many of them from the north and Normandy, were engaged in expeditions in the Iberian and Italian peninsulas, Sicily, and the Balkans. In many ways these operations were precursors to the First Crusade. Certainly the warriors from north of the Alps played a role out of all proportion to their numbers. Some, like the Hauteville clan, from the village of that name in Normandy, established new states and dynasties in the Mediterranean lands. Robert d'Hauteville became duke of Apulia and a papal banner-bearer; his nephew Roger conquered Sicily and was crowned its king. Robert and his son Bohemond even attempted to overthrow the Byzantine emperor by invading northern Greece in the 1080s and 1107-08.

A frieze above the north door of Bari Cathedral depicts aspects of the military conquest of southern Italy as the Normans liked to portray themselves: heavily armoured, charging knights. The reality, with its sieges and the interrelation of land and sea warfare, was more complex, involving a mastery of siege warfare and logistics which foreshadowed the crusades.

THE NORMANS IN ITALY

The military impact of northerners is exemplified by the successes of the Franks (called for convenience Normans) in Italy (map 1). Arriving around 1000 they soon found themselves in demand as mercenaries, fighting for Lombard rebels against the Byzantine rulers of the region in 1016-17. They also fought on a Greek expedition to Muslim Sicily (1038-40) led by George Maniakes, alongside Harald Hardrada's imperial Varangian Guard. After a dispute over booty, they defeated the Byzantines at Monte Maggiore in 1041, before Maniakes withdrew the rest of his troops to support his fruitless bid for the imperial crown in 1043.

It was clear that the Normans meant to stay. A certain Rainulf held Aversa from 1030, and Melfi was ruled by the sons of Tancred d'Hauteville, William, Drogo, and Humphrey. Another brother came south in c.1046, Robert, nicknamed Guiscard (or 'wily'), and outshone them all. These Normans were not united, but they could co-operate. In 1053, they defeated the forces of pope Leo IX at Civitate, and both the pope and the German emperor were obliged to recognize the reality of Norman power. In 1059, Guiscard became a papal vassal and duke of Apulia, and in the same year Rainulf's nephew was made duke of Capua.

Another Hauteville, Roger, arrived in 1056 and sought to make his name in Sicily. Allying himself with Abu Timnah, emir of Syracuse, he launched probing attacks into the interior in 1060 and early 1061. In May 1061, supported by Guiscard, he won a bridgehead at Messina. In 1064, they attempted a joint assault on Palermo, the key to the island, but despite Pisan naval assistance this failed and Guiscard returned to expelling the Greeks from southern Italy. His success was due to seapower, based on controlling Italian ports, and support from Sicily. Bari, the last Byzantine stronghold in Italy, was besieged from August 1068 until it fell in April 1071.

Immediately, Guiscard took his fleet, now augmented by vessels from Bari, for a combined attack on Palermo. This time it was successful. First, the Normans defeated a fleet from Zirid Tunisia, driving it into the harbour, breaking the defensive chain across its mouth and burning or capturing all the vessels. The city was blockaded by land and sea into starvation by January 1072. Back on the mainland, Guiscard employed the same blockade techniques to take Amalfi (1073) and Salerno (1076). Guiscard's ambitions now drew him east, for the Byzantine emperor, Alexius Comnenus, was deeply involved in recovering Asia Minor after a disastrous defeat by the Turks at Manzikert in 1071.

ASSAULT ON THE BYZANTINE EMPIRE

Guiscard launched a fleet across the Adriatic in May 1081 and besieged Durazzo (Dyrrachium, modern Dürres in Albania). The Greeks' Venetian allies proved more than a match for the Norman navy, but on land the Normans beat off a relief attempt by Alexius on 18 October, and the city fell the following February. Guiscard entrusted follow-up operations to his son, Mark Bohemond, but despite several successes in battle, the Normans were outmanoeuvred and lost the city in 1083. In 1084, Guiscard returned with a larger fleet and defeated the Greco-Venetian fleet off Corfu. Guiscard's death from disease in 1085 ended the ensuing campaign. Yet the same year saw Roger victorious over a Muslim fleet off Syracuse whilst besieging the city. In 1090, Malta and Gozo were occupied easily and Sicily was entirely in his hands by 1093, enabling attacks upon North Africa.

The preaching of the First Crusade in 1096 drew Bohemond to make a legitimate expedition into the Byzantine empire, from which he eventually wrung the city and territories of Antioch in Syria. Not satisfied with this prize, he launched his own 'crusade' in 1106, whose objective was Durazzo. He had made extensive preparations and gathered a large fleet, but Alexius Comnenus was ready for him. The Byzantine navy had been reconstructed, and after Bohemond settled down to besiege the city he found himself in turn blockaded and starved into a humiliating treaty. He died in 1108 after a remarkable military career, but it was peripheral to the creation, in 1130, of the kingdom of Sicily, built upon Hauteville gains.

In seeking to explain such success it is tempting to believe the Normans' own myth of their military virtue. The bravery of their men and the invincibility of their cavalry might seem reason enough. But good infantry were not easily defeated. At Civitate in 1053, the Swabian swordsmen put up a stiff resistance after the Lombards had fled. At Durazzo, the Byzantine emperor's Varangians had driven the Norman knights back into the sea. When rallied, heroically, by Guiscard's wife, they pinned the axemen in position by threatening to charge, while the crossbowmen shot down the now immobile infantry. There are obvious parallels with Hastings fifteen years earlier. It was the combination of arms which was important.

While repute in battle was clearly useful, most warfare revolved around sieges. It was in these operations that the Normans' ability to use fleets was crucial to their success. Early in the siege at Bari, ships were chained across the harbour. In 1081, the ships were fitted with siege towers before the crossing, although a fierce storm stripped them away before they could be brought into use. While these techniques failed, and blockade proved better, the drive for innovation was impressive.

Norman adaptability at sea was expressed by their victory at Bari in 1071. The last Byzantine relief force was defeated at night, losing nine of their twenty vessels captured and one sunk. In the battle off Durazzo in 1081, the Venetians had the advantages of a close formation known as the sea-harbour, bigger ships, 'bombs' dropped through the enemy ships' bottoms from the mastheads, and possibly Greek Fire. Yet by 1084, the Normans had developed a counter. Three squadrons of five large galleys, supported by smaller vessels, attacked the 'sea harbour' at different points and won an overwhelming victory: seven out of nine Venetian vessels sunk and two captured.

The use of horse-transports combined Norman expertise on land and at sea. Already, in the 1061 assault on Sicily, 13 vessels carried 270 knights' mounts to Messina in one crossing. By 1081, Guiscard may have had 60 horse-transports and 1,300 knights. The ability to deliver battle-winning troops by sea was emblematic of Norman military achievement.

MAP 1

Robert Guiscard's defeat of papal forces at Civitate (1053) was followed by campaigns to control the ports of southern Italy. He then used their fleets to support his nephew Roger's conquest of Sicily and his own attempts on the Byzantine empire. At Durazzo (1081) the Varangian Guard drove off the vaunted Norman cavalry before Guiscard achieved his victory.

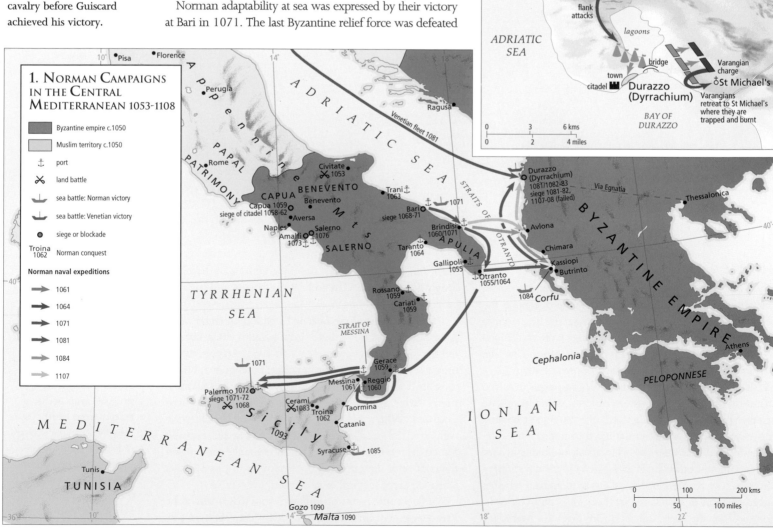

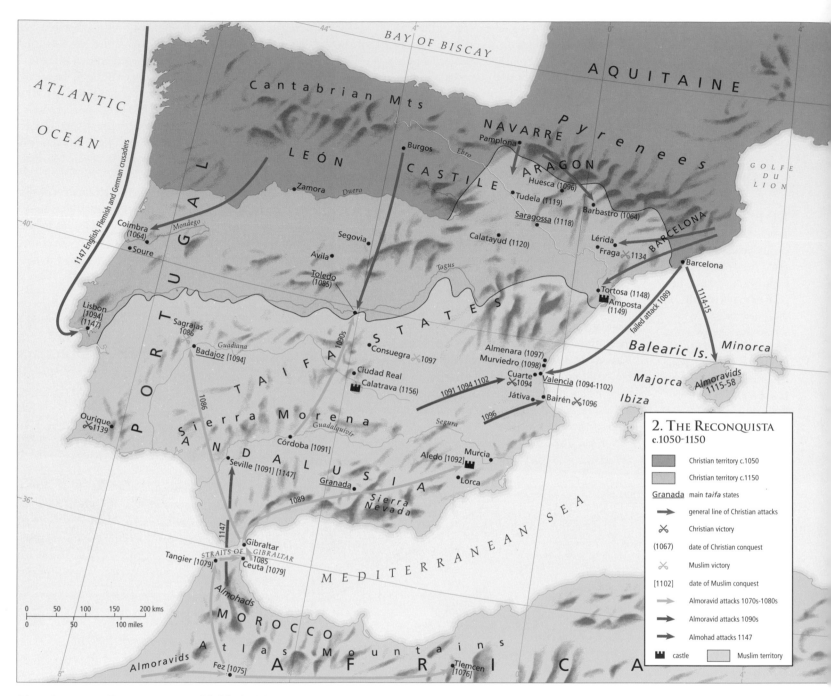

THE IBERIAN PENINSULA C.1050-1150

After 1031, the Umayyad Caliphate fragmented into small taifa successor states. Into the power vacuum stepped the northern, Christian kingdoms which began the Reconquista from Muslim Andalusia (map 2). But they were challenged by resurgent Berber powers from northern Africa. First, the Almoravids (1085-1147) and then the Almohads (1147-1220s) countered Christian advances. Campaigns revolved around raiding and the capture of cities. Initially private ventures by the Christian kingdoms, the reconquest became part of the pan-European crusading movement.

The Muslim taifa states proved incapable of uniting against aggression, and individually possessed only small military forces. In contrast, the kingdom of Castile, dominant whether linked to León or not, was a land of castles and warlords. Rodrigo Díaz de Vivar, called 'El Cid' from the Arabic for

'lord' (c.1040-99) was just the most famous of these. He fought for both Christian and Muslim rulers and in 1094 took Valencia for himself.

The Christian kingdoms operated a protection racket called parias, which extorted tributes from Muslim cities, but this did not prevent further conquests. In 1064, Aragon, newly united with Catalonia under its count, Berenguer I, briefly took the frontier town of Barbastro with the aid of Frankish mercenaries. In the same year the Portuguese captured Coimbra. When, in 1085, Alfonso VI of Castile-León conquered Toledo, al-Mu'tamid, the ruler of Seville, appealed for aid from northern Africa. This had recently come under the control of the Almoravids, religiously inspired Berber warriors, eager for further expansion.

Warfare in the peninsula differed from that north of the Pyrenees in that horses and equipment were lighter. The

MAP 2

Border warfare and fortress strategy characterized Iberian military activity. Mercenaries and opportunists like El Cid flourished while the Christian kingdoms struggled with Berber fanatics from North Africa. Crusaders and the military orders were vital to the success of a Christian advance which included the creation of the kingdom of Portugal.

in the south. By 1091 they were pressing on Valencia. The city had been the object of Catalan attack since 1086 and was besieged in 1088 and 1089. But count Berenguer fell out with El Cid and was defeated and captured. So, in 1092, Alfonso of Castile established a blockade, employing an Italian fleet. He too was deflected by a diversionary attack by El Cid, who began his own siege in July 1093. A year later the city had been starved into submission.

Almoravid forces which had been overrunning taifa Badajoz arrived in October, too late to save the city. El Cid secured his position by taking Almenara (1097) and the supposedly impregnable rock of Murviedro (1098), before dying in 1099. He epitomized the skill required by border warfare with its shifting alliances. He was missed: Valencia fell to the Almoravids in 1102.

THE EBRO VALLEY CAMPAIGNS

Although Yusuf died in 1106, Almoravid power was undiminished south of the Tagus. The Ebro valley became the main battleground. Alfonso I 'the Battler' of Aragon made his attack on Saragossa a crusade. In 1118, this was preached at Toulouse and drew recruits from among southern French lords. Many of them brought valuable military skills from the Holy Land. Drawing upon his experience at the siege of Jerusalem, Gaston de Béarn supervised the construction of siege towers and artillery. As a reward he was given the city when it fell in December.

The Aragonese advance continued, taking Tudela and Tarazona (1119) and Calatayud (1120), and pressed down the Ebro valley, but was halted in 1134 following Alfonso I's defeat at Fraga and subsequent death. It fell to the count of Barcelona, Ramón Berenguer IV, to take Tortosa (1148) and Lérida (1149). Christian rulers founded towns and created bishoprics in newly won territory. Frontier society also produced many caballeros villanos (commoner knights) whose social status depended upon their military equipment and activity.

As the Reconquista absorbed crusade ideology, the new orders of fighting monks began to play an important role. In fact, only the Knights Templar were fully established as such (1128), but the idea was popular and widely imitated. In a will of 1131, Alfonso I of Aragon intended to make the Templars his heir. In 1143, they entered into an agreement with the count of Barcelona; he also supported the Hospitallers, who were at the siege of Tortosa, and received the frontier castle of Amposta in 1149. When Portugal became a kingdom in 1143, the Templars were given the castle at Soure. But even they could not defend Calatrava, far south on the Guadiana river, so the first indigenous order of that name was created in 1156.

The Portuguese victory at Ourique in 1139 proved Almoravid military power to be on the wane. The Almohads seized their North African base and in 1147 crossed the Straits to capture Seville. In the same year, a crusader force composed of English, Flemish, and German seamen captured Lisbon after a remarkable siege. A military equilibrium had been established which was to last for half a century.

introduction of Frankish-style heavy cavalry, riding with a long stirrup, played its part in assuring Christian superiority in battle. Urban militias provided spearmen, crossbowmen, and siege troops for campaigns of conquest. In 1085, Yusuf ibn Tashufin led the Almoravids across the Straits of Gibraltar. Their tactics were a development of the ancient Berber techniques of forming a camel laager from which to launch attacks. They still used camels (which unsettled the enemy's horses) but relied upon a close and stationary phalanx of infantry spearmen, backed up by bow- and javelin-men, to withstand attack. Cavalry was generally unarmoured, although Yusuf had a bodyguard of 500 non-Berber troops including Franks and Turks. His disciplined troops manoeuvred silently to the sound of massed drums.

In battle at Sagrajas (1086) the Castilians were defeated, and the Almoravids went on to re-establish Muslim authority

THE FIRST CRUSADE

I N 1095, POPE URBAN II began preaching for an expedition to the Holy Land in response to a request by the Byzantine emperor, Alexius I Comnenus, for mercenary troops to fight the Seljuk Turks. But the western response was altogether more ambitious, involving huge numbers of military pilgrims under their own leaders, who crossed Europe and Asia Minor to reach Syria, and recovered Jerusalem in 1099. They initiated a series of overseas campaigns (crusades as they were later called) which mobilized the military potential of Christendom. Initially, the crusaders found the new conditions challenging: the heat, difficult terrain, and the fluid tactics of a nomadic enemy. The epic siege of Antioch taught them how to defeat the Muslims in battle and forged a veteran force. At Jerusalem, their mastery of siege technology achieved their goal.

Peter the Hermit, a popular preacher, used to be seen as the initiator of the First Crusade. He did lead the first forces to reach Constantinople; but lacking knights and armour, they were militarily ineffective and were massacred by the Seljuk Turks. Peter subsequently disgraced himself by running away from the siege of Antioch, and was captured and brought back ignominiously.

AN ARMED PILGRIMAGE

The Muslim powers around the Holy Land were chaotically divided. First there was the longstanding schism between the rival caliphs of Fatimid Cairo and Abbasid Baghdad. Then, in the 1060s, the Abbasids' Turkish soldiers began to assert their independence and semi-nomadic forces flooded into Asia Minor. At Manzikert in 1071, the Seljuk Turk leader, Alp Arslan, crushed a Byzantine army and captured emperor Romanus Diogenes. Turks overran the Syrian coast and took Jerusalem from the Fatimids in 1075. In 1085, they seized Antioch by treachery. Tutush controlled the Holy Land until his death in 1095, when his sons divided the inheritance, but Ridwan of Aleppo and Duqaq of Damascus felt threatened by the Abbasid general, Kerbogha, atabeg of Mosul. There would be no co-ordinated response to the unexpected crusader assault.

Crusading required a high level of organization. Forces had to be recruited which would retain military effectiveness for a campaign which might last years in hostile territory far from home. Logistical support would be a constant problem. The First Crusade, the first expedition of its kind, was a triumph of improvisation. The troops were raised by several powerful princes: Raymond, count of St Gilles from southern France; from the north, Godfrey of Bouillon, his brothers, the counts of Flanders and Boulogne, and Robert duke of Normandy who mortgaged the duchy to fund his forces; and the Normans of southern Italy, led by Bohemond of Taranto. He was experienced in war against Alexius and his Turkish mercenaries, and a man of boundless ambition and little scruple, like his nephew Tancred. There was no clear command structure among these princes.

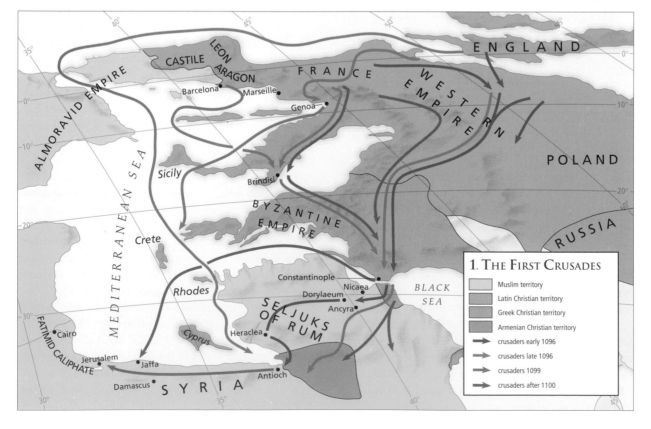

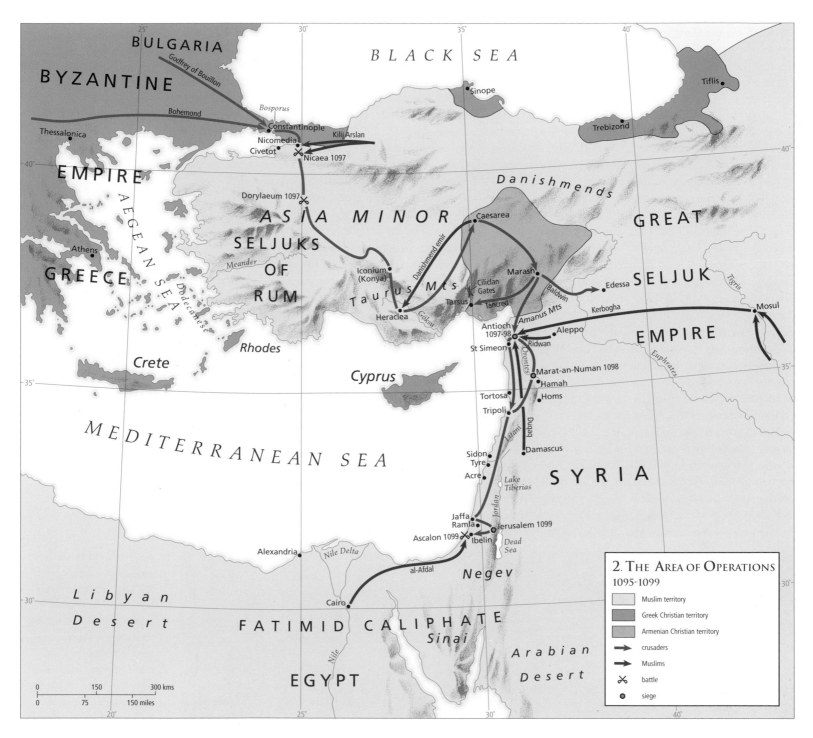

MAP 2

The disunity of the Islamic
world enabled the crusaders
to defeat six major Muslim
armies piecemeal, over two
years of hard campaigning.
Everything hinged on the
ten-month siege and
capture of Antioch. The
Syrian coastal cities paid
tribute and the Fatimid
attempt to save Jerusalem
was too little, too late.

Urban did not accompany the expedition, but sent as his
legate Adhemar, bishop of Le Puy. Raymond also claimed
leadership, but the other princes were unwilling to give
him precedence.

The mustering-point was Constantinople. The first arrivals
(August 1096) were ill-organized pilgrims under Peter the
Hermit and Walter Sansavoir. The Byzantine government
was surprised by their large numbers and poor military
quality. They were swiftly shipped to Anatolia where they
suffered two heavy defeats by the Seljuk Turks in September
and October. Most were killed or captured, only a few
surviving to be evacuated by sea from their base at Civetot.

In spring 1097, the princes' contingents entered Byzantine
territory. As they moved through northern Greece they

were harassed by the emperor's Turkic mercenaries. Each
side was suspicious of the others' intentions. After
negotiations, the crusader leaders swore to return to Alexius
all the former imperial territories and cities they recovered.
Then they were shipped to Asia Minor and approached
their first goal, Nicaea (map 2). Duke Godfrey's forces
included pioneers who prepared the line of march and put
up bronze crosses to mark the route. The Byzantines
provided supplies and logistical support.

THE SIEGE OF NICAEA

On 6 May, the first contingents reached Nicaea, although
the city was not completely invested by land until the
southern French arrived. Even then, the garrison was

supplied across Lake Ascanius by the Seljuk sultan Kilij Arslan. He attacked the besiegers, hoping to surprise and destroy them as he had the forces of Peter the Hermit. But in a battle on 16 May, he was soundly defeated. The crusaders may have numbered 100,000 (20-40,000 effectives?): about one-tenth were armoured cavalry (knights); there were substantial numbers of well-equipped footmen, some carrying the crossbow, which could outrange the Turkish bow; and many 'ordinary pilgrims' of limited military value. Kilij Arslan's troops were few, perhaps 6,000-8,000 Turkish horse-archers, who relied upon surprise and their showers of arrows for victory. Both failed them at Nicaea. The mining of the walls proceeded, although the defenders built a retaining wall behind the breach. The crucial development was the arrival of Byzantine boats dragged overland to Lake Ascanius. Cut off from supplies, doubting relief, and now under assault from all sides, the defenders surrendered to the Byzantines on 19 June to avoid the penalties of a sack, so denying the crusaders pillage.

The march was resumed in late June. Asia Minor was an extremely hostile environment for the passage of large armies. The Turks had destroyed the Byzantine system of water cisterns, and the crusaders were reduced to surviving on thorny plants at times. Many horses died on the march so later, goats, sheep, and even dogs had to carry their baggage. On the third day out (1 July) they were attacked at a river crossing by Kilij Arslan's forces and thrown into confusion. The vanguard, composed of the Norman contingents, was rallied by Bohemond, who ordered the foot soldiers to pitch camp, thus creating a defensible laager from which the mounted knights could make sorties. The

Turkish archery was especially fearsome and threw both crusader horse and foot into panic, but they held on through a long hot day, with the women pilgrims bringing water to the fighting men. Eventually, the main body came up. The knightly cavalry improvised a battle line and charged the Turks, while Raymond's contingent circled around a hill out of sight to attack their left rear. The Turkish rout was total, the crusaders taking their camp and much gold, silver, and livestock. The precious metals were essential to purchase supplies, while the animals provided food on the hoof and replacement mounts.

Reaching Iconium (Konya) in mid-August, the crusaders replenished their supplies and on the advice of the inhabitants prepared waterskins for the journey. At Heraclea, the Danishmend emir blocked their path, but fled with little resistance. Around 10 September, the army divided at Tyana, Baldwin of Boulogne and Tancred taking their followers south across the difficult pass of the Cilician Gates, while the main body proceeded north to Caesarea, which they saved from Danishmend siege. The expedition into Cilician Armenia was a piece of private enterprise, a reminder that the crusaders formed no unified army. In a quarrel between Baldwin and Tancred over the towns of the plain, Tancred was the loser.

FROM ANTIOCH TO JERUSALEM

The main body of the crusader army, supported by the Christian Armenian population, crossed the Anti-Taurus mountains and the Amanus range before arriving at Marash. In the process, the crusaders lost most of their remaining horses on the steep mountain paths and threw away much

Antioch, from an early nineteenth-century print. The city's walls had been built under Justinian I, over 500 years earlier, and improved in the tenth century. Without the Byzantine emperor Alexius' siege train they were effectively impregnable. The citadel held out when the city was betrayed to Bohemond, and only surrendered following the defeat of Kerbogha on 28 June 1098.

THE SIEGE OF ANTIOCH

The fortifications of Antioch were effectively impregnable if the defenders kept their nerve. They consisted of 33 feet (10m) high walls and 400 towers 65 feet (20m) high within mutual bowshot; the citadel was on the 1,000 feet (330m) high Mount Silpius, and to the north the river Orontes and its marshes gave further protection. The Turkish commander Yaghi-Siyan had a loyal and well-supplied garrison. Only the city's largely Armenian population gave him cause for concern.

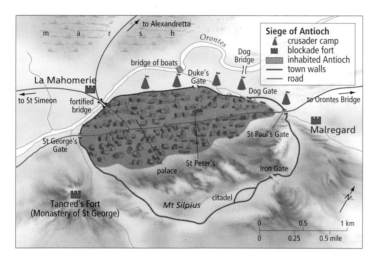

Alexius' representative, Tatkikios, urged an arm's-length siege strategy based upon the fortress of Baghras 12 miles (20 km) to the north, but the crusader leaders were conscious of the need to keep their forces united and preferred a close blockade. In November, the garrison launched cavalry sorties against foragers across the Orontes, so the crusaders built a pontoon bridge to enable them to deploy rapidly against such sallies. As winter drew on, supplies became short. At Christmas, Bohemond and Robert of Flanders led a raid against Aleppo, gaining flocks and booty. They also encountered and defeated a relief force under Duqaq of Damascus. Despite this, the supply situation became critical in January as camp prices rocketed and many poorer crusaders starved. The knights' horses suffered too; barely 1,000 were reckoned serviceable.

On 9 February, a relief force under Ridwan of Aleppo attacked, supported by a vigorous sally from the garrison. The crusaders, though weakened, repulsed both attempts and captured many desperately needed horses. In March, their situation began to improve, as ships arrived at St Simeon, Antioch's port. But the first food convoy from the coast came under attack and had to be rescued by a force led by Bohemond, which inflicted 1,500 casualties on the Antiochene cavalry. This was a crucial boost to crusader morale. They promptly constructed two siege castles to tighten the blockade of Antioch. In March, the mosque opposite the fortified bridge was provided with two towers and walls made from Muslim tombstones and put under the command of St Gilles.

In April, Tancred fortified the monastery of St George opposite the gate of the same name. The former protected crusader supplies from the coast, the latter prevented convoys reaching the city.

The tables had been turned and now it was the besieged's turn to starve. Firuz, a prominent Armenian Christian, negotiated secretly with Bohemond. On the night of 2 June, a tower was betrayed to the crusaders who broke into the city and ran amok. Large areas caught fire, while Yaghi-Siyan's garrison withdrew to the citadel. The events that followed seemed truly miraculous. On 5 June, the relieving army under Kerbogha of Mosul, sent by the Baghdad caliph, arrived to besiege the erstwhile besiegers. He had been delayed for a fortnight besieging Baldwin in Edessa. The fortified mosque (La Mahomerie) was wrested from crusader control by 8 June, leaving them in a dire situation, trapped between two forces in a devastated city exhausted of supplies, and with no escape route evident. Some notables did manage to slip away, including Stephen, count of Blois, and Peter the Hermit, who was caught and returned in disgrace.

Crusader morale was boosted by the discovery of the 'Holy Lance', supposedly a relic of the Crucifixion in St Peter's cathedral in Antioch. Not all the crusader leaders were convinced of its authenticity, but it served to inspire a desperate sortie. On 28 June, six 'battles' (divisions), each of infantry, and a few cavalry issued from the city to attack the besiegers. Perhaps taken by surprise, certainly disorganized by the lack of trust between Kerbogha and the Syrian emirs, the Muslim forces were driven back. Only on the western flank did Turkish horse-archers threaten to encircle the crusader battle line. The reserve division, mounted on the few remaining horses, drove off the outflanking attempt. Kerbogha's superior forces seem to have crumbled rapidly, firing the grass to facilitate their escape. The crusaders ascribed their surprising victory to the appearance of a supernatural host of men on white horses led by the military saints George and Demetrius.

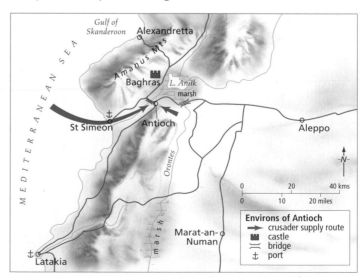

THE CASTLE OF SAONE

Saone stands in northern Syria, just inland from the important port of Latakia. It was of Byzantine construction, a rock-cut ditch isolating a spur between two steep river gorges. The 700-yard (640-m) long triangle created was surrounded by walls. The Franks took over the site soon after 1100 and built a tall keep to defend the gatehouse. They may also have raised the height of the circuit wall and its towers. The rock-cut ditch is 100 feet (30m) deep, and the bridge across it was supported in the centre by a pinnacle of stone.

T. E. Lawrence visited the site in 1911 when devising his theory that eastern styles of fortification were imported into the west. Modern experts believe that influences flowed both ways, although it is possible that Saone's towers being isolated from the wall-walk was a Byzantine device. Practically impregnable, Saone fell in 1188 to a commando-style surprise assault.

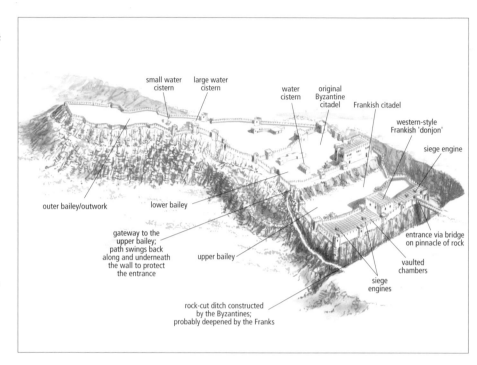

small water cistern large water cistern water cistern original Byzantine citadel Frankish citadel western-style Frankish 'donjon' siege engine outer bailey/outwork lower bailey entrance via bridge on pinnacle of rock gateway to the upper bailey; path swings back along and underneath the wall to protect the entrance upper bailey vaulted chambers siege engines rock-cut ditch constructed by the Byzantines; probably deepened by the Franks

of their equipment, even their arms and armour. But Marash provided a market and easy access to Antioch, which was reached on 20 October 1097. The siege of this city, lasting until 3 June 1098, was central to the First Crusade, which contemporaries often called the 'Antioch War' (page 89).

After the capture of Antioch and the defeat of Kerbogha's relief attempt, the crusade stagnated while the leaders squabbled. Bohemond held the citadel and claimed Antioch, to count Raymond's fury. Further advance was delayed until the wealthy count Raymond paid Godfrey, Robert of Normandy, Robert of Flanders, Tancred, and lesser lords to resume the advance. The siege of Marat-an-Numan, (28 November-12 December) featured the use of a huge siege tower and a brutal sack following the crusader assault. This ruthlessness paid off as few towns dared resist the crusaders as they advanced along the Syrian coast. Tortosa was taken by a ruse, but Arqah was too well-defended. The city survived a siege of four months (14 February-13 May 1099). By then, the crusaders' military effectives may have numbered only 1,000 knights and 5,000 foot, insufficient for a serious attempt at assault. The coastal route chosen for the advance allowed Italian and English ships to ferry supplies. The emir of Tripoli protected his town by providing money and supplies and the crusaders advanced into Fatimid territory. They marched quickly, taking tribute from Sidon, Tyre, and Acre.

By 3 June the crusaders reached Arsuf and turned inland to reach Jerusalem, via Ramla, on 7 June. Al-Afdal, the Fatimid vizier and effective ruler of Egypt, had taken advantage of the crusaders' arrival in the north to seize Jerusalem after a forty-day siege in 1098. The walls had been repaired and a strong garrison installed under ad-Dawla. Although not a formidable site, Jerusalem was well defended by walls and ditches and the garrison had poisoned all the nearby wells. Timber suitable for siege machinery had been cut down and some Christians expelled. An initial assault on 15 June was repelled, because although the crusaders got a foothold on the walls, they lacked enough ladders to exploit it. So they settled down for a siege.

The arrival of a Christian fleet at Jaffa on 17 June provided timber and nails for constructing siege towers. William Embriaco, a Genoan, supervised the construction of count Raymond's engines, while Gaston of Béarn advised the other leaders. Conditions were extremely harsh for the besiegers: it was midsummer, water had to be carried from 6 miles (10 km) away, and the defenders launched disrupting sorties. It took a month to prepare the assault. To the south, Raymond's siege tower had a level path prepared for its approach; to the north, Godfrey's assault tower was supported by a large covered ram. On the night of 9 July, the cumbersome equipment was shifted eastwards to a better site, and was fully operational by 13 July. On the next day, a combined assault from the north and south was repulsed. On 15 July, the northern tower was wedged against the wall near Herod's Gate, and the crusaders forced an entry. The defenders fled from the southern defences, allowing the crusaders to flood into the city from both sides. The discipline of the assault disintegrated into a

Despite a desperate lack of supplies, of food and especially water, and timber essential for siege engines, the crusaders improvised brilliantly. Breaking up ships from the supporting fleet in Jaffa, they constructed great towers with which to storm the walls of Jerusalem.

Duke Godfrey commanded the crusaders at Ascalon, deploying infantry in front of the knights to protect their horses from archery. Because the Egyptians had been surprised in their camp, the Fatimid house-hold and mercenary troops put up only a weak resis-tance. Once Godfrey had countered a flank attack by Bedouin light cavalry, the knights' charge swept the Muslims away.

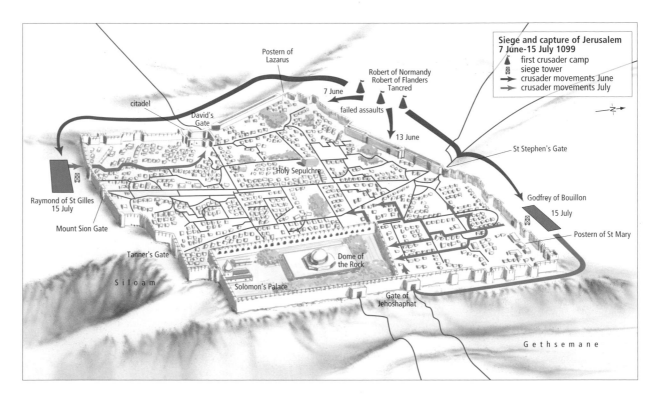

frenzied scramble for loot and the deliberate massacre of the Muslim population.

THE BATTLE OF ASCALON

Against all the odds the crusaders had achieved their objective. Their commanders immediately fell out over who was to control Jerusalem. Godfrey was elected 'Advocate of the Holy Sepulchre', while Raymond and Robert of Normandy left in disgust for the Jordan valley, until a new threat restored a temporary unity. Al-Afdal led a large force from Egypt to Ascalon, where he awaited his fleet. The crusaders mustered at Ibelin on 11 August, disputes temporarily forgotten, then advanced onto the plain of Ashdod, capturing the Egyptian supply herds. Al-Afdal's scouting was very poor, perhaps as a result of over-confidence, and he allowed his force to be surprised on the following day and routed.

The success at Ascalon was due to the veteran skills displayed by the Franks. Their order of march shows how much they had learnt since Dorylaeum. They formed nine 'battles', each composed of mutually supporting horse and foot, three in each of the van, centre, and rear. This created a 'box' which could turn to face wherever danger threatened. They then deployed into line for the attack. In fact, the crusaders' caution proved unnecessary for two reasons. First, because the Egyptians fought like the crusaders themselves, with cavalry and foot soldiers (some of the latter were the redoubtable negro regiments of spearmen and archers). This meant that they did not pose the same sort of threat as the mobile Turkish horse-archers. Secondly, the total surprise gave the Franks the initiative and left the Egyptians helpless. The victory at Ascalon secured the crusaders' grip on Jerusalem and made possible the conquest of the rest of the Syrian coastline.

The first crusaders were so successful because they possessed a fanatical determination, and because the three-year-long campaign created a veteran force. Although jealous of one another, their leaders managed to combine at critical moments. They overcame huge logistical problems, and their mastery of siege techniques gave them the crucial edge over their opponents.

THE LATIN STATES IN THE HOLY LAND

I F THE REMARKABLE military success of the recovery of Jerusalem in 1099 was to be secured, then the westerners needed to conquer the Levantine coastline and fortify both its ports and further inland. The Jordan valley formed a natural boundary with the Muslim powers of the interior, and new orders of military monks played a crucial role in defending it. They provided fortresses, garrisons, and field armies which remained in the east. Further crusades supplied valuable influxes of manpower, but often their leaders' objectives were overambitious for the time and resources available. The crusade following the loss of Edessa in 1144 achieved little, despite the involvement of the king of France and emperor of Germany. Almaric, king of Jerusalem, showed a much shrewder grasp of strategy when he chose to invade Egypt.

This mid-twelfth-century Egyptian paper fragment from Cairo shows the Fatimid defenders of Ascalon, which did not fall to the Latins until 1153. Their equipment is similar to that of the westerners, being distinguished only by the turbans they wear. The Fatimid mixture of heavy cavalry, spear-armed foot, and archers is well represented.

CONQUEST OF THE COAST

In 1099, the crusaders held pockets of territory around Jerusalem, Antioch, and Edessa. To secure these possessions it was essential to control the 625-mile (1,000-km) coastline of the Levant. In effect, this meant capturing and fortifying its ports, so castles were built to blockade the ports by land (map 1). In 1102-03, Raymond count of St Gilles built Mount Pilgrim 3 miles (5km) from Tripoli. Tyre was pressurized by Toron, 9 miles (15km) distant, in 1107 and Scandalion, only 4 miles (7km) away, in 1117. Blockade alone did not take fortresses, which required close siege and assaults. Latin forces, once committed, were then vulnerable to the relief attempts of Fatimid fleets and Damascene armies. When king Baldwin I besieged Acre in 1103, the port was relieved by twelve Fatimid vessels. The attack on Sidon in 1108 failed for the same reasons. There was also a shortage of manpower. In 1100, king Baldwin led only 200 knights and 1,000 foot soldiers; further crusades, especially naval expeditions, were essential.

Crusader fleets were important from the first; Haifa was taken in 1100 by a siege tower constructed from Venetian vessels. Genoa contributed to the storming of Caesarea in 1101 (when William Embriaco's sailors built siege machines), provided seventy beaked ships at Acre in 1104, and aided the capture of Tripoli, Beirut, and Jubail in 1109-10. The fleet of Sigurd, king of Norway, prevented a naval relief of Sidon, from Tyre, in 1110. But the supreme naval involvement was the Venetian crusade of 1123-24.

A winter siege of Tyre in 1111-12 by Baldwin I had failed to take this linchpin position. In May 1123, 120 Venetian vessels arrived in the coastal ports. In a rare sea battle off Ascalon, they routed a Fatimid fleet and captured ten supply ships containing timber suitable for siege engines. The siege of Tyre did not begin until 16 February 1124, but it soon became the focus of military activity. Fatimid forces attempted relief by sea and overland from Ascalon, while Tughtigin, atabeg of Damascus, approached from the east. The besiegers had entrenched themselves against attack, and were covered at sea by the Venetian fleet and on land by a force under Pons of Tripoli and the royal constable. Despairing of relief, Tyre surrendered on 7 July. Between

Cilician Armenia and Egypt, only Ascalon remained in Muslim hands.

A glance at a map of the crusader states showing the castles, forts, and walled towns might suggest that there was a kind of fortified frontier against the Muslim hinterland. Such an impression is misleading. First, these fortresses were not necessarily all in operation at the same time. Secondly, their role as centres of lordship – political dominion – did not always place them in the most strategically advantageous sites to protect the wider territories of the states. Thirdly, they could not interdict enemy movement in themselves. Their garrisons could go out and harry attackers, cutting lines of communication and restricting their opportunities to raid and forage, but it took a fully mustered field army to defeat invasion.

The County of Edessa was the most northerly and easterly crusader state, a vulnerable salient into Muslim territory. It survived the Seljuk sultan's attempts at reconquest in 1110-15. This was mainly achieved by the Latin field forces avoiding battle and hanging on to the fortifications. Edessa itself was especially well-fortified by walls and a rock-cut ditch. Antioch, centre of the principality established by Bohemond, possessed even stronger defences. The rulers of both cities sought to gain control of Aleppo, which would have secured their possessions as far as the Euphrates, but they were defeated twice in battle, first in 1104. On the latter occasion – 'The Field of Blood' (28 June 1119) – Roger of Antioch was killed and many fortresses east of the Orontes were lost. King Baldwin II marched north to rescue the situation after a hard-fought encounter near Hab (14 August 1119) and ruled the area for seven years. He pressed hard on Aleppo and was on the point of taking it after a three-month siege in 1126, but withdrew in the face of a relieving force. It was the only Frankish siege of this strategic city with its near-impregnable citadel.

When Bohemond II arrived from the west to take over Antioch in 1126, Baldwin transferred his attacks to Damascus, but a costly victory outside the city prevented further progress. The crusade of 1128-29 provided troops for another attempt, but insufficient supplies, linked to the

MAP 1

The castles and other fortifications of the Latin states are impressive survivals of the crusader era. Until the post-war revisionist work of R. C. Smail, they were interpreted as forming a defensive network. This they never were, and they only operated in conjunction with the Latin field armies. Since Muslim invasion routes were fairly predictable, they did play a role as bases for Christian forces and delayed Muslim campaigns by withstanding long sieges.

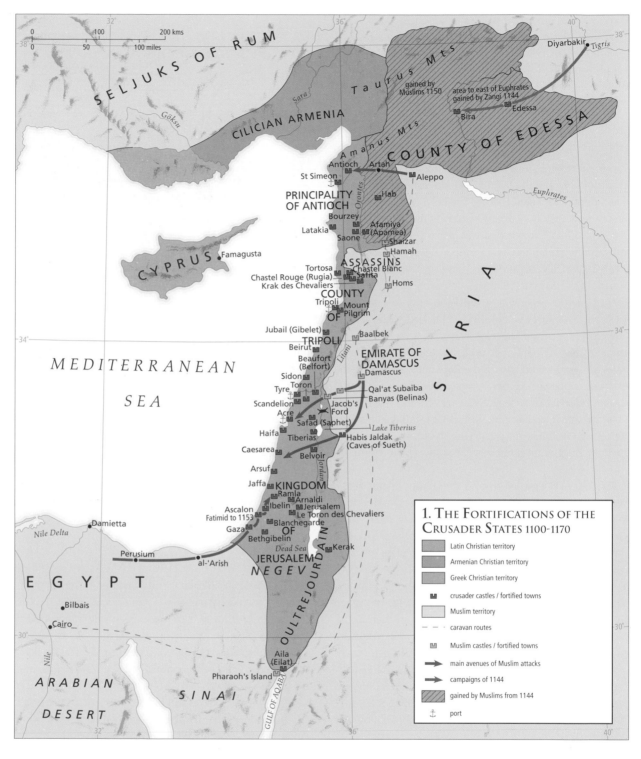

destruction of a foraging force, made a siege impossible. Damascus and Aleppo were the linchpins of the inland north-south route; in crusader hands they would have secured the coast from invasion. The arrival in 1127 of a new, energetic atabeg, Imad el-Din Zangi, who took over Mosul and Aleppo (1128), thwarted this aim.

The southern coast had been secured early on as far as Jaffa, and al-Afdal, the vizier of Egypt (1094–1121), attacked the region continually for several years. His one great victory over Baldwin I at Ramla in 1102 was not followed up. The Fatimids relied on raids from Ascalon after 1107, except for an expedition in 1121 which was decisively defeated

at Ibelin. The Ascalon garrison long remained a menace to pilgrims and settlers. Between 1136-41, a ring of castles was built to neutralize its activities: Ibelin, Blanchegarde, and Bethgibelin. Gaza was also fortified, cutting off the land route to Egypt, although Ascalon could still be reached by sea and had a vital role as the most northerly harbour for the Fatimid fleet. When this was lost, after an intermittent eight-month siege in 1153, the Egyptians also lost the possibility of naval intervention in the vital sea-zone between Cyprus, Tyre, and Acre.

The southern area of the kingdom was further secured by the great fief of Oultrejourdain. In 1131, Baldwin II died, and was succeeded by Fulk of Anjou. Fulk installed a new lord, Pagan the Butler, who proved energetic in defending his territory, which straddled the vital caravan route from Egypt to Damascus. He built the great castle of Kerak in Moab (1142) and strengthened the fortifications of Eilat on the Gulf of Aqaba.

THE FALL OF EDESSA AND THE SECOND CRUSADE

Zangi, meanwhile, was securing his hold on Syria, taking Homs (1138) and Baalbek (1139), threatening Damascus. The citizens appealed to Fulk for help, which he gave, cautiously at first, but effectively, forcing the atabeg to forgo a siege in 1140. The situation was not so good in the north. A Byzantine expedition led by emperor John Comnenus in 1138-39 was directed as much against the Franks of Antioch as against the Muslims. He was preparing to take the city in 1143 when he died as a result of a hunting accident (8 April). A similar fate befell king Fulk later in the year (7 November), giving Zangi new freedom of manoeuvre. In the autumn of 1144, he lured Joscelin of Edessa into supporting a Muslim ally on the Euphrates, and while the city was stripped of defenders, sent a subordinate to capture it after a four-week siege. Even his murder in 1146 did not save the situation. His son, Nur al-Din, inflicted a heavy defeat on Joscelin, who was trying to recover Edessa, and in 1147 he also rebuffed a royal army which attempted to intervene.

The loss of Edessa led to new crusading fervour in the west, stirred up by the preaching of the charismatic St Bernard. As a result, Louis VII of France and Conrad III of Germany both led large armies to Constantinople, then took the land route across Anatolia (map 2). Conrad set out first, only to have his army massacred near Dorylaeum by a Turkish ambush. The emperor Manuel, who had made a truce with the Turks, was blamed. The French (accompanied by remnants of Germans) did little better, as their army, lacking march discipline, almost fell apart under pressure from Turkish harassment. Fortunately, the Templar Master was able to reorganize the column and this enabled the crusaders to reach the coast at Antalya. Here Louis, his household, and much of the cavalry, took ship to St Simeon, Antioch's port, while the foot soldiers had to follow the coast by land, losing half their numbers on the way.

In 1148, Louis and Conrad persuaded Baldwin III to attack Damascus, reversing the recent policy of alliance. Despite the substantial forces at their disposal, the crusader leaders mishandled the siege (24-28 July). Attacking first through the orchards to the west of the city, but failing to make headway, they made the disastrous decision to transfer the assaults to the eastern walls. Here the besiegers were in open, waterless ground subject to attacks by Muslim cavalry. Eventually forced to retreat, the campaign ended amidst mutual recriminations between the settlers and crusaders, who left in spring 1149.

The situation only benefited Nur al-Din, who increased his pressure in the north. He besieged Inab and, on 28 June

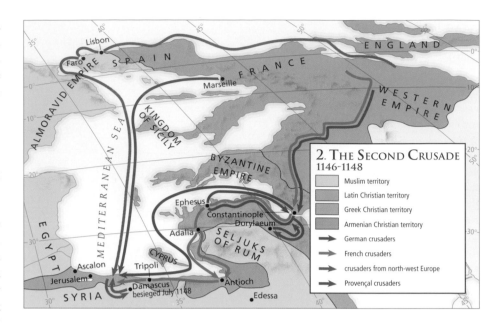

1149, inflicted a crushing defeat on a Frankish relieving force, killing its leader Raymond of Antioch. In April 1150, he captured Joscelin of Edessa, leaving both northern Latin states leaderless. Even accepting the suzerainty of emperor Manuel and his Byzantine garrisons did not save Edessa. Its last outlying castles were lost by the summer of 1151. Nur al-Din had already turned his attention to Damascus, which was only saved by a Latin royal army (May 1151). It eventually fell to him after a brief siege in 1154 (25 April). This more than outweighed Baldwin's capture of Ascalon in the previous year as regards the security of his kingdom. In 1158, he defeated an ailing Nur al-Din in battle outside Damascus, but died himself in February 1162.

THE STRUGGLE FOR EGYPT 1160-1170

In 1160, Baldwin III had extorted tribute from Egypt on threat of invasion, which was never paid. So, in September 1163, his brother and successor Almaric attacked and besieged Pelusium. Although unsuccessful, this initiated a series of campaigns into the Nile delta (map 3). The Egyptian government had been destabilized by several coups, and the ex-vizier Shawar fled to Nur al-Din for support. The Kurdish general Shirkuh and his nephew Saladin were sent to reinstate Shawar (May 1164), but then declined to leave Egypt, so the vizier called in Almaric to expel them. The king besieged Shirkuh in Bilbais, and the city was about to fall after three months' siege when news of a defeat outside Antioch forced him to agree to a mutual evacuation of Egypt. Bohemond of Antioch had been captured, along with his army, by Nur al-Din near Artah (10 August). Almaric had to rush north where, aided by Thierry of Champagne's crusaders, he ransomed Bohemond and restored the situation.

In January 1167, Shirkuh invaded Egypt again with 2,000 cavalry. Shawar called in Almaric, who made a treaty with the caliph and commanded the allied troops. At Cairo, Shirkuh kept the Nile between himself and the larger enemy forces, and in early March began a withdrawal southwards.

MAP 2

The loss of Edessa (1144) stimulated the largest western crusade since 1095. Both the French king and German emperor led large contingents through Asia Minor, where they were nearly destroyed by Turkish attacks. When the survivors reached Jerusalem, they insisted on attacking Damascus, but bungled the campaign badly. Only in Portugal, where Lisbon fell to northern crusaders after an epic siege, were they militarily successful.

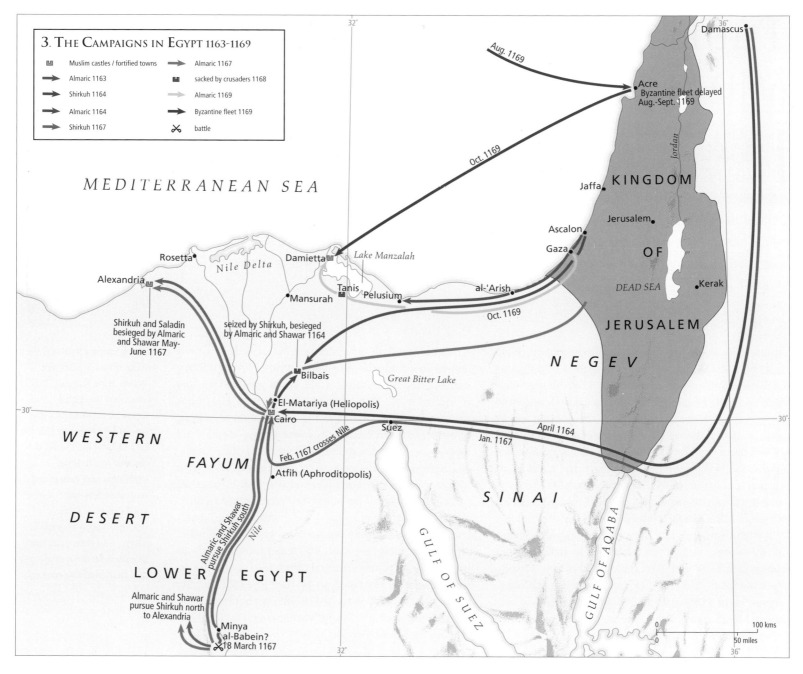

3. THE CAMPAIGNS IN EGYPT 1163-1169

- 🏰 Muslim castles / fortified towns
- → Almaric 1163
- → Shirkuh 1164
- → Almaric 1164
- → Shirkuh 1167
- → Almaric 1167
- 🏰 sacked by crusaders 1168
- → Almaric 1169
- → Byzantine fleet 1169
- ✕ battle

MEDITERRANEAN SEA

Damascus

Aug. 1169

Acre
Byzantine fleet delayed
Aug.-Sept. 1169

Oct. 1169

Jaffa KINGDOM

Rosetta Nile Delta Damietta Lake Manzalah

Alexandria

Ascalon Jerusalem OF

Gaza

Shirkuh and Saladin
besieged by Almaric
and Shawar May-
June 1167

Tanis Pelusium

Mansurah

al-'Arish

Oct. 1169

DEAD SEA Kerak

seized by Shirkuh, besieged
by Almaric and Shawar 1164

JERUSALEM

Bilbais

Great Bitter Lake

NEGEV

El-Matariya (Heliopolis)

Cairo

Suez

Feb. 1167 crosses Nile

April 1164

Jan. 1167

WESTERN

FAYUM

Atfih (Aphroditopolis)

SINAI

DESERT

Almaric and Shawat
pursue Shirkuh south

Nile

LOWER EGYPT

GULF OF SUEZ

GULF OF AQABA

Almaric and Shawar
pursue Shirkuh north
to Alexandria

Minya
al-Babein?
✕ 18 March 1167

0   100 kms
0   50 miles

MAP 3

In the 1160s Almaric, king of Jerusalem, made several attempts to conquer Egypt. Nur al-Din, ruler of Damascus, sent his general Shirkuh to intervene. With inferior resources, Shirkuh and his nephew Saladin kept the Franks at bay. When a combined Latin and Byzantine attack on Damietta failed, the Christians accepted defeat.

Almaric followed in such haste that he led only 375 knights and the Egyptian cavalry. When Shirkuh turned to fight at al-Babein, Saladin, commanding the centre, feigned flight, drawing the Frankish charge after him, leaving the Egyptians to be overwhelmed.

While Almaric struggled back to Cairo, Shirkuh swept north and captured Alexandria. Here he was besieged by the Franks and Egyptians, until food grew scarce and he broke out with half his force, leaving Saladin to defend the city (which was starved into surrender on 4 August). The expulsion of Shirkuh gave Almaric the upper hand in Egypt, which was forced to pay tribute. Latin conquest seemed imminent.

In 1168, emperor Manuel proposed a joint invasion of Egypt and a treaty was signed in September. Despite Almaric's misgivings about breaking a truce and the Templars' refusal to take part, hawks amongst the barons

and the crusader count of Nevers urged immediate attack. On 4 November, Bilbais was taken and sacked by the army, and a few days later Tanis was destroyed by the fleet. Such rigour proved to be mistaken, as the Egyptians now called in Shirkuh, who arrived swiftly with 8,000 cavalry, forcing the Franks to withdraw (2 January 1169).

They did not return until the autumn, by which time Saladin had made himself secure in Egypt. The Byzantine alliance bore fruit when a fleet arrived at Acre in July, but Almaric was not ready and the ships' supplies were almost exhausted when a combined siege of Damietta eventually began at the end of October. The Franks did not share their rations and the ensuing dissension, combined with the strength of the defence which was reinforced in December, soon ended the siege. The crusaders did not attack Egypt again for fifty years. Now the initiative had passed to the Muslims, and Saladin was ready to exploit it.

THE RESURGENCE OF ISLAM AND THE THIRD CRUSADE

I N THE 1170S AND 1180S, *the strategic balance shifted against the crusader states in the Levant. This was largely due to the influence of Saladin, an inspired military leader, who between 1174 and 1188 managed to unite the region from Mosul to Egypt and direct its military and naval resources for reconquest. Following his great victory at Hattin in 1187, his troops overran the Latin Kingdom and took Jerusalem. This provoked the so-called 'Third' Crusade of 1189-92, which drew forces to the Holy Land from throughout the Latin Christian west, including large armies under Philip II of France and Frederick Barbarossa. But its greatest leader was Richard I of England, who defeated Saladin at Acre and Arsuf in 1191. But even he proved unable to recover Jerusalem.*

SALADIN'S CAMPAIGNS

Saladin was a Kurd who served his military apprenticeship under his uncle Shirkuh in Egypt during the 1160s fighting for the Muslim leader Nur al-Din. In 1169 he was made vizier and in 1171 he deposed the last Fatimid caliph and restored Sunni Islam in the name of the Abbasid caliph. Egypt provided the resources to take Damascus on Nur al-Din's death in 1174. Saladin's shaky claim to power was legitimized by his religious orthodoxy and claim to be pursuing a holy war, or *jihad*, although other Muslim rulers saw his actions as aggressive opportunism. Indeed, between 1174 and 1186, Saladin spent thirty-three months fighting fellow Muslims and only thirteen campaigning against Christian states. During these campaigns he united regions from which he would draw the overwhelming force to attack the Latin states: in 1179 the Seljuks were defeated; Aleppo fell in 1183; and in 1185-86, despite his serious illness, Mosul and Diyarbakir were conquered. He then turned his attention to the crusader states.

Saladin's strength lay in the army he created. As a Kurd he was an outsider to the predominantly Turkish military establishment in the Islamic world, yet he possessed qualities of leadership which made him a fine general. His troops were bound to him in part by *iqta* (distribution of estates), in part by pay, and crucially by *asabiya* (group identity and loyalty). He used men well, chiefly members of his family. His nephews Taqi al-Din, Keukbir, and Farrukh Shah were inspirational field commanders. His brother, Turanshah (d.1180), conquered Egypt and the Yemen, while another, al-Adil, milked Egypt to pay for the army. From Egypt's revenues, five times more was spent on the army than under any other heading. Even this was inadequate, and Saladin had to resort to private loans and extortion to pay his troops, for when the money failed, so did their loyalty. This grew worse after the glory years of 1187-89, when plunder was not so freely available. Saladin's achievement in 1190-92, holding his forces together after blows to his prestige at

The crusaders believed they were divinely inspired. When Pope Gregory VIII launched the Third Crusade, provoked by the loss of Jerusalem to Saladin in 1187, he attributed this disaster to Christian sinfulness and demanded that crusaders 'turn to the Lord our God with penance and works of piety... and then turn our attention to the treachery and malice of the enemy.'

Richard I (left) and Saladin (right) had very different ways of commanding. Richard was always in the forefront of the fighting, leading the charge and restoring difficult situations through the strength of his own arm and moral presence. Saladin preferred to stand back and direct the action from high ground.

Acre and Arsuf, shows his strength of character. As a strategist he was supreme, and his skill at the operational and tactical level gave him his greatest victory, at Hattin in 1187.

The critical battle at Hattin (*page 98*) grew out of divisions amongst the Latin settlers. After king Almaric of Jerusalem died in 1174, leaving as his heir Baldwin IV, a leprous minor, opposing parties grew up in the Kingdom of Jerusalem. On one side were the native barons led by Raymond of Tripoli; on the other were the queen mother, Agnes of Courtney, and incomers such as Reynald de Châtillon (who married the heiress to Kerak in Oultrejourdain in 1175). Gerard de Ridefort, denied a profitable marriage by Raymond, joined the Templars, became their Master, and never forgot his grudge. Finally, there was Guy de Lusignan, who married the heiress apparent, Sibylla, in 1180 and became king of Jerusalem in 1186. Raymond refused him homage then, and they

were not reconciled until shortly before Hattin. Guy's supporters included the Ibelin family and the Hospitallers (who usually opposed the Templars).

Nor was help forthcoming from abroad. In 1176, the Byzantine emperor, Manuel I Comnenus, suffered a crushing defeat by the Seljuks at Myriocephalon, in Asia Minor. In 1177, though still supported by the Byzantine fleet, the crusade of Philip, Count of Flanders, made no impact. On Manuel's death in 1180 the Franks lost a valuable ally and Byzantium ceased to be an important player. While Henry II of England and Louis VII of France promised to crusade, in fact they failed to do so. Apart from the arrival of Henry of Champagne in 1179 and a force of Brabanters and Aquitainians in 1183, there were no significant reinforcements from the west until after 1187.

Saladin had first to learn how to fight the Franks. Usually he had a numerical advantage, especially in cavalry, which

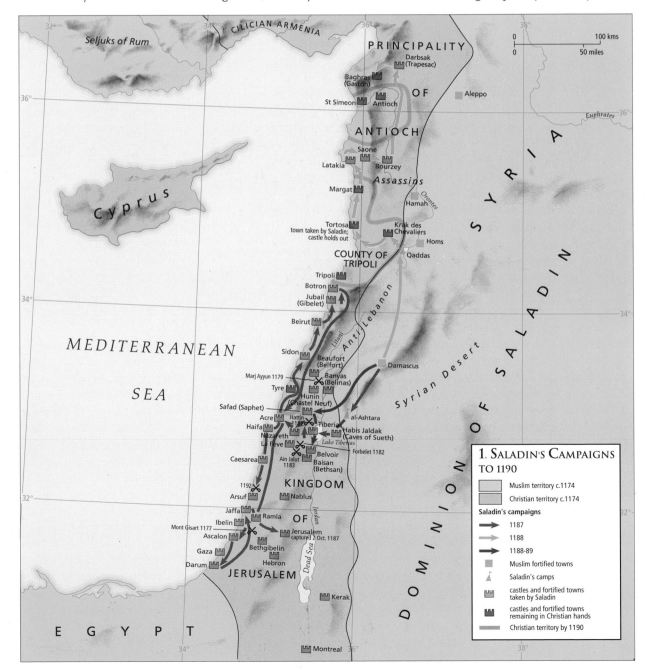

MAP 1

Saladin exploited his victory at Hattin in 1187 by energetic campaigning. That year, he conquered the coast from the frontier of Egypt north to Beirut. The next year saw the capture of valuable castles in Tripoli and Antioch, followed up by a winter campaign in the heart of the Latin Kingdom. Only Tyre held out and became the springboard for Frankish recovery. Saladin became bogged down in a counter-siege of Acre and lost the strategic initiative.

HATTIN 27 JUNE - 4 JULY 1187

Saladin's muster at Damascus was the largest he had ever assembled: 30,000 strong including 12,000 cavalry. On 27 June he set up camp south of Lake Tiberias and on 30 June he advanced to Kafr Sabt. This position was well provided with water, the key to the campaign. King Guy was encamped at the Springs of Saforie, his force estimated at 1,200 cavalry and 15-18,000 foot. Saladin advanced up to Saforie to offer battle, but, as in 1183, Guy was not tempted. So, on 2 July, Saladin attacked Tiberias and the outer town fell very swiftly. The motives behind Guy's advance on the following day remain controversial, but it is possible to make a case for Guy believing that he could trap the Muslim force against Mount Nimrin and the 'Horns' of Hattin with a well-judged charge. Certainly, his failure to engage in 1183, when he had been disgraced, may have weighed heavily with him.

On 3 July, the Franks set out from Saforie, probably taking the northern route on the Roman road to Tiberias. There were no more springs after the road divided and they took the northern arm to Maskana, where they made camp. There may have been some water here, but it was inadequate for such a large force. Further, they had been harassed by Muslim forces throughout the day, the rearguard coming under especially heavy attack. Once the Franks were stationary Saladin sent his right wing under Taqi al-Din and the left wing under Keukbir on a double-envelopment. The Franks were surrounded, both horses and men tortured by thirst. All night the Muslims kept

harassing the Frankish camp and Saladin called up 400 camel-loads of arrows for the next day. On the morning of 4 July, Guy's plight was desperate. The Franks advanced north-westwards to Hattin, where there were springs, although these were held by the Muslims. The Frankish cavalry and foot became separated as the infantry scrambled up the hillside to the illusory cover of the heights (the 'Horns'), and the ancient hillfort of Carn Hattin where, deluged by arrows and choking from grass fires started by the Muslims, they fought a last stand. The cavalry made two charges, probably to the west, aimed at Saladin himself. But they could not break through. Only Raymond of Tripoli's small force burst out and escaped. Guy ordered the pitching of tents and only when his tent fell did the Franks finally surrender.

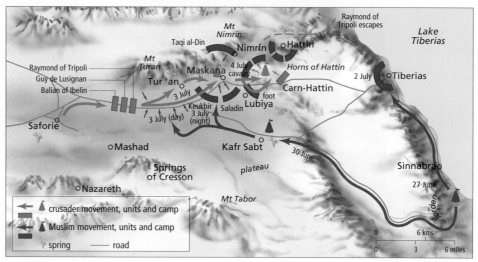

he had used to blunt the Franks' charge at al-Babein in 1167. His tactic was to withdraw the centre, allowing his wings to envelop and destroy the knights. At Darum in 1170, where Saladin mustered over 8,000 cavalry against Almaric's 250 horse and 2,000 foot, the latter remained on the defensive, sheltering his knights behind the infantry's bows and spears. In contrast, at Damascus in 1176, when his Muslim opponents offered battle, Saladin's veterans made short work of them. This may have made Saladin overconfident. In 1177, he led 8,400 well-equipped cavalry from Egypt, raiding as far north as Arsuf and Ramla, while Baldwin IV of Jerusalem sheltered his mere 500 knights under the walls of Ascalon. Summoning the Templars from Gaza and using the coastal route to avoid detection, Baldwin's general, Reynald de Châtillon, struck at Mont Gisart (Kefr Menachem, 16 miles, 26 km from Ascalon) and routed the scattered Muslims. Saladin learnt the lesson: dispersal and poor deployment were a recipe for disaster.

Strategically, Saladin was building a strong position. In 1177 he ordered the construction of new vessels to replace

the Egyptian fleet which had been destroyed by fire in 1168. By the spring of 1179, sixty galleys and twenty *taride* (horse-transports) were ready at Alexandria. In the early summer they raided Acre, taking 1,000 prisoners. At the same time Saladin threatened the new Frankish castle of Le Chastelet. This provoked Baldwin into a rash response. After an initial success against Farrukh Shah near Beaufort, the Latin infantry and cavalry became separated. On 10 June, at Marj Ayyun, Saladin and his nephew caught the Franks in a pincer movement, dispersing the infantry and capturing nearly all the notables except the king.

The arrival of Henry of Champagne delayed Saladin's exploitation of victory, but when he did move, Le Chastelet fell after only four days (29 August), and was followed up by raids to Sidon and Beirut. This campaign held the key to success over the Franks. A decisive victory in the field left their castles defenceless. Saladin repeated this line of approach in 1182, 1183, 1184, and 1187. It was a good strategy, which drove straight into the Frankish heartlands, impoverished them, and threatened their lifeline ports.

MAP 2

The Third Crusade drew on forces from all parts of western Christendom under the command of Frederick Barbarossa, Philip II of France, and Richard I of England. Frederick's force, which travelled overland, became depleted after he drowned in the river Göksu. Philip and Richard wintered in Sicily, and Richard went on to conquer Cyprus from the Byzantine Isaac Comnenus before joining the assembled forces at Acre in June 1191.

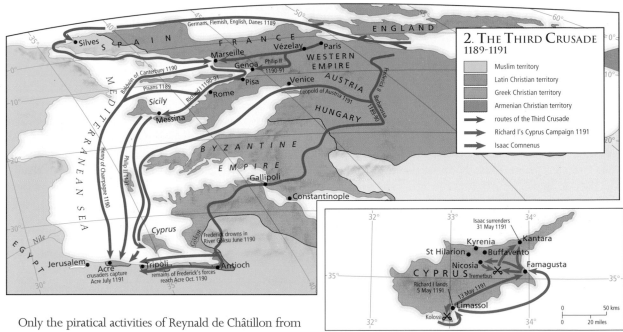

Only the piratical activities of Reynald de Châtillon from his castle of Kerak in the south distracted him. In summer 1181, despite a truce, Reynald raided towards Medina. Two years later he took Aqaba and constructed a fleet with timber carried overland to the port. However, Saladin's Armenian admiral, Lu Lu, responded quickly to crush the expedition. Strategically these were pinpricks, but as the defender of Islam, Saladin had to respond to these attacks on the holy cities of Islam. Sieges of Kerak in 1182 and 1184 were both unsuccessful, however.

More significant events took place in Galilee. In July 1182, Saladin provoked the Franks into a fighting march to relieve Baisan and they barely escaped intact to the shelter of Forbelet castle. In September 1183, Guy de Lusignan, now regent, led an unusually large force of 1,300 knights, 1,500 other cavalry, and 15,000 foot to 'Ain Jalut, in a fighting march against Muslim skirmishers conducted with exemplary cohesion. Guy did not attack Saladin's camp, was blamed for his lack of enterprise and lost the regency as a result. Memory of this humiliation probably influenced his actions four years later at Hattin. Saladin followed up with a combined land and sea assault (thirty Egyptian galleys) on Beirut, the linchpin to Frankish naval dominance in the Levant. But he lacked siege equipment and thirty-three Latin galleys from Tyre and Acre drove off his fleet. Saladin's weakness at sea was later to prove crucial.

THE CONQUEST OF THE KINGDOM OF JERUSALEM

Saladin attacked the heart of the kingdom again in 1187 (map 1), strengthened by forces drawn from Mosul and Diyarbakir and enraged by another attack by Reynald de Châtillon on a Muslim caravan. He was well aware of the Christian divisions between Guy, crowned king of Jerusalem in 1186, and Raymond of Tripoli (previously regent). A strong raiding party was sent through Raymond's lands, with the count's permission. Incredibly, Gerard de Ridefort led 140 knights against this force of 7,000 at the Springs

of Cresson (1 May) and was one of only three survivors. Only then did Raymond join Guy. On 2 July Saladin besieged Tiberias, held by Raymond's wife, effectively challenging Guy to relieve it. Guy accepted the challenge – perhaps because of his 'failure' in 1183, or because of his obligations to his vassal – and walked straight into a trap. The Christian army was destroyed at Hattin (4 July): the king was captured with most of the kingdom's nobility. Reynald de Châtillon and the knights of the Military Orders were executed.

Saladin moved swiftly to exploit the situation. Within days Acre surrendered. He sent emirs south along the coast to meet al-Adil advancing from Egypt and himself turned northward to Tyre. Conrad, the crusading count of Montferrat, who had just arrived, held the city against him, and Saladin moved north to take Sidon and Beirut. A month later he was back in the south. He used his prisoners to arrange submissions: king Guy persuaded Ascalon, and the Templar Master ordered Gaza, to surrender. Turning to Jerusalem, and despite the efforts of Balian of Ibelin, Saladin took it in a fortnight, but important as the Holy City was, it lacked the strategic significance of Tyre. When Saladin's weary troops refused to engage in a winter siege, the port became the centre for the revival of Frankish hopes. Success continued in 1188. Saladin swept through the County of Tripoli (although the major castles and ports held out) and into the Principality of Antioch. The port of Latakia fell first; inland, Saone, a seemingly impregnable castle, was captured in days by subterfuge. Bourzey, equally strong, was overwhelmed by numbers. Moving north, he took the Templar castles at Darsak and Baghras. Antioch seemed ready to fall, yet Saladin negotiated a truce with its ruler, Bohemond. His troops wished to enjoy their profits and their leaders were increasingly jealous or fearful of his power. Such factors limited what Saladin could achieve, and the nature of the war was changing. Despite success at

Safad and Belvoir (winter 1188-89) and Beaufort (April 1190), his attention was now drawn to defending Acre from Frankish counter-attack, having refused his emirs' advice to destroy its fortifications.

THE 'THIRD' CRUSADE

In the summer of 1189, Guy de Lusignan had led a small force to besiege Acre. This hopeless cause had become the focus for crusader activity. The news of the loss of Jerusalem had finally aroused crusade fervour in Europe. King Philip II of France, Richard I (the Lionheart) of England, and the German emperor Frederick Barbarossa all embarked on the expedition (map 2). Barbarossa, the first to set out (May 1189), was drowned in southern Asia Minor and his

army fell apart, only fragments reaching their goal. Richard and Philip II reluctantly made up their differences at Vézelay in July 1190. Philip contracted with the Genoese to move 650 knights, 1,300 squires, and 1,300 horses. Richard set off for southern France expecting to meet a fleet of ninety-three vessels coming out from England, but they were delayed at Lisbon, so he commissioned fourteen horse-transports at Marseille, each crewed by fifteen sailors and thirty oarsmen and carrying forty knights, forty horses, and forty footmen. These were substantial forces, but they were delayed and wintered with Philip's forces in Sicily. Philip arrived at Acre in March 1191, and left in July, though large French forces remained.

Richard travelled via Cyprus, where he conducted a brilliant campaign against Isaac Comnenus, the Byzantine governor who had detained English crusaders, including Richard's bride (map 2). On 5 May 1191, Richard led a beach assault at Limassol. The following day he landed his horses and won a battle at nearby Kolossi. He pursued Isaac, besieging his castles and routing his forces so consistently that the Greek surrendered within the month. The capture of Cyprus was of great strategic importance for the survival of the crusader states. It was typical of the impact Richard had on warfare in the Holy Land. Within two months of his arrival at Acre the city fell. Negotiations with Saladin

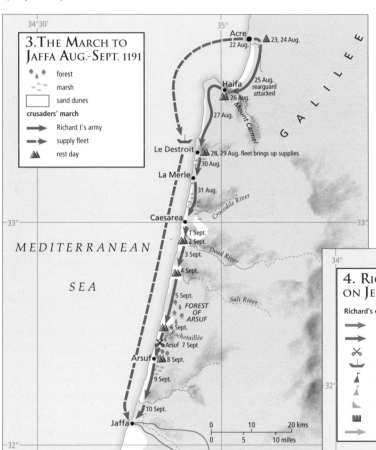

MAP 3

Richard I led his army on a fighting march south from Acre to Jaffa. With the sea covering one flank, where the crusader fleet cruised to supply and support the army, he proceeded under constant attack from Muslim forces. The advance was slow and well disciplined. Rest days, always near a water supply, when the fleet could bring up food and rescue the

wounded, alternated with marches. Only a few miles could be covered each day because of the heat and incessant attacks. Footmen collapsed from the heat; knights lost their horses to archery. Saladin only finally offered battle at Arsuf, a few miles north of Richard's destination.

MAP 4

Richard's advance on Jerusalem depended upon reconstructing fort-ifications destroyed by Saladin. Those on the coast were extensively rebuilt, but it was more difficult to do this inland. Advance beyond Beit Nuba proved impossible, as the wells had been poisoned. Richard's raid on an Egyptian caravan raised morale but had no long-term effect. Saladin's counter-strike at Jaffa, launched after Richard's retreat from Jerusalem, proved short-lived, but ensured the stalemate would not be broken.

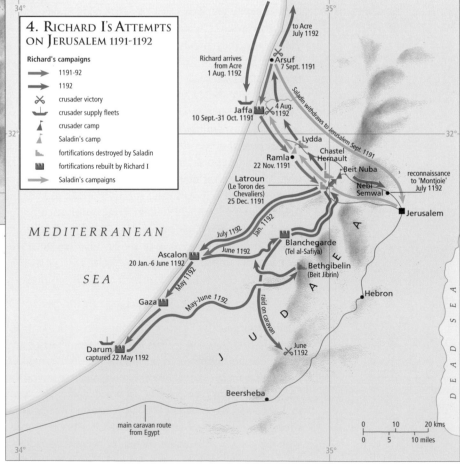

ARSUF 7 SEPTEMBER 1191

The battle at Arsuf proved the testing ground of Richard's move to take the crusade south from Acre to Jaffa, and thence to Jerusalem. On 6 September, the crusaders camped in the cover of a marsh. Morning revealed the Muslim army in the two-mile gap between the sea and the hills. Richard's cavalry comprised twelve units, each with perhaps 100 knights. The infantry wings may have numbered 10,000. Saladin may have had twice as many men, with a preponderance of cavalry. On the morning of 7 September, the crusaders set out for Arsuf. At mid-morning a mass of Muslim cavalry attacked in well-ordered squadrons. Their infantry also closed to skirmish with bows and javelins. The Hospitallers in the rear lost many horses, and eventually found themselves forced back upon the French squadrons in front. Richard was waiting until the

enemy's horses were exhausted. But the heat and casualties, especially among their horses, began to erode the crusaders' patience. The Hospitallers charged, taking some French knights with them. Richard reacted swiftly. As the crusader vanguard reached the gardens at Arsuf, his knights charged. They broke through and pursued the enemy for a mile. English and Norman squadrons advanced to support them. An attack by Saladin's 700 bodyguards was repulsed. Meanwhile, the camp at Arsuf now provided a base from which to launch counter-charges. In response to a last attack on his rearguard, Richard led a third charge and swept the Muslims back into the woods. Arsuf was not as 'decisive' as once thought. The alleged Muslim losses of 32 emirs and 7,000 men did not prevent them from returning to harass the next day.

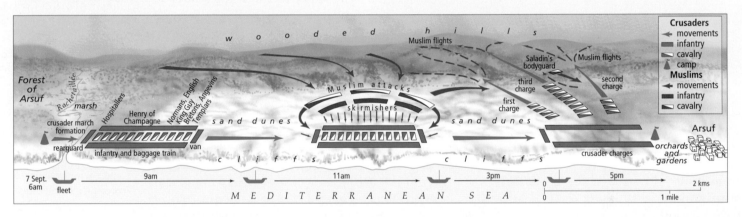

proved fruitless, and Richard had 3,000 prisoners massacred as a statement of intent before marching south down the coast to Jaffa (map 3). This 'fighting march' culminated in an encounter outside Arsuf (7 September) in which Saladin's forces were routed. While this victory was not decisive it made possible Richard's real task – the recovery of the coast and the approach to Jerusalem (map 4). First, he had to rebuild Jaffa as a base for the advance inland. This began on 31 October, but was very slow. Reconstruction of Ascalon and of castles to protect the route and line of communications took place at the same time as negotiations with Saladin. By 22 November the crusaders had reached Ramla. On 12 December, Saladin was compelled to disband his army and withdraw to Jerusalem. By Christmas, the main crusader force had reached Beit Nuba, 12 miles (20 km) from Jerusalem. However, torrential rain made further advance impossible and by 20 January 1192, Richard was back at Ascalon, where the army remained until the spring. Political machinations saw Guy replaced as king of Jerusalem by Conrad of Montferrat, who was promptly murdered and succeeded by Henry of Champagne. At least Henry could work with Richard, and by mid-June the crusaders were once more at Beit Nuba. They got no further. Saladin had a strong army and had poisoned the springs around

Jerusalem. Richard proposed a strike at Egypt instead, to deprive Saladin of his main strength and supply base, but too many crusaders refused. Eventually, on 4 July, the army withdrew.

Richard now marched north to attack Beirut. Aware of the move, on 27 July, Saladin made a dash for Jaffa and seized the town, although the citadel held out. Alerted to this threat at Acre, Richard embarked a small force, sailed south, and stormed the beaches to rescue the garrison on 31 July. After failed negotiations Saladin attacked at dawn on 4 August. A hastily gathered line of spearmen, shielding crossbowmen, beat off attack after attack. The Muslims had lost surprise and lost heart. They were unhappy that they had not been allowed to plunder Jaffa. Eventually Richard mounted up with a mere ten knights and drove the Muslims back. Once more his knightly qualities had achieved an extraordinary victory. But neither he nor Saladin could gain a decisive advantage. On 9 October, Richard finally sailed for home, having failed to recapture Jerusalem. Saladin, who was already ill, died the following spring. The military balance had swung to the Franks and was exploited in the confusion following his death. But Saladin's conquests were a remarkable achievement and it took an equally good opponent in Richard to begin rebuilding the crusader states.

THE LATIN CONQUEST OF CONSTANTINOPLE 1202-1311

T HE CONQUEST OF CONSTANTINOPLE during the Fourth Crusade was a major military achievement. The city's walls had defied the attacks of Goths, Avars, Arabs, and Russians for eight centuries. Nothing seemed surer than their invulnerability. Yet the crusaders, aided by Venetian vessels and engineering, captured the city twice within the space of a year. The Latin empire they set up was not successful and ended in 1261, when the Greeks recovered Constantinople. Other Frankish states in Greece were more long-lived, as the magnificent castles of the Peloponnese still bear witness. They survived under the successive suzerainty of Anjou, Aragon, and Venice until finally succumbing to the advancing Ottoman Turks in the fifteenth century.

This eleventh-century Byzantine military treatise envisages ships linked together to form siege towers for an amphibious assault. Ironically, it was just such devices which enabled the crusaders to storm Constantinople's walls in 1203 and 1204. Without Venetian naval expertize it would have been impossible to over-come the technological and navigational problems presented by such an assault. Robert of Clari, a crusader eyewitness, describes three armoured knights abreast crossing the 'flying bridges' suspended from the ships' mastheads onto the city walls.

THE FOURTH CRUSADE 1202-1204

In 1198, pope Innocent III encouraged a largely French crusade to be led by Theobald of Champagne. The count died before setting out, but his marshal, Geoffrey of Villehardouin, wrote a detailed account of the expedition (from the point of view of one of the leaders). Robert of Clari, an ordinary knight, also left a chronicle. They provide very important insights into the naval, military, and siege operations.

Villehardouin was amongst the ambassadors who negotiated a price with the doge of Venice for the transport of 4,500 knights, 9,000 horses and squires, and 20,000 foot soldiers. Barely half this number turned up at Venice in October 1202, and the crusaders found themselves in hock to the Venetians. In delaying payment, they became involved in expeditions for Venice's benefit: first against Christian Zara on the Dalmatian coast, and then against Constantinople in support of Alexius, son of the deposed emperor Isaac Angelus.

The Italian maritime republics, and Venice in particular, were in the forefront of developing naval architecture. Their 'roundships' were large by contemporary standards and tall enough to bring alongside Constantinople's walls and overtop them. The fleet arrived on 24 June 1203 and landed first at Scutari (map 1). On 6 July, while their ships broke the chain across the Golden Horn, the Franks stormed the Galata Tower. The Venetians had long maintained a quarter in the city and their advice must have been valuable in assessing where next to attack its walls.

The Blachernae Palace complex in the north-east corner was identified as a weak spot, a less well-defended salient accessible by land and sea. The Franks constructed a camp opposite and bombarded it with their siege engines. On 17 July, there was a combined assault. The Franks used a ram and ladders, briefly getting some men on the walls before being driven off. The seaborne attack was carried out by means of 'flying bridges', that is, bridges of planks wide enough for three men suspended from the mast-tops

so that they could be swung onto the walls. These were constructed of ships' yards and given canvas and leather coverings to protect the assault troops from Greek fire and artillery stones. While crossbowmen kept the defenders' heads down, the roundships' artillery and rams created a breach. As the flying bridges began to feed men onto the walls, Enrico Dandolo, the eighty-year-old doge, drove his galleys forward to seize gates in the Petrion sector. The Venetians gained control of some twenty-five to thirty towers (about a quarter of those on the eastern wall), but could not advance any further in the face of strong resistance.

The decisive encounter came the following day on the plain to the north of the city where emperor Alexius brought out his troops to attack the Franks. The crusaders reacted cautiously, deploying three 'battles', or divisions, of combined horse and foot against the Greeks' nine larger bodies. Baldwin of Flanders' battle led the way, followed by Henry of Hainaut's and Hugh of St Pol's. Fearing encirclement, Baldwin drew back, but confusion ensued when St Pol refused retreat as dishonourable. The Franks edged to within crossbow range, and probable disaster, when Alexius decided to withdraw. Relieved, and halted by a stream, Baldwin regained control and pulled the crusaders back into camp. Although there had been no fighting, Alexius' loss of nerve was his undoing; he fled, and Isaac Angelus was restored.

The crusaders became embroiled in Veneto-Byzantine politics. Alexius IV, now co-emperor, was unable to pay what he had promised, and it was too late in the year to sail to the Holy Land. They renewed their treaty with the Venetians, but friendly relations with the Greeks proved impossible. In August, the intolerant crusaders burnt half the city whilst attacking the Muslim quarter. In mid-December, the Greeks launched fire ships against the Venetian fleet, who avoided any loss, and repeated the exploit when the Greeks tried again, with a great line of fire ships chained together, on 1 January. The last straw for

MAP 1

Constantinople had withstood assault for 800 years; yet it fell to the maritime and siege technology of the Latins. By attacking the weak spot where the Blachernae Palace had been built, and combining with amphibious assault from the Golden Horn, the crusaders took the city twice in under a year.

the crusaders was when a coup within the city brought Alexius V to the throne (28 January), who began a more energetic campaign against them.

Within a few days Alexius V attacked a crusader force returning from a raid on Philia, on the Black Sea coast. Outnumbered, the crusaders discarded their lances in favour of swords and, despite the odds, routed the Greeks and captured the miraculous icon of the Virgin which the Patriarch bore. Although victorious in the field, the crusaders were forced to eat their horses as food ran out. Making an agreement to divide the spoils, the crusaders and Venetians set about peparing for a second assault.

Mangonels and petraries assailed Blachernae Palace from the land as rams and tortoises were prepared to attack the base of the walls. At sea, the Venetians mounted stone-throwers on their ships and covered the vessels with hides

on timber frameworks to protect themselves against Greek fire and artillery. They also raised up the flying bridges, for Alexius V had constructed timber hoardings to raise the wall height to that of the towers, and the towers still higher. He also had a double ditch dug in front of the walls to prevent the approach of siege engines. These precautions proved sufficient against an assault on 8 April, combined with a south wind which prevented the Venetian vessels from closing on the towers. Suffering some 100 casualties, the attackers withdrew. Four days later they returned, roping forty of the larger roundships together in pairs to attack each tower.

This time the north wind favoured the attackers, driving their ships against the towers. A courageous group established a foothold; then other towers fell. Meanwhile, Aleaumes of Clari, a fighting priest who was also the

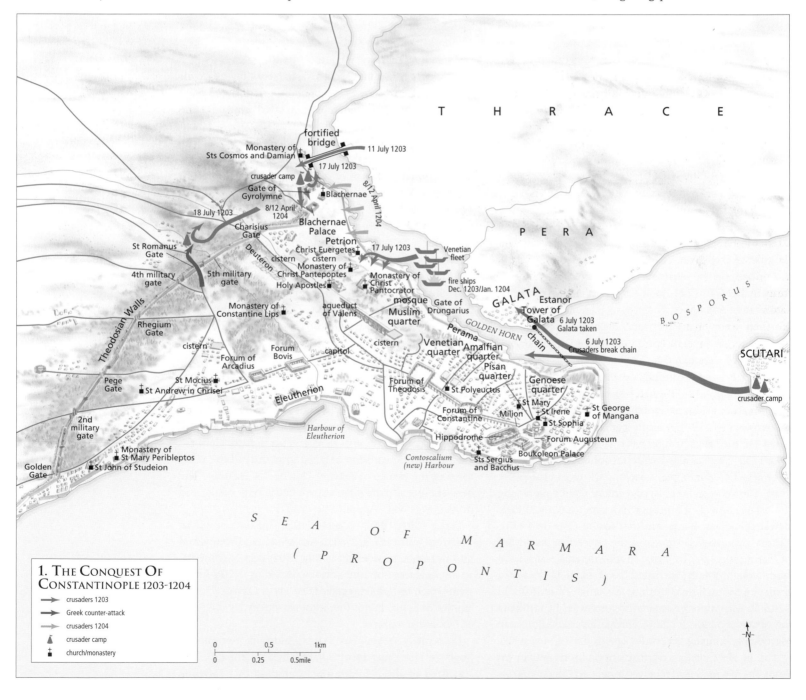

chronicler's brother, crept through a hole excavated in a postern gate, and, chasing off the defenders, bought time for others to unbar a larger gate. This let in the crusader cavalry and secured the bridgehead. Despite the emperor's encouragements, he could not get his troops or citizens to expel them. That night another great fire, the third since the crusaders' arrival, swept through the city, destroying half its houses. Alexius fled, leaving the crusaders to gain much booty, both in wealth and sacred relics.

THE LATIN EMPIRE

In accordance with the terms of the treaty made before the capture, an election was held and Baldwin of Flanders chosen emperor; but it was Venice which gained the financial rewards of victory. A year later, whilst trying to assert themselves against the Bulgarians in Thrace, the Latins suffered a disastrous defeat (*map* 2) in battle at Adrianople (5 April 1205). The Bulgarian tsar Kalojan planned an ambush with his horse-archers which trapped the western knights in a reckless charge. Baldwin was captured, and count Louis of Blois and many other leaders were killed. The remnants of the force, including Geoffrey of Ville-hardouin, were rescued by Dandolo and a relief column, the doge dying soon afterwards. Another crusader leader, Boniface of Montferrat, also died in an ambush in 1207. Meanwhile, in 1206, Baldwin's younger brother Henry became emperor and ruled for ten years, establishing a territory in Thrace and warring with rival Greek 'empires': Nicaea, Trebizond, and Epirus.

In 1211, Henry attacked Theodore Laskaris' Nicaean state in conjunction with Kaj-Khusrau I, the Seljuk sultan, and the ruler of Trebizond. Theodore's victory over the Seljuks at Antioch, on the Meander, secured a border-defining treaty in 1214. In 1224, John Vatatzes of Nicaea drove the Latins out of Asia Minor by defeating them at Poimanenon. He then went on to recover Adrianople and Thrace. Meanwhile, in western Epirus Theodore Dukas began a campaign of reconquest. In 1215 he took Macedonia, in 1221 Serres, and extinguished the Latin kingdom of Thessalonica in 1224. He had himself crowned emperor and threatened Constantinople, but was defeated by the Bulgarians in 1230. Yet in the generation following the conquest, the Latins had lost over half their territory.

In 1234, Vatatzes allied with tsar John Asen of Bulgaria to besiege Constantinople, assaulting the city in successive years. The Venetian fleet played a crucial role by preventing the establishment of a proper blockade (having already defeated Nicaean attacks on Rhodes and Crete in 1233). Victory by a smaller force over the Greek fleet in the Sea of Marmara in 1241 confirmed Latin supremacy at sea. On land, though, Vatatzes increased the pressure. He benefited from the Mongol defeat of tsar Koloman of Bulgaria in 1246. In Asia Minor he secured his territories by fortifying the Meander valley, while in Europe he seized Bulgarian Macedonia, bringing his border against that of Michael II's Epirus. In 1252, he forced a treaty upon his rival. Only his death in 1254 prevented renewed assault on Constantinople.

THE BYZANTINE RECONQUEST

In 1259, Michael VIII Paliaologos usurped the Nicaean throne. He moved swiftly to confront a dangerous alliance in western Macedonia comprising Michael II, William II of Villehardouin, prince of Achaea, and 400 cavalry sent by Manfred, king of Sicily. Exploiting differences in the enemy camp, Paliaologos surprised them at Pelagonia, routing them and capturing William and thirty of his barons. The next year he invaded Thrace and besieged Galata unsuccessfully (January-April). For 1261, he prepared carefully, securing pacts with Bulgaria, the Seljuks, and even the Mongols. He also arranged for Genoa to provide him with a fleet to counter Venice's. Yet the city fell almost by accident. A force of 800 Cumans under Alexius Strate-gopolous travelling to attack Epirus, were contacted by a group of *Thelematarioi* (independent farmers who lived around Constantinople). While they took care of the guards, Alexius' men broke through the Pege Gate on the night of 25 July. Astounded, emperor Baldwin fled without a fight.

William of Achaea was released in 1262 in exchange for the castles of Mistra and Monemvasia. He swiftly broke his oath to the new emperor, whose brother Constantine led forces into the Morea, attempting to take Andravida. The Byzantines suffered defeats at Prinitza (1262) and Makry Plagi (1263), securing Frankish rule for a generation.

In 1266, Charles of Anjou conquered Sicily and continued its traditional policy of hostility to Constantinople. He supported William of Achaea with 700 horse and foot in 1270, and infiltrated Albania in 1272. In 1274, his forces were driven back into Durazzo, but he allied himself with Epirus in 1276 and defeated imperial forces in 1277 and 1278. In 1280, an Angevin expedition of 2,700 knights and Muslim horse-archers, with 6,000 foot, attacked Albania, besieging Berat. But its leader fell into an ambush and his troops dispersed (March 1281). The 'Sicilian Vespers' of March 1282, a coup which lost Charles Sicily, ended his eastern ambitions.

During the reign of Andronikos II (1282-1328), military and naval developments weakened the Byzantine empire. Michael VIII had revived the fleet and by 1270 was no longer dependent upon Genoa, but in 1285 his son began cutbacks which undermined these reforms. The 1292 expedition against Epirus deployed some forty Genoese vessels, but the land forces failed to withstand the relief force of the prince of Achaea, Florence of Hainaut. The Genoese link also drew the empire into a long, costly, and fruitless war with Venice (1296-1302).

In late 1301, 10,000 Alans – Turkic Christians of whom half were warriors – arrived in Asia Minor, and were taken into Byzantine service. But in July 1302, near Nicomedia, an imperial force of 2,000 cavalry, including 1,000 Alans, were beaten by 5,000 nomadic horse under Osman, Turkish emir of Bithynia. In this first Ottoman victory lay the seeds of Byzantine collapse.

Desperately seeking any troops, Andronikos employed Roger of Flor's mercenary Catalan Grand Company. This consisted of about 6,500 foot, including the fearsome

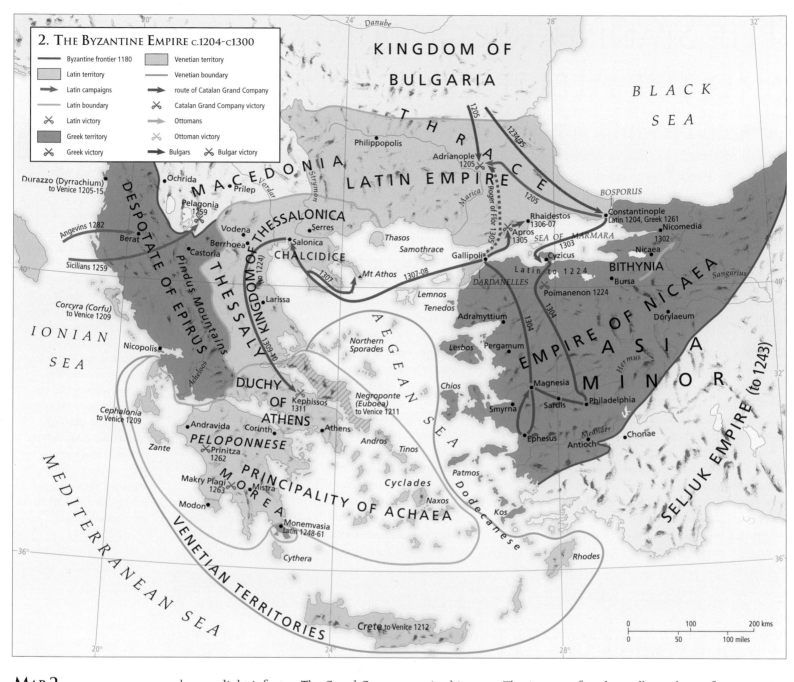

2. THE BYZANTINE EMPIRE c.1204–c1300

Byzantine frontier 1180
Latin territory
Latin campaigns
Latin boundary
Latin victory
Greek territory
Greek victory
Venetian territory
Venetian boundary
route of Catalan Grand Company
Catalan Grand Company victory
Ottomans
Ottoman victory
Bulgars
Bulgar victory

MAP 2

The Latin conquest of Constantinople in 1204 was to have a profound effect on the military viability of the Byzantine state. Although Greek rule was re-established in 1261, much territory remained in Frankish hands. After 1300, small forces of Ottomans and Catalans were able to carve out states amidst the ruins of empire.

almogavar light infantry. The Grand Company arrived in September 1303 and joined the surviving 1,800 Alans. But they fell out and the Catalans killed 300 Alans (including their leader's son) in April 1304, before embarking for Asia Minor. Once in the field they proved effective enough, conducting a wide-ranging raid through Turkish territories. But the Catalans' demands for money resulted in a rebellion, worsened by the revenge killing of Roger of Flor by the Alans. The Grand Company invaded Thrace and crushed a much superior imperial force – from which the Alans deserted – at Apros in July 1305. For the next few years, the Grand Company, now made up of 6,000 Spaniards and 3,000 Turks, ravaged northern Greece. In 1310, the duke of Athens, Walter of Brienne, employed the mercenaries, but they rebelled. At Kephissos, in 1311, they destroyed the Frankish cavalry, killed Walter, and seized his duchy. Their state lasted until 1388.

The impact of such small numbers of mercenaries illustrated how militarily weak the eastern empire had become, whether ruled by Greeks or Latins. Franks served widely both before and after 1204. The conquest did mark another downward step for the military structure of the empire. Greek emperors struggled to reassert the regionally based 'thematic' system which provided soldiers who were raised, supported by land grants, and employed in fortification and the field in their own locality. Michael VIII had successfully encouraged Cuman nomads to serve and to settle on the Anatolian frontier, but strategic necessity required pulling troops out of Asia Minor and into Europe. Despite its strong walls, Constantinople really depended upon Anatolian troops and a good navy for its protection. Once these were gone and northern Greece was prey to Ottoman 'razzias' (raids), the Turkish conquest could only be postponed.

THE SPANISH RECONQUISTA AND THE ALBIGENSIAN CRUSADES

CRUSADES WITHIN WESTERN EUROPE initiated campaigns against the heretics of southern France and the Muslims of southern Spain. The Albigensian crusades (1209-1229) enabled the French kings to extend their authority to the Pyrenees, despite Aragonese intervention (1213). This success sprang from a mastery of siege technique against strongly walled cities and inaccessible castles. In the Iberian peninsula, the Almohad caliph defeated the Christians at Alarcos (1195), but was in turn overcome at Las Navas de Tolosa (1212) by the combined efforts of the Spanish kingdoms. This led to the Reconquista, in which the Military Orders played a great part, of all Muslim Spain except for the kingdom of Granada. In both France and Spain, monarchs used the large forces raised by crusade preaching to good military effect.

Heavily armed Christian cavalry defeat lightly equipped Moors in this thirteenth-century manuscript. The victory is ascribed to the Virgin Mary, depicted on the banner, pointing out the religious inspiration of the Reconquista. Although battles yield colourful representations of warfare, the Christian reconquest really depended upon a fortress strategy based around castles and fortified towns.

THE RECONQUISTA

The arrival of the Almohads in the 1140s had thrown the Christians back on the defensive. In these circumstances, their kings were quite happy to sponsor Muslim buffer states. Sayf ad Dawla, the independent king of Saragossa, took Murcia and Valencia in 1146, but died soon afterwards. His successor in the region was Ibn Mardanish – 'king Wolf' – who although a Muslim spoke Spanish and used Christian troops and equipment. He survived until 1172 at Murcia, dying deserted by his Christian allies. The Military Orders now played the greatest role in frontier warfare, as the Knights of Calatrava illustrate.

They had been established in 1156 to protect Toledo and guard the route south. Alfonso VIII of Castile (1158-1214)

recognized the strategic importance of the 'Campo de Calatrava' and was an enthusiastic patron. By 1174, he had granted them rights to every castle captured from the enemy, one-fifth of his future conquests, and one-tenth of royal revenues. The king of Aragon also rewarded them for the capture of Cuenca in 1177, with Alcañiz castle, to help advance his borders further south of the Ebro (map 1). In 1182, the Order was further strengthened by a pact with the rival Knights of Santiago, reinforced in 1188.

In 1190, the Almohad caliph, al-Mansur, responded to truce-breaking Castilian raids by bringing a large invasion force from Africa to Córdoba. In June, Alfonso VIII mustered at Toledo and then advanced to Alarcos, where he was

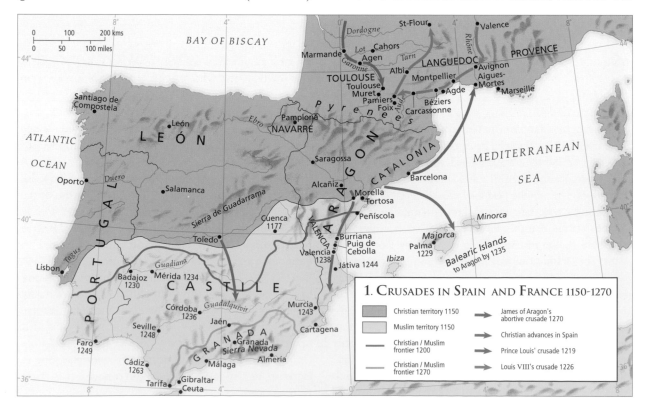

MAP 1

In southern France, prince Louis (later Louis VIII) twice campaigned to mop up the last remnants of resistance to royal control. His successor, Louis IX, was able to devote his crusading activities against the Holy Land. In Spain, the dissolution of the Almohad caliphate by 1231 made possible a rapid conquest of all but Granada in the deep south.

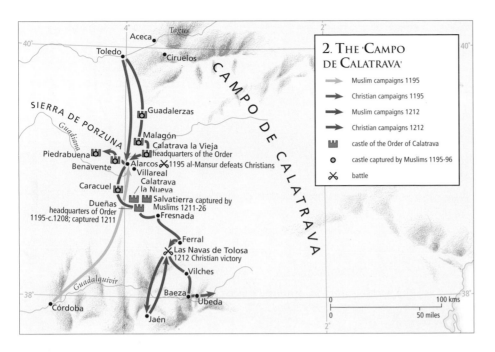

2. THE 'CAMPO DE CALATRAVA'

→ Muslim campaigns 1195
→ Christian campaigns 1195
→ Muslim campaigns 1212
→ Christian campaigns 1212
castle of the Order of Calatrava
castle captured by Muslims 1195-96
battle

MAP 2

Lying between Christian Toledo and Muslim Cordoba, the plains around Calatrava were strategically crucial during the decades on either side of 1200. That is why the Knights of Calatrava had fortified the site and constructed other castles in the region. In 1195, caliph al-Mansur won a victory at Alarcos, and seized the fortresses; but in 1212 the combined forces of Christian Spain turned the tables at Las Navas de Tolosa. This was to prove a decisive point in the progress of the Reconquista. From now on the Muslim states were militarily outmatched.

constructing a town. In early July, his reconnaissance force was annihilated at Salvatierra. Al-Mansur then out-manoeuvred the Christians and inflicted a heavy defeat upon them at Alarcos. As a result, the Knights lost Calatrava and many other castles (map 2). When the Almohads followed up by attacking in the Tagus valley, the Order's Master made the daring decision to occupy Salvatierra, now deep in Muslim territory (1196). While Alfonso VIII made a truce with the Almohads, Peter II of Aragon (1196-1213) went on the offensive, and gave the Knights strong support in the Ebro valley area.

The Castilian truce expired in 1210, and Alfonso resumed his attacks in 1211. Caliph al-Nasir reacted by assembling a large force at Córdoba and advancing on Salvatierra. After destroying a detachment of Knights below its walls, he besieged the castle and its twin fortification of Dueñas. This fell quickly, but the well-supplied main stronghold held out against heavy siege artillery until September. Despite this actual and symbolic loss, it had bought the Christians time, since the campaigning season was now over.

In 1212, the Christians mustered at Toledo. Three kings led forces from all over Spain, all the Military Orders, and substantial numbers of crusaders provided by Innocent III. Setting out on 20 June, the host captured Malagón (24 June) and Calatrava (1 July). At this point the French crusaders abandoned the expedition, dissatisfied with little booty. But the advance continued, to confront al-Nasir at Las Navas de Tolosa on 13 July. In a battle fought on 16 July, the Almohads were defeated and never recovered the initiative.

THE ALBIGENSIAN CRUSADES

By 1200 the dualist heresy of Catharism had taken a strong hold in south-western France. The murder of a papal legate in 1208 led to Innocent III preaching a crusade directed at Raymond VI, count of Toulouse, in 1209. Raymond quickly came to terms, but in 1210 the crusaders invaded the lands

of his neighbour, Raymond Roger of Trencavel. He was viscount of Béziers, which was sacked amidst terrible slaughter of its citizens in July, and of Carcassonne, which promptly surrendered in August (map 3). A minor northern baron, Simon de Montfort, was given the Trencavel lands and set about subduing them. This proved far from easy, for Peter II of Aragon refused to accept de Montfort as his vassal, which encouraged resistance. Pierre-Roger, lord of Cabaret, secure in his inaccessible castle, prosecuted a war of great ferocity against the northerners, but de Montfort held on until spring brought new groups of crusaders.

The siege of Minerve (3 June-22 July 1210) was a blue-print for the Albigensian campaigns. Standing 300 feet (90m) above river gorges which defended it on three sides, it was impregnable to assault. But the northerners' trebuchets were able to batter it into submission. In mid-August 1210, de Montfort besieged Termes, strategically unimportant but a strong Cathar base. Although the outworks fell swiftly, the castle was so high above as to be almost out of range from trebuchets. The siege revealed a weakness in crusading armies. In October, many who had completed their vows departed, encouraging the defenders to hang on. Only the arrival of Lorrainers in November kept the siege going until the construction of a mine (22 November) forced the defenders to break out and flee.

In 1211, the count of Toulouse's failure to root out heresy provided an excuse for an attack on the city. As preliminaries, Cabaret was pressurized into surrender and Lavaur was mined and stormed, its garrison massacred in retaliation for the ambush of some German crusaders (3 May). There seemed plenty of campaigning season left in which to besiege Toulouse. But despite the arrival of Tibald, count of Bar, and his German troops, the task proved too great. Count Raymond was well provided with vassals, notably the contingents of the viscounts of Comminges and Foix. Above all, the city's 3-mile (5-km) circuit of walls made blockade impossible; it was the besiegers who starved. So, after two weeks, on 29 June, the crusaders withdrew, humiliated.

De Montfort could now muster only 800 men at Carcassonne, while Raymond now led 5,000. But, acting on the advice of Hugh de Lacy, a longtime companion, de Montfort advanced to block Raymond's approach at Castelnaudary. This ill-defended town he defended aggressively, while awaiting reinforcements from Lavaur. But their route was blocked by count Raymond Roger of Foix at St Martin-la-Lande, 4 miles (6km) away. De Montfort took the daring risk of sending forty knights, almost half his cavalry, to their aid. In the ensuing battle the crusaders were worsted, but at the last minute de Montfort arrived on the scene with the remaining fifty knights and turned the tables. Raymond lifted the siege of Castelnaudary and retreated. Yet, overall, rebellion and defection left de Montfort in his weakest position so far.

The preaching of crusade in 1212 drew many knights to Spain, but de Montfort also benefited from recruits from Germany, Austria, Dalmatia, and from parts of northern

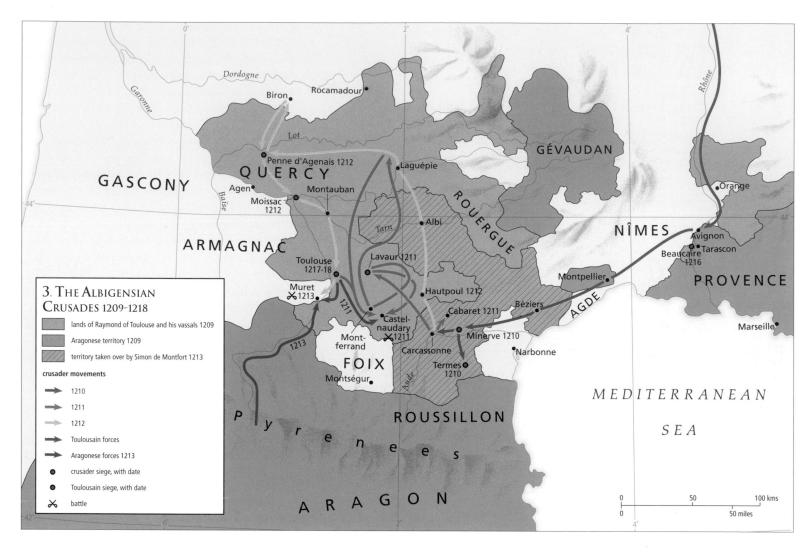

3. THE ALBIGENSIAN CRUSADES 1209-1218

- lands of Raymond of Toulouse and his vassals 1209
- Aragonese territory 1209
- territory taken over by Simon de Montfort 1213

crusader movements

- → 1210
- → 1211
- → 1212
- → Toulousain forces
- → Aragonese forces 1213
- ● crusader siege, with date
- ● Toulousain siege, with date
- ✕ battle

France. In early April, Hautpoul (modern Mazamet) fell. This proved a turning point. The arrival of reinforcements allowed Guy de Montfort to lead the Norman and Champagnard crusaders against the count of Foix, while Simon attacked in the Laurageais with his men from Germany and the Auvergne. Raymond dared not oppose him and Simon de Montfort went on to conquer the areas of the Tarn and the Agenais. Even the strong castle of Penne d'Agenais fell after only seven weeks as its garrison of mercenaries knew that they could expect no relief from the count of Toulouse. The important town of Moissac fell for the same reason, and later Muret, 12 miles (19km) from Toulouse. Only Toulouse and Montauban now opposed de Montfort, as the southern barons brought him their homage.

De Montfort's success brought greater players into the game. Suggestions that he might become count of Toulouse displeased the pope, king Philip of France, king John of England, and king Peter of Aragon. The last was well placed to intervene, being a victorious crusader himself. After Christmas 1212, he marched across the Pyrenees to defy de Montfort, while using his ambassadors at Rome to have the crusades suspended. Despite Innocent III changing his mind about the legitimacy of intervention, Peter took a large force to Muret in September 1213, but de Montfort's victory against Peter, who died in the battle, assured his

supremacy in the region. He became 'dominator' (though not count) of Toulouse. The city still rejected him though, and repulsed an attack in the spring of 1214. When king John, a supporter of Raymond VI, arrived in Aquitaine he looked to restore the count. But the defeat of Bouvines ended the threat. In April 1215, prince Louis arrived with an army which persuaded Toulouse to submit and accept the destruction of its defences.

While the father had been defeated, Raymond, his son, led a resurgence supported by the Rhône towns of Marseille, Avignon, and Tarascon. He challenged de Montfort by besieging Beaucaire (on that river) in late April 1216. The crusaders were too dispersed to react quickly and no relief force arrived until 5 June. By this time the besiegers had taken the town and outworks and entrenched themselves against attack. De Montfort was unable to prevent the surrender of the castle on 24 August. Returning to Toulouse, he vented his anger on its citizens, provoking a riot. Establishing his son Guy as lord of Bigorre and attempting to oust the count of Foix further increased his enemies.

When, in September 1217, Raymond VI launched a long-delayed invasion from across the Pyrenees, he reoccupied Toulouse and feverish refortification began. Although this was extemporized around churches and towers, 1,000 yards (900m) of trenches proved enough to keep the Montfortians

MAP 3

The initial invasion of 1210 took Raymond, count of Toulouse, off guard. Simon de Montfort proved an able commander. He pursued sieges to their conclusion, and his heavy cavalry won victories at Castelnaudary (1211) and Muret (1213). Although crusader numbers fluctuated wildly, their determination in difficulty and constant reinforcement from all over Europe guaranteed their triumph. De Montfort's death in 1219 enabled a Toulousain recovery, but this lasted only until 1226.

at bay. They spent the winter south of the city, and only resumed assaults in the spring. Despite reinforcements, de Montfort could make no headway on the east or west sides of the town, and the Toulousains still held the river between. On 25 June, they launched a sally against a great *cat* (mobile shelter). Rushing to its defence de Montfort, in the thick of the fight, was struck on the head by a stone from a trebuchet and killed. De Montfort's heir, Aumary, lacked his father's drive and military skill; between 1218 and 1224, the southerners recovered all they had lost.

The next crusade was a royal one, led by Louis VIII of France in May 1226. As a result of an attack on the vanguard of the royal host by the citizens of Avignon, Louis besieged the city until it surrendered on 9 September. But Raymond VII had been unable to raise forces from his war-weary vassals, and the belated campaign became little more than a royal progress. Although Louis died on the way home, the south had finally been conquered.

JAMES THE CONQUEROR 1213-1276

When his father died at Muret, James was a hostage of Simon de Montfort, and only five years old. But in 1214 he was recognized as ruler of Aragon and Catalonia. He survived internal dissensions to attack the Moors in 1225-26, although without success. His conquests began in 1228 with an attack on Majorca. On 5 September, 150 ships, 800 knights, and several thousand foot set out. They met little resistance on landing, but the siege of the

island's capital took until 21 December, ending in a bloody sack. This encouraged quick surrenders elsewhere, although further royal expeditions were necessary in 1231-32. Minorca submitted in 1231, and Ibiza fell in 1235, completing the conquest of the Balearics.

James also advanced into Valencia, taking the castles of Morella, Burriana, and Peñíscola (1232-33). The Aragonese baronage initiated such attacks, while the king insisted on hearth taxes to pay for expeditions. The conquest of Valencia itself began by using the Puig de Cebolla as a base for attacks on the city. By having his expedition preached as a crusade, James raised forces from as far afield as England. The siege lasted from April until 28 September 1238. The taking of Játiva (1244) and Biar (1245) completed the conquest, although rebellions continued for longer.

In general, James worked in co-operation with the kings of Castile. In 1264, Alfonso X asked for aid against revolts in Andalusia and Murcia, which were sponsored by the Muslim king of Granada. James responded by taking Murcia in a winter campaign (January 1266), and handing the city over to Castile. James' ambitions were thwarted north of the Pyrenees, but his reputation spread as far as the court of Kublai Khan. The Mongol offered a joint expedition against Islam, and James even set out in 1269. But the bulk of the fleet was driven by a storm into Aigues-Mortes and only a few vessels reached Syria. Denied glory in the Holy Land, James had to remain satisfied with his achievements at home.

THE BATTLE OF MURET

'William des Barres took command, deploying the three divisions leading the charge against the Toulousain camp. They galloped across the marshy plain, banners flying and pennons on high. Gold flashes on helmets and shields, hauberks, and swords glitter in the sunlight. The good king of Aragon, when he saw them, rallied a small group of companions and vassals to oppose them; but the Toulouse militia fled, despite the pleas of king and count. They knew nothing of the attack until the French arrived in the vicinity of the king. He yelled "I am the king!"; but no one heard and he was struck and badly wounded, his blood pouring on the ground. There he lay dead. The rest gave themselves up for lost, one running here, another there, while the French rode amongst them, cutting them down... The Toulousains, rich and poor, dashed into the river Garonne, some swam across, but many drowned.' *The Song of the Crusade against the Albigensians*, William of Tudela c.1220.

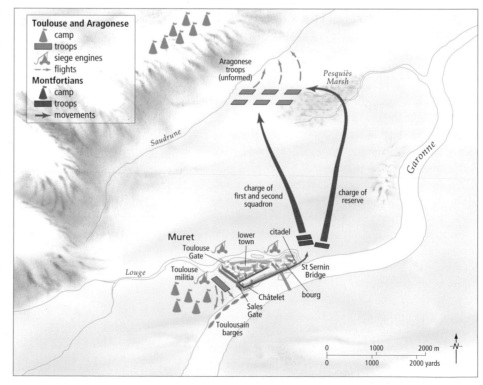

THE CRUSADE IN AFRICA IN THE THIRTEENTH CENTURY

T HE THIRTEENTH-CENTURY CRUSADES *saw a decisive shift of emphasis to attacking Egypt. The expeditions of 1217-21 and 1248-50 became bogged down in the Nile Delta, and both ended with the crusaders captured and subject to heavy ransoms. These disastrous campaigns bracketed the successful expedition of the German emperor Frederick II, who recovered Jerusalem by diplomacy, not in battle. The second crusade of Louis IX of France, against Tunis in 1270, ended with his death, although Edward of England did reach Syria. The real military contribution to the defence of the Latin Kingdom was St Louis' extensive modernizing of its coastal fortifications in 1250-54. That this proved inadequate was due to Egypt's military renaissance under the Mamluks, notably sultan Baibars.*

THE FIFTH CRUSADE

The failure of this crusade has been blamed on the interference of the papal legate, cardinal Pelagius. This is unfair, although it is true that divisions between the leaders undermined consistent strategy-making. This was a result of the continual arrival and departure of prominent lords and their contingents, who campaigned for perhaps only one or two seasons.

The first wave came in autumn 1217 (map 1), and included Leopold, duke of Austria, a veteran of the Third Crusade, and Andrew, king of Hungary. Together with John of Brienne, king of Jerusalem, they campaigned ineffectually in Syria, whilst building up huge supplies of food and fodder. King Andrew and many Hungarians left in January 1218, but Rhenish and Frisian reinforcements arrived in the spring. The attack on Egypt (map 2) was launched by sea, which required besieging Damietta, a fortress town in the Nile Delta. Only when this was taken could the crusaders advance on Cairo.

Damietta stood 3 miles (5km) from the mouth of the Nile, on the right bank. Behind the town lay Lake Manzalah, making it accessible only by water. The eyewitness account of Oliver of Paderborn describes three defensive walls, each higher than the other. The middle wall had twenty-eight towers and there was a moat between it and the outer wall, wide enough to accommodate vessels. A chain stretched across the river, secured in a wall-tower and a tower on the left bank, protected by a bridge of boats. The crusaders had to overcome this barrier and set up camp opposite the chain-tower, which they bombarded with artillery. The water surrounding the tower was too shallow for their vessels, yet it would only fall to close assault. This type of fighting put a premium on leadership and heroism, in which duke Leopold excelled.

On 23 June, there was a general assault of seventy to eighty ships, but without success. Flying-bridges were employed, and during another assault, on 1 July, a ship's mast broke under the weight of the armoured knights, who

fell into the river. The defenders fought back stoutly, aided by numerous engines and Greek fire. Technology was needed to back up heroism. Oliver of Paderborn designed a floating siege tower made of two ships bound together, bearing four masts which formed the uprights of a square wooden tower, covered in hides. Projecting from the tower was a bridge extending 30ft (9m) beyond the prows, with another at forecastle level. Despite a vigorous defence, the chain-tower was taken on 24 August. The crusaders were

This picture of the sea walls at Acre represents St Louis' real achievement: the rebuilding of fortifications on the Syrian coast. Even so, they were unable to repel the determined attacks of the Mamluk sultans without the manpower provided by crusading expeditions.

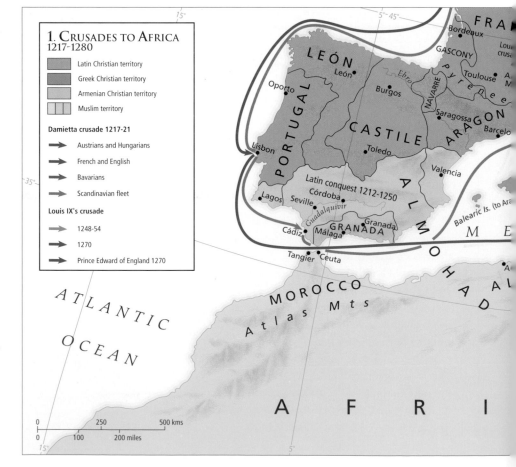

gaining the upper hand and received large reinforcements from England, France, and Italy in the autumn, accompanied by the papal legate Pelagius.

Al-Kamil, son of sultan al-Adil, had been commanding Egyptian forces in the area since June, but had made no move. His father's death on 31 August freed him to act. He launched attacks on the crusaders on 9 and 26 October; both were repelled with difficulty. Seeking freedom to manoeuvre upriver, the crusaders re-excavated an old canal to bypass Damietta and the river now clogged with wrecks. A fierce winter storm on 29 November ended these works and almost swamped their camp. Stalemate set in and the crusaders began to suffer from scurvy which devastated their number in the winter of 1218-19.

In the spring of 1219, al-Kamil moved again, launching a heavy attack on 31 March, supported by seventy ships. Leopold's heroism was crucial in finally repelling the assaults. The ordinary crusaders felt the loss deeply when he left for home with his contingent in May. Unhappy with their leaders' defensive strategy, they demanded an attack on the Muslim camp (29 August). But the Egyptians feigned retreat and drew the crusaders after them into the desert. Lacking discipline, the crusaders began to withdraw and then to flee. The Templars, Hospitallers, Teutonic Knights, and great feudatories covered the retreat, but there were heavy losses. Al-Kamil attempted to exploit the situation by negotiations and bribery, but to no avail. Aware of the desperate state of Damietta's defenders, he attacked again in early November, only to be repulsed from the crusader

camp. On 5 November, the city finally fell to assault, the crusaders finding the defenders either dead or dying from starvation.

The year 1220 was spent in consolidation. The crusaders established another camp on the right bank of the Nile and awaited the arrival of Frederick II. But he never came. His absence emphasized the lack of leadership and lack of momentum; crusaders left the camps, but only a few Italians arrived. Meanwhile, al-Kamil received Syrian reinforcements led by his brother al-Mu'azzam. When the crusaders began their advance in July 1221 they numbered 1,200 knights and 4,000 archers, supported by 630 ships. Cairo was in panic and al-Kamil offered peace terms. But the crusaders had overreached themselves. They advanced into a narrow triangle of land between branches of the Nile opposite Mansurah and were trapped as the river began to rise. Pelagius may have been responsible for this strategic blunder. Al-Kamil surrounded them by sending ships down the al-Mahallah canal, sinking four to block the Nile. Meanwhile, his brother's land forces circled around to the north-east. Forced into retreat, the crusader army collapsed and surrendered at Baramun on 29 August 1221. They bought their freedom with the hard-won town of Damietta.

ST LOUIS' CRUSADE IN EGYPT

Louis IX of France set out for Egypt in August 1248. His was a well-planned expedition, centrally directed and funded by the richest kingdom in Europe. Perhaps it could succeed where the Fifth Crusade had failed? He had constructed the

MAP 1

Thirteenth-century crusaders saw control of Egypt as essential to recovering the Holy Land. The Nile Delta campaign of 1218-21 was almost successful, but it collapsed when lines of communication stretched too far inland. St Louis' crusade followed much the same course. From 1250, the Mamluk sultanate proved a formidable opponent. St Louis' 1270 crusade was diverted to Tunis, although the lord Edward's was helpful in northern Syria.

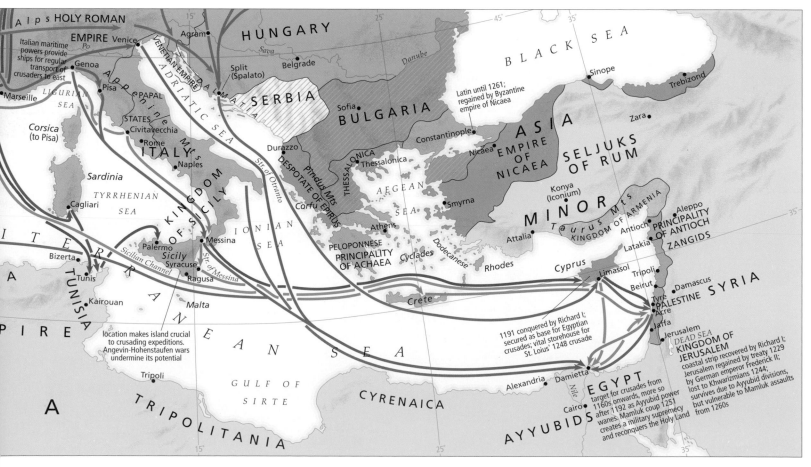

fortress-port of Aigues-Mortes as a base, and had a large and well-equipped fleet of the most modern vessels. It sailed first to Cyprus in September, and then wintered there while the island was made a vast forward supply dump. His forces were large by contemporary standards: about 2,500 knights and 10,000-12,000 foot soldiers. His strategy was designed to take the Nile floods into account. He reached Damietta on 4 June 1249 (map 3); two days later it was in crusader hands. Sultan Ayub was very ill and its defenders could elicit no message of support from him.

Yet Louis did not move on Cairo immediately. He waited for the Nile floods to subside and for reinforcements led by his brother Alphonse of Poitiers to arrive from France. Only in October did the advance to the next objective, Mansurah, begin. A huge fleet carried supplies and siege engines while the army marched down the left bank. Progress was slow because of the feeder streams and canals running into the Nile, and it was not until 21 December that the host reached the city. The crusaders made camp between two branches of the river and sought to cross the canal which still separated them from Mansurah.

First, they built a causeway, protecting the engineers with covered sheds; but the defenders dug out the far side as fast as the attackers advanced. The Muslims also bombarded the crusaders with Greek fire, whose terrifying effects are so vividly described by Joinville, Louis' biographer. Since the causeway approach was proving futile, Louis sought to find a ford and outflank the town. Early in February 1250, a renegade Muslim brought news of one; the attack was launched on the night of 7 February.

The order of march was carefully planned, with a vanguard under the king and his brothers, and a rearguard left in camp under the duke of Burgundy. The infantry missilemen were to cross the river by a pontoon bridge to bring archery support to the knights. Initially the attack went well, as the vanguard fell upon the sleeping Muslims and destroyed their artillery. But Robert of Artois, despite the advice of the Templar Master, charged ahead into the town. Once caught in the narrow streets and unsupported by their crossbowmen, the count and many other knights were massacred. Some fought their way out to be rescued by the rest of the cavalry, this time covered by bowmen who kept the Muslim cavalry at bay. The crusaders were forced onto the defensive by determined attacks on 11 February. Egyptian forces grew with the arrival of the new sultan, Turanshah (28 February). They dug in at the canal bridgehead, but now were themselves besieged in unhealthy conditions. Turanshah had galleys taken overland from a tributary to the Nile, cutting off the crusaders' supplies. On 16 March, thirty-two of their vessels were captured, and eighty in all before Louis finally recognized the inevitability of retreat.

The crusaders were suffering from heavy attacks and succumbing to dysentery and typhus. On 5 April, with the sick and wounded loaded onto ships, the retreat began. Louis, however, insisted on accompanying the march by land, yet he was so ill that he had continually to be helped from his horse, and progress was pitifully slow. The pontoon bridge across the Bahr al Saghir was left intact, a mistake which enabled the Muslims to swarm over in pursuit.

MAP 2

The siege of Damietta was central to the Fifth Crusade. The city held out from June 1218 to November 1219, until the crusaders' floating siege towers breached its defences. In July 1221, the long-delayed crusader advance on Cairo began. But surrounded and forced to surrender short of their objective, they bought their freedom with the return of Damietta.

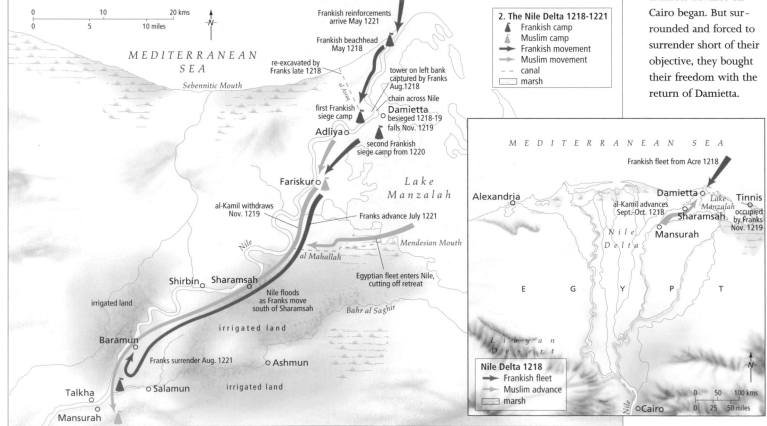

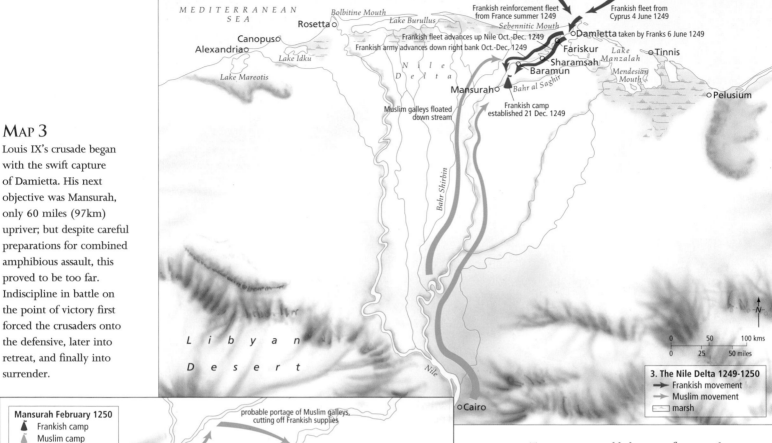

MAP 3

Louis IX's crusade began with the swift capture of Damietta. His next objective was Mansurah, only 60 miles (97km) upriver; but despite careful preparations for combined amphibious assault, this proved to be too far. Indiscipline in battle on the point of victory first forced the crusaders onto the defensive, later into retreat, and finally into surrender.

Meanwhile, the fleet was attacked by Muslim galleys and the wounded slaughtered, save for those wealthy enough, like Joinville, to offer a ransom.

This was to be the fate of the entire army; Louis was forced to surrender. As in 1221, the crusaders had to buy their freedom. Damietta was returned to Turanshah with 400,000 *bezants* in payment. The coup engineered by the Mamluk Baibars, who assassinated the sultan, made no difference to the outcome. In fact, the ransom was less than a year's income for Louis. After his release he remained in the Holy Land for another four years, spending huge amounts on reconstructing and improving the fortifications of the coastal ports.

THE TUNIS CRUSADE

Louis' second crusade in 1270 is more interesting from the point of view of its careful organization rather than its outcome. Tunis was an unlikely target for crusader activity, for the Latin East was under severe pressure. The Greeks recovered Constantinople in 1261, expelling Baldwin III. The Mongols sacked Baghdad in 1258 and presented both a threat and a potential ally against the Muslims. But sultan Qutuz had decisively defeated the Mongol thrust into Syria at Ain Jalut in 1260. He fell victim to Baibars soon afterwards and it was Baibars who began the reconquest of Syria.

In 1265, Baibars took Jaffa, Arsuf, and Caesarea, settling Mamluks in the captured territories. In 1266, the huge, seemingly invulnerable Templar castle of Safad fell after an eighteeen-day siege. In 1268, he force-marched north, surprised and stormed Antioch. In the circumstances, French resources were badly needed. In addition to his refortification of the coast, Louis had maintained a 'French Regiment' of up to 100 knights, plus support, since his departure in 1254. When he set out in 1270, it was not generally known where he intended to land.

But the target had been chosen as long ago as 1268, and its choice had more to do with the ambitions of Charles of Anjou, Louis' brother, who had recently conquered Sicily, than the needs of the Holy Land. The campaign was a disaster, as the army fell prey to diseases of the camp in the hot July weather. Louis himself died on 25 August, leaving his heir Philip III to make a treaty and withdraw. Edward of England did sail on to Acre, where he played a role in securing a ten-year truce with Baibars in May 1272. This was only a stay of execution for the remnants of the Latin states. Acre fell to the Mamluks in 1291; the last, tiny foothold at Gibelet in 1302.

IV

EUROPE DIVIDED

Wars between England and France were not unusual; but in the mid-fourteenth century there began a series of campaigns called, by nineteenth-century historians, the 'Hundred Years' War'. The struggle for the throne of France dominated the politics and warfare of most of Europe, drawing in not just France, England, and Scotland, but the Empire and its satellites, the Iberian kingdoms, and spilling over into Italy also, creating far-ranging military alliances. The wars' main interest lies in the opportunity they provide to analyze the strategy and tactics of later medieval warfare.

Warfare in the fourteenth and fifteenth centuries was marked by technological developments. Improvements in metallurgy, combined with a desire to combat increasingly effective missile weapons, produced the full suits of shining plate which epitomize the knight to a modern audience. This was essentially a fifteenth-century phenomenon though, and restricted to the wealthy before 1450. Most soldiers still wore coats of plates (brigandines), and were only partly armoured on their limbs.

Gunpowder was first used in warfare in the 1330s, and the early guns were only crude firepots. Cannon did not assume their distinctive cylindrical shape much before 1400, when they were still largely restricted to use in sieges. But there was an acceleration in the development of all types of guns. In the 1420s, Jan Zizka taught the Bohemian Hussites the importance of firepower in his wagon-forts, and these tactics were taken up further west. The fashion in the 1450s was for artillery camps, in other words dug-in guns, especially following the French victory over the Anglo-Gascons at Castillon in 1453, but such was the pace of change that this was comparatively short-lived. By the time of the wars of Charles the Bold and the Swiss in the 1470s, a thoroughly modern army deployed handgunners and mobile artillery on carriages, in a style that prefigured the warfare of the next 300 years.

This did not make the mounted knight redundant. Despite chivalric reverses such as Agincourt (where the bulk of the French men-at-arms fought on foot), the heavily armoured gen d'armes of the French and Burgundian Ordinance Companies enjoyed a revival on the battlefield that lasted until the 1570s. As the French king asserted his authority and the English were expelled from France, large numbers of English longbowmen were employed as mercenaries, or in the series of civil wars which became known as the Wars of the Roses. Like most civil wars where the crown was at stake, these consisted of short, sharp campaigns with high-risk strategies, including many battles. Unfortunately, this unusual form of warfare has been taken by military historians to characterize medieval warfare; something the exploits of Charles the Bold of Burgundy seems to confirm.

But this is a mistaken view, for fortress warfare was as dominant as ever elsewhere. The developments in fortifications represented by the construction of thick, low-lying brick and earth bastions in Italy and bulwarks in north-western Europe, designed to counter gunpowder artillery, quickly remedied any advantage which the attacker possessed over the defender. There was no dramatic change in warfare after 1500, although there were developments, many of which had been prefigured in the preceding two centuries.

THE HUNDRED YEARS' WAR 1337-1396

THE HUNDRED YEARS' WAR *as a term is an invention of nineteenth-century historians. There had been earlier wars between England and France in 1294-97 and 1324-27, over the profitable territories of Gascony. In 1339-40, the stakes were raised by Philip VI's attempts to conquer the region and Edward III's response in claiming the French crown. But, except in Brittany, the first phases of the war saw only brief periods of campaigning: 1345-47, 1355-56, and 1359-60. There were twice as many English expeditions from 1369-89, and the war spread to include Flanders and the Iberian peninsula. This international nature of the conflict — ranging from Scotland to Portugal — made it distinctive and gave the campaigns a kind of unity. It also placed an emphasis upon naval activity.*

CAMPAIGNS 1337-1360

In 1337, the military reputation of the English was not high, but they soon became the most feared troops in Europe. The battle tactic of dismounting men-at-arms and combining them with flanking archery, developed against the Scots, proved almost unbeatable. Numbers of archers grew during the wars from one to one or less in proportion to men-at-arms, to two to one or more. In addition, English armies were very mobile. Experience in Scotland and Ireland had developed the *hobilar*, a light horseman useful in raids. A rising proportion of archers served mounted, as their status and income rose, squeezing out peasant participation. English armies increasingly served for pay through 'indenture', whereby captains, ranging from great lords to esquires, contracted to provide an agreed number of men. This was a flexible system well-suited to overseas expeditions and created 'professional' armies.

In contrast, French royal armies depended heavily upon the military obligations of the chivalrous classes, providing men-at-arms, and a levied infantry or town militias, often of poor quality. Missile-men were commonly Genoese mercenary crossbowmen, drawn from the royal fleets. Such forces proved difficult to muster, being tied down in garrison duty, and being tactically inflexible in the face of the English 'system'.

Certainly English tactics were crucial in providing victories, often against the odds, but this does not mean that the English strategy of *chevauchée* was a battle-seeking one. The *chevauchées* resulting in the battles of Crécy (1346) and Poitiers (1356) were untypical, although both gave Edward important political advantages. The *chevauchées* of the 1370s and 1380s were less successful. The French had learnt not to offer battle, and the English gained no fortifications. They needed to form part of a coherent strategy such as was achieved in 1346-47 and 1356 when Edward co-ordinated attacks in Flanders, Gascony, Brittany, and Normandy to great effect (map 1).

In 1339, Edward's strategy was the traditional one against France – based in Flanders and depending upon large numbers of mercenary knights. After unsuccessfully besieging Cambrai, he settled for devastating the region (map 2).

Philip mustered his army at St Quentin and pursued Edward to La Capelle, wisely refusing battle.

In 1340, the 200 vessels which Philip had collected threatened England with invasion. Crossing in his own smaller fleet, Edward surprised the French and their Genoese allies at Sluys, in the mouth of the Zwijn. The French ships were chained together and, in what was effectively a land battle at sea, English archery swept the enemy decks, allowing their men-at-arms to board. Unable to manoeuvre, the French were overwhelmed, losing '10,000' casualties and all but 30 ships. But the following land campaign achieved no more for Edward than an unsuccessful siege of Tournai. These costly expeditions bankrupted the government and forced a change of strategy.

Edward now exploited divisions within the French kingdom. He supported John de Montfort's claim to the duchy of Brittany, which was strategically placed between England and Gascony, against Philip's candidate Charles of Blois. A French expedition led by Philip's son John, duke of Normandy, captured Nantes (and de Montfort) in November 1341. So in 1342, Edward first sent sir Walter Mauny in March, the earl of Northampton in July, and brought 5,000 to Brest himself in October. He besieged Vannes and once again Philip led an army against him but avoided battle. There had been a battle at Morlaix (30 September), where Northampton's outnumbered force had taken up a strong defensive position and inflicted substantial casualties with the bow before withdrawing. But the support of the lesser nobility and control of a string of fortifications which could be relieved by sea gave the Montfortians the real advantage. When John de Montfort died during the siege of Hennebont in 1345, he left a young heir under English protection. On 20 June 1347, sir Thomas Dagworth surprised and captured Blois at La Roche Derrien. Almost two decades of guerrilla warfare followed. The English established oppressive 'ransom districts' to support their garrisons in Brittany, whose captains made fortunes.

In Gascony, Bertrand de l'Isle was reconquering territory for the French crown. In response, in 1345, Henry de Grosmont, earl of Derby and Edward's lieutenant, took 500

While Edward the 'Black Prince' clearly inherited his father's military virtues, he lacked Edward III's humanity. His gilded tomb in Canterbury Cathedral represents him as a paragon of chivalry – which he was – but although brave in battle and a good general, he failed as a ruler in Aquitaine (1362-72). The disastrous resumption of the war after 1369 was a direct result of his harsh taxation following the great expense of the Castilian expedition.

MAP 1

Edward III's 1339 campaign in Flanders ended in stalemate. Despite his naval victory at Sluys in 1340, his siege of Tournai proved equally fruitless. The Brittany expeditions of 1341-42 were more profitable, and presaged a change in English strategy. Edward's *chevauchée* of 1346 brought victory at Crécy and the capture of Calais in 1347, whilst Henry of Lancaster campaigned equally successfully in Gascony and Poitou. In 1355, Edward, prince of Wales, *chevauchéed* from Bordeaux to the Mediterranean, and in the following year captured king John at Poitiers. The treaty of Brétigny (1360) gave Edward one-third of France in return for renouncing his claim to the throne.

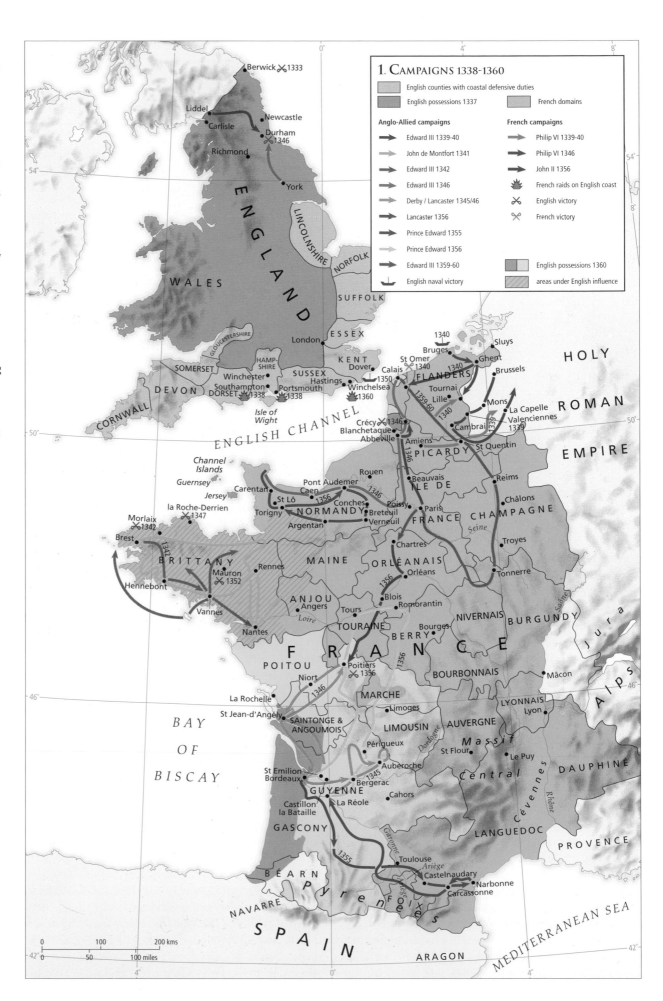

1. CAMPAIGNS 1338-1360

English counties with coastal defensive duties
English possessions 1337
French domains

Anglo-Allied campaigns
Edward III 1339-40
John de Montfort 1341
Edward III 1342
Edward III 1346
Derby / Lancaster 1345/46
Lancaster 1356
Prince Edward 1355
Prince Edward 1356
Edward III 1359-60
English naval victory

French campaigns
Philip VI 1339-40
Philip VI 1346
John II 1356
French raids on English coast
English victory
French victory

English possessions 1360
areas under English influence

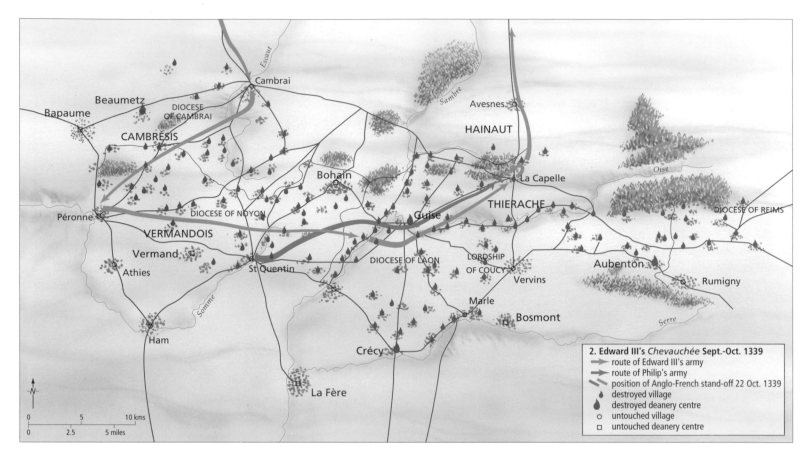

2. Edward III's *Chevauchée* Sept.-Oct. 1339
→ route of Edward III's army
⇒ route of Philip's army
⤢ position of Anglo-French stand-off 22 Oct. 1339
🌢 destroyed village
🌢 destroyed deanery centre
○ untouched village
□ untouched deanery centre

men-at-arms and 2,000 archers and landed at Bayonne (6 June). Advancing on Bergerac, on the Dordogne, with a river fleet, his men immediately stormed the town's suburb. A subsequent assault by men-at-arms on foot, supported by archery from the ships, persuaded the place to surrender (26 August). In October, Derby, with 300 men-at-arms and 600 archers, surprised and captured de l'Isle with many notables while they were besieging Auberoche castle. With no forces left in the field to oppose him, by the end of the year Derby was able to besiege and take La Réole and Aiguillon. It was not until spring 1346 that John of Normandy moved to recover Aiguillon with a large army, including five cannon cast at Cahors and eight trebuchets from Toulouse. That city also provided four barges mounting artillery but, despite heavy bombardment, Aiguillon held out until the news of Crécy forced John to abandon the siege (20 August).

Henry (now duke of Lancaster) resumed the offensive into Poitou in September 1346, capturing towns and castles en route. A forced march and surprise assault took Poitiers (4 October), which was sacked. By the end of October he was back in Bordeaux. He had advanced English authority south along the Garonne, north to the Dordogne, and into the Saintonge and Poitou. The significance of the achievement has not always been recognized because of the prominence given to the Crécy campaign.

A dissident Norman faction encouraged Edward to try his hand in the duchy. He gave out that he was embarking for Gascony, but actually landed in the Cotentin peninsula in Normandy (11 July) with 15,000 men, aiming to join

up with a Flemish force advancing from Flanders. Caen was stormed by land and from his ships (26 July), and sacked. He then made for Rouen, but this was too well-defended and he was forced upriver toward Paris. He challenged the French king to battle at Poissy, but then withdrew across the Seine and made to cross the Somme with Philip in hot pursuit. The English were nearly trapped against the river but fought their way across the ford at Blanchetacque. Edward halted his 10,000 men in a strong defensive position at Crécy. Philip, who had wisely avoided battle previously, found himself carried by the tide of events and the enthusiasm of his nobles (*page 120*). His army was double that of Edward's, but it came on in no real order and was crushingly defeated (25 August). This severely damaged Philip's authority and enabled Edward to besiege Calais largely undisturbed.

Following his defeat at Crécy, and to divert Edward's siege of Calais, Philip VI appealed to king David of Scotland to attack in the north. Early in October, a Scottish army over 10,000-strong captured Liddell castle and advanced on Durham, ravaging as it went. As the city's bishop was with Edward in France, it fell to the archbishop of York to muster the English forces: some 3,000-4,000 men from Cumberland, Northumberland, and Yorkshire. All men from the southern and Midland counties were required for Calais. Without waiting for the Yorkshire contingent, the archbishop marched swiftly to Durham where his forces blundered into the Scots in the fog and repulsed them. He then took up position at Neville's Cross, just outside the city. The Scots were unwilling to attack across ground broken by

MAP 2

A papal envoy's survey of the devastation wreaked by Edward's army in 1339 makes it possible to examine the mechanics of *chevauchée*. Although attempts were made against Cambrai, the bulk of the campaign consisted of ravaging and burning its region, the Cambrésis. Interspersing stops of several days with 10-15 mile (16-24km) marches enabled maximum destruction. Philip VI force-marched to challenge battle, but Edward slipped away unpunished.

ditches and walls in the face of English archery. However, late in the day the archers advanced and stung the Scots into attacking. The result was predictable. First the left and then the right Scots' 'battle' (division) broke and fled, leaving only David in the centre. Although he displayed personal bravery, he was captured along with many of his nobles. David remained in Edward's hands until 1358.

The strategic importance of Calais may be judged by the effort Edward devoted to its capture. He was able to supply his initial besieging force of 10,000-12,000 men both overland from Flanders, despite French attempts to cut this route, and by sea. In fact, the first supply fleet of twenty-five ships was destroyed by Philip's Genoese galleys, but this was the last French success (17 September). Lancaster's operations in Poitou caused Philip most concern and defeat caused severe financial problems. French military operations ceased from the end of October until mid-March 1347. Fighting then focused on the Flanders border, represented by an Anglo-Flemish attack on St Omer and a French assault on Cassel, both unsuccessful. The French also failed to break the dam which would have flooded the land-route to Calais. In late April, the English captured and fortified the sandbank forming the harbour, with a fleet of almost 100 fighting ships. The town's isolation was confirmed by the scattering of a fifty-strong relief convoy (25 June). Philip mustered some 20,000 men at Hesdin, about half of them men-at-arms. However, on arriving outside Calais on 27 July, he found himself outnumbered. Men had flocked to Edward's banner and 5,000 men-at-arms with 6,000 infantry and 20,000 archers, together with 15,000 sailors, served during the siege. His camp was entrenched by land, and the sea was covered by ships. After skirmishing, the French withdrew and Calais surrendered the next day (3 August).

The onset of the Black Death in 1348 brought campaigning to a halt. Its successive ravages, combined with a lack of money and papal peace diplomacy, postponed any large-scale English military activity. When operations resumed in 1355, Edward pursued the same strategy as a decade earlier with attacks in Normandy, Brittany, and Aquitaine, but he did not campaign himself. The *chevauchée* of Edward the 'Black Prince' of Wales, from 5 October to 1 December 1355, is characteristic of the warfare of the period. He led a mobile Anglo-Gascon force of about 4,000 men on a 700-mile (1125-km) raid from Bordeaux to Narbonne. His initial objective was to ravage the lands of the French king's lieutenant, Jean d'Armagnac, but Edward seized the initiative and marched on Toulouse. This city proved too powerful to assault without a siege train, so Edward surprised the French by fording the dangerous Garonne and Ariège rivers and plunged eastwards (28 October). Lands unused to war were ravaged and fired. Small towns like Castelnaudary were stormed, sacked, and burnt. Carcassonne offered a ransom, but the *bourg* (town) was burnt (6 November), while the *cité* (citadel) defied attack. Narbonne suffered the same indignity, but the resistance offered by its *cité* (9-10 November) persuaded the prince to retreat, which was managed with great success, despite large quantities of booty, severe rains, boggy roads, and deaths among the horses. The swollen Garonne was crossed again and contacts with French troops occurred only in late November, none serious. By 1 December, the raiders were back at La Réole. The expedition had been a huge success, both financially and in terms of political influence, as southern lords sought English protection. The French forces had been supine, though, weakened by disagreements between Armagnac and the royal constable.

In April 1356, John II (king of France since 1350) arrested Charles, king of Navarre, for treachery. This brought Philip of Navarre, Charles' brother, into Edward's camp and opened up strategic possibilities, as the brothers' estates in Normandy were now justifiable targets for relief. The forces intended for Brittany were redirected under Henry of Lancaster's command: 500 men-at-arms and 800 archers. In addition, Robert Knollys brought 500 men-at-arms and

The conduct of warfare for soldiers' profit meant that plundering was common practice. In the wake of the Black Death (from 1348) and the huge expense of king John's ransom (after 1356), the French peasantry suffered horribly. They rose in revolt (the *Jacquerie*) in 1358 but, after the 1360 treaty, unpaid mercenary bands ravaged uncontrollably for almost a decade.

THE BATTLE OF CRÉCY
25 AUGUST 1346

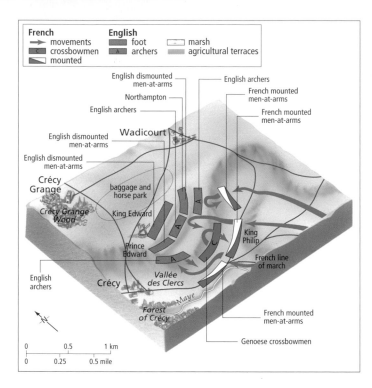

French
→ movements
C crossbowmen
mounted

English
foot
A archers

marsh
agricultural terraces

English dismounted men-at-arms
Northampton
English archers
English dismounted men-at-arms
English dismounted men-at-arms
Wadicourt
English archers
French mounted men-at-arms
French mounted men-at-arms
Crécy Grange
baggage and horse park
Crécy Grange Wood
King Edward
King Philip
Prince Edward
French line of march
English archers
Crécy
Vallée des Clercs
Maye
Forest of Crécy
French mounted men-at-arms
Genoese crossbowmen

0   0.5   1 km
0   0.25   0.5 mile

Although he was retreating in haste before the French, it is possible that Edward had chosen the position at Crécy beforehand. Its steep, terraced hillside allowed him to deploy his archers to best advantage around the dismounted men-at-arms. Woods protected the English rear and wagons the flanks, while a windmill provided a command post.

Philip had lost control of his troops and could not deploy them properly. Specially recruited Genoese crossbowmen were sent forward to exchange fire with the English archers, but they lacked the protection of their pavises (which were still on the baggage wagons) and with their slower rate of fire they were comprehensively outshot. As they fell back, the French chivalry rode them down in disgust. Unsupported cavalry charges could make no headway against the combined archers and men-at-arms of the English. The hardest fighting was against the prince of Wales' battle, where the French broke into the archers' formation but, by the end of the day, 1,500 knights and nobles lay dead. The key to the English victory was their strong position, good discipline, and firepower.

500 archers from Brittany, while Philip of Navarre provided 100 Norman men-at-arms. This small force, all mounted, set out on 22 June, and a week later raised the siege of Pont Audemer. Henry advanced to Breteuil, which was resupplied, and stormed Conches (4 July) and Verneuil (5 July). King John had mustered troops to oppose Lancaster too slowly, and the English slipped away when offered battle (9 July). Two long marches, on successive days, of 35 miles (56km) to Argentan, then 52 miles (84km) to Torigny (10 July) got them clean away. This was a different kind of *chevauchée* from the Prince's, moving an average of 22 miles (35km) a day, too swiftly to ravage effectively, but still bringing relief to two friendly fortresses, destroying two enemy ones, and capturing 2,000 horses. A few days later, Lancaster launched another *chevauchée* out of Brittany to join up with prince Edward, advancing north from Bergerac. The French royal army spent a month fruitlessly besieging Breteuil, before marching south against the prince.

Prince Edward led a fully mounted force of 3,000 men-at-arms, 3,000 archers, and 1,000 *hobilars*. Averaging 10 miles (16km) a day, they rode unopposed to Bourges, ravaging for miles on either side (4-28 August). From prisoners taken at the raid on Aubigny, king John learnt of Edward's position. The prince spent 7-11 August at Tours, perhaps awaiting Lancaster, whose advance was barred by the swollen Loire and French forces, so that he got no further than Angers. Unaware of his danger until it was too late, prince Edward was trapped just south of Poitiers (*page 121*). However, by taking up a strong position in broken ground, he was able to nullify John's numerical superiority and capture the French king (19 September).

Wrangling over the royal ransom provoked Edward to invade northern France again in 1359. Intending to take Reims and be crowned king there, he led a large army of 4,000 men-at-arms and 5,000 mounted archers. When the city defied siege, Edward, ever the opportunist, gave up his claim to the French throne in return for confirmation of the widest extent of lands held by the English crown for 200 years (Treaty of Brétigny, 1360). His original aim of securing Gascony had been greatly exceeded as the campaigns of the 1340s created their own momentum of plunder and glory, and the windfall of king John's capture gave him a trump card in negotiation. The *chevauchée* strategy had won huge gains, but it was to prove fallible.

Campaigns 1360-1396

By the time king John died in 1364, still a prisoner, his son Charles V had spent almost a decade exercising the reins of power. He never intended to abide by the Brétigny treaty of 1360 and he had surrounded himself with experienced warriors. Bertrand du Guesclin, a minor noble from Brittany, was one of the most successful *routier* (mercenary) captains. He rose to fame through his defence of Rennes in 1356-57, and in 1364 defeated the Navarrese royal army at Cocherel in Normandy (16 May). On 29 September, he challenged the English at Auray. He had devised a tactic for neutralizing English archery by dismounting his men-at-arms and advancing behind pavises. This worked in so far as the French reached the Anglo-Breton battle line, but they were then defeated, Charles of Blois being killed and du Guesclin captured. Brittany remained in the English camp until 1379.

Charles V valued his Breton captain so highly that in

1365 he paid a huge ransom. This freed du Guesclin for private enterprise in supporting Henry of Trastamara's claim to the throne of Castile against his half-brother Pedro I, 'the Cruel'. He led one of the 'Great Companies' which had flourished since the end of royal campaigns in France. A contingent of 800 men was led by the Englishman Hugh de Calveley, a former opponent in Brittany, and the Companies made up half the 10,000-12,000 men gathered at Saragossa in 1366. With this force, Henry swiftly chased Pedro from the throne. This coup alarmed Edward prince of Wales who, as ruler of Aquitaine, perceived a threat from a French-dominated Castile. In 1367, he marched into Spain (*map 3*), where Calveley and the English companies joined him. At Nájera, Edward's army faced a much larger Franco-Castilian force, but despite du Guesclin urging caution on his allies, they charged recklessly against the English bowmen and were routed (3 April). In fact, Edward won the battle but lost the war. In 1368, Henry returned

THE BATTLE OF POITIERS
19 SEPTEMBER 1356

Poor scouting had put prince Edward into a far more difficult situation than Crécy, but he managed to find a defensive position just north of Nouaille wood. This lay in ground broken by vines and other agriculture, behind a hedge, protected by the woods to its rear, marsh on the left flank and on the right, open, flank a hillock and wagon-fort. No map can accurately depict his deployment, as groups of men-at-arms and archers were scattered in the cover. Edward may still have been trying to escape, as early in the day the baggage was taken across the river Miosson.

This encouraged a cavalry charge led by 200 picked knights under the command of the two French marshals, Clermont and Audrehem, along the road and at a gap in the hedge. It failed due to English bowmen shooting the horses, aiming at their unprotected rumps if they were barded. Then the dauphin's battle advanced on foot, and hard fighting ensued all along the line. Once more the French were thrown back, with heavy casualties. The third battle, presumably mounted to exploit any retreat by Edward's men, gave up the fight for lost and dispersed.

With difficulty, the prince held his men back from pursuit. Finally, king John led up the reserve of dismounted men-at-arms, probably still equal in numbers to Edward's exhausted force. The prince seized the initiative and mounted up his men-at-arms and many archers, also sending the Captal de Buch with a cavalry flank attack around the hillock. While the English fought with desperation, the Gascons arrived with a shout in the French rear, so that they broke under the double pressure. Around 3,000 French were killed and king John was captured in the melee, along with many of his nobles and some 1,000 more worth a ransom. Despite the French attempts to counteract English tactics, they still delivered separate attacks which were defeated piecemeal.

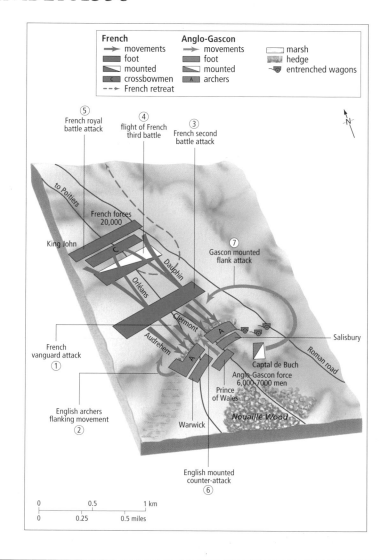

to Spain, then captured and murdered Peter. The huge cost of Edward's expedition, paid for out of heavy taxes in Gascony, undermined English rule there.

In 1369, Charles V renewed the war in Gascony, using the Castilian fleet against English communications, and built up a Channel fleet. Edward III responded by sending another son, John of Gaunt, to Calais with 4,000 men, later reinforced by 2,000 men of the royal household. Gaunt maintained an army of 5,000 men in France over four successive campaigning seasons, but to little effect (*map 4*). In 1370, sir Robert Knollys led an unsuccessful *chevauchée* from Normandy to Poitou. In 1371, prince Edward sacked Limoges. This was a political mistake which further undermined his support. In 1373, John of Gaunt led an ambitious *chevauchée* from Calais to Bordeaux, covering 1,000 miles (1600km) in five months. But the French strategy was now to contain English ravaging, by withdrawing into refortified towns and denying them provisions, plunder, and an opportunity for battle. This proved successful, for when Gaunt's men staggered into Bordeaux at Christmas, they were exhausted and starving, and had lost many of their horses.

With both Edwards ill, there was a lack of leadership and direction. By 1374, the French recovery in the south-west had pinned the English back into the territories they held in 1337. Prince Edward died in 1376, and Edward III in 1377, leaving Richard II to succeed as a minor. Campaigns

in 1380-81 to Brittany and Portugal failed miserably. The Breton campaign foundered when its duke repudiated the English alliance and submitted to Charles V. The duke of Cambridge's expedition to Portugal ended in humiliation – shipped home in Castilian vessels.

After French raids on southern England in the 1330s, and a brief seizure of the Channel Islands, Edward's victory at Sluys assured English dominance at sea for almost two decades. The French kings immediately recruited twenty Genoese galleys and looked to Spain for more. In 1350, Edward fell upon forty Castilian vessels heading for Flanders, destroying them off Winchelsea in a sea battle known as 'Les Espagnols-sur-Mer'. So, in 1359, Charles began to rebuild his navy, based on the *Clos des gallées* (galley yards) at Rouen, while Harfleur was developed as a bastion at the mouth of the Seine.

In 1372, a combined Genoese-Castilian fleet in French service defeated the English off La Rochelle and recovered the port. In 1373, the appointment of Jean de Vienne as admiral led to a further dramatic improvement in French fortunes. He built up the Rouen fleet from ten vessels in 1376 to fifty-six by 1379. With this new strength he began raids on England's southern ports, causing great destruction in 1377 (*map 4*), and burning Gravesend in 1380. Between 1385 and 1387, Charles VI mustered 180 French vessels 'between the Seine and the Zwijn' and hired many more. Charles was able to threaten a full-scale invasion of England

MAP 3

In 1362, Edward III allied with Castile to benefit from her fleet. The Black Prince campaigned to aid Pedro I, but Henry of Trastamara, the French-supported claimant, seized the Castilian throne in 1368. In the 1380s, John of Gaunt unsuccessfully attempted to claim the kingdom by right of his wife. Despite victories in battle at Nájera (1367) and Aljubarrota (1385), English strategy failed.

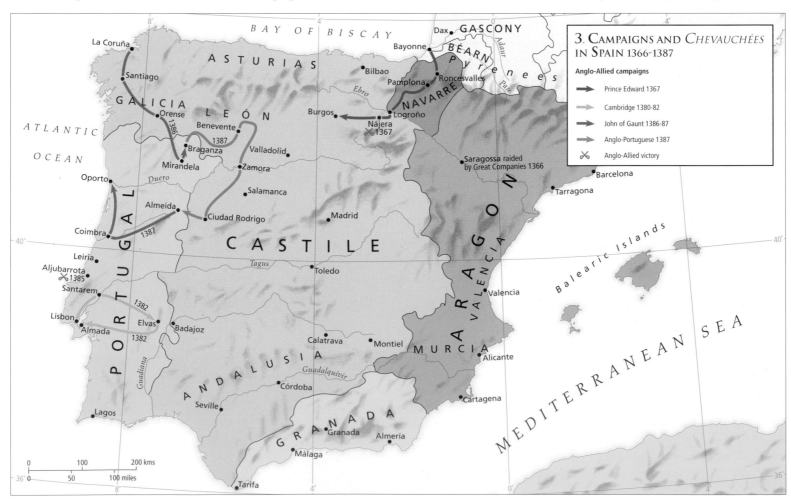

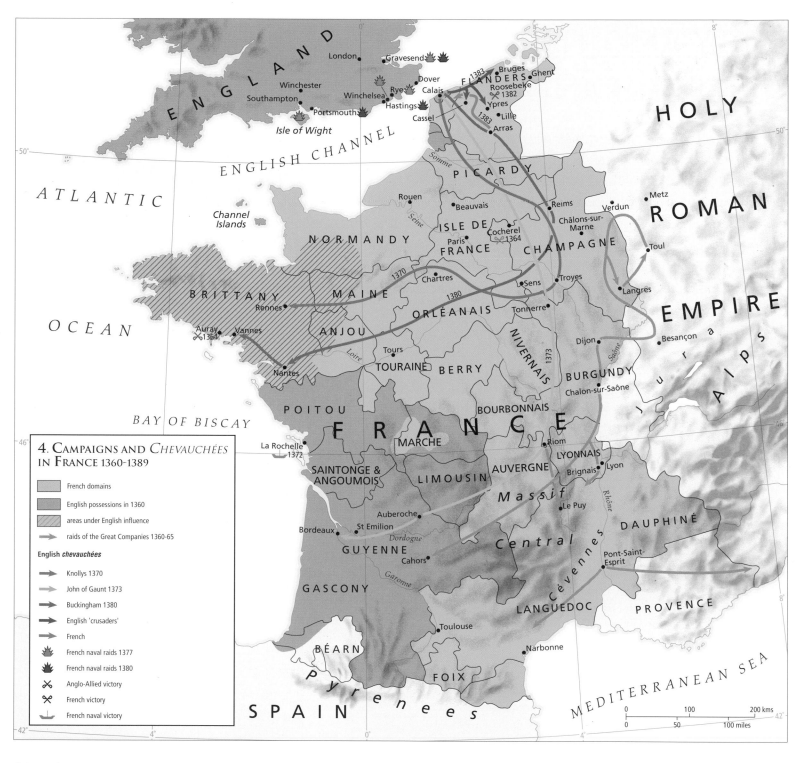

4. CAMPAIGNS AND *CHEVAUCHÉES* IN FRANCE 1360-1389

French domains

English possessions in 1360

areas under English influence

raids of the Great Companies 1360-65

English *chevauchées*

Knollys 1370

John of Gaunt 1373

Buckingham 1380

English 'crusaders'

French

French naval raids 1377

French naval raids 1380

Anglo-Allied victory

French victory

French naval victory

MAP 4

From 1369, Charles V's battle-avoiding strategy successfully neutralized English *chevauchées* in France. His victory off La Rochelle with a Genoese-Castilian fleet (1372) began a French naval supremacy which led to raids on the English south coast and a genuine invasion threat.

for the first time for half a century. The English found a defensive war increasingly expensive to pursue, and heavy taxation provoked the Peasants' Revolt of 1381. English strategy became increasingly disjointed. In 1382, there were plans to unite with Flemish rebels, but they were crushed at Roosebeke (27 November). In 1383, it was only possible to raise an army under the auspices of a crusade which besieged Ypres (July to October), until French royal forces relieved the city.

In 1385, at Aljubarrota, an Anglo-Portuguese force prevented Henry of Trastamara from conquering Portugal. John of Gaunt turned his attention to the Iberian peninsula

once more, to press his claim to the throne of Castile, but after the failure of his expedition in 1386-87 he allowed Henry to buy off his claim.

From 1390 to 1396, there were a series of complex peace negotiations in which Charles VI's madness (since 1392) gave England the upper hand and resulted in Richard II marrying the French king's sister. Even so, English territories in France were reduced to Calais and a coastal strip from Bordeaux to Bayonne in Gascony. Decades of failure had dulled memories of Edward III's successes; but with good leadership the claim to the French throne might yet be revived.

ITALY AND THE MEDITERRANEAN ARENA c.1350-1480

AFTER THE LOSS of the crusader states, Venice, Genoa, and Pisa haggled over the remnants of Byzantium and often proved the only determined opposition to the Turks. The Knights Hospitaller, first on Cyprus, then on Rhodes, remained in the front line. Catalan naval power made inroads in the central Mediterranean, winning control of Sardinia, Sicily, and eventually a mainland base in southern Italy. The maritime city-states fought in all waters, and victories on land created a Venetian terra firma. Contrary to the myth, the condottieri warfare of Italy was not a genteel game, but a fierce contest which saw Milan emerging as the foremost state under the Visconti and Sforza dynasties. As a result, little thought was given to rescuing Constantinople, which finally fell to the Ottomans in 1453. By 1480, the Turks were besieging Rhodes and landing in Italy.

THE OTTOMAN CONQUEST OF THE BYZANTINE EMPIRE

By 1350, the Byzantine military position was dire. John V, effective ruler from 1357, toured western courts in 1369-71 in search of troops, even reaching England. While he was away, sultan Murad II defeated the Serbs at Marica (1371). In 1373, John led a contingent on Murad's campaign in Asia Minor, effectively accepting vassal status until his death in 1392. Thrace was conquered by the Turks during the 1360s, Adrianople falling in 1369 (map 1). In 1377, it became the Ottoman European capital and Murad provided troops for the Byzantine coups of 1376 and 1379. The last pitched battle against the Turks was fought by Manuel II outside Salonica in 1384, the city surrendering after a three-year siege in 1387. Meanwhile, Sofia (1385), Nis (1386), and Verria (1387), also fell to the Ottomans. The Serbian defeat at Kosovo (1389) forced them into vassal status. Murad was assassinated during the battle, but his son Bayezid besieged Constantinople for eight years from 1394. He easily defeated a crusade at Nicopolis in 1396, before falling captive to Timur-lenk at Ankara in 1402.

Civil war over the succession meant that Constantinople was not besieged again until 1422. Once more the city survived, and the Byzantines staged a recovery in the Morea, taking over all except the Venetian possessions and holding out until 1460. The final siege of 1453 merely confirmed a military situation long lost. Mehmet II's great artillery train smashed the 1,000-year-old walls and the 6,000-7,000 defenders could do nothing in the face of overwhelming numbers.

THE ARAGONESE EMPIRE

In 1282, through the coup known as the Sicilian Vespers, Peter III of Aragon had seized Sicily from Angevin control. Charles of Anjou's brother, Philip III of France, then invaded Aragon with 8,000 men, capturing Gerona. But the Catalan fleet returned from Sicily and destroyed the French support-ships in the Bay of Roses (2-3 September), forcing Philip

into ignominious retreat. Aragon's naval power enabled the conquest of Minorca (1287) and Sardinia (in 1297 briefly, and then in 1323). Following civil war in the 1340s, Corsica was lost through defeat by the Genoese fleet. In 1351, Peter IV of Aragon allied with Venice, and in the following year their fleets, together with Byzantine and Catalan forces in Greece, combined to defeat the Genoese in the Bosporus. In 1353, admiral Bernat de Cabrera repeated

Although representing an imaginary twelfth-century sea battle, this fresco from the Palazzo Publico in Siena depicts warfare in around 1400 perfectly. The ships are designed to grapple and, while missilemen play an important role, the decision is achieved by boarding and hand-to-hand fighting.

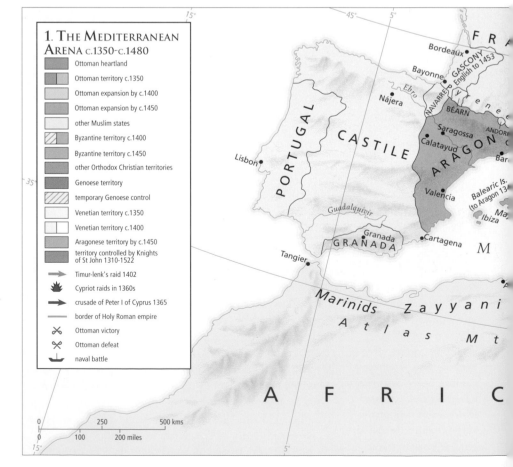

1. THE MEDITERRANEAN ARENA c.1350-c.1480

- Ottoman heartland
- Ottoman territory c.1350
- Ottoman expansion by c.1400
- Ottoman expansion by c.1450
- other Muslim states
- Byzantine territory c.1400
- Byzantine territory c.1450
- other Orthodox Christian territories
- Genoese territory
- temporary Genoese control
- Venetian territory c.1350
- Venetian territory c.1400
- Aragonese territory by c.1450
- territory controlled by Knights of St John 1310-1522
- Timur-lenk's raid 1402
- Cypriot raids in 1360s
- crusade of Peter I of Cyprus 1365
- border of Holy Roman empire
- Ottoman victory
- Ottoman defeat
- naval battle

MAP 1

By the mid-fourteenth century, western maritime powers were disputing control of Italy, and Italians and Spaniards fought even in the waters of the Golden Horn. The Greeks had their own concerns, because the Ottoman Turks were encroaching in Europe. Sultan Bayezid dispatched the 1396 crusade with ease, before falling prey to Timur-lenk (1402). But in the absence of a co-ordinated crusader response, Constantinople fell in 1453. Only the Hospitallers at Rhodes effectively opposed the Turks.

the treatment in Sardinian waters. The wars with Pedro 'the Cruel' (1356-69) and Enrique (to 1375) of Castile delayed further expansion. As Castilian galleys attacked the Balearics, Pedro seized Tarazona (1357). Peter successfully defended Barcelona in 1359 against a combined assault from land and sea, the Castilian fleet comprising thirty galleys and forty great ships. But in 1362, Pedro took Calatayud after a long siege and detached Aragon's ally, Muslim Granada. The mercenary Great Companies, left unemployed by the Treaty of Brétigny (1360), also began to operate in Spain (*page 121*), and in 1366 their leader, Bertrand du Guesclin, joined Peter's allegiance. This brought in the English under Edward, prince of Wales, and resulted in defeat for Aragon at Nájera (1367). After Pedro was murdered and replaced by Enrique in 1369, the conflict ended in 1375.

Peter IV tried to re-establish his weakened authority in Sicily through his grandson duke Marti (1378-84). In 1386, he was succeeded by John I, who also sent Marti with a fleet in 1392, capturing Palermo before meeting stiff resistance. In 1393, the overseas empire of Aragon shrank further with the loss of the Greek provinces of Neopatria and Athens to the Turks. When Marti became king in 1396, he was constrained by financial difficulties, but visited Sardinia and Corsica to re-enforce his rule. This provoked war with Genoa, who continued to raid the islands despite the peace of 1402. Only the Valencian 'crusades' of 1398-1400 proved profitable, and his heir died on campaign in Sicily in 1409. As a result, in 1410 the throne fell vacant,

and Ferdinand of Trastamara officially united Sicily to the crown of Aragon. His successor, Alfonso V (1416-58), took a fleet to reconquer Sardinia from Genoese partisans in 1420, and in 1423 blockaded recalcitrant Naples and attacked Angevin Marseille. After a decade spent in Spain he returned to Sicily in 1453, for good.

Despite defeat and capture by the Genoese in a sea battle that year, Alfonso was soon released and began a determined assault on Naples. He besieged the city from 1438, until eventually capturing it in 1442. He has been called a 'condottiere king', who devoted himself to Italian affairs but proved unable to intervene to save Constantinople. Catalan maritime power was not used as aggressively as formerly, Alfonso contenting himself with trading posts in the Morea, Crete, and Ragusa in Dalmatia, and support of the Hospitallers of Rhodes. After his death in 1458, civil wars in Catalonia absorbed Aragonese energy.

CRUSADING ACTIVITY

With the conquest of Acre by the Mamluks in 1291, the military orders lost their rationale. Philip IV of France overthrew the Templars (1307-14), a warning which the Hospitallers heeded. They had already established themselves on Cyprus and, in 1310, on Rhodes. Wealthy from inheriting Templar possessions, the Knights spent lavishly on a galley fleet (usually ten-strong) and constructing fortifications. The crusading activities of Peter I of Cyprus (1359-69) helped to increase their territories. His initial raids along the southern Turkish coast established

enclaves at Adalia and Corycus, then after a recruiting tour of Europe he launched an attack on the Mamluk sultanate. Raids on the Syrian coast were followed by a serious, though futile, attempt to capture Alexandria in 1369.

The Hospitallers made more solid gains on the west coast of Asia Minor. Izmir had been captured by crusaders in 1344, and was handed over to the Knights in 1374, to be held until Timur-lenk's conquests in 1402. Then St Peter's Port, Bodrum, was fortified and not lost until the Ottoman capture of Rhodes itself (1522). The island had successfully repulsed Mamluk attacks in 1440 and 1444, and survived an epic Ottoman siege in 1480 – the first flexing of new Turkish naval power.

ITALIAN MARITIME POWER

In 1350, the Genoese seized Venetian ships at Caffa, the beginning of a fifty-year conflict which turned Venice into a colonial power. In response, the Venetians conquered Negroponte island (modern Evvoia). In alliance with eighteen Aragonese and twelve Byzantine galleys, they were defeated by Pietro Doria's Genoese at Galata (1352). The victorious Genoese fleet returned to raise the blockade of Alghero on Sardinia by the Aragonese, but lost heavily; out of sixty vessels, forty-one were captured (29 August 1353). As a result, Genoa found herself cut off from eastern trade and became dependent upon Milan. Next year Vettor Pisani, the Venetian admiral, pursued Genoese raiders in the Adriatic to their base on Chios. Here, on 4 November 1354, it was the Venetians' turn to suffer catastrophic defeat: fifty-six ships were captured, including thirty-three war galleys. This rapid reversal of fortunes was typical of sea warfare.

In 1377, war resumed over the island of Tenedos. Venice signed a treaty with Milan, dividing sea and land conquests between them respectively. On 30 May 1378, Pisani led the Venetians to victory over the Genoese off Anzio and then pursued them to the east, wintering at Pola. This proved a mistake, as his vessels deteriorated without the annual refit in the Arsenal. When a twenty-five-strong Genoese fleet attacked on 7 May 1379, Pisani only escaped with six battered vessels. Deprived of their fleet, the Venetians were soon blockaded in their own lagoon by the forty-seven ships of Doria and besieged by land by their old enemy Francesco Carrara of Padua.

Gradually though, the tables turned as Venice recovered the Lido (shoreline) and pushed the Genoese back into Chioggia harbour. Here the besiegers became the besieged. In January 1380, Carlo Zeno returned with eighteen vessels of the Venetian Levant fleet (the Arsenal having made good other losses). The Genoese began to starve, especially after Taddeo Guistinian captured twelve ships destined to collect Sicilian grain. On 24 June 1380, the surviving 4,000 Genoese surrendered. In the next twenty years, Venice expanded her overseas territories, taking Corfu and Dalmatian ports, Nauplia and Argos in the Morea, and most of the Cyclades and Dodecanese islands. She still held Crete, despite frequent rebellions, the island containing 132 knights fiefs and over 400 infantry sergeantries. Genoa held Cyprus (Venetian from 1489), Lesbos, Samos, and Chios, but was now playing second fiddle.

A concomitant to seaborne empire was Venice's expansion on land, its *terra firma*. This was achieved sometimes in alliance and sometimes in opposition to Milan (*map 2*). In 1388, Venice even sided with its old enemies the Carrare of Padua, in defence of Florence and Mantua against Gian Galeazzeo Visconti. In 1402, he defeated the western emperor designate, Rupert of the Palatinate, and took Pisa, Siena, Lucca, and Bologna, before dying whilst besieging Florence. Venice was then able to capture Padua in 1404.

By 1400, Venice was an international power, with some 3,300 ships, 36,000 sailors, and a potential militia of 30,000 men of all arms (although it turned increasingly to mercenaries). The Arsenal had 16,000 workers, almost one-third of the city's active male population, and was the engine which drove the military and naval machines. As well as producing arms and armour, its workers could produce a 200-man war galley more quickly than any competitor.

The Sienese army sets out to defeat the freebooting Company del Capello at the battle of Sinalunga (1363) in this fresco by Lippo Vanni. It is a well-balanced force of men-at-arms, spearmen, and archers, with the infantry marching to music and the missilemen at least, under unit banners. The heraldry is that of the actual participants.

MAP 2

Italy was full of states made rich by overseas trade but in close geographical proximity. Competition was intense both at home and abroad, and there was an increased militarization in terms of the growth of armies and fortifications throughout the period. Venice carved out a large territory, and Milan sought to dominate all other cities. The use of mercenaries did not demonstrate any Italian unwillingness to fight, rather the desire to pay for the best troops in Europe.

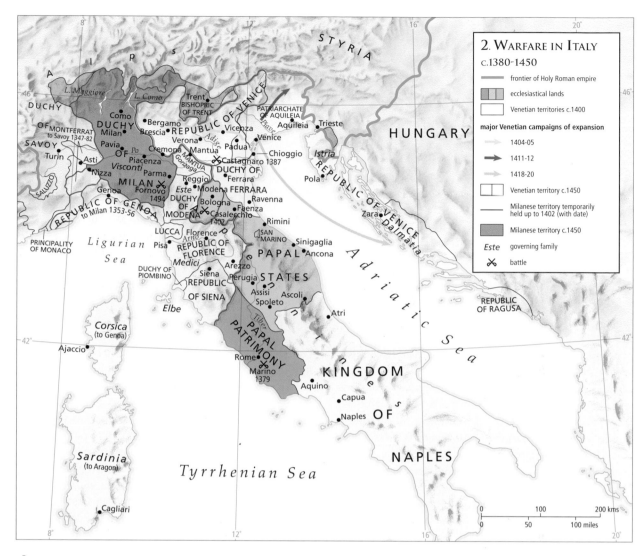

ITALIAN LAND WARFARE AND THE CONDOTTIERI

Between 1300 and 1350, Italian cities shifted from deploying a citizen militia to an increasing use of mercenaries. These were known after the contract – condotta – by which they were retained, and have acquired a bad reputation, both as cynical exploiters and protagonists in 'bloodless battles'. Both stereotypes were wrong. Nor was Italian warfare dominated by foreigners, despite Machiavelli's propaganda. True, the Great Companies (c.1353-64) and Hawkwood's White Company (1363-75) did make an impact, especially the English style of fighting practised by the latter (dismounted men-at-arms and archers). But such companies were short-lived, and Italian captains were common. Alberigo da Barbiano (1378-c.1400), although he came to be celebrated as the first native captain to defeat foreigners (Bretons) at Marino (1379), was not exceptional. The captain-generals of cities had long employed mercenaries: in 1359, Pandolfo Malatesta of Florence fielded 4,000 mercenary cavalry when he routed the Great Company. Italy was a good recruiting ground for mercenaries because its numerous city-states provided many competitive employers, not because its citizens were feeble. Nor were the condottieri as fickle as has been assumed: most

of them remained loyal to their employers, like Hawkwood to Florence.

In the early fifteenth century, the Malatesta brothers represent the committed mercenary. The elder was lord of Rimini, giving the younger a base for wider condottieri operations. Their cautious approach to war proved victorious over Pippo Spano, Ladislas of Naples' dashing cavalryman, in 1412. At this time the condotte began to list mixed companies of horse and foot, with an increased number of missilemen. Armies grew in size as well. In 1439, the Venetian chronicler, Sanuto, assessed the cavalry strength of Venice at 16,100, Milan at 19,750, and the Aragonese at 17,800 (with the expectation of equal numbers of infantry). By 1472, Sforzan Milan hoped to mobilize 43,000 (although this was never realized), and had a genuine standing army some 4,000-5,000 strong. Lesser powers, such as Florence or the papacy, were capable of maintaining 10,000 men on campaigns of several years' duration. There was nothing 'old-fashioned' or ad hoc about Italian armies, condemning them to inevitable defeat by Charles VIII of France in 1494. In fact, the French king was lucky to escape capture at Fornovo (1495) during a well-planned ambush by an allied army under the command of the captain-general of Venice, Francesco Gonzaga.

THE HUNDRED YEARS' WAR:
THE FIFTEENTH CENTURY

ALTHOUGH HENRY IV'S USURPATION of the English throne (1399) did not end the truce with France, the French harassed Calais and Gascony up to 1408. After 1410, the condition of France, where Charles VI was frequently insane and the Burgundians and Armagnac factions struggled for dominance, invited intervention. Expeditions in 1411 and 1412 alerted the English nobility to French weakness. Henry V (1413-22) took advantage of French divisions to conquer Normandy and negotiate the French crown for his dynasty, and English successes continued until 1428. The French recovery inspired by Joan of Arc gathered pace during the 1430s. Failure to conclude a negotiated peace in the 1440s was followed by the rapid collapse of English rule in Normandy (1449-50) and Gascony (1451-53).

The siege of Rouen lasted from 1 August 1418 to mid-January 1419, the second consecutive winter Henry's army spent in the field. Henry had a ditch and bank built around the city to seal it off and protect his men. An iron chain suspended across the Seine prevented supplies coming from upstream, while the English used the river to ship in their own supplies.

ENGLISH EXPANSION

When Henry V became king, the Lancastrian dynasty was secure enough for him to spend much of his reign campaigning in France. He was already experienced in war and in government, and immediately began military preparations. When the French refused his vast territorial demands, he invaded in 1415 with some 10,500 soldiers, three-quarters of them archers, plus hundreds of siege specialists and military craftsmen, contracted for one year (map 1). Taxation was secured from parliament, and shipping impressed to transport the host, its equipment, and over 10,000 horses. Two-thirds of the army was mounted, indicating a *chevauchée* was planned to Bordeaux via Paris, while early contracts mentioned Gascony, but by June Henry had decided to besiege the key Norman port of Harfleur. The siege took five weeks, much longer than Henry had anticipated, and cost him many men, particularly from dysentery, and for a garrison. Yet with barely 6,000 soldiers, Henry decided to ride 120 miles (193km) across hostile territory to Calais with eight days' food, despite the late season and against the advice of his nobles.

French occupation of the Somme crossings enforced a wide detour, and it was a hungry and tired army which faced the French near Agincourt (page 130). French blunders and the traditional virtues of English men-at-arms and archers brought Henry a great victory on 25 October. It confirmed English support for Henry and hardened French resolve. However, the death of over 600 French nobles and knights, and capture of 1,000 more, deprived them of leaders and made them unwilling to face Henry in battle.

While Henry V spent 1416 in diplomacy, his brother John, duke of Bedford, raised the French blockade of Harfleur (15 August 1416). The destruction of the French flotilla based at Honfleur (29 June 1417) made the Channel safe for English shipping for several years. On 1 August 1417, Henry landed in Normandy with nearly 11,000 combatants, bent on the capture of its fortified and garrisoned towns. Keeping his army in the field for two

consecutive winters, supplying it from England without the incentive of plunder, and its pay frequently in arrears, was Henry's greatest achievement. But it was only feasible because the bitterly divided French allowed him to disperse his army in prolonged sieges. Henry's strategy was to isolate western Normandy first. It took a month to capture Caen, a useful port. He then secured the southern border. The neighbouring princes sued for truces (16 November), permitting the reduction of Falaise. In the spring, the western fortresses were mopped up. Only Domfront and Cherbourg resisted for long, the latter occupying the duke of Gloucester with 3,000 men for five months (to 29 September). In early summer, the duke of Clarence cleared the way to the Seine. The fast-flowing river was a major obstacle. A bridgehead was secured by a ruse, and the English crossed by a prefabricated pontoon bridge. The blockade of the Norman capital, Rouen, began at the end of July. It had

Henry V was one of the most remarkable men ever to rule England. His grim determination and effectiveness were apparent as much in his government as in his military command. But his ambition to rule France exceeded his resources and the willingness of his English subjects to foot the bill.

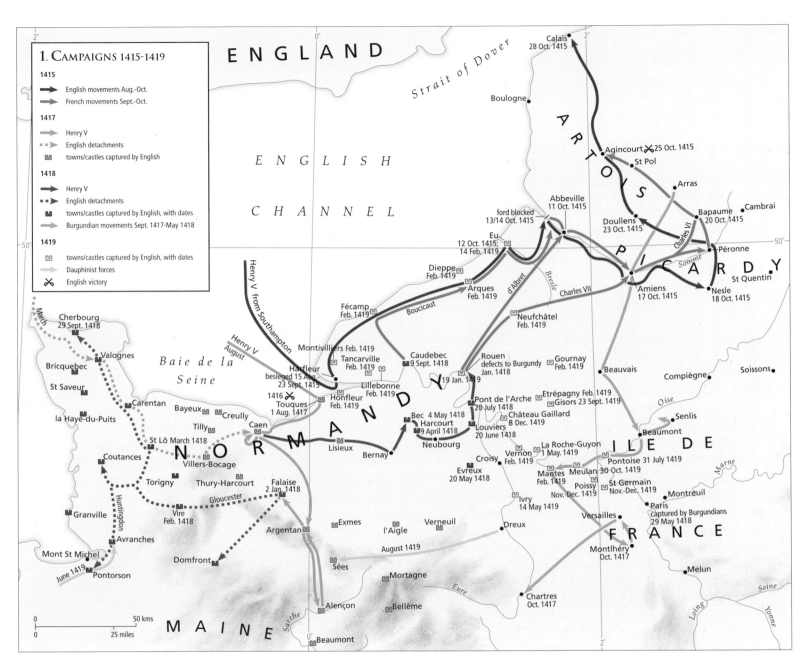

1. CAMPAIGNS 1415-1419

1415

→ English movements Aug.-Oct.

→ French movements Sept.-Oct.

1417

→ Henry V

⇢ English detachments

🏰 towns/castles captured by English

1418

→ Henry V

⇢ English detachments

🏰 towns/castles captured by English, with dates

→ Burgundian movements Sept. 1417-May 1418

1419

🏰 towns/castles captured by English, with dates

→ Dauphinist forces

✕ English victory

MAP 1

After capturing Harfleur as a foothold in Normandy, Henry V started a *chevauchée* to Calais. The French decision to fight at Agincourt gave Henry a great victory whose moral effects made it much easier for him to conquer Normandy in a continuous campaign between 1417 and 1419. The division of the French nobility into warring factions also allowed Henry to disperse his forces for a war of long sieges.

had ten months to prepare, but was full of refugees who quickly consumed the stores. Henry's army was depleted by detachments, casualties, and desertion, but duke John 'the Fearless' of Burgundy, who took Paris from the Armagnacs in May 1418, failed to relieve Rouen (November-December 1418) out of fear of the Armagnacs. Their raids from the Loire valley did not distract Henry. In January 1419, Rouen capitulated, and Normandy north of the Seine fell quickly. While his captains overcame strong resistance as they reduced the strongholds towards Paris, Henry V spent the rest of 1419 negotiating with both French factions. Whatever his plans, Burgundy's murder by the Armagnac leader, the dauphin Charles, brought the French crown within his grasp.

The treaty of Troyes (21 May 1420) was ostensibly a peace treaty. It made Henry V regent of France and Charles VI's heir, and committed Henry and Philip, the new duke of Burgundy, to conquer central and southern France from

the dauphin Charles. Two days after marrying princess Katherine (2 June 1420), Henry set out to reduce the dauphinist strongholds south of Paris (map 2). Melun defied the battering of heavy cannon and mining for four months before hunger led to its surrender (18 November 1420). Only then did Henry visit Paris (1 December 1420), then England for the first time since 1417. Burgundy was inactive, while Henry's brother Clarence raided up to Angers, but was killed when he rashly attacked a dauphinist army containing 6,000 Scots at Baugé (22 March). The dauphin besieged Chartres, wasting the chance to regain Paris, and allowing Henry's lieutenants to restore stability. Henry landed at Calais (10 June) with 4,000 men, abandoned his campaign in Picardy, and made for Chartres. The dauphin's retreat allowed Henry to take Dreux and recover most of the summer's losses. Unable to bring the dauphin to battle, he turned on Meaux, the last significant dauphinist stronghold near Paris. The siege lasted seven months: despite strong defence furnished by the river Marne, flooded siege lines, shortage of men, provisions and money, and active resistance, Henry prosecuted it to the end. Its capture secured Paris and communications with Burgundy. By the end of June, Henry was boasting that only Guise, le Crotoy, and St Valéry-sur-Somme remained to the dauphinists in northern France, but two months later he was dead (31 August 1422), apparently of dysentery.

Henry V was a remarkable soldier. He prepared meticulously and was expert in overcoming the strongest defences. He ensured his army was supplied from England and later by merchants in France. He kept strict discipline, but shared his soldiers' dangers. He created a network of garrisons to preserve his conquests, and granted land in Normandy on condition of military service for its defence. He also recognized the importance of seapower, and built up a royal fleet of thirty-nine ships by 1418 (a figure not surpassed until the reign of Henry VIII), with an administrative organization to service it. Annual patrols helped keep the Channel clear, but once the war was pushed deep into France the navy was run down to cut costs. However, Henry's vision of conquering France before crusading against the Turk was unrealistic. In England there was waning enthusiasm for funding what became a French civil war, and most Frenchmen saw the dauphin as the rightful heir. Charles VI died two months after Henry. The infant Henry

THE BATTLE OF AGINCOURT 25 OCTOBER 1415

The survivors of Henry V's 6,000 men who reached Agincourt were exhausted, but they had no choice but to fight their way through to Calais, although outnumbered by at least three to one. Henry placed his men-at-arms (perhaps 900) in the centre, the archers (under 5,000) on each flank, then advanced to within bowshot (200-300 yards, 180-275m) of the French. His front of about 800 yards (730m) rested on two woods. The archers made an irregular hedge of sharpened stakes, since Henry had learned the French intended to disperse them with cavalry, then shot to provoke the French. The plan devised by the experienced Boucicaut and d'Albret, to scatter the archers with cavalry on armoured horses, was not put into effect properly. The two small cavalry squadrons made little impact on them, and in fleeing smashed into the advancing French main battle of some 8,000 heavily armoured men-at-arms on foot, struggling across rain-sodden ploughed land.

The plentiful French archers and crossbowmen were not employed. Exhausted by the clinging mud, the French men-at-arms had little impetus when they reached the English line. In the intense mêlée, Henry V sustained a blow to his helmet, but gradually the French were pushed back, their flanks harried by the nimble archers. The second French battle (3,000-6,000 men-at-arms) joined in, but on the constricted field their numbers were no advantage. The closely packed soldiers could not wield their weapons and those who fell to the ground could not regain their feet. Probably within an hour the English were victorious. Some 2,000 French surrendered and hundreds were dead, including many leaders. The third French battle of several thousand men-at-arms remained. A few hundred made a fruitless charge, the rest rode off. About this time, the English camp was attacked, perhaps also part of the original French plan. Fearful that the prisoners might rebel, Henry ordered their murder. His men-at-arms refused such an ignoble act and the massacre was begun by archers, striking at the heads of the heavily armoured prisoners. Since Henry took at least 1,000 noble prisoners to England, he must have called a halt. Nevertheless, he had demonstrated the coldly professional approach to war which made him so successful. English dead numbered about 300. One retinue of twenty-five men-at-arms and archers lost three casualties at Harfleur, as well as seven who were killed at Agincourt; another of forty-eight men suffered five casualties at Harfleur and none at the battle; of a company of fifty archers, Harfleur accounted for twenty-four men (sixteen casualties and eight garrison), seven men were captured the night before Agincourt, and none were lost in the battle.

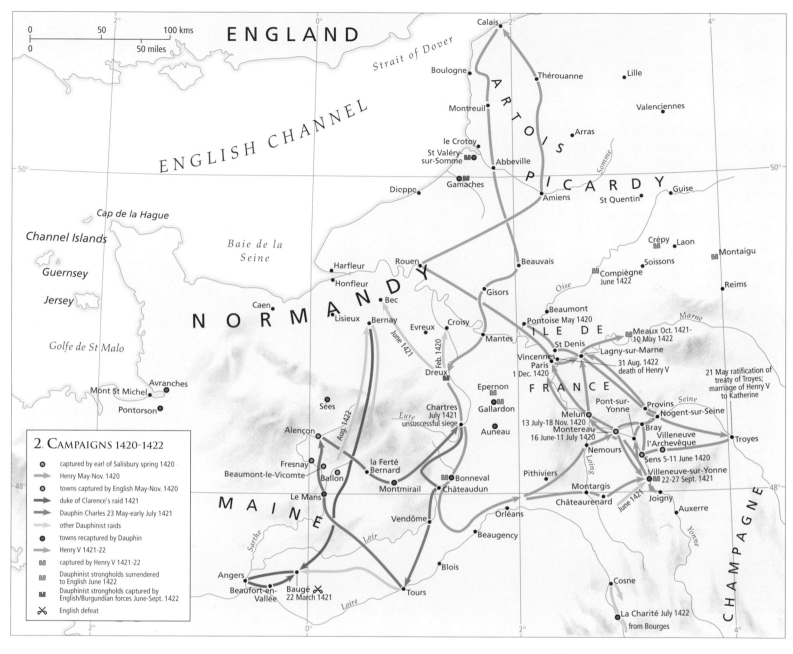

2. CAMPAIGNS 1420-1422

- ● captured by earl of Salisbury spring 1420
- → Henry May-Nov. 1420
- ● towns captured by English May-Nov. 1420
- ➡ duke of Clarence's raid 1421
- ➡ Dauphin Charles 23 May-early July 1421
- ➡ other Dauphinist raids
- ● towns recaptured by Dauphin
- ➡ Henry V 1421-22
- 🏰 captured by Henry V 1421-22
- 🏰 Dauphinist strongholds surrendered to English June 1422
- 🏰 Dauphinist strongholds captured by English/Burgundian forces June-Sept. 1422
- ✗ English defeat

MAP 2

The treaty of Troyes allied Henry V with Burgundy, but the dauphin Charles refused to accept disinheritance. In 1420, Henry reduced the threat to Paris from dauphinist garrisons, but while he visited England (winter 1420-21) the French won a morale-raising victory at Baugé. Henry was able to regain the ground lost, but the dauphin refused to fight. Henry's capture of Meaux secured northern France.

VI of England and the dauphin (as Charles VII) were both declared king of France by their partisans.

Henry VI's uncle, the duke of Bedford, took command in France. He was an able commander and diplomat, aided by experienced captains. However, England and Lancastrian France no longer had a single government. The English administration sent what help it could, and Bedford raised funds in France, but men and money were always in short supply. Duke Philip was a lukewarm ally, interested mainly in expanding in the Netherlands. Only Bedford's skill kept the alliance alive to 1435. The nineteen-year-old Charles VII, based at Bourges, was at this stage an uninspiring leader dependent on foreign troops. Bedford, with some 15,000 English troops scattered in garrisons and sieges, needed to mop up Charles VII's strongholds in Champagne, Brie, and around Paris (map 3). The capture of le Crotoy (1424) secured the east flank, but in the west Mont-St Michel was never captured. The French seized Meulan in 1423, and

Gaillon in 1424, both on the Seine below Paris, showing the vulnerability of Lancastrian Normandy. However, two Anglo-Burgundian victories stemmed the French revival. At Cravant in July 1423, the earl of Salisbury crushed a French thrust into Champagne. In a hard-fought battle at Verneuil in August 1424, Bedford prevented a Franco-Scottish relief of Ivry castle, seized in April. 'Verneuil was no Agincourt, yet its effects were greater' (C. Allmand). Charles VII's Scottish field army was destroyed, removing the threat to Normandy, and leaving him unable to prevent the capture of Maine in small-scale operations between 1425 and 1426. Bedford, who methodically reduced French fortresses on a broad front from Montargis to Mont-St Michel, both of which the English failed to take, has been criticized for not striking at Bourges. He lacked men, despite reducing the Norman garrisons, while the defection of Brittany and revolt in Maine delayed him. When Salisbury brought over 2,500 men with a siege train, an attack on

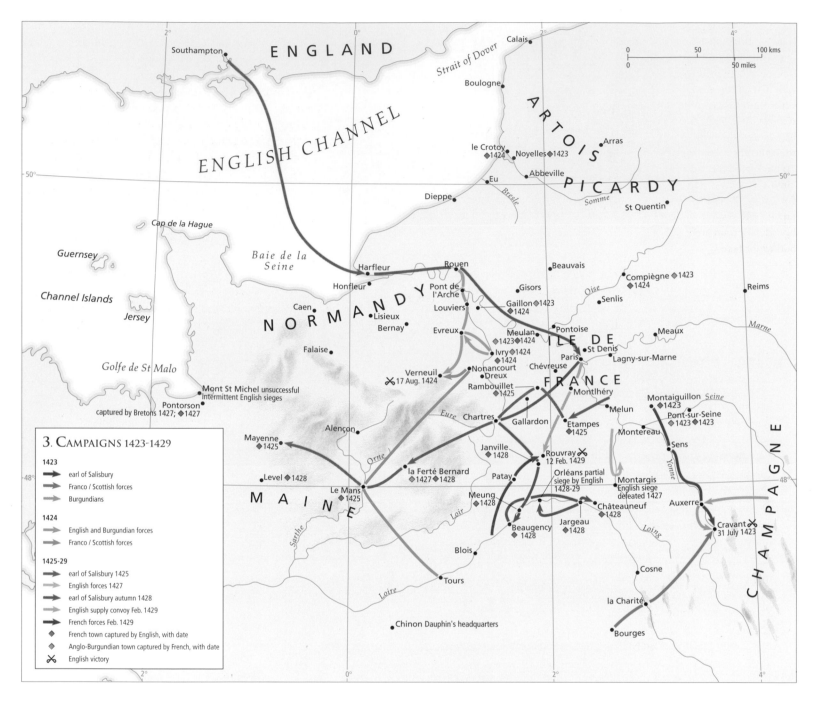

3. CAMPAIGNS 1423-1429

1423

➔ earl of Salisbury

➔ Franco / Scottish forces

➔ Burgundians

1424

➔ English and Burgundian forces

➔ Franco / Scottish forces

1425-29

➔ earl of Salisbury 1425

➔ English forces 1427

➔ earl of Salisbury autumn 1428

➔ English supply convoy Feb. 1429

➔ French forces Feb. 1429

◆ French town captured by English, with date

◆ Anglo-Burgundian town captured by French, with date

✗ English victory

Orléans was launched in 1428 to carry the war across the river Loire.

THE FRENCH RESURGENCE 1429-53

Salisbury's army comprised his own retinue, some 1,500 Burgundians, and troops from the English garrisons. It was too small to invest Orléans fully, but for seven months the French were passive, despite the withdrawal of the Burgundians. The turning point was the miraculous intervention of Joan of Arc, a peasant girl from eastern France, who inspired the French forces (map 5). The relief of Orléans was followed by the capture of the English-held bridges over the Loire, and the rout at Patay (18 June 1429) of the only English field army in France. Although the English garrisons had been weakened, Joan insisted on crowning Charles at Reims (July 1429) to end any doubts

about his legitimacy before she would countenance an attempt to recover Paris. Charles VII avoided Bedford's attempts to bring about battle, but when Joan was eventually allowed to assault the city (8 September 1429) she was repulsed. This was her first setback, and Charles closed the campaign. The French revival undermined the English position, despite Joan of Arc's capture and her execution in 1431. The French noose tightened around Paris, raiders penetrated Normandy, there were conspiracies to deliver Rouen and Paris to them, and increasing popular resistance to English occupation. In 1430-31, Henry VI was brought to France with substantial reinforcements, but Anglo-Burgundian failure to recover Reims made his coronation in Paris (1431) a pale imitation of Charles VII's. However, in the early 1430s, the English did recover losses in the Seine valley and elsewhere, while the French attacked the

MAP 3

Between 1422 and 1428, Bedford consolidated English control north of the Loire. Although Anglo-Burgundian victories in 1423-24 destroyed the French field army, Bedford lacked the resources for a major offensive. When Salisbury arrived with reinforcements in 1428, the objective chosen was Orléans, but after his death the siege was not pressed with urgency.

Joan was a peasant girl who convinced the dauphin Charles of her divine mission and inspired his demoralized forces. Her triumphant campaign resulted in Charles' coronation, immeasurably strengthening his standing. To the English she was a 'limb and disciple of the fiend [Devil]'. After her capture she was condemned by a church court and burned for heresy.

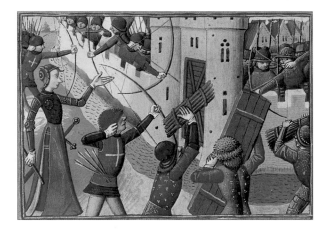

duke of Burgundy to force him to change sides. Moreover, the effort since 1429 had drained Charles VII's resources as much as those of the English.

In 1435, the course of the war changed decisively. The death of Bedford, whom the French respected, was followed by Burgundy's defection after abortive peace talks at Arras. While Burgundy's commitment to Troyes had been waning, his desertion left the English a longer frontier to defend. At the end of 1435, the French overran eastern Normandy (the 'Caux') with the help of a peasants' revolt. In the next year, Paris was lost and Calais besieged. For a while there was panic in Rouen, but the French forces were unco-ordinated. The peasants were brutally dispersed and sub-stantial reinforcements from England ended the crisis. Up to 1442, the English recovered most of eastern Normandy in small-scale sieges dictated by their growing financial crisis. Dieppe was never recaptured, and the loss of Louviers (1440) brought a French garrison to within 20 miles (32km) of Rouen. English raids and French companies living off the land, bands of brigands (a mixture of partisans and robbers), plague, and famine devastated large tracts of the countryside.

The English still won local successes. In December 1439, the French besieging Avranches were routed by John Talbot,

THE FRENCH AND ENGLISH ARMIES

By 1400, nobles and vassals provided the French men-at-arms again, and their servants (called *coutiliers* after their long knives) served as light cavalry. Specified towns furnished infantry (crossbowmen and halberdiers). At Agincourt, the French host of 20,000 men or more lacked cohesion and discipline. Crushing defeat and civil war led to military collapse. In the 1420s, Charles VII relied on Armagnac garrisons, free companies, and foreigners. In the period 1418-23, more than 16,000 Scots fought for him. The defeats of 1423-24 cost Charles his field army. His troops were poorly paid and their marauding, exceeding that of the English, earned the nickname 'skinners' (*écorcheurs*). The French resurgence in the 1430s eased manpower problems, so that Charles could afford to reject Scottish offers. In the late 1430s, the French artillery was reorganized by the Bureau brothers. However, not until 1445 did Charles succeed in asserting control over the rapacious companies serving in his name which were liable to support rebellious magnates. His 1445 ordinance selected permanent companies of veterans 600-strong, a total of 1,800 men-at-arms, 3,600 mounted archers, and 1,800 *coutiliers* billeted about his realm. A militia of 8,000 'free-archers' and more 'ordinance' companies were quickly organized. The *écorcheurs* were sent to campaign in Lorraine. When the English broke the truce in 1449, Charles possessed effective artillery, a nucleus of permanent units, and above all adequate finance. However, he still needed forces raised by nobles, and the rapid decay of English resistance may have made his army appear more effective than it really was.

By 1415, the English crown raised forces by standardized contracts (indentures) with captains, specifying the number in each retinue, wages, length of service, discipline, and division of spoils.

Henry V preferred three archers to each man-at-arms. Later the proportion of archers, who were easier to recruit, increased. Between 1415 and 1450, the English government sent 90,000 soldiers to northern France, and far smaller forces to Calais and Gascony. Often individuals served more than once and many stayed on in France. Up to forty-five royal garrisons were maintained, constituting a standing army. Its numbers fluctuated with the military and financial situation: in 1436, there were about 6,000 men in 38 garrisons. An elaborate system of inspection attempted to maintain discipline and avoid fraud, with nineteen documents being required each year to authorize quarterly payment. The garrisons also contributed men to field armies, which could denude them dangerously. Henry V's land grants provided a further 1,400 men, but absenteeism and the devastation of estates after 1435 made their contribution negligible. The same may be said of native Normans. The English artillery, which was well organized, played an important part in the advance up to 1428.

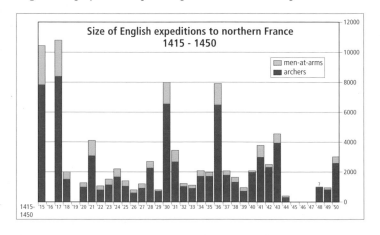

Size of English expeditions to northern France 1415 - 1450

men-at-arms
archers

a leading English commander, in a daring attack. In a ten-day campaign in 1441, Talbot and the duke of York relieved Pontoise. They pursued Charles VII and came close to capturing him, but their men were exhausted. Charles followed his long-standing policy of refusing battle, and a few weeks later stormed Pontoise, while another force took Evreux, closing in on Rouen. By 1442, English weakness was increasingly apparent: French ships operating from Dieppe made the Channel unsafe in the absence of Henry V's navy; and Charles VII's Gascon campaign (1442) further taxed scarce English resources. Defensive war with little prospect of plunder was a costly affair, and the government depended on loans from cardinal Beaufort, which gave him control of strategy. The 1438 expedition was used to establish his nephew Dorset in Maine. In 1443, the duke of Somerset, another nephew, led the last major English expedition of the war: 4,500 men with artillery and bridging equipment, with a commission to wage war across the Loire and force Charles VII to terms. While Somerset's plundering benefited himself and alienated Brittany, Charles refused battle. At least he did not resume his Gascon campaign and offered to negotiate, but the English did not have a strong hand. The result was a mere two-year truce.

The intermittent negotiations of the 1430s foundered on the English claim to the French throne. The great English nobles were bitterly divided over what course to follow, although the traditional division into 'peace' and 'war' factions is inaccurate. All wanted to retain as much as possible of Henry V's conquests. In the early 1440s, Charles VII overcame English attempts to stir up the French princes. Henry VI, who began to influence policy in the late 1430s, believed that concession could secure peace. This, and financial exhaustion, brought about the two-year truce of Tours in 1444.

Although Charles VII later claimed that he was poised to drive out the English, the first break in the fighting since 1420 allowed him to reorganize his armies and to attack the Burgundians in Lorraine. Henry VI's marriage to Charles' niece Margaret, and his highly unpopular surrender of Maine, stripping Normandy of its protective shield, brought peace no nearer. Meanwhile, the English garrisons in Normandy were unpaid and run down: the key fortress of Gisors was held by only forty-three men in 1448, compared to ninety in 1438. The king's lieutenant, Somerset, complained that 'there is no hiding place in the king's obedience purveyed, neither in reparations, ordnance, nor any manner of artillery.' The government had no funds and the taxpayers in parliament were indifferent. In such circumstances, provoking the French was insanity. In March 1449, an English force of some 6,000 men seized the Breton town of Fougères in a well-executed operation. The English government was fully implicated, hoping to strengthen their influence in Brittany. The attack gave Charles the pretext to attack. The French seized Pont de l'Arche on the Seine, and several Norman towns opened their gates before Charles declared war on 31 July 1449.

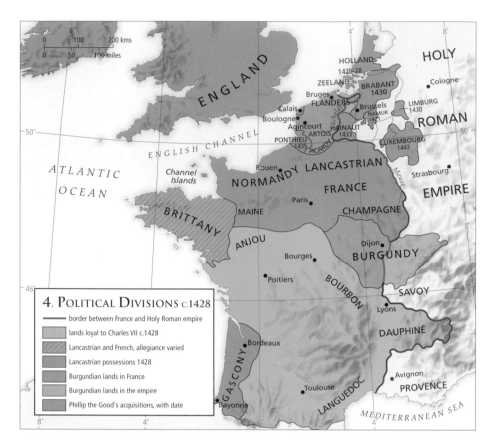

The French and Bretons assaulted with at least 20,000 men, well-supplied with artillery. One column from the east took Pont-Audemer, Pont l'Evêque, and Lisieux, before clearing the English garrisons east of Rouen. A second column took Verneuil, Mantes, Vernon, and Argentan. By mid-October, twenty English garrisons had surrendered without a fight; there was no effective central command. In October, the French converged on Rouen. At first the English fought determinedly, but the defection of the citizens was crucial. On 29 October, Somerset capitulated, saving himself and his garrison but surrendering neighbouring fortresses. In the west, the Bretons overran the Cotentin. During the winter, the English government struggled to raise and transport an army of 4,000-5,000 men, but when it finally landed in March, it was annihilated at Formigny (15 April 1450) by two smaller French forces. The fate of Normandy was, however, decided by the exhaustion of English resources and by the French siege artillery. The English garrisons in Bayeux and Caen each resisted bombardment for over a fortnight, before surrendering to vastly greater forces. The last important English fortress, Cherbourg, surrendered on 12 August 1450, barely one year after the campaign had opened.

Meanwhile, Charles VII's lieutenant in the south-west, the count of Foix, subdued the region around Bayonne with his seven culverins. The royal artillery arrived in autumn 1450, facilitating the capture of Bergerac, followed by Charles VII's captain-general Dunois (May 1451) with 7,000 men. While French, Breton, and Castilian ships blockaded Bordeaux, the key fortresses nearby fell: Bourg and Blaye without a fight, and Fronsac after heavy bombardment. Cut

MAP 4

English success required French divisions. Although an unreliable and lukewarm ally, Burgundy was vital to the Lancastrian Dual Monarchy, and its defection in 1435 made Normandy more vulnerable. Other French princes, like the duke of Brittany and the count of Foix, hoped to benefit from the situation, but after Henry V's death the likelihood of any other princes joining the English side receded.

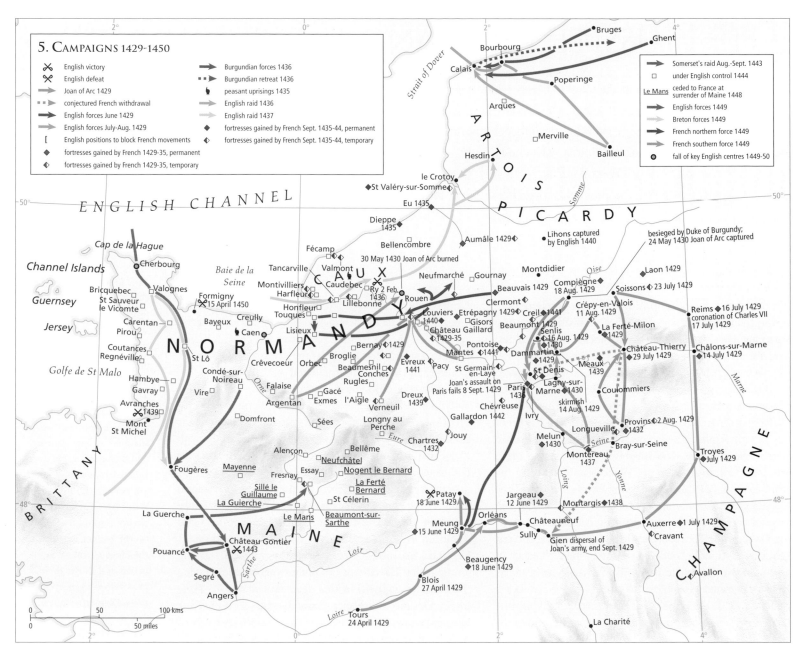

5. CAMPAIGNS 1429-1450

- ✗ English victory
- ✗ English defeat
- → Joan of Arc 1429
- ⇢ conjectured French withdrawal
- → English forces June 1429
- → English forces July-Aug. 1429
- [English positions to block French movements
- ◆ fortresses gained by French 1429-35, permanent
- ◆ fortresses gained by French 1429-35, temporary
- → Burgundian forces 1436
- ⇢ Burgundian retreat 1436
- 🔥 peasant uprisings 1435
- → English raid 1436
- → English raid 1437
- ◆ fortresses gained by French Sept. 1435-44, permanent
- ◆ fortresses gained by French Sept. 1435-44, temporary
- → Somerset's raid Aug.-Sept. 1443
- ☐ under English control 1444
- Le Mans ceded to France at surrender of Maine 1448
- → English forces 1449
- → Breton forces 1449
- → French northern force 1449
- → French southern force 1449
- ⦿ fall of key English centres 1449-50

MAP 5

The English lost the initiative after Joan of Arc revitalized Charles VII's forces, but in the 1430s, and after Burgundy's defection in 1435, they stabilized their position and in 1444 they retained the bulk of Normandy. In the 1440s, Charles VII's resources grew; he overcame the French princes and reformed the army. The bankrupt English government's decision to provoke war in 1449 was criminal folly.

off, Bordeaux surrendered on 29 June, followed by Bayonne on 22 August after a siege of a fortnight. Relief forces, which the English government had been organizing for ten months, never sailed.

THE END OF THE HUNDRED YEARS' WAR

The development of effective siege guns allowed the French to eject the English from Normandy and Gascony with astonishing speed. Effective artillery, available since about 1400, had also been important in English successes, but by the 1440s the English position had decayed from within; even in Gascony, enthusiasm for independence from France, which had preserved English rule in the last resort, was exhausted. It is feasible that, had Henry VI been prepared to lead, a negotiated peace might have been reached. But while Henry never led his troops, Charles VII became a more impressive leader in the 1440s. Above all, his attention to finance made possible his overwhelming superiority

in men and artillery. His refusal to engage the English in battle negated their remaining advantage, until the English lost even that.

The epilogue to the French victory of 1449-51 underlines this conclusion. While Charles massed his troops in Normandy against expected English attack, Talbot with 5,000 men was admitted to Bordeaux by Anglophile citizens in October 1452. Reinforcements brought his army to over 7,000, whose poor discipline contrasted with Charles VII's well-paid companies. In June 1453, three French columns closed in on Bordeaux. Talbot attempted to destroy one by storming their siege camp outside Castillon. His army was committed piecemeal and suffered badly from the French siege guns. He was killed, and his army was annihilated. Bordeaux held out for a further three months, cut off by land and sea, but in England there was indifference to the governments' attempts to raise help. In retrospect, the Hundred Years' War was over.

THE HUSSITE WARS AND LATER CRUSADES

THE BURNING of the Czech religious reformer Jan Hus for heresy in 1415 provoked a revolt amongst his Bohemian followers who expelled their new king, Sigismund of Hungary, in 1420. The Hussite leader Jan Zizka provided inspirational leadership and tactical genius in turning the wagenburg (wagon-fort) into a mobile artillery camp. The crusader hosts sent to put down the Hussites proved helpless against this new tactic. After Zizka's death in 1424, his 'Orphan' army and its successor generals carried the war into Germany in a series of great raids (1429-33). Only internecine warfare was capable of destroying these veteran forces, culminating in the victory of Lipany (1434) by the moderate Utraquists over the Taborites.

THE HUSSITE ARMIES AND THE BOHEMIAN CRUSADES

Although the Bohemian uprising was not a purely peasant revolt, many soldiers were equipped with simple infantry weapons like the flail. Recreating 'biblical' communities, as at Tabor, the Hussites possessed strict discipline and high morale from their religious inspiration. Their 'heresy' related to the laity receiving wine as well as the wafer at Communion, so their symbol was the chalice. Their greatest leader, Jan Zizka, took this as his personal arms. Born of gentry rank around 1378, he was a career soldier who had fought against the Teutonic Knights at Tannenberg in 1410, and later lost an eye serving Wenceslas IV. During the revolution of 1419, he came to the fore as a leader of the Hussite cause. Zizka's rapidity of strategic movement and shrewd battlecraft in choosing strong defensive positions for a wagon-fort, brought the Hussites remarkable success. His strict disciplinary code (surviving in the Ordinance of 1424, and strikingly similar to that of his contemporary, Henry V) created a tough, veteran army. Men such as Borek of Miletinik, Prokop the Great, and Procupek, whom he trained as leaders, continued this tradition to the end of the wars (map 1).

Contemporary chronicles describe '100,000-strong' crusader cavalry armies against few Hussites. Actually, the Bohemians were made up of half-a-dozen factional armies, each capable of putting 5,000-6,000 men into the field; united they made a formidable force. Sigismund had great difficulty recruiting a cavalry strike-force. In 1422, the second of the two armies he raised that year contained only 1,656 cavalry, but 31,000 foot.

In 1420, Zizka had only 400 men and 12 wagons when confronted by royalist forces. Baffled by the wagon-fort, they attacked dismounted, to be rebuffed after a hard fight. This first victory, at Sudomer (25 March), was vital. It emboldened the Taborites to march on against Sigismund (20 May). The proclamation of crusade (1 March) brought Sigismund into Bohemia in April, heading for Kutná Hora, with its supportive population of German miners. Sigismund then advanced on Prague and attacked the Hussite entrenchment on the Vitkov Hill (14 July), but suffered a bloody repulse. Rivalries and plague within the crusader

camp compelled his withdrawal a fortnight later. Zizka had secured the Hussite rebellion and now besieged Hradcany and Vysehrad, the royalist fortresses which dominated Prague. Sigismund's attempt at relief was defeated on 31 October, and Vysehrad surrendered.

Hussite columns fanned out from Prague and by mid-1421 they had taken Hradcany and most of central Bohemia. The Congress of Caslav (3 June) elected twenty regents from the nobles and the cities to rule the country. Although Zizka was wounded at the siege of Rabi, and became completely blind, he continued in active command.

In the autumn of 1421, Sigismund invaded Moravia from Hungary. Supported by the *condottiere* Pipa of Ozora and duke Albert of Austria, he captured Brno (1 November) and advanced to Kutná Hora. Zizka held the city and on 21 December marched out to challenge the crusaders, forming a wagon-fort. The citizens promptly switched sides, leaving the Hussites trapped. In this desperate situation, Zizka inspired his men to advance, drove the enemy off the Kasik Hill, and rebuilt his wagon-fort. (This manoeuvre has been mistakenly understood as 'charging' the enemy with the battle-wagons). Still vulnerable but not attacked, he withdrew under cover of night to Kolin. Despite the freezing weather, Zizka soon returned, and this time Sigismund withdrew. On 8 January, the Hussites caught up with his rearguard led by Pipa of Ozora at Habry and routed it with heavy loss. The crusade dispersed.

As external threats fell away, the struggle for an alternative regime began. The Bohemian nobility had a wavering relationship with Sigismund and constantly threatened defection under the banner of the Utraquist (moderate) religious position. In 1422, Zizka defeated them at Hořice (20 April) in a battle which epitomized his tactical method. In mid-May, prince Korybut (nephew of Vitold, grand duke of Lithuania) arrived in Prague to present himself as a candidate for the throne. He began an unsuccessful siege of nearby Karlstein castle, an immensely strong royal fortress. In fact, Hussite siege technique proved inadequate generally. The wagon-train's limitations were also exposed by Zizka's invasion of Hungary in 1423. The mobile Hungarian cavalry

This fifteenth-century German manuscript presents a compendiumized view of a Hussite wagon-fort. All the essential elements are there, although reduced in scale. The baggage wagons and horses stand within linked armoured war-wagons manned by handgunners and flail-men. Large quantities of guns and weapons are portrayed, indicating a formidable firepower. The chalice symbol that appears on the banner represents the Hussite's religious beliefs and shows their importance in motivating these Christian soldiers.

withdrew before him, avoiding combat. Unable to force a decision, Zizka was forced to retreat to Moravia, only extracting his forces with some difficulty after a ten-day fighting march.

In 1424, Zizka, opposed by the Praguers, put into operation his standard plan of a strong defensive position which he had chosen. At Malešov (7 June) he set up his wagon-fort on a hill, whilst sending light cavalry to harass the enemy and goad them into attack. When the mass of their infantry crossed the valley he had stone-filled wagons rolled into their ranks, followed by a vigorous attack. As the infantry panicked and fled, their mounted noble allies rode off unscathed. This victory enabled Zizka to bring the cities of central Bohemia under his control. On 29 June, prince Korybut returned to Prague from Poland with 1,500 cavalry. Zizka advanced on the city and set up camp nearby. Following negotiations, a united campaign began against Moravia; but Zizka died at the siege of Pribyslav and the campaign was abandoned.

THE GREAT RAIDS AND THE BATTLE OF LIPANY

In spring 1426, duke Frederick of Saxony attempted to seize Usti (map 1), which had been pledged to him by Sigismund. The Hussites united again to oppose this invasion under the leadership of the priest, Prokop. Imitating his master's tactics to the letter, he defeated the enemy's attack on the wagon-fort. The crusaders, having promised no quarter, received none, even the ransomable nobles being cut down in the ensuing pursuit.

During 1427-28, Sigismund was busy fighting the Turks, so it fell to the German princes to continue the crusades. The Diet of Frankfurt (April 1427) planned a four-pronged assault on Bohemia, but this proved impossible to co-ordinate. The main attack in the west faltered at Stříbro (besieged 23 July). Hussite forces under Prokop were only mustered by forced marches and arrived exhausted (2 August). Their mere presence was enough to cause the crusaders to dissolve into flight, much to the annoyance of the late-arriving cardinal Beaufort with 1,000 English archers. Prokop went on to capture Tachov on 11 August.

The Hussites now moved on to the offensive. The combined armies of the 'Orphans', Taborites, and Praguers raided into Hungary, reaching Pressburg. In early 1428 they devastated Silesia as far as Wroclaw (Breslau). By December 1429, Prokop mustered a credible '4,000 cavalry, 40,000 infantry, and 2,500 war-wagons' at Prague to invade Saxony. They marched in five parallel columns, avoiding sieges, but raiding open towns. Unopposed, they continued into Franconia and only withdrew after securing payment from the elector of Brandenburg. Prokop was back in Prague by 21 February 1430, his winter campaign a brilliant success. In March, the combined forces of the 'Orphans' and New Town Praguers ('10,000 foot and 1,200 horse') invaded Silesia, and then Hungary in April. In battle at Tyrnau, the Hungarian horse penetrated the wagon-fort, killing a Hussite commander, but were eventually defeated with heavy loss on both sides. As greed for plunder replaced religious fervour, Hussite armies were losing the iron discipline necessary for victory.

MAP 1

In 1420, Zizka's wagon-fort defeated king Sigismund on Vitkov Hill, outside Prague, and in 1421 repelled the second Crusade, at Kutna Hora. Victories at Horice (1422) and Malesov (1424) secured his power over Bohemia. Even after Zizka's death the Hussites defeated attacks on Usti (1426) and Stribro (1427). From 1428-30, Prokop led great raids into Germany, and the fifth crusaders fled in panic (1431). Eventually, internecine warfare amongst the Hussites destroyed Zizka's veterans at Lipany in 1434, and Sigismund regained his throne.

Hoping to profit from divisions within Bohemia, Sigismund launched a fifth crusade in the summer of 1431. Once again, the line of advance was through Tachov, moving on to besiege Domazlice. The Hussites united to muster at Karlstein and moved quickly to its relief. The mere sound of their battle hymn 'All ye warriors of God' was enough to cause a flight. Only the 200 Italian mercenaries of cardinal Cesarini's bodyguard stood to fight within their own wagon-fort, where they were overwhelmed. The crusaders left an enormous booty in Hussite hands, losing almost all of their 100 bombards, and saving only 300 from 4,000 wagons. This was Sigismund's last attempt at military conquest.

In autumn 1431, the Taborites and Orphans raided Silesia and Slovakia, but fell out over the spoils. Whilst Prokop withdrew, the Orphans' expedition into Hungary met with disaster. From 7 November they engaged in a fighting retreat under appalling weather conditions, during which 120 wagons were lost. A Taborite column was also defeated whilst pillaging Austria. Retreating with the booty, it was trapped near Waidhofen losing 1,000 killed and 500 captured, together with all the wagons. Despite these setbacks, in 1432 the Hussites campaigned in Lusatia. In 1433, the Orphans served with the Poles against the Teutonic Knights, reaching the Baltic (April-September). Meanwhile, Prokop began a siege of Pilsen (Plzen) with the other combined armies, but he was unable to prevent his troops from pillaging within Bohemia or raiding without. A column operating in Bavaria was trapped at Waldmunchen by the burgrave of Nuremberg. He was joined by numerous peasants outraged by Hussite brutalities. The wagon-fort was stormed and of 1,800, only the leaders and 130 men escaped. When Prokop imprisoned the defeated general, he provoked a mutiny and was himself briefly held captive.

This evident anarchy encouraged the formation of an Utraquist noble league at Kutna Hora, mustering some 600 horse and 10,000 foot. Marching on Prague, they dragooned the citizens' aid. The Taborites and their allies abandoned the siege of Pilsen and withdrew to Kolin, then advanced to relieve the Utraquist siege of Cesky Brod. After negotiations failed, reportedly, 25,000 leaguers confronted Prokop's 18,000-strong wagon-fort. Borek of Miletinik, commanding the Utraquists, had devised a plan of attack. As flanking artillery bombarded the wagon-fort, he waited until the defenders had fired, then attacked rapidly before they could reload; but instead of closing, ordered his troops to feign retreat. The Taborites poured out in pursuit, to be enveloped by larger numbers and then massacred. Two years after the battle of Lipany, Sigismund of Hungary was reigning in Prague.

THE LATER CRUSADES

The loss of the Syrian coastline in 1291 proved final, but contemporaries were unaware of this and 150 years of crusades – either planned or actual – followed. The Hospitallers built up an impregnable base at Rhodes and nibbled at the Turkish coastline. In the early thirteenth century, the Venetian theorist, Marino Sanudo, drew up ambitious plans for conquering Mamluk Egypt. He hoped to mobilize a massive army of 2,000 knights and 50,000 foot in Europe, to be preceded by an advance guard of 200 knights and 15,000 foot. Unsurprisingly, this did not materialize.

Expeditions did leave the west though. King Peter of Cyprus had some success recruiting for his raids in the 1360s; but by far the largest expedition was the Nicopolis crusade of 1396. An outbreak of peace in the wars between France and England freed many noblemen to revive the crusader spirit. John of Nevers, heir to Burgundy, was a principal leader, accompanied by 150 men-at-arms, while the next-largest contingent was that of marshal Boucicault of France with half this number. In total, there may have

---

THE HUSSITE WAGON-FORT

'When the Hussites marched against the Germans to fight, they enclosed themselves with their carts, chained together, and carried chain flails with lead balls...and every time they struck they felled a man and by this method they remained always in their fortified wagons' (Berry Herald).

The Hussite war-wagons (page 136) have often been represented as forerunners to the modern tank, but they were only mobile on the march. For battle, the draught horses were unhitched and wagons' wheels interlocked to form a wagon-fort made of an inner ring of baggage wagons and an entrenched outer ring of 'armoured' wagons. These latter were bound in iron, with protective hoardings and planks underneath pierced for firing, with ten-man 'crews' of handgunners and flail-men. The artillery, which travelled on small carts, was dismounted and dug in behind pavises

between the wagons. Within the fort, small cavalry forces were poised near a rear exit and an infantry strike force at the front, ready to sortie out upon disordered attackers.

At the battle of Hörice in 1422, 'He [Zizka] took up his position with his men near the church of St Gothard, to be able to place his soldiers and his artillery on a height, and also so that, as the enemy were cavalry, they should be obliged to dismount... When they advanced against the position they were more burdened by their heavy armour than Zizka's infantry. When they were near the summit and attempted to attack the wagons he received them with fire from his guns and constant attacks by his infantry; and before they could capture his wagons he beat them back as he pleased; and after he had driven them away from the wagons he sent fresh soldiers against them.' (Contemporary Bohemian account)

BATTLE OF NICOPOLIS 25 SEPTEMBER 1396

Whilst besieging Nicopolis, the crusader army became aware of Bayezid's advance. It was Sigismund's intention to deploy his unreliable vassals, the voivodes of Wallachia and Transylvania, in front of his main body in order to force them to fight. But the French demanded the honour of the van and charged directly at Bayezid's position. Behind a screen of Akinji light cavalry, and invisible to the westerners, lay a belt of sharpened wooden stakes, at chest height to the horses, full of Janissary archers. As the Turkish light cavalry melted away to the flanks, the crusaders lost their horses to both the arrows and the obstacles. Undeterred, they abandoned their mounts and attacked on foot, routing the unarmoured bowmen. Unfortunately, when they saw the crusaders' horses galloping back across the plain, the Wallachians and Transylvanians made off. Meanwhile, the French arrived at the top of the hill, exhausted by their efforts, to find the cream of Bayezid's heavy cavalry – the Spahis – awaiting them. Surrounded and overwhelmed, they surrendered en masse. Sigismund's Hungarians arrived too late, and were themselves driven off by the flanking attack of Bayezid's Christian Serbian vassals. The outcome epitomized the difference between Bayezid's well-balanced defence in depth and a headstrong western charge. Numbers on both sides are difficult to assess, but there is no reason to believe that the Turks greatly exceeded the crusaders. They were simply better disciplined and better led.

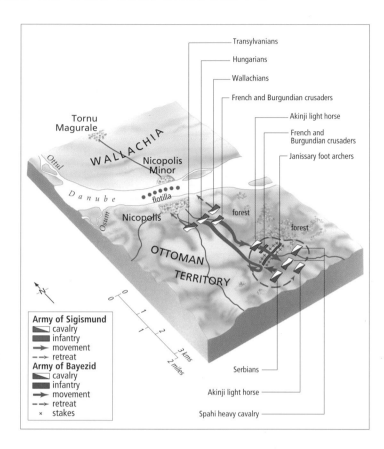

been 1,000 heavy cavalry with concomitant support troops.

The call for crusade came from the Christian ruler most threatened by the advance of the Ottoman Turks. This was king Sigismund of Hungary, who hoped to operate defensively against sultan Bayezid. But he was overruled by the crusaders who, after storming two smaller fortresses, insisted upon a siege of the strongly fortified town of Nicopolis on the Danube, despite lacking any siege engines. This enabled Bayezid to draw them into battle on unfavourable terms which led to the defeat and capture of the entire force.

Bayezid was himself overthrown by the Mongol leader Timur-lenk at Ankara in 1402, but the Ottoman momentum was proving unstoppable. Under Murad II (1421-51) the Turks resumed their attacks on Constantinople and pushed further into the Balkans. The only real opposition came from Janos Hunyadi, regent of Hungary and voivode of Transylvania. When Murad attacked Transylvania in 1438, Hunyadi allied with the king of Poland and the despot of Serbia to defeat him at Hermannstadt (modern Sibiu). In 1442, Murad suffered another defeat there, losing '20,000' men, and a third defeat soon after. The arrival of western crusaders in 1443 encouraged Hunyadi to go on to the offensive, and drew in the Albanian ruler George Castriota, known as Iskander Beg. The combination was able to

impose a humiliating ten-year truce on the sultan, which drove Murad to abdicate. The next year, the crusaders insisted upon breaking the treaty and attacking Varna. Murad then promptly emerged from his retirement, leading a force of 40,000 men transferred from Asia Minor in Genoese ships, and attacked the besiegers, eventually forcing them into retreat.

Hunyadi returned to the offensive in support of Iskander Beg and to relieve pressure on Constantinople in 1448. He met Murad at Kosovo, but after a tough contest was defeated. This was the last gasp for Byzantium, and the city was finally overwhelmed by Mehmed II in 1453. The Ottoman victory was one of logistics, technology, and vastly superior manpower. Mehmed had ships dragged overland into the Golden Horn to outflank its chain barrier. He possessed massive cannon, one shooting 800-pound stones, eleven 500-pounders, and over fifty 200-pounders. They battered down the thousand-year-old walls, allowing the Janissaries to storm the breaches, slaughtering the last emperor and his paltry, largely mercenary, garrison.

Hunyadi raised the siege of Belgrade in 1456, with the help of German and Hungarian crusaders, but died in the same year. Iskander Beg died in 1468 and Albania was absorbed into the Ottoman empire, although Hungary survived as a result of Hunyadi's efforts.

THE WARS OF THE ROSES 1452-1487

THE 'WARS OF THE ROSES' is a convenient label for three English civil wars. First (1459-61) two factions competed to control the imbecilic Lancastrian Henry VI (1422-61) — Lancastrians led by Edmund duke of Somerset, then queen Margaret, and Richard duke of York backed by the Neville family (earls of Salisbury and Warwick). York's son, Edward IV (1461-83), won the throne in 1461. In 1470, Warwick joined the Lancastrians against Edward IV, whose victories in 1471 extinguished the direct Lancastrian line. The usurper Richard III (1483-85) was overthrown by Henry VII (1485-1509) with Yorkist and Lancastrian backing. In the civil wars, both sides followed battle-seeking strategies to win political power. Their mainly unprofessional forces reinforced the tendency to short campaigns.

The phrase 'Wars of the Roses' is derived from the badges of the rival families descended from Edward III. The white rose was York's most famous badge, and Henry VII adopted the red rose to show he was the true heir of Lancaster. Edward IV also used a sunburst, Richard III a seated boar, and this shows Henry VII's banner and Tudor devices, including double roses.

THE FIRST WAR

In February 1452, Richard of York first tried to remove Henry VI's favourite, Somerset, by force. The Lancastrian army at Northampton cut off York at Ludlow from his partisans in eastern England. When London and Kent failed to support him, he 'marvellously fortified his ground with pits, pavises, and guns' (Benet's Chronicle) — a tactic from the French war — south of the Thames near Dartford. When the king's army arrived, neither side was eager to fight and after negotiations York disbanded his forces. In 1455, York tried again, backed by two powerful lords, Salisbury and his son Warwick. Avoiding the mistakes of 1452, they swooped on the royal army (map 1) at St Albans (22 May 1455) before it was assembled. Lancastrian forces held the narrow streets of the unwalled town for an hour, but fled leaving around fifty dead when Warwick's men broke through some back gardens into the market place. The Yorkist lords killed their rivals, the duke of Somerset, Percy the earl of Northumberland, and lord Clifford, but could not control Henry VI for long. The slide into war was led by the dominant figure at court, Henry's wife Margaret. The armies mustered in September 1459. Salisbury won a stiff skirmish at Blore Heath (23 September), but only poor co-ordination of the royal forces let him join York at Ludlow. The Yorkists boldly advanced to Worcester to avoid entrapment west of the Severn, but then fell back before the Lancastrians, until near Ludlow at Ludford Bridge they made 'a great deep ditch and fortified it with guns, carts, and stakes' (Gregory's Chronicle). The same night, the Yorkist leaders fled, dishonourably but sensibly: their army was demoralized; its elite troops from the Calais garrison were about to defect; and the presence of Henry VI with many lords in the Lancastrian army made many on the Yorkist side unwilling to fight.

The most intense fighting of the Wars of the Roses took place between 1460-61. While Margaret waited at Coventry for York to invade from Dublin, she failed to send adequate forces to defeat the Yorkists at Calais. Some 2,000 Yorkists seized a bridgehead at Sandwich (June 1460), and by promising good government attracted men in Kent, and cash and transport in London. Warwick advanced in two columns (4 and 5 July) until the Lancastrian position was known. Rain and negotiations slowed the advance. Although many contingents were still on the road, the Lancastrians were confident in their fortified camp near Northampton. But when the Yorkists attacked on 10 July, 'the ordnance of the king's guns availed not, for that day was so great rain that the guns…were quenched and might not be shot' (Anonymous London chronicler). The Kentish foot played a notable role in the assault. In barely half an hour, the Lancastrian army was in flight, betrayed by lord Grey who let Warwick in. The casualties, around 300 in number, were mainly Lancastrian, and king Henry was captured.

York was no longer content to rule through Henry VI, but by claiming the throne himself (October 1460) he rallied support for Margaret and her son Edward. Margaret's army mustered at Hull (December), advancing to Ponte-fract (map 2). Rather than allow winter to discourage the Lancastrians, York and Salisbury marched north (9-21 December) to rescue their partisans in the north and to forestall defections. At York's castle of Sandal (Wakefield), they were dangerously isolated, and were surprised and defeated outside their defences in an obscure fight (30 December). York and Salisbury headed the list of the dead. Margaret's army then advanced menacingly southwards. Warwick's decision to fight close to London was wise, but at St Albans he first moved his army out of its fortified camp, then failed to locate the Lancastrian army. Somerset skilfully approached from the north-west to attack the York-ist rear (17 February 1461) with his most reliable troops, the lords' retinues. In both armies food was scarce and the levies unreliable. The Yorkist vanguard put up a fight, but Warwick failed to rally the main body, and his Burgundian gunners could not get their cumbersome weapons into action. The Yorkists escaped into the dusk, abandoning Henry. Margaret then made a crucial error. Her withdrawal to Dunstable to await supplies from London allowed York's son Edward, victorious over the Welsh Lancastrians at Mortimer's Cross (2-3 February 1461), to reach the city, where he was proclaimed king as a last resort to justify continued rebellion. Margaret fell back in order to raise fresh troops in the north. Edward's vanguard followed on 9 March, the main division two days later, joined by contingents en route.

The armies raised for the March 1461 campaign were the largest of the Wars of the Roses – possibly over 20,000 on each side, many of whom had been under arms since before Christmas. On 28 March, Yorkist patrols found the bridge over the river Aire destroyed and defended so, as the Yorkist bishop George Neville wrote 'our men could only cross by a narrow way which they themselves made and over which they forced a way at sword point, many men being slain on both sides'. Lancastrian failure to reinforce their vanguard, while Edward fed in his whole army, led to them losing a strategic obstacle. The Yorkists camped in snow and bitter cold, and next morning found the Lancastrians drawn up 6 miles (10km) away near Towton, anxious to settle the matter. A strong wind favoured the Yorkist archers, but the Lancastrian cavalry routed Edward's cavalry and pursued them. The battle was decided in their absence by the mêlée between the dismounted men-at-arms. The Lancastrian army, composed of many different retinues, may have lacked cohesion, and

MAP 1

In these early campaigns, the issue was control of Henry VI. In 1452, York failed owing to his political isolation. In 1455, he was joined by the Nevilles, but victory at St Albans could not guarantee control of Henry VI for long. The stakes were raised in 1459 when queen Margaret determined to remove York. His army refused to fight the king in person, but the Yorkist leaders escaped. They invaded from Calais and captured Henry at the battle of Northampton. Subsequently, York claimed the throne himself.

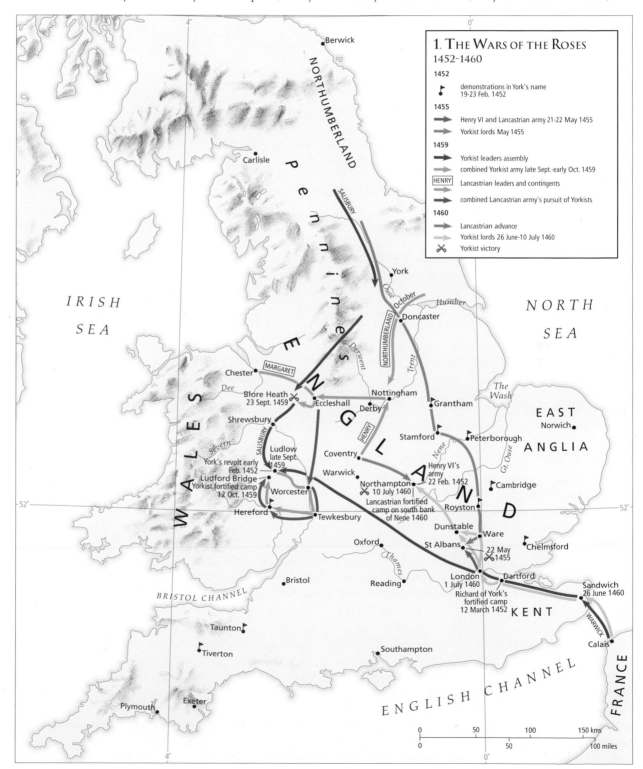

1. THE WARS OF THE ROSES 1452-1460

1452
- demonstrations in York's name 19-23 Feb. 1452

1455
- Henry VI and Lancastrian army 21-22 May 1455
- Yorkist lords May 1455

1459
- Yorkist leaders assembly
- combined Yorkist army late Sept.-early Oct. 1459
- HENRY Lancastrian leaders and contingents
- combined Lancastrian army's pursuit of Yorkists

1460
- Lancastrian advance
- Yorkist lords 26 June-10 July 1460
- Yorkist victory

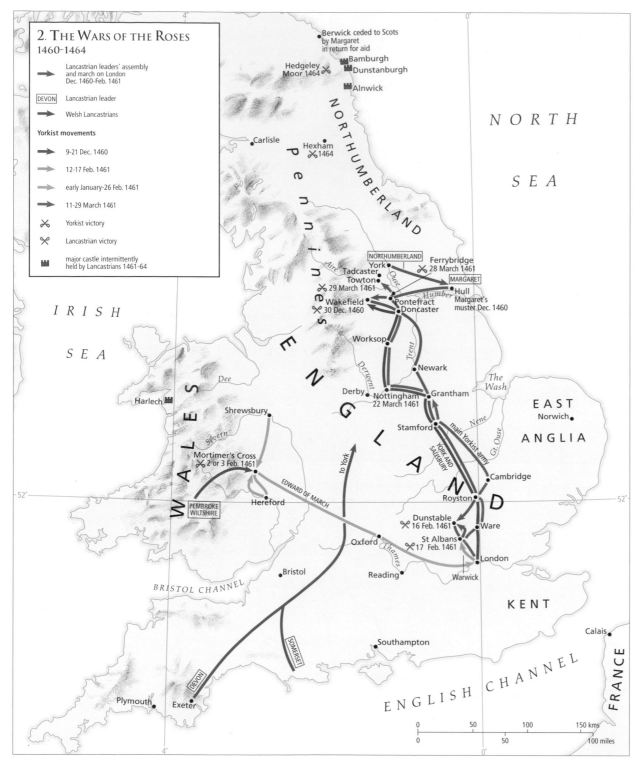

2. THE WARS OF THE ROSES
1460-1464

➤ Lancastrian leaders' assembly
and march on London
Dec. 1460-Feb. 1461

DEVON Lancastrian leader

➤ Welsh Lancastrians

Yorkist movements

➤ 9-21 Dec. 1460

➤ 12-17 Feb. 1461

➤ early January-26 Feb. 1461

➤ 11-29 March 1461

✗ Yorkist victory

✗ Lancastrian victory

▥ major castle intermittently
held by Lancastrians 1461-64

MAP 2

In December 1460, the
Lancastrians mustered a
new army, and killed
Richard of York at
Wakefield. This began
a prolonged mid-winter
campaign, involving most
of the English nobility.
Margaret brushed War-
wick aside at St Albans,
but failed to occupy
London, allowing Edward
of York to be declared
king. He pursued the
Lancastrians to Yorkshire,
where two days of heavy
fighting culminated in his
victory. Although he was
dilatory in snuffing out the
last Lancastrians in Northumberland, they were not
a serious threat.

---

it broke after a long struggle. Many were killed as they fled,
especially at Tadcaster, where the bridge had been broken
to impede the Yorkists. Towton has the reputation as one
of Britain's bloodiest battles, but even figures reported at
the time of from 9,000 to 28,000 dead, would seem to be
exaggerations. It effectively gave Edward control of England,
but Henry VI escaped and Lancastrians maintained a foothold
in Northumberland. Edward's inability to find reliable
constables for border fortresses allowed the Lancastrian
cause to revive, until his diplomacy ended Franco-Scottish
support for Margaret. Then, in 1464, Warwick's brother,

lord Montagu, defeated the Lancastrians in two skirmishes.
The royal siege guns, sent by sea from London, were needed
only at Bamburgh. The execution of captured Lancastrian
leaders, and the capture of Henry VI in 1465, extinguished
support for the Lancastrian cause in England. Their last
stronghold, Harlech, fell in 1468.

THE SECOND WAR 1469-1471

In 1469, Warwick and Edward's brother Clarence harnessed
popular discontent to gain control themselves. Warwick
met up with an army of his Yorkshire tenants to isolate

Edward from London and intercept the earls of Pembroke and Devon who were leading men to Edward at Nottingham. Pembroke's Welsh men-at-arms were defeated near Banbury (battle of Edgecote, 26 July) where he fought unsupported by Devon's West Country archers, possibly due to a quarrel. However, Warwick could not command obedience; in September he released Edward, who apparently forgave him. In early 1470, Warwick tried again. A Lincolnshire rising was intended to join Warwick at Leicester on 12 March, to trap Edward between them and a Yorkshire army. However, Edward was alert. The Lincolnshire rebels tried to ambush Edward near Stamford, before he could unite his forces at Grantham, to save their leader's father from execution. Warned by his spies and scouts, Edward routed them at 'Lose-cote field' (map 3). By 18 March, his army growing every day, Edward had put his army across Warwick's way into Yorkshire. But then Warwick's vanguard feinted towards Rotherham and, as Edward advanced to fight, he escaped across the Pennines. Edward could not follow at once, owing to the lack of provisions in the thinly populated uplands and the need to

pacify Yorkshire. Warwick and Clarence escaped to France where king Louis XI, in order to gain English support against Burgundy, reconciled the arch-enemies Margaret and Warwick and funded an invasion. Although Edward easily dealt with a rising of Warwick's retainers in Yorkshire (August 1470), in early September a storm scattered Anglo-Burgundian ships in the Channel, allowing Warwick to land. When Warwick's brother Montagu defected, Edward barely escaped to Burgundy, and Henry VI was restored to the throne.

In March 1471, Edward sailed for England with almost 2,000 troops, including 300 hand-gunners provided by the duke of Burgundy. An Italian diplomat reported that 'men think he will leave his skin there'. In the following weeks, Edward took calculated risks to defeat Warwick and Margaret (who was still in France) separately, while they failed to concentrate their forces. Since Edward landed in Yorkshire where he had few supporters, he claimed only his family lands. The dominant local landowner, Northumberland, let him pass, while Montagu at Pontefract failed to intercept his small force (map 3). A bold advance on Newark dispersed some 4,000 Lancastrians, and then lord Hastings led in the first significant support of 3,000 well-equipped men. At the end of March, Warwick sensibly withdrew into the walled town of Coventry, refusing battle. Although Clarence, with 4,000 men, defected to Edward (3 April), greater reinforcements joined Warwick. Edward broke the deadlock by seizing London (11 April). Warwick had to follow, and Edward advanced with less than 10,000 to confront his larger army at Barnet. In the dark, Edward pushed his men forward for a dawn attack to neutralize Warwick's artillery. Owing to this, the armies were not aligned, so when Edward attacked after four o'clock on Easter Sunday (14 April), his outflanked left fled, pursued by Warwick's right. But in the dense mist, the rest of his army fought on, oblivious. His right enveloped Warwick's left, but the battle was decided in the centre. After three hours of intense combat, in which Edward fought prominently, Warwick's army broke. Casualties were heavy: more than 1,000 dead were reported, among them Warwick and Montagu. The same evening, Margaret landed in the south-west.

Rather than strike before Edward replaced his losses, the Lancastrians decided to join their supporters in the north-west and Wales, which required them to cross the Severn. To deceive Edward they made feints towards London. Edward remained in the Thames valley, keeping both routes covered, then advanced 30 miles (48km) on 29 April to guard the Severn at Gloucester. The Lancastrians successfully lured Edward south by appearing to offer battle, while their army refreshed itself at Bristol before a forced march overnight to Gloucester. Fortunately for Edward, the constable refused them entry, condemning them to march to the next crossing at Tewkesbury. Having covered 50 miles (80km) in 36 hours, the Lancastrians were too exhausted to cross that afternoon. Consequently, Edward's army was able to catch them, covering more than 30 miles

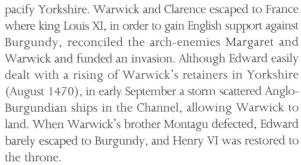

The pictures in this French copy of the *Historie of the Arrivall of Edward IV*, by an eyewitness, are less useful than the text. The battle of Barnet took place in dense mist, increasing the 'fog of war' which bedevils battle reconstructions. In the mist, Edward's troops were unaware that their left wing had been routed, and fought on to win.

BATTLE OF TEWKESBURY
4 MAY 1471

Tewkesbury is the only Wars of the Roses battle whose precise site is known. A Yorkist eye-witness gave a sequence of events, but they cannot be related to the ground exactly. The Lancastrians were in a 'marvellously strong ground…[with] so evil lanes, and deep dykes, so many hedges…that it was right hard to approach them near'. Edward had about 3,000 foot, plus men-at-arms and artillery; Margaret's strength is unknown. The Yorkist vanguard (Gloucester) assailed Somerset with arrows and shot. He charged down 'by certain paths…afore purveyed, and to the king's party unknown, he departed out of the field, passed a lane…and came into a…close… and, from the hill that was in one of the closes, he set right fiercely upon the end of the king's battle'. The remaining Lancastrians stayed put, allowing Edward and Gloucester to 'with great violence, put them [Somerset] up towards the hill'. An attack by 200 cavalry Edward had sent to clear a wood routed Somerset's men. Edward then put the Lancastrian centre and left to flight.

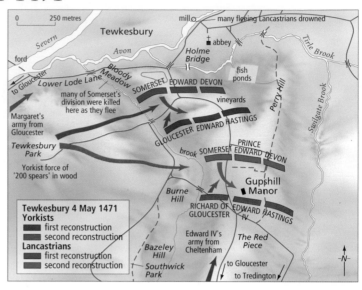

(48km) on 3 May on the open downland, to camp 3 miles (5km) away. Although the Lancastrian strategy had failed, they held a strong site on a low ridge for the now unavoidable battle. Goaded by Yorkist artillery and archery, Somerset led the Lancastrian right down to attack Edward's centre, using the close terrain to approach unseen. However, his division was squeezed between the Yorkist centre and left, then routed by a surprise attack by 200 men-at-arms Edward had concealed in a wood. The Yorkists then defeated the Lancastrian centre and left separately. The Lancastrians in the north collapsed following Tewkesbury, but in Kent, Thomas Fauconberg (a cousin of Warwick) threatened London with a considerable force. News of Edward's victory emboldened the city authorities to resist, a course of action unusual in the Wars of the Roses. Guns were mounted on the river wall and the gates were protected with bulwarks and guns. Fauconberg's assaults on London Bridge and the city gates (12 and 14 May) were beaten off. His ships' guns mounted on the south bank of the Thames were overwhelmed by London's artillery. The approach of Edward's advance guard hastened the dispersal of Fauconberg's men.

THE THIRD WAR 1483-1487

After the murder of Henry VI in the Tower, and the death of his heir Edward in 1471, Edward IV enjoyed twelve years of peace. He died prematurely in 1483, leaving as heir the twelve year-old Edward V. Edward IV had made his brother Richard the greatest noble in the north, a power he now used to usurp the throne, causing a new civil war. During August 1483, former servants of Edward IV, his widow's family, and the duke of Buckingham (who was instrumental in Richard's usurpation), accepted that Edward V was dead, and plotted to make an obscure Lancastrian exile, Henry

Tudor, king. There were risings across southern England in October, but in Wales, Buckingham attracted no support and Richard encountered little resistance. By the time Henry was proclaimed king in Cornwall (*map 4*) the revolt was dead. Richard survived in 1483 because his magnate backers, Norfolk, Northumberland, and Stanley, remained loyal. The surviving Yorkist plotters joined Henry and his Lancastrian companions in Brittany.

During 1484, Richard was based centrally at Nottingham awaiting an invasion which never came, as Henry Tudor was unable to secure foreign backing. This waiting exhausted Richard's resources. Henry Tudor finally landed in Wales on 7 August 1485, with a few hundred mainly Yorkist exiles and 4,000 French mercenaries. They marched rapidly through Wales, seeking to fight before Richard could complete his muster. Henry gained little support, but no attempt was made to stop him either. He was in touch with the Stanley family, who promised to defect. Richard, at Leicester, was also eager for battle as he detected signs of crumbling loyalty.

The battlefield at Bosworth cannot be located precisely, but a broad outline of the fighting is possible. The battle lasted some two hours. Richard's forces considerably outnumbered Henry's army of around 5,000 men. His large vanguard of cavalry, infantry, and archers attacked and was pinned by Henry's smaller vanguard. Richard led his household around the mêlée to attack Henry's own force, threatening Henry's life. However, sir William Stanley, waiting on one side, committed his force of 3,000 to crush Richard's isolated troop. According to Henry's court historian, Polydore Vergil, 'king Richard alone was killed fighting manfully in the thickest press of his enemies… his courage was high and fierce and failed him not even at the death which, when his men forsook him, he preferred to take by the sword rather than, by foul flight, to prolong his life'. Richard's death ended the battle. Richard's charge was a desperate gamble rather than a brilliant manoeuvre: he had failed to keep the loyalty of the nobles who brought him to the throne (lord Stanley and Northumberland, who profited greatly from the usurpation, did not fight) and risked his life before committing his whole army.

Henry VII represented Yorkist legitimism as well as Lancaster, making his position more stable than Richard's, but early in his reign he was vulnerable. In 1487, an impostor was crowned in Ireland as 'Edward VI'. In June, two surviving Ricardians, the earl of Lincoln and lord Lovel,

landed in Lancashire with 2,000 German mercenaries, paid for by Edward IV's sister Margaret of Burgundy, and up to 5,000 Irish levies. Support in Yorkshire was disappointing, despite the region's connections with Richard III, and York refused to admit the ill-disciplined Irish. However, Northumberland failed to deal with the rebels. Henry awaited the support of the Stanleys and precise news of Lincoln's route in the east Midlands, before intercepting the rebels at East Stoke, south-west of Newark. He had a large army, whose vanguard alone sufficed to defeat Lincoln's forces. The poorly equipped Irish were of little threat to Henry, and the German mercenaries were too few

MAP 3

In 1469, Edward IV was captured after his former ally Warwick destroyed his forces at Edgecote. He was more alert in 1470, defeating the rebels at 'Lose-cote field', but Warwick escaped after both sides manoeuvred skilfully. By the end of 1470, Edward was an exile, after Warwick's alliance with Margaret revived the Lancastrian cause. Edward IV invaded in March 1471, seizing the initiative to defeat his enemies separately, forcing battle at Barnet and Tewkesbury, before they joined forces. Fauconberg's attack on London was the only town siege of the wars. The city authorities resisted, knowing that Edward was approaching.

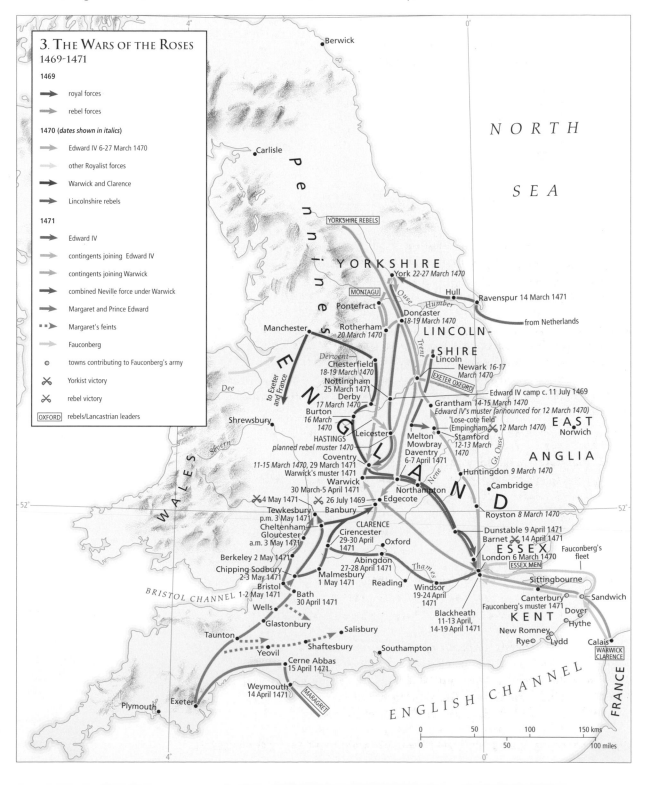

in number. Unlike in 1485, this time there was no treachery among the king's chief supporters. This battle of Stoke marked the end of the Wars of the Roses because it was the last time Henry VII had to fight a pitched battle against a pretender.

ARMIES OF THE WARS OF THE ROSES

The Calais garrison of over 1,000 men was England's only standing army. The town was a vital Yorkist base in the winter of 1459-60, and Calais troops formed the core of

the Yorkist army which invaded in June 1460. However, Andrew Trollope, a Calais commander and renowned soldier, refused to fight Henry VI (October 1459) and became a leading Lancastrian captain until his death at Towton. The government also paid the wardens of the northern marches (usually from the rival Neville and Percy families) to retain a few hundred soldiers, but their private forces were more important. French and Burgundian rulers supplied mercenaries to back invasion in 1470-71 and 1485-87. Their importance grew as noble participation

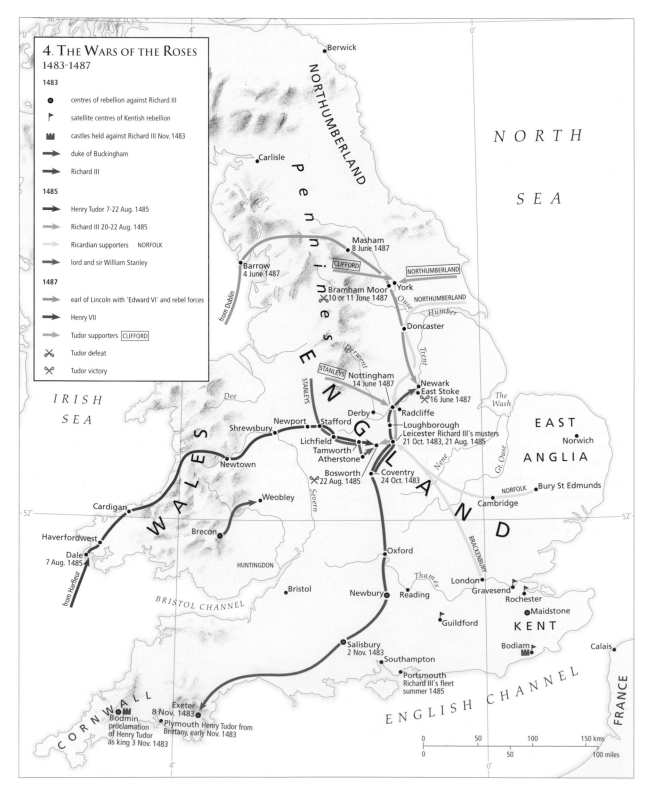

MAP 4

Richard III's usurpation drove many Yorkists to support Henry Tudor, the hitherto hopeless last Lancastrian. The 1483 rebellion was easily sup-pressed. In 1485, Henry Tudor's rapid march made Richard fight before his muster was complete. But at Bosworth he was be-trayed by the nobles who backed him in 1483. The invasion of the 'Yorkist' imposter Lambert Simnel in 1487 did not seriously trouble Henry VII, since he attracted little support. Stoke, the last battle of the Wars of the Roses, has the reputation of a close-run affair. It was not. Henry VII was not be-trayed by his partisans, unlike Richard III.

The increasing sophistication of fifteenth-century armour, which was designed to deflect sword and spear, made crushing weapons more popular. Noblemen tended to use maces, battle axes, and hammers. Common infantry made more use of staff weapons, combining axes, spikes, and hooks. They were intended to knock an armoured opponent off his feet, rather than to pierce his armour.

in the wars declined after 1461. The major source of soldiers was noblemen's retainers and tenants. The Percys and Nevilles could field up to 10,000 men each for short periods, many of whom were experienced in border warfare. The Yorkist lord Hastings raised 3,000 men in 1471, and the Stanleys fielded large contingents between 1485 and 1487. The reluctance of tenants to serve far from home, and the nobles' ability to pay them were the main limitations.

At Towton (1461), seventy-five per cent of lords and much of the gentry fought on the Lancastrian side. The Yorkists had fewer lords, but they were the wealthier. Armies became smaller in later wars. At Bosworth, twenty-eight of thirty-five lords failed to turn out for Richard III. Experience taught them it was safer to wait and accept the victor, who could then summon soldiers from towns and counties: in 1455, Coventry equipped 100 archers for Henry VI, and sent the same number with Warwick to Towton. However, by 1470-71, their daily wages had to be raised by fifty per cent to attract recruits.

The largest armies fought at Towton, over 20,000 men on each side; Edward may have had 9,000 at Barnet (1471), Warwick more; at Bosworth, Richard heavily outnumbered Henry Tudor's 5,000 men, although sir William Stanley's army redressed the balance, and not all of Richard's army was engaged. Archers predominated, outnumbering men-at-arms by seven or more to one. English archers were highly rated in Europe. In the civil war battles both sides had them and they were less influential than in the Hundred Years' War, their main function being to cover the men-at-arms and to break up defensive formations. However, their absence compromised the Yorkists at Edgecote. Other footmen were armed with bills (poleaxes). The elite men-at-arms, all landowners, were encased in expensive armour. Nearly all battles of the civil wars became slogging matches in which the men-at-arms on foot played the dom-

inant role, though cavalry were also used, as at Towton, Tewkesbury, and Bosworth. Most armies had field artillery, although this was used only at the start of battles because its rate of fire was relatively slow; mounting it in field defences went out of fashion after 1460. There were few sieges in the civil wars, although Edward IV possessed an impressive siege train. The English made little use of handguns, and the mercenary gunners from the Continent made little impact in the wars.

The main goal in the civil wars was political power rather than control of territory, so the camapigns of the Wars of the Roses were brief and ended in battles. This was not due to lack of military skill; many of the nobles who commanded in the 1450s had experience in the French wars, and younger captains like Somerset, Warwick, and Edward IV, who learned from experience, were capable soldiers. It was desirable to limit campaigns to avoid causing damage by foraging, and to reach a conclusion before the levies dispersed. Analysis of the campaigns of 1470-71, for which there is detailed evidence, shows that both sides manoeuvred skilfully. York (in 1459) and Warwick (in 1461) paid dearly for failure to reconnoitre. Edward IV's handling of his men before Barnet and at Tewkesbury also shows some tactical skill and, in contrast to the English experience in the French wars, it was often the attackers who won battles.

Sources rarely refer to the crucial role of logistics. To invade Scotland in 1481, 500 carts were requisitioned to carry supplies, and more would ferry provisions from Newcastle. In civil wars such preparations were impossible, and the mobility of armies suggests that there were no large wagon trains. Armies carried a few days' provisions and equipment in wagons. In 1459, the Yorkists used wagons for protection at Blore Heath and Ludford Bridge. In 1460, London furnished Yorkist transport. Supplies were purchased or seized from towns, depending on their lord (Stamford, Wakefield, and Ludlow were York's towns) and the state of discipline. The best sources were the largest towns like London (1461), York (1470), and Bristol (1471). Requisitioning and looting were often indistinguishable, but living off the country meant dangerous dispersal (as the Yorkists found in December 1460), while plundering alienated the population. Margaret kept her northerners, who had a bad reputation, out of London in February 1461 in deference to fears of pillaging, thus leaving the city open to Edward.

An army on the march was preceded by light horse called 'scourers', harbingers, or aforeriders whose tasks included arranging billets and victuals, and scouting. Accurate reconnaissance gave Edward a crucial advantage in 1470 and 1471, whereas the failure of York's and Warwick's scouts (December 1460 and February 1461) resulted in defeat. Contact between opposing harbingers provided knowledge of the enemy's location, and thus sending aforeriders in one direction, and the main body in another was used to deceive the enemy by Warwick in March 1470, and by Margaret in April 1471.

THE ARMY AND CAMPAIGNS OF CHARLES THE BOLD OF BURGUNDY C.1465-1477

I N THE CENTURY between its foundation in 1363 and Charles the Bold's accession, the Valois duchy of Burgundy grew to become a veritable middle kingdom between France and the German empire. Burgundy's military resources were always limited, although Flanders provided good infantry, and the dukes made great use of mercenaries. Charles the Bold's solution was to create a modern-style army with full-time soldiers, uniforms, units, and banners. He also built up his train of artillery for a campaign of conquest. Despite his nineteenth-century epithet 'the Rash', Charles operated very cautiously, until he challenged the Swiss in 1475-77. Their massed infantry could be quickly mustered, but were difficult to hold together. By seeking battle, Charles chose the wrong strategic option, suffering three defeats and eventual death at their hands.

THE BURGUNDIAN TERRITORIES

Although Valois Burgundy was comparable in size to England, its territories stretched 500 miles (800km), from Holland to Lake Geneva, and were considerably more disjointed. Despite the efforts of Philip the Good (1364-1404), the northern and southern parts of the state were still separated by the duchy of Lorraine (map 1). Charles held effective power from 1464 and, nourishing imperial ambitions, was determined on further expansion. In 1473, he almost settled for a kingdom comprising his inheritance, the ecclesiastical principalities within them, and the duchies of Cleves, Lorraine, and Savoy. But ambition pushed him

into opposition to France (over the Somme towns), and the Swiss Federation of Upper Germany, chiefly Bern.

Burgundian forces had previously been small, and mercenaries made up at least thirty per cent of any force. Charles' household troops still formed the core: 40 mounted bodyguards and 126 each of men-at-arms and archers in 1474, increased by 400 infantry and 400 mounted English archers (each in four companies) in 1476 to over 2,000 in total. In addition, he strove to create permanent troops in mixed Companies, made up of cavalry, foot, and missilemen, supported by the most modern artillery, to

Charles' rash attempt to recapture Nancy over a bitter winter left him vulnerable to counter-attack. Duke René's forces outnumbered the Burgundians by three to one. His forces also possessed the tactical flexibility to outflank the dug-in guns and surround their enemy. Charles died in the ensuing massacre.

This illustration from Diebold Schilling's chronicle shows the Burgundian defeat at Grandson and represents the different composition of the opposing armies. The Burgundians are a mixture of gens d'armes, artillery, and infantry, including a substantial proportion of archers. The massed Swiss halberds and pikes are preceded by handgunners. The bear standard of Bern and blue-white diagonal banner of Zurich are prominent.

MAP 1

Charles the Bold inherited a wealthy duchy composed of scattered territories, which he set about unifying. He disputed the Somme towns with Louis XI of France, conquered Guelders (1473) and Lorraine (1475), and tried to capture the imperial town of Neuss (1474-75). Following Charles' defeats by the Swiss in 1476, duke Rene of Lorraine recaptured Nancy. Whilst besieging the city, Charles met his death in battle on 5 January 1477.

four squadrons, each of twenty-five men-at-arms, twenty-five *coustiliers* (light horse), twenty-five valets, and seventy-five archers (all mounted), and twenty-five each of crossbowmen, pikemen, and handgunners (all on foot). In fact, these numbers proved hard to achieve, notably amongst specialist troops such as handgunners. So Charles continued to employ condottieri such as Cola de Montforte, who signed up in November with 400 four-horse lances, 400 mounted crossbowmen, and 300 infantrymen, and served until his defection just before the final battle at Nancy in 1477.

CAMPAIGNS IN FRANCE, FLANDERS, AND THE EMPIRE 1465-1475

While still count of Charolais, Charles was involved in a princely revolt against Louis XI. He seized the Somme towns before taking part in a confusing encounter at Montlhéry, just south of Paris (14 July 1465), where the archers alone fought well. Despite losing control of his troops and being wounded in the neck, it made his reputation as a a soldier.

Between 1465 and 1468, Charles conducted a four-campaign war against Liège. In 1466, he took Dinant, and as duke in 1467 fought a battle at Brustem against the Liègeois. They had dug in and defied both artillery bombardment and cavalry charges. Significantly, it was the archers who stormed the camp on foot, although looting prevented a pursuit. Liège was demilitarized, but rebelled in 1468, and after a desperate night-attack by its defenders, which almost captured the duke, was razed.

Charles seized Louis XI by a trick at Péronne in 1468, and extracted a favourable treaty, but the French king recaptured the Somme towns in 1471, and held them in 1472. So Charles looked for conquests elsewhere.

Charles' next area of operations was in the Rhineland, where his control of the archbishopric of Cologne was opposed by Neuss. The siege of this small town took from July 1474 to June 1475 and, although unsuccessful, displayed the new potential of Burgundian forces (*page 150*). Charles mustered 12,000 men and 229 guns against 3,000 defenders. By Christmas 1474, the town's walls had been battered down and food supplies were exhausted. Yet the citizens hung on, raiding the besiegers' camp at night for supplies.

They were waiting for relief by the emperor Frederick III, who eventually mustered enough strength to advance cautiously in May 1475. Charles took the initiative and marched against his camp on 23 May, and his letter describing the Burgundian deployment survives. Mobile artillery, supported by Italian infantry, was advanced some 800 yards (730m) in front of the battle-line, and bombarded the imperial camp. The main body was made up of two 'battles' (divisions) of infantry and flanking mounted men-at-arms. The infantry of the first battle were made up of one pikeman to every four archers. The bodyguard cavalry made up the centre of the second battle, flanked by archers and handgunners. This was a flexible formation combining firepower with mounted shock troops.

give him not a host, but an army. If his losses to the Swiss are to be believed, he possessed over 1,000 guns, many on new, mobile carriages.

Charles published three detailed military ordinances (instructions) every year from 1471-73. These set out details of uniforms (blue and white with a St Andrew's cross), armour, and weapons for each man, and grouped them under *conducteurs* (condottieri, leaders) with a designated hierarchy of numbered banners. Each arm was also drilled in peacetime for its respective role in battle. The cavalry were taught to charge in close formation with lances, to retire, and rally. The horse archers practised dismounting, leading their horses, and also shooting whilst advancing. They were accompanied by the pikemen in close order, ready to kneel in front, pikes presented, while the archers shot over their heads.

The proposed composition of each Company changed over time, but in its final form of 1473 numbered 900 men. This was based on a nine-man lance, made up into

No battle ensued, the rulers made peace, and Frederick agreed to support Charles.

In September 1475, after carefully isolating its duke, René II, by diplomacy, Charles invaded Lorraine. Using an indirect strategy, he advanced up the Moselle, taking towns with exemplary brutality, and only returning to take the surrender of the capital Nancy on 30 November. This was the peak of Charles the Bold's power, although he held Lorraine for less than a year.

THE ATTACK ON THE SWISS FEDERATION

Alarmed at Burgundian expansion, Strasbourg led some Rhine towns (the Lower Union) into an alliance with the Swiss cantons (the Upper Union) to form the League of Constance. Bern, especially, found itself in conflict with Charles over the areas of Vaud and Savoy. Following a rebellion against his tyrannical governor in Alsace (April 1474), the League declared war on Burgundy. In the autumn, a large allied army besieged Héricourt on the frontier of the Franche-Comté and overwhelmed a Burgundian relief force (13 November). More castles in the region were destroyed in the summer of 1475. Charles, meanwhile, had constructed the League of Moncalieri with Milan and Savoy agaisnt Bern, and spent Christmas at Nancy. But Bern seized the Vaud and prevented troops from Italy reaching him. As a result, he began operations in 1476 with 11,000 men, but the League of Constance mustered 20,000 (one-third from Bern).

Charles' objective was to recover fortifications in the Vaud held by Bern and then to attack the city itself. On 21 February, he laid siege to Grandson castle on the shore of Lake Neuchâtel (map 2). When the garrison surrendered a week later, he had them hanged. The next day he personally led a reconnaissance to Vaumarcus, which he garrisoned.

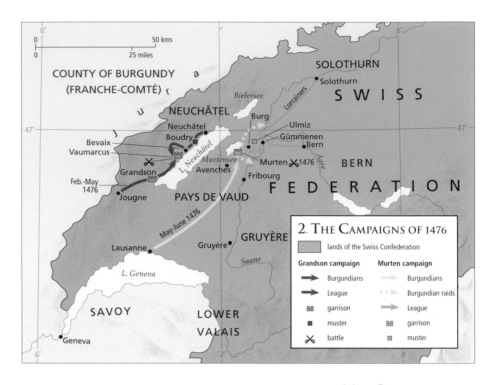

2. THE CAMPAIGNS OF 1476

lands of the Swiss Confederation

Grandson campaign	Murten campaign
Burgundians	Burgundians
League	Burgundian raids
garrison	League
muster	garrison
battle	muster

This castle dominated a possible ambush point on the road where forested Mount Aubert came close to the lake shore. On 2 March, the Burgundians marched north in order to set up camp there. Meanwhile, the League forces were intent on attacking Vaumarcus.

Reconnaissance was poor on both sides, and the League's van emerged from the woods high on the mountain slope, to see the Burgundians in march columns below. Charging impetuously downhill, the van found itself surrounded and attacked by infantry and cavalry. Its 10,000 men formed a great, impenetrable block which suffered from missile fire but repelled the Burgundian cavalry. Duke Charles' own horse was wounded in a charge. After three hours' fighting, Charles ordered a partial withdrawal intended to bring more archery and artillery fire to bear. This manoeuvre, coupled with the sudden arrival of the Swiss main body on the Burgundian flank, led to a

MAP 2

Charles' ambitions in Savoy and Vaud brought him into conflict with Swiss and German towns, specifically Bern. Advancing on the city, he was ambushed by Lake Neuchâtel, and forced to abandon his artillery and baggage (2 March). Returning in May to besiege Murten, he was again surprised in the siege lines (22 June). This time casualties were heavy as the Burgundians were driven into the lake.

The eleven-month siege of Neuss deployed Charles' reformed army to full effect. Despite overwhelming numbers, the citizens held out, and the Burgundians were forced to deploy against emperor Frederick III's relief attempt. Their model order of battle combined an artillery screen with a balanced mixture of horse and foot.

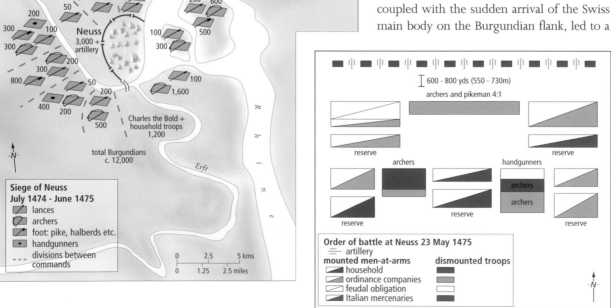

Siege of Neuss
July 1474 - June 1475
- lances
- archers
- foot: pike, halberds etc.
- handgunners
- --- divisions between commands

Neuss 3,000 + artillery

Charles the Bold + household troops 1,200

total Burgundians c. 12,000

I 600 - 800 yds (550 - 730m)
archers and pikeman 4:1

reserve · archers · handgunners · reserve
archers · archers · reserve
reserve · reserve · reserve

Order of battle at Neuss 23 May 1475
=== artillery
mounted men-at-arms   dismounted troops
- household
- ordinance companies
- feudal obligation
- Italian mercenaries

panic-stricken flight by his unengaged troops. Losses were light, but all the Burgundian baggage, treasure, and 400 guns were lost.

Charles' setback appeared temporary. He regrouped at Lausanne and ordered 8,000 reinforcements from Flanders. Bern could find no support amongst the cities and cantons of the Upper Union for defending her recent conquests. Only René II of Lorraine went onto the offensive against Burgundy, beginning the reconquest of his duchy by taking Vaudemont (14 April). By 27 May, Charles resumed operations with his, as yet, unreinforced army, marching on Bern via Murten. He knew that he was risking 'his state, his life, his everything' but 'he could not live with the disgrace of having been defeated by these beastish people' (the Swiss). However, his next encounter with the Swiss, at Mürten, proved a disaster.

Duke René of Lorraine, who had fought at Murten, now took the opportunity to recover his duchy. Nancy fell just before Charles could come to its relief (6 October), but he was unable to drive off René's small force and besiege the city. This was ill-advised, as the winter drew in and there was a weak line of supply from the north. René, meanwhile, could not get the Swiss to venture out, although they agreed that he could recruit mercenaries. He raised 6,000 veterans which, supported by the troops of Basle, Strasbourg, and his own Lorrainers, gave him a total of nearly 20,000 men.

Charles' force had been worn down to no more than 7,000 men. He planned to block the likely line of attack with his artillery, but the Swiss reacted by swinging through the forest and around his right flank. Attacked on two sides by overwhelming numbers, the Burgundians were overrun, and this time Charles himself was killed in the rout.

Charles the Bold's failure stemmed from taking on the best infantry in Europe, on ground of their own choosing, and with a faulty strategy. Swiss armies were large and rapidly mustered, but could not be held together for long. Charles' battle-seeking strategy exposed the weaknesses of his heterogeneous force. Nevertheless, his combination of horse, foot, and artillery was to become the model for armies for centuries to come.

MURTEN 22 JUNE 1476

Charles besieged Murten on 11 June, but his aggressive scouting against the crossings of the rivers Aare and Saane suggests that he was trying to bring on a decisive engagement. The terrain was utilized to construct a ditch and palisade entrenchment, the *Grünhag*, manned by archers and guns producing a killing ground to be exploited by flanking cavalry. Charles prepared for an attack on 21 June, but the League forces were still mustering. Their 25,000 men were drawn together by forced marches and went straight into battle the next day.

Charles had stood his men down, the defences being manned by only 2,000 archers and handgunners, with 1,200 horse in support. The rest of his troops were lunching in the camp; even so he was outnumbered by two to one. The Swiss came on in three great blocks of foot: the *Vorhut* (van) of 5,000, half missilemen, half pike, which was flanked by Lorrainer cavalry; the *Gewalthut* (centre) of 12,000 halberdiers; and 7,000 more in the *Nachhut* (rear). Advancing through the woods, this force was concealed until it was a mile from the Burgundian lines. The defenders had twenty minutes to arm and form up. It was not enough. Piecemeal cavalry charges were ineffectual and the *Grünhag* was soon overrun. There was no escape route, the Swiss were pledged to no quarter, and a sortie from Murten caught the fleeing Burgundians in the rear. In the ensuing massacre, Charles lost one-third of his army, cut down or drowned in the lake, and another '400' guns.

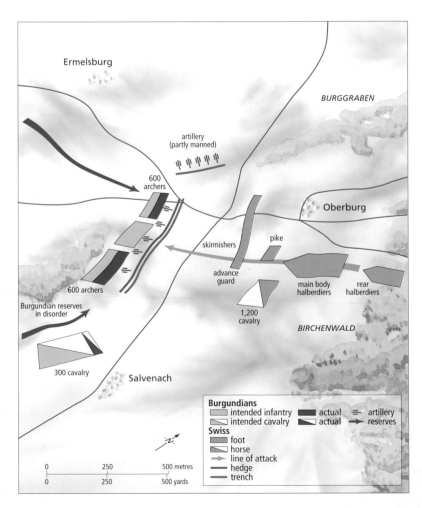

Ermelsburg

BURGGRABEN

artillery (partly manned)

600 archers

Oberburg

pike

skirmishers

advance guard

main body halberdiers

rear halberdiers

600 archers

Burgundian reserves in disorder

1,200 cavalry

BIRCHENWALD

300 cavalry

Salvenach

Burgundians
intended infantry — actual ═ artillery
intended cavalry — actual → reserves
Swiss
foot
horse
→ line of attack
— hedge
— trench

0   250   500 metres
0   250   500 yards

A MILITARY REVOLUTION?

The idea of a sixteenth-century 'military revolution' which transformed European warfare was formulated by Professor Michael Roberts in the mid-1950s. Historians have argued over the precise timespan of this revolution and some of its details, but the concept that such a revolution occurred has been widely accepted. By contrast, the preceding Middle Ages have been presented as an era when the practice of war was unprofessional and changed little. They have been characterized as 'the long interregnum between the disappearance of the disciplined armies of Rome and the appearance of state forces in the sixteenth century' (John Keegan, *A History of Warfare*). As this suggests, historians have seen the military revolution in the context of the growth of the modern state after a long period of stagnation following the collapse of the Roman empire. However, while important changes did occur in war and military organization in the sixteenth and seventeenth centuries, it is arguable that their extent and novelty have been exaggerated.

According to Professor Roberts, the century after 1560 witnessed critical changes: a tactical revolution, in which musketeers in linear formations replaced lance and pike, and massed firepower 'blew away' feudal cavalry and blocks of pikemen; a massive growth in the size of European armies; and the adoption of more complex strategies to bring those armies into action. All these increased the burden of war on society, requiring the development of 'modern' states to recruit, pay for, and supply the new

armies. Professor Geoffrey Parker's influential revision of 1976 pushed the starting date of the transformation back to the late fifteenth century, as well as stressing the importance of siege warfare, which Roberts had underestimated. The French invasion of Italy in 1494-95, with a horse-drawn siege train which demonstrated the power of new siege artillery was, according to Parker, a 'new departure in warfare'. It necessitated the development of costly new defensive systems of low bastions built of rubble and brick (known as the 'trace Italienne'). Parker concluded, however, that he had 'failed to dent the basic thesis', and that a 'new use of firepower, leading to a new type of fortifications and an increase in army size' still deserve to be interpreted as a revolution.

Seventeenth-century historians have raised important doubts about the Roberts-Parker thesis. In tactical terms, the pike only became obsolete with the invention of the ring bayonet in about 1670. Rising population and price inflation in the sixteenth century to some extent explain increases in overall army sizes and the cost of war. The force actually deployed in the field remained small. For example, the Swedish king Gustavus Adolphus had 175,000 troops under arms in 1632, but managed to bring barely 19,000 to the battle of Lützen in that year. It is now clear that a great many troops were employed in enforcing the collection of dues to support the soldiers at the 'sharp end'. The growth in army sizes was much more marked after 1660, and

One aspect of the military revolution which is alleged to have begun at the end of the fifteenth century is that infantry became more important in the field. This nearly contemporary picture of the battle of Nancy (1477) shows the power of Swiss infantry armed with pykes and halbards. Infantry armed with similar weapons were important in warfare as early as the twelfth century.

Professor Jeremy Black has argued that the most revolutionary changes date to the late seventeenth century. Before about 1660, most troops were still raised by private contractors, and the development of state institutions to control and finance large armies is again a phenomenon of the late seventeenth century.

The creation of the concept of a military revolution which began around 1500 also relied upon a simplified caricature of medieval warfare and government (see, for example, Keegan's comment above) which has been epitomized in English in sir Charles Oman's works on military history (originally published between 1885 and 1924), although his continental contemporaries, such as Delbrück, reached similarly negative conclusions. Unfortunately, this caricature has been influential. The era of the alleged military revolution coincided with the intellectual movement of humanism which depicted the millennium between the end of the Roman empire and the late fifteenth century as the 'Dark Ages'. The sixteenth century is generally, and inaccurately, referred to as the Renaissance. Earlier centuries had their own 'renaissances', but the invention of printing in the mid-fifteenth century has meant that humanist prejudices have been widely popularized and accepted. Consequently, historians conventionally date the beginning of the 'early modern' period to around the year 1500, and sixteenth-century historians have tended to be ignorant about earlier centuries. The result has been exaggerated claims for sixteenth-century developments in warfare and government.

MILITARY CHANGE BEFORE 1500

The history of gunpowder, weapons, and fortifications emphasizes the artificiality of portraying the late fifteenth century as a turning point in European warfare. Gunpowder weapons appeared in Europe in the fourteenth century, but it required improvements in the manufacture of guns and gunpowder around 1400 before sieges were appreciably shortened. The improved siege artillery played an important role in bringing the Hundred Years' War to an end in mid-century, long before the French invaded Italy. The last phase of the Hundred Years' War also saw the development of a new system of circumvallation, elaborate systems of trenches which allowed besiegers to bring their artillery close to the walls of a town and defend themselves against assault, which replaced the older method of building separate siege castles (bastilles). Important steps to counter the improved techniques of attack date to the same period. The construction of 'boulevards', outworks of earth and timber, is found at Harfleur in 1415, and regularly in Gascony. They not only protected gates, but enabled crossfire to be directed against attackers. Indeed, it is possible that the origins of the bastion are to be found in mid-fifteenth-century France, rather than in Italy half a century later.

Looking further back, many claims made for the sixteenth-century military revolution can be disproved: for example, that sieges became longer; that 'the old rhythm of summer fighting followed by disbandment or winter-quarters ease' ended; and that 'battle came to be avoided' (both J. R. Hale, *War and Society in Renaissance Europe 1450-1620*). The preceding chapters include plentiful examples of prolonged sieges and military operations which continued throughout the year. The tactic of avoiding battle whenever possible, unless conditions were favourable, was understood and observed by commanders for much of the Middle Ages. Hale's 'printed flood' of treatises on war should perhaps be attributed to the development of printing, rather than to a military revolution. Another alleged development of the late fifteenth century, 'a new respect for the infantry's power to resist cavalry charges' (Hale), is not borne out by a study of battles of earlier centuries. The well-known victories of Scottish, Flemish, and Swiss pikemen, and of English longbowmen, in the fourteenth and fifteenth centuries, have been described as adding up to an 'infantry revolution' which prepared the way for sixteenth-century developments. In fact, even this interpretation is based on the misconceptions that infantry eclipsed cavalry in these centuries, and that infantry had been unimportant before about 1300. Historians of the later Middle Ages have also tended to be ill-informed about earlier centuries!

REVOLUTION OR EVOLUTION?

The concept of a single military revolution located in the sixteenth and seventeenth centuries oversimplifies military developments which occurred over several centuries. Even such an apparently radical change as the introduction of gunpowder was worked out over the course of several centuries, and in fact consisted of periods of rapid change in artillery manufacture, infantry weapons and tactics, and fortification, combined with periods of gradual evolution. Indeed, the idea of a military revolution which occurred over centuries raises doubts as to whether the very concept of revolution is at all appropriate. One 'early modern' historian describes the military revolution as an 'improbable thesis'. Moreover, many historians are now reluctant to see progress following a straight line: in the sixteenth century, as in the twelfth, armed forces were built up during periods of conflict and paid off when peace came; prolonged wars saw the development of military professionalism, while prolonged peace saw its decline, arguably until military academies were established.

Many of the changes which are alleged to have happened in the so-called military revolution were already commonplace long before the sixteenth century. This is not to deny that significant changes did take place in the sixteenth and seventeenth centuries, but in military history, as in other fields of historical study, the arbitrary selection of a year which is supposed to have witnessed a turning-point, whether it be 1500, 1485, or 1453, is redundant. Since the 1950s, medieval historians have been demonstrating the levels of organization and discipline medieval commanders achieved – not all of them, by any means, but then the Middle Ages had no monopoly of the militarily incompetent. It is time modern military historians took note of this research and incorporated it into their surveys.

THEORY AND PRACTICE OF MEDIEVAL WARFARE

CAVALRY, CHIVALRY AND CHEVAUCHÉE

HEAVY CAVALRY

Many commentators continue to peddle the chivalric myth that knightly cavalry dominated medieval warfare, and that their sole concept of war was glorious, undisciplined charges. The destruction of an East Roman army by Goths at the battle of Adrianople (378) has been seen as opening the new era, during which infantry were unimportant. It is said that, in the eighth century, the Frank Charles Martel created a heavy cavalry force, seizing church lands to share among his followers in return for military service; that the introduction of the stirrup soon after 700 made the new heavy cavalry possible, employing the technique of 'mounted shock combat' in which the lance was held firmly in the armpit ('couched'); and that this made heavy cavalry masters of the battlefield. Thus, a respected historian of war described medieval warfare as 'the war of the knights' (Michael Howard, *War in European History*). This interpretation was also attractive since it seemed to explain the development of feudalism, a method of organizing society in which knights granted land to their greater subjects in return for military service, and bound them by oaths of loyalty.

Historians now recognize that the Roman cavalry saddle gave considerable support and that the stirrup made relatively little difference. The stirrup was adopted in western Europe in a patchy way, not in one revolutionary instant, and Charles Martel seized church lands in order to break the power of the regional aristocracies which opposed his expansion, rather than to endow his warriors with property. The couched-lance technique in fact dates from the late eleventh century. This makes far-fetched the idea of a revolution between 378 and c.1100. This is not to deny that heavy cavalry did become important. Charlemagne legislated about the equipment of his horsemen (and infantry too), and the German king, Henry I, created a force of *milites armati*. The rising cost of military equipment increasingly excluded all but landowners and their followers from warfare. But the idea that cavalry dominated medieval warfare is false. Many writers have been misled by sources which, produced by members of the ruling elite, concentrated on the exploits of the *milites* (generally translated as 'knights' or 'men-at-arms'). This does not mean common infantry were unimportant. In fact, while heavy cavalry were important in battle, battles were relatively rare. Cavalry were of course useful for reconnaissance and escorts, but infantry were a necessity in the attritional, fortress-based warfare and deliberate destruction of opponents' resources which dominated medieval campaigns.

What may have been most significant about Carolingian and Ottonian cavalry was the armour they wore, rather than simply being cavalry. Their main weapon was the sword. The development of the couched-lance technique ('jousting') in the eleventh century made western European cavalry more potent, especially with the adoption of high 'wrap-round' saddles after c.1100. The astute Byzantine princess Anna Comnena noted that 'a mounted Frank is irresistible; he would bore his way through the walls of Babylon'. The impact of a well-delivered charge could shatter any body of troops. A successful charge needed discipline to maximize its impact. Knights fought in small groups (*conrois*) of friends, and practised together in tournaments. These tactical units were the building blocks from which larger battles (*batailles*) were formed. It was normal to keep close order, endure enemy provocation, and to charge in line. Jousting was the preliminary round – the main action was conducted with sword and mace. Timing was vitally important, particularly against the Turks, whose light horse-archers were like swarms of gnats who evaded a poorly-timed charge, returning when Frankish horses were exhausted to shoot them before closing in. But as early as 1097, the crusaders used their infantry as a shield to protect their vulnerable horses before charging. This was possible because infantry were already significant in western warfare. This view of disciplined knights fits ill with the traditional view of knightly warfare. However, as the twelfth-century Syrian Usamah observed, 'the Franks – may Allah's curse be upon them – are of all men the most cautious in warfare'.

Mounted shock combat was designed for use against cavalry. When cavalry from northern France encountered specialized infantry – Germans at Civitate (1053), Anglo-Scandinavian at Hastings (1066) and at Durazzo (1081) – they were victorious. But the knights did not overrun the sword or axe-bearing infantry, and victory was achieved by co-ordination between cavalry and archers. Only disciplined infantry was likely to have the nerve to stand before a heavy cavalry charge. Knights also had to be prepared to dismount. This long predates the fourteenth century, to which it is frequently dated. In 891, for example, a Frankish army dismounted to storm a Viking fort at the river Dyle. In several encounters in the first half of the twelfth century in northern France and England, knights dismounted to strengthen common infantry, combined with archers and mounted reserves. This was often to neutralize the effect of the enemy's cavalry charge, and to stiffen resolve: men on foot could not escape a mounted enemy. At the siege of Damascus (1148), the German knights also dismounted to fight, 'as is their custom in a desperate situation in war' (William of Tyre). In the fourteenth century, English men-at-arms began habitually to dismount for battle alongside massed archers. The dismounting was not novel, but the large numbers of archers involved was. In the same century, densely packed common infantry armed with spears and pikes – Flemings, Scots, and Swiss – defeated mounted chivalry, for example at Courtrai and Bannockburn. This has led to the argument that feudal cavalry were now eclipsed, but in the later fifteenth century 'super-heavy cavalry', with effective plate armour and armoured horses, enjoyed a revival. From the late 1300s, the lance became much heavier and the breast-plate was equipped with a rest, enabling the lance to be held steady at speed. This development made the 'mounted man into a form of living projectile whose force of impact against both horse and foot was greater than it had ever been' (Malcolm Vale).

Mounted men-at-arms combined with archery and gunfire were able to crack open the enemy formations, a renewed effectiveness which continued into the sixteenth century. Throughout the Middle Ages, unsupported heavy cavalry never possessed the vast superiority often attributed to them, but, combined with infantry, especially archers, they played a significant part in war.

KNIGHTHOOD

In eleventh-century Burgundy, the Latin term *miles* ('soldier') began to imply nobility. This occurred unevenly in the Christian west – in twelfth-century Germany there were *ministeriales* (unfree knights) – but gradually the knights became a socially distinct elite, a fellowship embracing lords, even kings, and their followers. The cost of arms, armour, and horses, always high, increasingly separated knights from other soldiers. To meet this burden required land, or membership of a

South German 'Gothic' armour of c.1475-85, whose fluted and rippled surfaces gave good protection against arrows and bolts. Smooth, rounded Italian armour was more suited to cavalry warfare. The horse armour, providing some protection against archery and pike hedge, gave heavy cavalry new force in the later fifteenth century.

lord's following. Many twelfth-century knights were waged members of a royal, noble, or episcopal household (*mesnie*). The knight needed a war-horse (*destrier*), riding horse ('palfrey') and pack animals, and servants. The principal aide was the esquire, often a mature servant rather than a boy apprentice, who had an auxiliary combat role. From the late fourteenth century, a 'lance' consisted of one heavy cavalryman with an armed servant, a page, and three to six variously armed infantry. The number of knights, however, shrank drastically as costs mounted. 'Serjeants' (from the French for servant) provided lighter, and non-noble, cavalry. Their role was to act as supporting ranks and to back up the knights' charge in battle. In the later Middle Ages, historians prefer to refer to men-at-arms since, while knighthood became a distinct social rank, heavy cavalrymen could be esquires or gentlemen.

Rituals associated with 'knighting' were based on royal coronations. The giving of arms, particularly tying on the sword belt (a symbol of knighthood), was an ancient bond between lord and follower. In the twelfth century, knights could be created en masse on the eve of battle, but by the end of the century the church had added a ritual bath, white tunic, and overnight vigil to sanctify knighthood. This legitimization reached its apogee with the creation of monastic knighthood, beginning with the Order of the Knights Templar in 1128, knights who originally helped protect Christian pilgrims in the Holy Land. Donations made the military orders very wealthy. In the Holy Land, the Templars and Hospitallers played a crucial role in constructing fortresses and providing troops; in the thirteenth and fourteenth centuries, the Teutonic Knights ruled Prussia and Livonia. Knights who wished to fight the infidel or pagans did not have to join the military orders, but were able to campaign with them in the east, Spain, and the Baltic to gain the spiritual advantages of crusading vows.

Heraldry developed to distinguish knights who were otherwise difficult to identify in their armour. While the Bayeux Tapestry (c.1080) depicted decorative mythical beasts on shields, there is no sign that they were specific to individuals. Heraldic designs were. The lion was the most popular early choice, but there were many other symbols, both natural and geometric. Many designs were puns on the bearer's name, for example Richard de Lucy's bore a pike (*luce* in French). In the twelfth century, members of a *mesnie* wore their lords' colours. The development of heraldry mirrors another twelfth-century trend, the process by which knighthood developed into a hereditary warrior caste with its own code.

TOURNAMENTS

Military games were ancient, and cavalry manoeuvres had been practised in front of ninth-century Carolingian rulers. Around 1100, more realistic combat games became popular in northern France, made possible because wider use of high-quality body armour minimized the risk to participants. By 1138, when Geoffrey of Monmouth composed his Arthurian fantasy *The History of the Kings of Britain*, tournaments were well-established. The twelfth-century tournament was a real training for war: teams of knights with their infantry participated in contests ranging over several fields. The bulk of the fighting was with sword and mace, and a skilful young warrior such as William Marshal could make a good living through knight-errantry on the north French tournament circuit. As in real war, ruses were appreciated, such as pretending not to be participating, then joining in when the other teams were exhausted. Also in common with real war, defeated knights gave their *parole* (word of honour) and paid ransoms. Some twelfth-century rulers promoted tournaments because of their role in training and as publicity opportunities; others banned them since such assemblies could be the cover for conspiracies, which tells us more about such rulers than about tournaments. The Church was unenthusiastic about legitimized 'brawling' which deflected knights from crusading. Jousting between pairs of knights in the 'lists' (across a barrier) gradually emerged as a popular spectator sport. Blunted weapons and special tournament armour limited the probability of serious injury. But as the rules became more formal, the lists became less valuable as a training for real war. Jousting for honour also occurred in war, especially during prolonged sieges. In the 'Combat of the Thirty' in Brittany in 1350, the victorious French suffered three dead and the vanquished English and Bretons twelve. The survivors were all wounded.

CHIVALRY AND CHEVAUCHÉES

'Chivalry' is used to describe the code of values of knights – kings, aristocrats, and their *milites* – which originated around 1100. The values of chivalry were expressed in vernacular literature: the *chansons de gestes* ('songs of deeds') and stories of king Arthur and the knights of the Round Table celebrated legendary heroes, while Ambroise's *History of the Holy War* (the Third Crusade) and the *History of William the Marshal* celebrated real warriors. Contrary to the popular view of undisciplined knights, the military values they celebrated were prudence, cunning, and caution, as well as bravery. Thus, 'chivalric' commanders were masters of ambushes, sudden attacks, night marches, and deceptions. The medieval French *chevalerie* means 'knighthood' and 'deeds of horsemanship and arms'.

Chivalry was not unique in appreciating courage, loyalty, generosity, and military skill. The special quality of chivalry was that a vanquished fellow knight's life was spared: instead of death or slavery, which he might have expected in the seventh century, for example, he would be ransomed. However, this code only governed relationships between knights, so relatively few were killed when knight fought knight. Non-knights or 'barbarians', for example common infantry or the Welsh, Irish, and pagan Slavs, were not covered by it. Knights who did not observe it in dealings with other knights were unpopular. Thus, king John's brutal treatment of prisoners taken at Mirebeau (1202) drove many nobles into rebellion, and Henry V's men-at-arms refused his command to kill their noble prisoners during the battle of Agincourt (1415). Outside this group, chivalry did little to limit the brutality of war. The plundering raid (*chevauchée*), the normal practice of chivalric warfare, was aimed at the civilian population in order to put pressure on their rulers, much as indiscriminate 'area bombing' was in the Second World War.

It is often said that the *chevauchée* was an invention of the English in Scotland and France in the fourteenth century. The French term, literally meaning 'to be on horseback', appears in the late twelfth century to describe a plundering expedition into enemy territory, and the long-distance mounted raid is found in Frankish, English, and British (Welsh) warfare at least as early as the seventh century. According to

king Henry V (1413-22), 'war without fire is like sausages without mustard'. Why that was so is made specific in the thirteenth-century *History of William the Marshal*, 'for when the poor can no longer reap the harvest from their fields, then they can no longer pay their rents and this in turn impoverishes their lords'. Despite the fact that it meant poor men suffered, pillaging was not considered dishonourable. Nor was this destruction mindless, the soldiers' love of burning. To Vegetius (q.v.), 'the main and principal point in war is to secure plenty of provisions for oneself and to destroy the enemy by famine. Famine is more terrible than the sword.' The lesson was applied diligently by medieval commanders. Thus, in his *Chronicle*, Jordan Fantosme put these words of advice into the mouth of count Philip of Flanders, in 1173:

> Destroy your foes and lay waste their country,
> By fire and burning let all be set alight,
> That nothing be left for them, either in wood or meadow,
> Of which in the morning they could have a meal.
> Then with his united force let him besiege their castles…
> Thus should war be begun: such is my advice.
> First lay waste the land.

In addition to strategic ends, plundering also provided the incentive for soldiers to participate in war, to make them wealthy. If an army could not plunder, then war lost its appeal. For the civilian population, perhaps the one improvement they enjoyed was that war ceased to be a slave raid after the eleventh and twelfth centuries.

INFANTRY

Infantry are generally regarded as having had little importance in western warfare until the fourteenth century. This is an illusion created by the sources of information about early medieval warfare, whose clerical authors dwelt on the doings of their relatives among the social elite, who were horsemen (*chevaliers*, *caballeros*, or *Ritter*). The exceptions are England and Scandinavia, where there was apparently no tendency to fight on horseback before the eleventh century. Vikings and Anglo-Saxons certainly used horses for travelling, and dismounted to fight but, since only two Anglo-Saxon battles are described in any detail, it would be unwise to insist that they never fought on horseback.

Two eleventh-century examples, for which detailed sources exist, show infantry's great importance in the field. William of Normandy's army in 1066 contained a significant component of mailed spearmen and archers. The victory of 'Norman' cavalry over English infantry required sophisticated tactical combination with the archers. Spearmen and archers were prominent in the First Crusade, where they formed a barrier protecting the Christian knights until ready to charge. Hastings and the Crusade did not teach western generals the value of infantry – they were already aware of it, which is why they took infantry with them. The dominant type of warfare was siege and ravaging, in which infantry were vital as garrison troops, bowmen, foragers, and fire-raisers. A distinction must be made here between the *vulgus inerme* ('unarmed rabble') who could only labour, and men wealthy enough to possess military equipment – at least spear and shield or bow and arrows, and some armour.

The sources fail us on where eleventh-century infantry were recruited. On crusade, some were knights without horses, and in several battles in the first half of the twelfth century, Norman knights dismounted alongside common infantry. This was a tactical reaction to strengthen infantry against the charge with the couched lance. Archers were ordered to shoot the enemy horses. In the twelfth century, Angevins and Capetians employed large numbers of infantry in the French wars. At Gisors (1188) the spears of Henry II's foot sergeants beat off French cavalry charges. His 'Assize of Arms' (1180-81) details the equipment required of a footsoldier, including a helmet and mail-coat. Richard I's infantry were effective on the Third Crusade against Saladin's Turks – especially in the coastal march, and at Jaffa (4 August 1192). Spearmen and crossbowmen fought in combination as pikemen and musketeers did in the sixteenth century.

An important group of twelfth-century mercenary infantry were 'Brabançons' from Flanders, Brabant, and Hainaut, who served in Germany, France, and Italy. The Angevins hired Welsh troops and Genoese crossbowmen. In addition, the thriving towns of western Europe, many of whose citizens were wealthy enough to arm themselves, had effective militias. The Flemish already had a reputation as pikemen. The Angevins and Capetians granted a measure of self-government to some towns (communes) in return for military service. At Bouvines (1214) the French communes contributed 3,000 infantry to Philip II's army. Well-drilled communal militias and experienced mercenaries were already capable of worsting knightly cavalry. At Legnano (1176), the German cavalry routed the Italian horse, but the Milanese militia with grounded spears and shields repelled their charges before counter-attacking.

The idea of a fourteenth-century 'infantry revolution' is based on an underestimate of the importance of earlier infantry in the field and in more quotidian operations, and upon a rash of infantry victories shortly after 1300. Flemish communal spearmen defeated French chivalry at Courtrai in 1302. Bogged down in marshy ground, they were slaughtered. At Bannockburn (1314) Scottish spearmen achieved a similar result. But these victories can be attributed to bad generalship. The French simply should not have attacked at Courtrai – on more favourable ground they defeated the Flemish at Cassel (1328). In 1314, Edward II failed to use archers to open up the Scottish 'schiltrons' (hedgehogs of spears). His father, Edward I, had used his English archers to do this successfully at Falkirk (1297). After 1314, the English abandoned spearmen and relied entirely on massed archers, but their role in the victories over Scots and French in the century after 1332 can be exaggerated. Each battle was actually won by the English men-at-arms in the climactic mêlée. In Italian service, at least, they grounded their lances as pikes. The English were mainly successful in defensive positions, and the simplest counter-measure was to refuse battle.

The other famous late medieval infantry were the confederate cantons of upper Germany (later, the Swiss Federation). Their fourteenth-century victories were won largely with polearms (halberds etc.) and they only switched to the pike in the mid-fifteenth century. Like the Flemish and Italian militias, the Swiss fought in dense, well-drilled formations. They were capable of all-round defence and had the cohesion to advance rather than fighting solely defensively. Most armies which encountered them were bloodily repulsed. French nobles present at the Swiss defeat by French *Ecorcheurs* at St Jakob-an-der-Birs (1444) noted 'they had never seen nor met men who resisted so strongly or were so willing to sacrifice their lives'. Mercenary service in France in 1465, and the Swiss part in the defeat of Charles the Bold of Burgundy

(1474-76) made them highly prized as mercenaries and much copied by the end of the century.

It is important to recognize that there was no dramatic break in 1500. Footsoldiers had played an important role for centuries earlier. The halberd or pike block supported by 'shot' (at first bowmen, later handgunners of growing sophistication) was, like so many things that are taken to be characteristic of the 'Early Modern' period, a medieval invention.

MERCENARIES

In today's world of citizen armies the word 'mercenary' is pejorative. When Robert Curthose, son of William the Conqueror, complained he did not wish to be his father's mercenary, he expressed distaste; but this was because he was impatient to be king. While some mercenaries earned a bad reputation for greed and cruelty, it was also a respected profession. One problem of interpretation is that, contrary to the popular myth of 'feudal' society, many soldiers received pay in the field because customary service was usually inadequate for a campaign. Also, the military households of princes included many knights who received pay (called 'stipendiaries' in Latin) who are widely found. English household *thegns*, Scandinavian and Anglo-Scandinavian *huscarls*, and the household *milites* of the Norman kings, to name only three groups, were essentially the same – individuals serving a king or prince for pay, hoping in the long term for land or a good marriage. The term mercenary is perhaps better reserved for bands who received pay through their captain, who was a military entrepreneur, and were generally foreigners to the region in which they operated.

Scandinavians were widely hired from the mid-ninth century until the eleventh century. In England in 1012 a special tax (*heregeld*) was used to hire a Danish fleet. Byzantine emperors recruited Scandinavians into the Varangian Guard from the tenth century until the fall of Constantinople. In the mid-eleventh century, Harald Hardrada, a future king of Norway, served there with his warband. The Byzantines had a long tradition of using specialist mercenary corps and saw no weaknesses in this system (unlike nineteenth- and twentieth-century historians). In the twelfth century, Flanders, Brabant, and Hainaut, an over-populated region, provided the most successful mercenaries of the period, the Brabançons. A contemporary described them as: 'foot certainly, but in knowledge and courage in war not inferior to knights'. Their special weapon was the pike. William of Ypres, king Stephen's much-reviled mercenary captain, was forced 'into service' when his claim to the duchy of Flanders failed. Many other regions, often poor areas, produced specialized mercenaries – Genoese crossbowmen, Saracens from Lucera in south Italy, Gascons, Provençals, Welsh, and many more – enticed by the long-running struggles in France, Germany, and Italy.

The fourteenth and fifteenth centuries were the second heyday of medieval mercenaries, owing to the extended Anglo-French conflict. The contemporary term for such troops was *routiers*, which suggests their mobile nature; they also became known as *écorcheurs* ('skinners') because of their brutal exploitation of civilians. In 1327, Edward III employed large numbers of mercenary knights against the mobile Scots, with little success. In his later campaigns in France, he used wild Welsh and Irish troops for their skills at ambush and ravaging so essential to medieval warfare. Spain produced the fearsome light infantry *almogavars*, who served the Byzantines (until they broke away to form their own state based on Athens in 1311). Their leader, called Roger de Flor in the Catalan source describing their exploits, was actually a German, Rutger von Blum. The international nature of mercenary companies is one of their defining factors.

Mercenaries were useful to princes who needed armies 'off the shelf'. Whether a ninth-century Viking warband, twelfth-century Flemings, or fourteenth-century English, in peacetime they became a nuisance. Mid-fourteenth century France was full of mercenary companies. After the Peace of Brétigny (1360) work dried up, and many took to open brigandage, as opposed to the covert brigandage justified by war. In the 1360s, the 'Great Company' rampaged through France until eventually it was deflected to fight in Spain. One of the best known mercenary captains, John Hawkwood, and many like him, made careers serving the Italian city-states. He was largely committed to Florentine service from 1380 until his death in 1394, but he fought for other cities. The Italian *condottieri* have been condemned for the worst sins of 'professionalism', putting their own interests first, reducing warfare to bloodless and pointless manoeuvres. Michael Mallet's book, *Mercenaries and their Masters*, reveals that the captains who commanded city forces were professional in the best sense: they knew their job.

Fashion was important in the history of medieval mercenaries. The fifteenth century saw English archers as a popular choice, particularly valued and on the market after the end of the wars in France (c.1450). Then the Swiss came to prominence as useful infantry, having proved their worth against Burgundy's expensively concocted army in 1475-77. The French saying '*Pas d'argent, pas de Suisse*' ('No money, no Swiss') has become proverbial, and is used to encompass the problem with

mercenary troops. In reality, paid troops formed the core of many medieval armies and were an essential component of warfare.

ARMOUR

The medieval soldier had to come ready-armed, since state production of equipment had ceased in the west by the sixth century. Armour circulated through purchase, gift, inheritance, and looting. Before c.1000, knowledge is derived from rare archaeological finds and artistic depictions, which may draw on life or earlier manuscripts. Later illustrations are more reliable, and are supplemented by sculpture, brasses and tomb effigies, and surviving items. Some matters are mysteries for much of the period under review – whether, for example, padded garments (thirteenth- and fourteenth-century 'hacketon' and 'gambeson') were always worn under mail, as seems likely.

Illustrations and finds of eighth- to tenth-century helmets show great variety. They were based on the late Roman *spangenhelm* of metal strips joined at the apex, with triangular metal or horn plates. Some examples had nasals, cheek-pieces, and mail neck-guards. Most warriors probably only had leather caps. The precise form of body armour shown in depictions from this period is uncertain. The *brunia* (Anglo-Saxon *byrnie*, Latin *lorica*) was a short shirt of interlocking metal rings (mail), but metal scales or rings sewn to an undergarment may also have been used. Carolingian palace troops may even have copied the Roman cuirass. Both armour and helmets could be afforded only by wealthy landowners, who may have armed some of their followers. All warriors had a shield, in this period round or oval, concave or flat, giving protection from neck to thighs. Their sugarloaf iron bosses could be used offensively in combat, and contained the handgrip. Shields could be leather-covered, with metal rims and riveted strips forming radial patterns. The paucity of iron armour meant a few well-armed warriors had a disproportionate significance, for example the tenth-century German *milites armati*. In the late tenth century, the English seem to have been outclassed by the new wave of Viking invaders, which may explain their defeats and the efforts of Aethelred's government to produce body armour and helmets.

By the late eleventh century, armour like that shown by the Bayeux Tapestry had become more common and is illustrated all over western Europe. The 'hauberk' was a mail-shirt stretching to the knees and split for mounting. The English generally fought on foot and seem to have tied the hauberks' skirts to protect their inner thighs, something the Bayeux Tapestry mistakenly depicts on the Normans, too. A mail hood (coif), integral or separate, had a flap (ventail) which strapped across the lower face. In the later 1100s, lengthened sleeves were provided with mittens, and mail leggings became more common. From about 1150, knights wore a loose textile garment (surcoat) over their armour. The eleventh-century *spangenhelm* developed several variations. A round-topped, single-piece helmet became popular in the late twelfth century, sometimes with a face mask (apparently favoured in Spain). By the 1200s, the flat-topped, cylindrical 'great helm' had been developed, and a hemispherical iron cap was worn under the coif. The long kite-shaped shield, used by eleventh-century cavalry and infantry, was cut down in the later twelfth century to become smaller and triangular in shape. As before, however, it was suspended around the neck by a strap.

From at least 1200, metal plates were sometimes worn under the

Before about 1000, helmets were expensive items possessed only by the wealthy. Few such helmets survive. The three known Anglo-Saxon helmets follow the same pattern of frame and plates, but appear very differently. This mid-eighth-century helmet found in York includes nosepiece, cheek guards, and a curtain of mail for the neck.

hauberk or surcoat, riveted to a garment, and about 1250, shaped plates of boiled leather or metal were worn over the mail to protect knees and elbows. Despite the development in the fourteenth century of the coat of plates (a garment lined with metal plates), infantry armed with longbows, spears, pikes, and halberds inflicted a series of defeats on knightly heavy cavalry. The coat of plates was worn over a coifless mail 'haubergeon', with shaped and hinged plates for arms, thighs, shins, and feet. The development of full plate armour ('white armour') followed. In the fifteenth century, the fully equipped man-at-arms was encased from head to foot in articulated metal plates. The haubergeon was no longer required, nor was the shield; the great helm was abandoned in favour of the visored bascinet, then armets and long-tailed sallets, whose weight was supported on a gorget. This occurred across western Europe, although more slowly in Spain and Italy. A

A long-tailed sallet, of the type favoured among German men-at-arms in the second half of the fifteenth century, offered good protection against vertical archery. This model has a movable visor, and the paintwork would have served merely a decorative purpose.

The mail armour on this English tomb (c.1250) covers the whole body. The mittens were thrown back when not in use. The shield strap is clearly visible. Small metal plates strapped to the body beneath the surcoat, for additional protection, developed into the fourteenth-century 'coat of plates'. In battle, a closed 'great helm' (not shown) was worn.

heavier lance was adopted to counter the improved protection, which necessitated a lance-rest to be attached to the breastplate from c.1390.

In producing such armour, improved metal-working techniques were employed: steel with a high carbon constituent and hardening techniques for outer surfaces were used; surfaces were rippled and fluted to deflect lances, swords, and arrows; vulnerable areas were reinforced. The best armours were tested at point-blank range against steel crossbows. Improved protection was achieved without reducing the man-at-arms to immobility. A mid-century armour weighed about 50-60lbs (23-27kg) – comparable to infantry equipment in the nineteenth and twentieth centuries – but the weight was better distributed than earlier mail. Only the attempt to proof armour against firearms made it impossibly heavy in the sixteenth century. The horse was not neglected, and by c.1450 the neck, breast, and flanks were given some protection against pike and arrow. This required breeding heavier horses. The expense of cavalry warfare was mounting inexorably. By no means all knights or men-at-arms could afford full equipment. Those without horse armour or full body armour fought behind the front ranks, adding weight, or performing auxiliary tasks.

The infantry could not hope to possess the armour their social and economic superiors had, but the best equipped were not undefended. At the battle of Hastings, William had mailed footmen, and the Bayeux Tapestry depicts one Norman archer in mail. The mailed English infantry depicted on the Bayeux Tapestry were landowners, thegns, or household warriors, the social and economic equivalent of the Norman knights. The better armed twelfth-century infantry as far apart as England and Outremer wore iron caps, body armour of mail, quilted linen or leather, and carried shields, spears, bows, or crossbows. Thus equipped, infantry were able to act as a shield to their own cavalry, repelling cavalry charges or Turkish archery attacks. Both the helmet, according to the fashion of the time, and the padded jacket remained standard infantry equipment, although some paid troops were expected to have more. English mercenary archers serving in Italy in 1369 were expected to have breastplate, iron helmet, and mail gloves. The French mounted archers of Charles VII's new standing army were clad in brigandines (cloth waistcoats with metal plates riveted in), leg armour, and sallets, or good jacks (quilted coats) with haubergeons.

How much protection did this armour afford? In the view of the twelfth-century historian Orderic Vitalis, only 3 out of 900 knights engaged in the battle of Brémule (1119) were killed because all were mail-clad. Knightly armour did afford a good deal of protection. The Muslim Beha ad-Din described Christian infantry in 1191 with ten arrows stuck in their quilted armour, and it was easier to batter a well-armed man to the ground than to kill him. However, when mail was pierced the rings were driven into a wound. In chivalric warfare it made sense not to kill a ransomable knight or man-at-arms since he represented a profitable asset. But when knocked to the floor (heavy armour made it difficult to rise), if his opponent did not wish to ransom him, the heavily armed knight was vulnerable. Even the fifteenth-century carapace had vulnerable points – the visor being forced open followed by a dagger in the eye.

The study of medieval armour presents many difficulties and risks of creating a false impression of standardization. Although medieval rulers legislated for the equipment to be owned, it is difficult to determine how often ideal standards were met. Individual wealth and personal inclination determined the equipment possessed, and at times of low military activity there was no incentive to maintain readiness.

WEAPONS

CAVALRY WEAPONS: THE SWORD AND THE LANCE

The sword was the principal cavalry weapon. Made of high-grade steel, it was a rare and expensive item. The western sword was principally a slashing weapon throughout the period, although around 1100 there was a change from a parallel-sided to a tapering blade, which became accentuated with time. There were other specialist swords which emerged in the later Middle Ages: broad-bladed falchions and thin, square-sectioned, armour-piercing weapons popular in eastern Europe. These were introduced in response to plate armour. In the Islamic world, while scimitar and light sabres were used, they were by no means universal. The traditional Turco-Iranian weapon was a long, straight-sided type, also used for slashing.

Until around 1300 the lance was a simple pole, usually of ash, 10-12ft (3-4m) long. It then grew heavier and thicker, and broadened into a handguard. About 1390, the new, solid breastplates begin to sprout a device known as the arrêt, as a support for the heavier lance (which had previously been rested on the pommel). This further refinement of the couched-lance technique is one reason for the revived use of knightly

This early fifteenth-century sword has an especially long grip to enable it to be wielded in two hands. Such 'bastard swords' (as contemporaries called them) or hand-and-a-half swords (as they are known today) were wielded by men-at-arms fighting on foot. This weapon is quite possibly English, of the Agincourt (1415) period.

These five swords represent archetypal fourteenth- and fifteenth-century forms of the weapon, and demonstrate the typological development of the blade, pommel, and quillon (cross-guard) formations. Although these swords are designed primarily for thrusting, the weapons at either end are in the form of earlier, slashing types. Dates, from left to right, are pre-1350, post-1350, post-1450, c.1380, and post-1350.

lancers in the fifteenth century. Although seen as the archetypal knightly weapon, the lance had limitations. It often broke on impact and needed replacing, which was more easily achieved in the sporting joust than in battle. Dismounted knights often used the weapon defensively, shortening it for extra rigidity. In the fourteenth century, the English developed the technique of pairs of men-at-arms holding one lance for foot combat. Although the Byzantines and Muslims used lances too, they tended to be longer and lighter and were not so narrowly specialized as the western weapon.

INFANTRY WEAPONS

Spears, about 9ft (2.75m) in length, were used universally by foot soldiers (a hedge of spears held by resolute infantry could resist cavalry charges). Other staff weapons included a range of broad-bladed types, known as polearms, based upon agricultural implements like the bill-hook. When the halberd emerged c.1300, it had an axe-shaped head, often with a hammer or spike opposite the blade. Polearms looked like huge tin-openers and shared some of their characteristics, allowing a foot soldier to hook a cavalryman out of the saddle and jab through or crush his armour. Against footmen, halberds were equally effective, and the Swiss made terrifying use of them. The Swiss are usually associated with the pike, a spear lengthened to about 15-18ft (4.5-5.5m), but this did not predominate in their forces until the later fifteenth century.

Urban militias seem to have produced the most pikemen — for example, Flanders and northern Italy in the twelfth century — perhaps because urban life made the requirements of pike-drill more easily practised. Pikemen seem to have been used defensively until the advent of the Swiss, who were able to manoeuvre their massed pikes aggressively. In the sixteenth century, 'pike-blocks' with their attached handgunners, became effectively mobile castles of men.

Most countries mixed pike and polearm men. The Flemish had the *goedendag* ('good-day'), a 3-4ft (c.1m) club, wider at the top, bound in iron and capped by a spike. The Hussites used the flail, developed from agricultural use, with added balls on chains. The Swiss *Morgenstern* was a club bristling with spikes. All combined weight with spikiness. From c.1350, dismounted knights favoured the poleaxe, a 5-ft (1.5m) long weapon with a spike and an axe head. The English archers adopted the leaden-headed mallet at Agincourt (1415), used for driving in their defensive stakes, and employed ever after as a similar weapon. Short

Four late fifteenth-century poleaxes, featuring a spike, axe-like blade, and 'meat-tenderiser' form of spiked club. This enabled the wielder, often a dismounted man-at-arms, to puncture or crush the defences of a plate-armoured opponent. Poleaxes caused devastating casualties during the fierce foot-mêlees of the English Civil Wars of the Roses.

hand-maces were favoured by Muslims, so that they were described as 'Turkish arms' in the west, where they were also adopted by horsemen. These might be round and spiked, flanged, or in axe-form.

Swords were used on foot, too, there being specialized two-handed versions. These were certainly used by 1300, and were popular in the fifteenth century, when there were some monstrous examples, 5ft (1.5m) long, used very much like polearms. Daggers and other light hand-arms proliferated also. Their principal use in battle seems to have been to despatch the wounded or to find the chinks in a knight's armour once he was down. At Crécy (1346), Edward III's Welsh troops carried long knives with which they slit the bellies of the French horses by creeping underneath them.

MISSILE WEAPONS

Hand-thrown stones continued to play a role, and slingers were still in evidence, although they were being overtaken by archery. The bow was the hunter's weapon and was widely available. Western bows were all self-bows, that is simple wooden staves (unlike eastern composite bows of wood, bone, and sinew). There is a common misapprehension that until about 1300 these self-bows were also 'short bows', to be overtaken by the new 'longbows' of the Welsh. In fact, the term 'longbow' has no contemporary validity; the sources only distinguish between bows and crossbows. The mechanics of a self-bow dictate that the longer its arms, the more potentially powerful it is. The bows which Gerald de Barry describes the Welsh wielding c.1200 were short, but thick and strong. Manuscript illustrations often show English bows as knobbly, for to smooth out the knots weakened the weapon.

Archers had always been important. Carolingian capitularies required footmen to possess bows and arrows; at Hastings, the archers may have won the day. In the thirteenth century, the English kings started to build up large forces of archers. These were not just Welsh, as in 1217 archers from the (forested) Weald of Kent were deployed against the French besiegers at Dover. But the English achievement was in taking the weapon out of the wooded areas and diffusing it throughout agrarian society, thus generating a large pool of potential archers. It was the weight of numbers, rather than the power of the bows alone, which made the English so feared in the later Middle Ages. Although it is possible that the bows of 1545 found on *The Mary Rose*, with their 180lb (100kg) draw-weights, may represent a peak of development, such simple technology was incapable of great improvement. Much depended upon the quality of the wood used, Iberian yew being most favoured. Arrow heads did change over time, though. Broad-heads were used against unarmoured men and horses, while the narrow, square-sectioned bodkin-head was developed to punch through plate.

The eastern composite bow was also an ancient weapon. It had been perfected half a millennium before the time of Christ. It was short and strong for use on horseback. Its power, especially in comparison with self-bows, has been the subject of much debate. Both weapons have had ranges of 400yds (365m) claimed for them, although 200yds (182m) seems to have been the longest effective range. Even the English 'longbow' was probably armour-piercing only at short range (30yds, 27m), although it could wound unarmoured men and horses at longer distances. The Turkish composite bow may have been limited by the lightness of its arrows. On crusade, western foot-bowmen kept horse-archers at bay.

Even more dangerous to such light cavalry was the crossbow. It had been developed in late antiquity, and is represented in a tenth-century manuscript, but only seems to have been widely used from c.1050. Anna Comnena treats it as a new weapon on the First Crusade. In 1139, the Second Lateran Council banned its use against Christians, and sanctioned it against unbelievers. It was also a composite bow, set on a shaft and so very stiff that it could only be 'spanned' by using the feet or, later, hooks and ratchet devices. It had the advantage that it could be kept loaded, because a 'nut' held the cord in place. As the machines grew heavier they took so long to load that the user needed an assistant to carry a pavise (large shield) to protect them both. Without them crossbowmen proved very vulnerable to faster-shooting archers. When used on the defensive or behind fortifications the weapons were still valuable. Fifteenth-century steel crossbows had draw-weights of 1,000lbs (450kg) and even lighter machines were capable of sending their square bolts ('quarrels') through most armour.

SIEGE TECHNIQUES

In order to control territory, it was necessary to occupy its fortified places. Much warfare consequently concerned the capture of fortresses. The quickest method of attack was to storm the defences, using siege ladders. But frequently this was not feasible, and to be successful an attacker had to be able to go over, through, or to mine under the walls and towers of a fortress. The alternative was blockade, but this could be extremely time-consuming. The main technique for mining was the digging of a tunnel under the wall or a tower, under which a chamber was hollowed out, supported by wooden props; when these were burned the masonry above collapsed, creating a breach. With the invention of gunpowder, it became possible to bring down fortifications by subterranean explosions; but this was not a widely-used technique before 1500. It is still possible to visit the sixteenth-century mines at St Andrews castle (Fife, Scotland). At Rochester castle in Kent, the effects of king John's mining in 1215 can be seen – the corner quarter of the keep was brought down and subsequently rebuilt in a different style. The defenders' counter-measure of counter-mining involved intercepting the besiegers' tunnel.

A breach could also be made above ground. This could be done by miners working with picks at the base of a wall; or by use of a 'ram', a thick beam with a pointed iron head which was supported by ropes and swung against the masonry to break it down by impact; or by use of a pointed 'bore'. The 'sappers' or engineers who managed it required protection from above, and so rams were frequently protected by roofed and wheeled sheds. This type of engine was called a 'mouse', as it was reminiscent of the creature creeping up to the walls. Its roof was often 'armoured' with metal bands, and the men within it also wore armour and helmets to protect themselves. For battering down walls at longer range there were many kinds of artillery pieces deployed. The oldest type, used at Paris in the siege of 885-86, was the *ballista*. This was a kind of giant crossbow, with the motive force provided by torsion, its two arms held between twisted rope and sinew braces within a wooden frame. Torsion was also the method used to power the 'mangonel', only this time a vertical arm was inserted into the

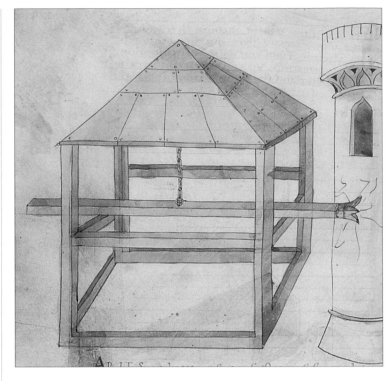

A covered battering ram (Aries). This illustration shows the kind of shed, with an armoured roof, used throughout the medieval period to protect engineers in their attempts to knock down walls. Although not shown here, they were frequently wheeled constructions.

horizontal brace, producing a lobbing motion. In the mid-twelfth century the trebuchet first appeared in Europe. It had been invented in China centuries earlier, and gradually made its way west via the Arab world. It worked on the sling principle. A tall frame supported a giant beam which was pulled around and over it to hurl its missile. Originally, the motive power came from men (or women, who operated a machine at the siege of Toulouse, 1218) pulling the ropes. Later, a counterweight device was used. Trebuchets were considered to be the most powerful form of artillery before the development of gunpowder weapons. One of the earliest examples of its use in western warfare was at Acre in 1191, when the crusaders had machines nicknamed 'Bad Neighbour' and 'God's Own'.

The range of these weapons depended upon their size. Mangonels normally reached about 200yds (183m), but large trebuchets may have been capable of double that. Most battering was done at close range, even gunpowder artillery being brought as close to the walls as possible for maximum effect. Indeed, stone-throwers (*petrariae*) and cannon were used in tandem well into the fifteenth century. Both types of weapon shot stone balls, usually worked by masons on the spot, although they could be pre-prepared. Other projectiles included dead horses or other animals to spread disease in a fortification, dead bodies of the defenders' comrades to spread dismay, or exotica such as beehives to spread disorder. Pre-gunpowder engines could be extemporized on the spot, provided suitable timber and skilled engineers were available. The former was a major problem on the First Crusade – when available, ships were broken up. The Vikings at the siege of Paris (885-86) are alleged to have employed renegade Franks skilled in such matters. Or engines could be kept dismantled in arsenals, as was the case in thirteenth-century England. In the 1260s, sultan Baibars possessed a siege-train of prefabricated siege engines for use against crusader fortifications. Artillery was used in defence too, to bombard attackers' engines, which could also be burned in sorties if they were not well-guarded.

The purpose of mining and battery was to cause a breach which could then be stormed. Siege towers ('belfries') were employed to get troops safely up to the walls. They could be several stories high, built of huge timbers (often taken from ships) and bound in iron. Like all wooden siege engines, they were covered in untanned hides, flesh-side out and soaked in water or vinegar, since defenders attempted to burn them, using 'Greek fire' where its composition was known. Dating back to the classical world, this was an oil-based fuel which stuck to anything it was squirted at. Originally a Byzantine 'secret weapon', by the eleventh century Muslim troops were using 'naphtha' compounds, and the recipe was later known in the west. Greek fire was a much feared weapon, since such fires could only be extinguished by smothering them to cut off oxygen. Getting a belfry up to a wall required that the ditch be filled in. The easiest method was using bundles of branches (faggots). At the siege of Acre (1191) pilgrims were paid for each stone they brought to fill the ditch, one woman pilgrim requesting that her

A siege tower and bridge used for approaching and storming fortifications. This diagram shows how the wicker bridge could be lowered onto the walls. It also enables the attackers to cross the defensive ditch around the fortress. Frequently, such towers (belfries) had several enclosed storeys filled with missilemen; they were propelled by oxen or manpower.

corpse be used if she died in the attempt. When a belfry did reach the walls, the attackers attempted to drop a bridge onto them, in order to cross. To prevent this, defenders used wooden beams to keep the attackers' tower out of range, or could use wood to build up their own walls opposite the belfry. Siege towers were also constructed on floating platforms. At Constantinople in 1203-04, the crusaders adapted large Venetian ships by building 'flying bridges' suspended from their masts to assault the sea-walls.

Frequently, fortifications could not be taken by assault, despite the use of whichever of the techniques described above was appropriate. Starvation was the final method. It was cheaper in both men and material, but it was time-consuming. Indeed, no fortress was expected to hold out forever, but only to buy time for a relieving force to arrive. This, or exhaustion of a besiegers' interest or resources, could result in a siege being raised. To continue a siege for months, through winter and with little plunder or entertainment, required great powers of organization and motivation. And the fact that medieval warfare contained so many prolonged sieges is an underestimated tribute to the skills of medieval commanders and the discipline of their forces. Negotiations to enable a defender to surrender could result in a date for surrender being set if relief did not arrive after a castellan sent an appeal to his lord. But a fortress commander was expected to put up a fight before taking this option, and there are plentiful examples of castles and towns being reduced to desperate straits before asking for terms. Knights would consume their horses – which represented a considerable investment to them – before surrendering. In famous cases like Rouen (1418-19), *bouches inutiles* (useless mouths) were ejected in order to save supplies. This meant that the elderly, women, and children were forced to starve in the 'no-man's-land' between the walls and siege lines. If a fortress was stormed, then there was no quarter given and the besiegers were allowed to indulge in rapine. Of course, siege warfare predates the medieval centuries, and even as this was being written, such tactics were being repeated in Bosnia, at Sarajevo, and elsewhere.

FORTRESSES

Medieval fortification is usually characterized as the castle. In fact, fortresses could be anything from 'strong' houses, small towers and forts, castles of a primarily residential or military nature (usually both), fortified churches, monasteries and castles designed for the Military Orders, town-walls, city-complexes, to ports and specialist fortifications concerned with bridges or harbours. Control of such fortifications was crucial to the conduct of warfare. Sometimes the fate of a campaign could hang on the resistance of one tower, as at Damietta (on the Nile in Egypt) in the thirteenth century.

It used to be thought that castles formed part of a system of 'defensive networks', especially along frontiers. R.C. Smail debunked this idea for the Latin crusading states (*Crusading Warfare*), and his criticisms are valid elsewhere. Certainly frontier zones could be heavily fortified; for example, on the borders of Christendom in Latin Syria, Spain, or in the Baltic lands. But this was also the case within Europe, as the study of the Vexin shows (*page 53*). Castles had a wider role than the purely military though: they were symbolic of power and wealth. Often they were the creation of an ambitious individual rather than the conscious product of 'national strategy', such as Vauban's schemes of fortress-building for Louis XIV in the later seventeenth century. Nor could individual castles obstruct the movement of enemy armies. What they could do, like fortresses throughout time, is provide bases from which an invading force could be harried, or cut off from its supply routes. So long as the castles and fortified towns of a region held out, an invader could plunder, but would not be able to make permanent gains. So there was frequently a need to capture fortifications in order to make them work for an attacker. Consequently, Henry V's conquest of Normandy (1417-19) took the form of the systematic reduction of the province's fortresses.

Rulers expended vast sums on the construction of fortifications, often substantial proportions of their total incomes. Funding the building of Belvoir c.1160, on the river Jordan, drove the Hospitaller Master mad with worry. Richard I's Château Gaillard and Edward I's Welsh castles are significant examples of the cost of major programmes of castle-building. Popes built fortified palaces at Rome and Avignon at the expense of the faithful. During the Hundred Years' War, there were plans for constructing entire defensive systems for England and France. Spain was recovered from the Muslims by a fortress strategy of building and manning castles and towns, and eastern Europe was colonized in the same way. Fortification was an integral part of government since administration, justice, and tribute or tax collecting, and the display of lordship, were based on fortified centres. Whatever was spent on military building repaid the cost in the long run. However, it often served a purpose to destroy fortifications in order to prevent a 'colonial' power regaining an effective foothold. Saladin's activities after his victory at Hattin (1187) or Robert Bruce's in 1306-14, are good examples of this. Oliver Cromwell still found this approach necessary in the mid-seventeenth century, because quite small fortifications provided significant points of resistance.

The development of the castle is often represented as a move from timber to stone, yet some of the earliest fortifications described in this book were the stone towers built in Anjou c.950-1000. The Carolingian royal palaces had been largely undefended, but the *casa firmissima* (strong house) begins to appear in ninth-century Frankia. There were stone buildings from an early date, such as at Doué-la-Fontaine, which was gradually transformed from Carolingian stone hall to a tower, then to a keep with a motte around it .

It is true that the 'motte-and-bailey' castles, particularly associated with the conquest of the British Isles, had wooden towers in the eleventh and twelfth centuries, but these may have been specifically designed as temporary forts, even though some later developed into more permanent stone fortresses. Timber was also used much later in heavily wooded regions such as eastern Europe (where stone was also scarce). Earth-banked fortifications also remained popular, especially for long circuits such as town walls. These were not mere ditches and banks, but often elaborately constructed internally for permanence. Such mottes as have been excavated share the characteristic of being composed of layers of different types of earth, braced with timber. Many motte castles had the earth banked up around the wooden tower, rather than it being perched on top. Much later, with the development of gunpowder weapons, low earthen banks regained favour for their ability to absorb shot. Earth and timber bulwarks were the first anti-gunpowder works.

The late eleventh century appears to show a technical explosion in castle-building, although the rarity of earlier survivals may exaggerate this. The White Tower in London, and the keeps at Colchester and Rochester (all built by the architect-monk Gundulf) literally rose to new heights. Twelfth-century developments have often been associated with knowledge acquired on the crusades, but this is an over-simplification. After all, there were plentiful examples of Roman military architecture in the west. Square towers were characteristic of twelfth-century fortification, although those of Roman forts had been round. There was a general trend from tall tower-keeps, popular to about 1180, to more complex multi-walled fortresses. Much depended upon the fortress's origins, however. A castle like Dover was shaped by Iron Age, Roman, and Anglo-Saxon work on the site, while others were built as a piece. Richard I's Château Gaillard is a classic example. Its central tower was built *en bec* (wedge-shaped) in order to deflect artillery stones. There was also a general move away from square to round towers for the same reason, although this change varied a great deal from region to region. Around 1200, towers and walls, which had always been capped with wooden hoardings to give a projecting platform against besiegers, began to be equipped with stone 'machicolations' for the same purpose.

The thirteenth century was probably the highpoint of the castle proper. It witnessed the building of Edward I's concentric castles in Wales; Krak des Chevaliers (Hospitaller) and Safad (Templar) in Syria; and others in Spain and Germany. Wide water defences, where feasible, could keep besiegers at arms' length and remove the danger of mining. Another reaction in castle design to resist mining was to make the base of a wall very broad, with a sloping *glacis* (where the base of a wall was broad, with a triangular profile). Castles continued to be valued into the later Middle Ages. Only the advent of effective gunpowder siege trains after 1400 reduced their viability as strongpoints. The emphasis then shifted to larger fortifications which took longer to reduce.

Town walls were always important, though few now survive because of nineteenth-century urban growth which swallowed them up; most can only be observed as shadowy influences on current street plans. Rare examples such as the fortress town of Carcassonne (itself largely a nineteenth-century reconstruction) give an idea of how such fortresses worked. All needed an inner citadel as a refuge when the longer, outer circuit was breached. Most were rebuilt from the sixteenth century onwards in the *trace italienne* style of masonry and brick, most easily seen in northern France, Flanders, and Italy. The presence of town walls indicated the prevalence of a threat. Peaceful England was panicked into rapid construction of town walls during the fourteenth century both on the south coast where French invasion seemed imminent, and in the northern borders. Before that, Edward I had built fortified towns in association with his Welsh castles; and the same was true in Ireland. Further examples in Spain and the Holy Land indicate that this was a 'colonial' form of fortress warfare employed on expanding frontiers. In contrast, it is important to remember that England, insulated by its natural water defences, was a relative backwater. After about 1300, military architecture in England stagnated and many fourteenth- and fifteenth-century castles, like Bodiam (Sussex), Raglan (Gwent), and Tattershall (Lincolnshire) have a large element of decoration. Few modern bulwarks were constructed in fifteenth-century England, the south-coast port of Sandwich being one of the rare exceptions.

THE IMPACT OF GUNPOWDER ON WAR AND FORTIFICATIONS

Gunpowder, known in China by the eleventh century, reached western Europe in the mid-thirteenth century, probably via the Muslim world. There are illustrations of primitive cannon (the French *canon* is derived from Latin *canna*, a tube) from around 1320. Within twenty years, their use was widespread in sieges, defending towns, and in battle, although of limited value. A great advance occurred in the 1370s. By 1420 there were cannon capable of firing projectiles of nearly 800lbs (363kg).

GUN MANUFACTURE

By 1400, a bewildering variety of guns existed: from large bombards, through medium-sized veuglaires, crapadeaux, mortars, and serpentines, to small culverins, either handheld or mounted on walls or stands. Guns were made from iron or bronze. Early guns tended to be of iron bars welded together and bound by hoops. Most guns were cast from iron or preferably bronze. Gun-makers were often the master-gunners, although bell-founders could cast bronze guns. Many cannon were loaded with removable chambers wedged in place. They shot iron or stone balls, or lead in the case of culverins, and were fired by applying a heated iron bar. Bombards had custom-made projectiles and many had names, like 'De dulle Griet' ('Mad Margot'). Heavy guns were most easily moved by water or travelled on four-wheeled carts. When they reached their destination, special mounts were constructed. Trunnions, for mounting on two-wheeled carriages, are mentioned in the mid-fifteenth century. This, and the rejection of gigantic bombards for more, smaller, faster-firing culverins, improved mobility after c.1450.

'Mons Meg', a Burgundian iron bombard cast in 1449 (now at Edinburgh castle), is 15ft (250kg) long, weighs 8.5 tons (8.63 tonnes), and used over 100lbs (45kg) of gunpowder to fire its 549lb (250kg) ball. Guns like this were so heavy that they were most easily moved by water, limiting their deployment. In the later fifteenth century, they were superseded by more mobile culverins.

ARTILLERY IN ACTION: SIEGES

The rapid development of cannon by about 1380 threatened to take the advantage in warfare from the defence. Medieval fortifications did not become redundant overnight, but, in general, high stone walls which defied stone-throwing engines for centuries collapsed under the impact of massive projectiles from bombards. In 1405, a single shot made the Scots of Berwick surrender. The Burgundians fired three shots at Ham in 1411: the first missed, the second destroyed a tower, and the third breached the walls. By the 1440s, the French developed new siege techniques, constructing fortified camps, surrounding strongholds with trenches, and using lighter pieces to prevent defenders from repairing damage caused by slow-firing bombards. Not all sieges were over quickly, but the pace of siege warfare quickened during the fifteenth century. The rapid ending of the Hundred Years' War is testimony to the power of siege artillery.

Defenders reacted rapidly. The first response was to thicken walls and to scarp them. Guns were quickly employed in defence. Hand culverins required little modification to defences, but they were only useful against assault parties. In the fifteenth century the *bulwark* (or *boulevard* in French), an outwork of earth and timber mounting defensive artillery, was rapidly developed to protect vulnerable features like gates and to keep the attackers at a distance from which their guns could do less damage. By 1465 the French, again, used trenches and *boulevards* against a besieger. Ultimately the bastion, an angled gun platform at the same level as the walls so artillery could be moved easily, projecting from the walls to give the widest possible field of fire, was developed by the early sixteenth century.

THE BATTLEFIELD

Firearms had less impact in battle, not least because battles were uncommon. Slow rate of fire generally limited artillery to opening salvoes, although the invention of trunnions and wheeled carriages improved mobility. Hand culverins and 'arquebuses' were increasingly used in the second half of the fifteenth century. Charles the Bold of Burgundy, a self-consciously modern general, employed hand-gunners, mobile culverins, and English archers in the 1470s – although nothing could save him from his lack of skill as a general. Handgunners were also to be found in the armies of France and Italian states near the end of the century, suggesting they were valued.

Kings and princes rapidly recognized the importance of firearms and enthusiastically adopted the new weapons, as did town councils. There was no room for chivalrous luddism, and the church gave gunners a patron saint (St Barbara). Guns claimed many noble victims – like the earl of Salisbury at Orléans in 1428 – but there was no outcry against firearms. Indeed, the French king Louis XI's master of artillery was a nobleman. The ruling classes, too often caricatured as empty-headed and interested only in jousting, promoted the manufacture of improved types of artillery and new methods of attack and defence.

SHIPPING AND AMPHIBIOUS WARFARE

Military histories tend to leave out navies in their accounts. To do so in an account of medieval warfare is to omit a very important aspect of its history. Fleets moved much faster than land armies and vessels were valuable as transport, warships, and siege weapons. They were deployed at sea and on inland waters, as specialized and multi-purpose vessels. There were also considerable developments in ship design from 800-1500 which led eventually to the production of ocean-going vessels capable of world exploration.

Viking longships dominated the North Sea from the ninth to eleventh centuries. Up to 100ft (30m) long, with 20 to 30 oars (and crews perhaps 3 times as large), they were both sailed and rowed. Their shallow draught (3ft, 1m) allowed them to penetrate the riverine coasts of the British Isles and Francia, while their seaworthiness was good enough to bring the Mediterranean within reach. The dominant ship type there was the galley, usually powered by a double bank of oars and about 50 rowers, although the largest Byzantine dromons boasted 200. The ram was no longer used, having been replaced by a beak that was designed for transfixing an opponent prior to boarding.

The Muslim contribution to ship types was a horse-transport (*usari* or *tarida*) ship that unloaded directly onto the shore by a stern ramp, used by the Byzantines in the reconquest of Crete and Cyprus in the mid-tenth century. It was possible to transport horses in longships, too. Vikings already used them cross-Channel in 892, and William the Bastard's 1066 fleet carried perhaps eight to ten per ship. Other Normans in the Mediterranean used *taride*, loading twenty horses; but

this maritime technology was not used in northern waters. In 1123, the Venetians were the first to transport horses on crusade, swiftly followed by the Sicilians. By the 1190s, a tarida's load had increased to 40, and by the 1270s large roundships (*see below*) carried 100 mounts.

The Christians dominated the naval contest in the Mediterranean. In the west, Iberian and Sicilian fleets proved superior to those of Muslim north Africa. As the crusaders gained control of the ports of the Syrian coast, the Fatimid navy was marginalized. After the loss of Ascalon in 1153, its galleys could not interfere with the crucial sea-route between Cyprus and Acre, as they could not carry enough water to sustain them in the area. The Mamluks and later the Ottomans deployed large navies, but Muslim fleets were vulnerable to superior western technology.

By 1200, the Mediterranean roundship developed to a massive size and played a crucial role at Constantinople (1203-04) and Damietta (1221). For his crusades, St Louis ordered to be built two-deckers 90ft (29m) long of 325 tons, and three-deckers 115ft (35m) long of 800 tons (broadening the beam increased the tonnage with small

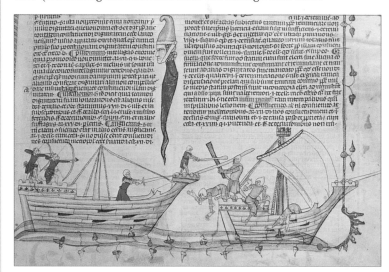

A mid-fourteenth-century depiction of two cogs fighting. Ships of this type were used by the English at Sluys (1340). As well as being taller than galleys, the construction of castles gave an extra dimension to the use of missilemen (such as the archer shown here) and were useful in boarding enemy vessels.

lengthening of the keel). An 800-ton ship had 80 crew and could carry between 500 and 600 passengers or 100 horses. Roundships were regularly used to transport crusaders with horse and arms on a package-tour basis, often arranged by the Military Orders, to provide fighting men for Outremer. Journey times were swift in comparison with the long and dangerous land route. In 1248, Louis IX's fleet travelled the 2,000 miles (3,380km) from Aigue-Mortes to Cyprus in only 24 days (although this was with the prevailing wind). To some extent this was offset by the danger of shipwreck, but on the later crusades a Mediterranean crossing became the favoured route until the Ottomans sealed off the Levant. Even then, the Knights Hospitaller at Rhodes organized crusading and raiding expeditions until they were finally expelled in 1522.

With the development of the cog, ship design in the North Sea and the Baltic took a new turn. The Carolingians employed naval troops called *cokingi*, which suggests that a ship type, shorter, broader, and

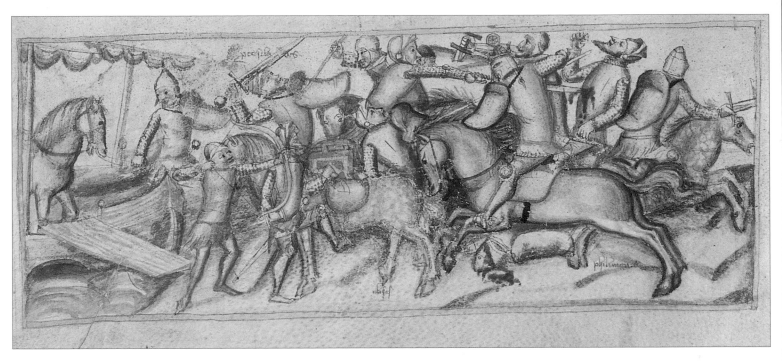

This lively scene from a mid-fourteenth-century manuscript is a good example of amphibious warfare. The warhorses are shown being disembarked from a horse transport and then mounted, on land, under cover of archery, before joining the fray.

higher than longships, already existed. Around 1200, the cog appears extensively in written and pictorial records. Originally a bulk carrier, it became a warship of great versatility. Although vessels of between 150 and 200 tons are recorded, most were 100 tons or less. They could be equipped, fore and aft, with wooden 'castles', which, when filled with archers and men-at-arms, improved their fighting capabilities. English cogs defeated the galley fleets of the French (1340) and Castilians (1359) with such vessels, while they proved invaluable in the Baltic crusades against lighter skiffs. In the English Channel, small, oar-powered vessels known as barges or balingers, had an important military role in coastal raids and river operations. French and Castilian galleys were also suited to raiding England's Channel coast.

In about the mid-fourteenth century, the northern and Mediterranean traditions of naval architecture came together to create a sailing ship known as the carrack. Originally a two-masted vessel, by c.1425 a third, the mizzen mast, had been added. The creation of an English navy by Henry V included a three-masted 'great ship', *Grace Dieu*. Although at 500-600 tons, the tonnages were smaller than some of the earlier roundships, carracks were swift, fully rigged ships, with stern- and fore-castles. They mostly only mounted stone-throwing artillery, however. The first reference to a gunpowder weapon employed at sea is on an English royal ship in 1338. Until the creation of gun-decks on sixteenth-century galleons, the number of cannon on board remained few. Of Henry V's fleet, the fifteen ships equipped with cannon had only two to three each. So battles at sea remained like land battles throughout the medieval period, with vessels closing to allow boarding and hand-to-hand combat as a way of reaching a decision.

By 1500, there had been great technological developments. Because these happened fairly slowly in comparison to the rapid advances made

after the Industrial Revolution, they have tended to be overlooked. There were still important operational constraints. Ships lacked the sailing capabilities to hold station, making the naval blockades typical of

This illustration contains fantastical elements, but shows a form of siege weapon which was actually used, for example, in the early thirteenth-century crusader attacks on Constantinople and Damietta. Ships were bound together in pairs, with siege towers erected on the broad platform this provided.

the eighteenth century impossible. Limited water supplies also restricted the length of their cruises to a few weeks. But whether as transport, fighting ships, or floating siege towers, medieval fleets made a substantial contribution to warfare.

MILITARY MANUALS

Theoretical studies, personal memoirs, and pragmatic manuals born of experience provide plentiful evidence that medieval commanders could take a systematic approach to war. The *Epitome de rei militari* (Digest on Military Matters) by Vegetius Renatus, a late fourth-century Roman, was the most widely read work. It exists in over 300 medieval manuscripts, showing its popularity. Although it describes the deployment of the Roman legion, Vegetius' advice was 'eternal common-sense principles' (R. C. Smail, *Crusading Warfare*). A ninth-century reader highlighted the use of cavalry, while an English translator in 1408 added a comment on 'great guns…that nowadays no wall may withstand them'. Vegetius emphasized the importance of logistics and starving out opponents, in fortress or in the field, and not risking battle, a lesson medieval generals often put into practice. His work contains appendices on fleets and siege warfare. Possession of a manuscript was the mark of a serious interest in war; in 1266 a copy was to be found in the library of the future Edward I of England, one of the great generals of his age.

Folding, pocket-sized manuscripts show that the *Epitome de rei militari* was used in the field. In 1147, count Geoffrey of Anjou called for it at a siege in order to use its recipe for Greek fire. That the recipe is not in any surviving manuscripts suggests that it was especially augmented for this most significant area of warfare. Over four centuries later, a Castilian knight versed in the text advised Charles the Bold of Burgundy on the construction of a mobile tower for the siege of Neuss (1474-75). Count Geoffrey had struggled with the Latin, so it is not surprising to find vernacular translations from the mid-thirteenth century onwards. The earliest is in Italian (c.1250). The first English translation was made for Thomas, lord Berkeley, in 1408, and the fifteenth century saw a rash of translations.

Vernacular works on warfare were original productions springing directly from the medieval experience. One of the earliest is *La Règle du Temple* ('The Rule of the [Knights of the] Temple'). The Templars received a short Latin Rule of seventy-two clauses from their patron, St Bernard, in 1128, dealing with monastic matters. Within two decades, over 120 additional clauses had been added in French detailing their military life. These described the dress, armour, horses, and servants allowed to the knight brothers, from the master to ordinary knight, then the more lightly armed sergeants and skirmishing horse archers ('turcopoles'). The Rule then outlined how the Templars were organized on campaign – in camp, on the march, and in battle – and a unique section described how the Knights were to deliver their cavalry charge, following the Piebald Banner carried by the Marshal. These instructions compare well with cavalry drill books from the eighteenth century onwards. The Rule is elitist, however, in dealing only with mounted men and ignoring infantry, even though their role, especially on crusade, was vital.

Later treatises on crusading corrected this omission. Marino Sanudo envisaged 50,000 footsoldiers in his plan to recover the Holy Land (c.1320). Bertrand de Brocquière analyzed Turkish tactics for duke Philip of Burgundy (1432). He pinpointed the Muslims' weakness in the area of solid infantry and advised the creation of a crusader host embodying the best features of the Christian nations: French chivalry, German crossbows, and 10,000 English longbowmen. He drew up an order of battle for this imagined force. Another old soldier was Jean de Beuil, whose *Le Jouvencel* ('The Youth', c.1466) was an imagined biography based upon his own experience in the last decades of the Hundred Years' War. He had commanded the French forces at Castillon (1453), the last and decisive battle of the war, deploying large numbers of artillery pieces to defeat the English. Although a 'Renaissance' soldier, he drew on earlier chivalric works and passed on their ideas: since 'The Youth' was printed five times between 1493 and 1529, the message must have been popular.

THE LAWS OF WAR

In his book *The Laws of War in the Late Middle Ages*, Maurice Keen showed that the ideas of chivalry 'prepared the way for the notion of a law of nations'. The medieval concept of a 'Just War' (derived from the fourth-century writings of St Augustine), as refined in the thirteenth century, required that war be waged under proper authority, that of the Church against infidels, that of a prince or judge, or in self-defence. To Augustine, 'the final object of war is peace…unjust war is no more than robbery on a majestic scale'. There was concern to distinguish the legitimate war of princes (*guerre ouverte*, open war) from private war in pursuit of noble feuds (*guerre couverte*). Reality did not always comply. Where princely authority was weak, lords waged unrestrained 'private' wars. Marcher lords conducted cross-border quarrels under the guise of the war of princes. Some actions 'open war', especially burning. This was a legitimate activity for princes, but was deemed arson by lesser men, although it was central to the plundering raid (*chevauchées*) which characterized warfare. As in all law, the principle was more important than its evasions. Rulers arranged for their bishops, and later representative institutions or courts, to endorse their campaigns. In the prolonged struggles between the German king-emperors and popes, the latter's blessing legitimized civil war, while the former set up alternative popes as part of the war of ideas.

The concept of *jus militare* (military or chivalric law) was only concerned with soldiers of knightly rank. It dealt with issues such as ransom and the division of plunder. The idea of ransom was that a man who possessed a coat of arms (nobility) could preserve his life by surrender, in return for a sum to be agreed with his captor. In the case of a monarch, like king John of France captured at Poitiers (1356), the price agreed was enormous (and not paid in full – John returned to captivity where he died). It was forbidden to abuse a captive in order to extort a higher ransom (such as knocking out his teeth with a hammer), as a court confirmed. Indeed, many men contracted to fight, a phenomenon not restricted to the later Middle Ages, in the hope of profit. Much medieval warfare can be seen as a 'joint stock' operation, by which participants invested heavily in campaigns in the expectation of recouping the cost from the spoils of war. If they were captured, however, payment of a ransom could be ruinous.

The law of ransom allegedly spared Christian lives, but ordinary soldiers were not protected by it and were slaughtered or, in the case of missilemen especially, subjected to mutilation. Infidels who refused to convert were liable to death. On the marches with Islam, the heathen, or other 'barbarians' (such as England's Celtic fringe), slave-taking continued to be widespread. From around 1000, in areas of France and the Empire where royal authority was weak, bishops tried to restrain warfare under the Peace and Truce of God, by outlawing fighting on holy days, effectively confining it to between Tuesday and Thursday. The crusading movement intended to direct military energies against non-Christians or heretics, but this required the co-operation of rulers.

The law of sieges was well-developed since so much warfare revolved around fortresses. Defenders were allowed to request relief from their lord by a certain date and, if it did not materialize, surrender with honour, protected from reprisals. Should they refuse all calls to surrender, a fortress taken by storm was entitled to no quarter (the lives and property of the inhabitants were at the mercy of the besiegers). This law was still observed in nineteenth-century warfare. Any 'useless mouths' expelled from a fortress during the course of a siege in order to conserve supplies had no right to pass through the siege lines, and were frequently left to starve in 'no-man's-land'. Such was chivalric warfare, although questions of personal morality were considered of the utmost importance. By 1400, a genre of writing on warfare had developed which, while drawing heavily upon Vegetius, made efforts to define modes of Christian warfare. In the fifteenth century, both Christine de Pisan's *Book of Deeds of Arms and Chivalry* and Honoré Bovet's *Tree of Battles* were as concerned with proper knightly behaviour as with the management of war. Both were translated into English in the later fifteenth century. Christine de Pisan's work entered the Renaissance canon both via Jean de Beuil's plagiarism, and by the publication of an edition by Caxton.

THE REALITY OF WAR

The danger of military history lies in presenting war in an acceptable form. It is not our intention to glorify war. However, much literature produced for medieval ruling elites did precisely that, in their celebration of martial values. It contains descriptions ranging from sober reportage to fictional deeds of arms. Medieval depictions of military scenes are important sources for arms, armour, and techniques, but the written sources are rarely first-hand, and the visual representations are not 'photographic'. Some indication of the nature of combat is provided by the gruesome contents of three graves, containing 1,185 corpses from the battle of Wisby (1361), in Gotland, Sweden. The skeletons display the effects of crossbow bolts descending vertically, piercing mail coifs, sword and axe cuts, and blows from maces and morning-stars (spiked balls attached by a chain to a handle). In one case the lower legs were severed, and several skulls exhibited deep cuts. The lower legs below the protection of shields suffered many deep wounds. Many corpses were stripped, but some were buried with their armour, owing to advancing decomposition. The finds are in the National Museum of Antiquities in Stockholm, Sweden, and are analysed in B. Thordeman, *Armour from the Battle of Wisby, 1361*.

Losses in battle were perhaps twenty to fifty per cent higher on the losing side. The knights' armour and ransom value meant that most of the dead were commoners, although the French nobility suffered heavily at Courtrai (1328) and Agincourt (1415). Commanders had to lead from the front, so death was always a risk. Harold's death at

Hastings (1066) made it a decisive victory for William. Nor was battle the only cause of death. Emperor Frederick I drowned in a river in 1190. Although Richard I survived a crossbow bolt in his knee in 1196, in 1199 a similar wound in his shoulder, sustained during a siege, killed him. The barbed arrowhead had to be cut out with no anaesthetic, and without antiseptic the wound became gangrenous. Surgery was primitive, as it would remain until the second half of the nineteenth century.

After the sixteenth century, records show how armies wasted away through disease and desertion (see Geoffrey Parker, *The Military Revolution*, pp.53-58), and this must have been true earlier. Armies, with their attendant horses, produced sewage which bred dysentery when they were static, when mustering or during sieges. Professor Bachrach's speculations concerning the by-products of the Norman army in 1066 illustrate the problem commanders faced, and frequently coped with successfully (Bachrach, 'The Military Administration of the Norman Conquest', *Anglo-Norman Studies*, pp.1-25). Of a list of ninety-eight dead on the Third Crusade, eighty-four apparently died through sickness. An eye-witness reported that 'by famine and by malady more than 3,000 were struck down at the siege of Acre' (cited by John Gillingham, *Richard Coeur de Lion*, p.221). Henry V's army lost at least fifteen per cent of its strength to dysentery at the siege of Harfleur, and more on the way to Agincourt. English casualties in the battle of Agincourt were about five per cent (Christopher Allmand, *Henry V*, p.211-12). Henry's own death was caused by the unhealthy conditions of siege lines. Supply and disease were closely related, and most medieval commanders were well aware of the need to supply their armies in the field and to stock their fortresses in wartime.

Few sources dwell on ravaging, the central feature of medieval warfare. Bertrand de Born, a late twelfth-century chivalric writer, greeted the onset of the campaigning season: 'I love the gay Eastertide, which brings forth leaves and flowers…it gives me great joy to see, drawn up on the field, knights and horses in battle array. And it delights me when the skirmishers scatter people and herds in their path.' (from John Gillingham, *Richard Coeur de Lion*, p.243). What this entailed is described in a *chanson de geste*: 'Out in front are the scouts and incendiaries. After them come the foragers…soon all is in tumult…the incendiaries set the villages on fire and the foragers visit and sack them. The terrified inhabitants are either burned or led away with their hands tied to be held for ransom…money, cattle, mules and sheep are all seized.' (Gillingham, *Richard Coeur de Lion*, p.118). According to Orderic Vitalis, after William I's harrying of northern England in 1069-70, 'so terrible a famine [fell] upon the humble and defenceless populace, that more than 100,000 Christian folk of both sexes, young and old alike, perished of hunger'. The figure simply means 'a large number'. This was the deliberate creation of a zone of 'scorched earth', but an army a few thousand strong, with its horses and camp followers, was equal to a major town and was a severe drain on provisions. Armies and garrisons could scour a region for supplies, and the result could easily be described as a 'desert'. Even in friendly territory, armies often took what they wanted, including labour and carting services from the peasantry. However, war gradually ceased to be a slave-hunt, although this occurred at different rates. In eastern Europe, where *sclavus* (Slav) displaced the Latin *servus* as the word for a slave c.900, this development was slower than in the west.

GLOSSARY

Albigensians Christian heretics based in south-western France (*see* **Catharism**). The 'Albigensian crusades' were directed against them between 1209 and 1229, and resulted in the culturally distinct south being brought under north French control.

Almohads Islamic Berber tribesmen from North Africa who invaded the Iberian Peninsula in 1145 and maintained a caliphate there until the 1230s.

Almoravids Islamic Berber tribesmen from North Africa who invaded the Iberian Peninsula in 1085, in response to the Christian conquest of Toledo, and maintained a state there until the 1140s.

Angevin Literally meaning 'from Anjou', applied to the first English kings of the Plantagenet dynasty i.e. Henry II (1154-89), Richard I (1189-99), John (1199-1216).

Asabiya A sense of community or a brotherhood of arms amongst Muslims.

Assassins A revolutionary Islamic sect formed in 1094 in northern Iran, which soon spread to Syria where its leader was called 'The Old Man of the Mountain'. They used murder as a political weapon, for their own ends or on hire to other rulers. Their name is derived from hashish, which their enemies accused them of using to make them fearless, since their assassination missions meant certain death.

ballista A giant crossbow weapon known from the Romans, used across Europe in sieges and occasionally in the field, for shooting darts or stone balls, for example, the Franks are alleged to have taught the Vikings how to construct one at the siege of Paris 885-86.

ban Royal power to command, including military service, and punish. It was delegated to lower lords like dukes, counts, and bishops. Where public authority fragmented, as in tenth- and eleventh-century France, it was frequently usurped by castellans, before being reasserted by the crown. The arrière-ban has an imprecise meaning, of the summons of all free men or all who held land for military service, no matter who was their lord. It was frequently replaced by a tax.

barded horses A general term used to describe armoured horses, used in west-ern Europe in the fourteenth and fifteenth centuries.

battle A division of an army. Typically in the later Middle Ages there were three. On the march they formed van, main body, and rearguard; they could go into action in line abreast, or one behind the other.

belfry *See* **siege tower**.

blockhouse A square wooden fort used extensively in the piecemeal conquest of the eastern Baltic lands (e.g. Pomerania, Prussia, Livonia) by the Danes, Swedes, and the military orders.

bolskip A light vessel widely used in the Baltic Sea and rivers flowing into it dur-ing the period of the Baltic crusades.

boulevard Term appearing in France at the start of the fifteenth century to describe works generally made in front of gates, initially of earth, timber, and straw, and later of stone. Their function was to protect the structure behind from enemy gunfire, and to mount the defenders' guns to fire against the besiegers. Also 'bulwark' in English.

bridgehead fort Small fortress at each end of a bridge, a type of fortification developed to block rivers against the Vikings in France in the 860s. Some use was made of fortified bridges in England from the 890s to the 920s. London Bridge was the greatest work of this type, defying attacks from the eleventh to the fifteenth centuries.

bulwark *See* **boulevard**.

burh Old English word for a walled, for-tified site, generally of earth and timber, from which the modern English 'bor-ough' is derived.

Cabaleros villanos 'Commoner knights'; frontier warriors in Reconquista Spain.

Capetian Dynasty of French kings which ruled 987-1328.

carroccio An ox-drawn wagon carrying the banner of an Italian city-state. Manned by priests and soldiers, it was placed in the centre of the army, as a command and rallying point. A similar device was also used by Flemish city forces, and by English forces at the Battle of the Standard (1138).

cat A type of siege engine used through-out medieval Europe, consisting of a mobile shed to protect miners or men operating other battering or boring engines at a siege.

castellan Literally, a man entrusted with the command of a castle. In late tenth-century France, castellans exercising the royal 'ban' established effectively inde-pendent lordships. The French king and princes began to reassert their power over such lords and their castles from the late eleventh century onwards.

Catharism A Christian dualist heresy, whose followers believed that the world was created by the Devil. Popular in south-western France, where it attracted considerable support from local princes around 1200, because its ascetic holy men and women (*perfecti*) seemed closer to the Christian ideal than the wealthy contemporary Church. It was crushed by the combined forces of the Inquisition and the Albigensian crusade.

chevauchée A mounted raid intended to destroy an enemy's resources, damage his prestige, and enrich the soldiers involved. A French term first encountered in twelfth-century sources, but a tactic central to warfare throughout the medieval period.

chiliarch A Greek term meaning 'com-mander of a thousand'. It was used loosely in tenth-century France, where it it simply meant a military leader. There was no regular division into military units of one thousand (with their sub-divisions of hundreds). The latin *legio* meaning 'legion' was similarly misused in tenth-century Germany, meaning no more than a unit of soldiers.

circumvallation Works surrounding a besieged fortress. Generally, from the eleventh century, individual siege castles ('bastilles') were built outside the gates. In the fifteenth century this could consist of a complete circuit of trenches, faggots, bundles of branches, and wooden mantlets (large screens) to protect gun-ners. Intended to cut off relief from out-side and protect the besieging army.

cog A high-sided vessel with square sails, clinker-built hull, flat bottom, and square stern, developed in the Baltic and capable of carrying 300-400 tons. Cogs were employed by German and Scandinavian towns and rulers as transports and warships from c.1150, and spread to the North Sea. Merchant vessels were easily adapted to warships by the addition of 'castles' (fighting platforms) to prow and stern.

commissariat General term for organization responsible for provisioning an army on campaign. Soldiers generally carried food for a few days in wagons and/or on pack horses. Commanders encouraged merchants to sell supplies at an army camp. This essential aspect of military command features rarely in medieval sources, but the necessity to supply an army was fully understood, and cutting off supplies was used as a defensive tactic. Richard I captured Cyprus (1191) as a safe source of supplies for the crusaders in Palestine.

condottieri Mercenaries employed by fourteenth- and fifteenth-century Italian city-states (for example, Florence, Pisa, Milan), serving under a contract called a *condotta*. They were recruited from all over Europe. *See* **White Company**.

coutiliers Servants of a fifteenth-century French or Burgundian man-at-arms, more lightly armoured, but able to fight as auxiliary cavalry with lances. Name derived from long, two-edged knife.

Danishmends Turkish dynasty in central and northern Asia Minor in the late eleventh century, nomadic and warlike, and committed to the idea of holy war against Christians.

Fatimids Caliphs and rulers of Egypt from 969 until overthrown by Saladin in 1171. They were of the minority, Shi'i form of Islam, and therefore bitter enemies of the majority Sunni form.

field army Mobile forces, as opposed to those in garrisons in castles and towns. Frequently, contingents from the latter were drawn on to reinforce field forces, especially in the crusader kingdom of Jerusalem.

flail-men Hussite troops carrying weapons based on the flail, an agricultural instrument used for threshing grain, consisting of two hinged pieces of wood.

flying bridge A bridge suspended from the top of a ship's mast used for assaulting coastal fortifications in crusading warfare, notably at the sieges of Constantinople in 1203 and 1204.

fodrum Theoretical right for German kings to claim food and lodging for himself and his following from anyone. Frederick Barbarossa gave up his right to

regalia (q.v.) from the Italian cities of the Lombard League in 1183 (Peace of Constance), but retained *fodrum* which was vital for provisioning his armies on expeditions to Italy.

forced march Abnormally rapid movement, travelling by night and day, to achieve surprise. For example, in February 1183 Richard I rode almost non-stop for two days and nights with a troop of cavalry; in 1471 the Lancastrian army covered almost 50 miles in 36 hours.

freebooters Soldiers owing allegiance to no lord, fighting on their own behalf; raiders, pirates.

gallo glach Heavily-armoured Irish foot soldiers. Tomb sculptures show their typical equipment to have been a round helmet, a mail cape (camail) over either mail coat or a knee-length, long-sleeved, padded leather coat (jack). They carried long, double-handed swords or axes, or shorter axes and spears. They formed the rearguard on the plundering raids which made up much of Irish warfare.

Golden Horde One of four successor states to the Mongol empire, ruled by antagonisitc branches of Chingiz Khan's dynasty, its khans dominated Russia after 1242. It was enfeebled by Timur-lenk's attacks around 1400, and it collapsed in 1502.

Grand Company/Great Companies The title of a combination of mercenary bands based in central-southern France in the 1350s and 1360s, fighting in the name of Edward III, then on their own account. There was also a Catalan 'Grand Company' in Greece 1304-11.

Greek fire An inflammable mixture made from a now-lost recipe originally known by the Byzantines and later used in the Islamic world and the west. The Greeks used syphons to squirt it at defences or enemy ships, otherwise it was hurled in clay pots which smashed on impact.

halberdiers Soldiers carrying pole-arms with blade or axe-shaped heads, swung in close combat. In the thirteenth and fourteenth centuries, the Swiss infantry were mainly armed with these fearsome weapons in their victories against the Austrians. The pike only became their main arm in the fifteenth century.

harry To lay waste, ravage, plunder. The normal behaviour of medieval armies, a combination of foraging, looting, and destructiveness.

hearth taxes A widely-used later medieval form of direct taxation based on family units (literally payable on each hearth or fireplace). For example, it was introduced in fourteenth-century France as the *fouage*, with differing rates of payment. In 1355 it was decreed that 100 hearths would pay for a man-at-arms and an archer.

hide An Anglo-Saxon measure of land used in southern and Midland England. Obligations to the crown, including military service and taxation, were performed at a certain ratio per *hide*. In eleventh- century England, an estate of 5 *hides* was required to provide a well-armed warrior for two months service.

hobilar A light horseman initially found in Ireland c.1300, employed on the borders of the English kingdom, and later under Edward III during the Hundred Years War in France.

Hospitallers The hospital of St John, a charitable foundation, assumed military functions in the mid-twelfth century. Most brothers were western knights, mainly French, who led a monastic life. Like the Templars, the Hospitallers acquired land in the west, and played an important role in defending the crusader states. They were later notable for their role in defending Rhodes and Malta against the Ottoman Turks.

host Employed by historians as an alternative to 'army', to avoid comparisons with modern standing armies. A host was a temporary gathering which might be as little as a few dozen warriors.

housecarl Member of a Scandinavian lord's military household; they are found in England after Cnut's conquest (1016) until 1066. Often identified as a unique standing army, they were identical to military households all princes maintained. Some became landowners in their own right.

Hussites Bohemians who followed the ideas of the Czech church reformer Jan Hus, who was burned for heresy at Constance in 1415, and were allied to Czech national fervour. Five crusades between 1420 and 1431 failed to crush the Hussites.

Il-Khanate One of four successor states to the Mongol empire, ruled by often antagonistic branches of Chingiz Khan's family. The Il-Khans were based in Iran, Iraq, and part of Asia Minor from 1256 until 1352, and converted to Islam.

invest To lay siege to a fortified place.

indenture Sealed contract specifying the terms of an agreement between a magnate and a knight or esquire. The latter might be retained for one campaign in return for wages, or for life, receiving an annual fee for service in war and in peace. The retainer brought his own followers with him.

iqta' A grant of land or revenues by an Islamic ruler to an individual. From the eleventh century, the most important iqta's were those held by emirs, who were required to bring military contingents with them when summoned.

Janisseries The *yeni áeri* ('New Troops' in Turkish), raised by the Ottomans in the mid-fourteenth century to provide their largely cavalry forces with reliable infantry. They gained a reputation for ferocity, and were the first Ottoman troops into Constantinople in 1453, when there were 12,000. They followed the Muslim pattern of elite slave-soldiers (like the Mamluks), and were recruited as children, often from the Balkans.

jihad Islamic holy war, the duty of Muslims to wage war on non-Muslims until they submit. In fact the obligation on rulers was frequently ignored. In the later twelfth century, Saladin invoked jihad as a force capable of uniting Muslims against the crusaders.

kern (s) Unarmoured Irish foot soldiers, ubiquitous in the medieval period and later. Often barefooted and bare-headed, they carried only a sword and several light javelins. Their main task was burning down houses and running off cattle, usually leading the beasts on ahead during a raid while the better-armed troops formed the rearguard. *See also* **gallo glach**.

Knights of Calatrava A monastic military order based at Calatrava in central Spain, set up around an existing crusading brotherhood (1158), owing to the Templars' and Hospitallers' reluctance to use resources in Spain. Until 1212, they held important frontier castles, and with the Order of Santiago formed the backbone of the advancing armies up to 1248. They were fragmented in 1288 by suspicious kings.

Knights of Dobrin Small monastic military order formed to convert the pagan Prussians. They had little success, and in the early thirteenth century were absorbed into the Teutonic Knights.

Knights of Santiago A monastic military order set up in Spain in 1170, whose history was very similar to that of the Knights of Calatrava.

Knights Templar The knights of the Order of the Templar, founded in 1128 for the protection of pilgrims on the route to the river Jordan, and later a potent military force on the boundaries of Christendom.

lager An encampment, made by drawing an army's baggage wagons into a circle/square. In the later Middle Ages, guns could be mounted on the wagons.

limes (Lat.) Literally, border or wall, hence a fortified frontier region or defensive works on a border, for example, Hadrian's Wall.

longship General term for warship of Viking design. Surviving examples are 16 to 28 metres long, and 2.7 to 4.5 metres broad. They had masts, and 24-50 oars, but their crews included a complement of warriors as well as oarsmen.

loricati Literally men with body armour (from the Latin, *loricum*) of uncertain form; it could be mail, strips of metal sewn to a garment, or a solid breastplate.

mangonel A torsion-powered stone-throwing siege-engine, with a vertical arm.

marches/marcher lords Any border region; after 1066, the Anglo-Norman lords of Wales and the neighbouring English border counties (the Marches) had legal privileges which included the right to wage private war.

men-at-arms Heavily-armoured soldiers trained to fight as cavalry, by the fourteenth century in addition to knights, these included lesser nobles, such as esquires and gentlemen.

milites armati Literally 'armoured soldiers', a term used to describe the heavy cavalry force established in tenth-century Germany by Henry I and his Ottonian successors, synonymous with *loricati* (q.v.). They were generally maintained by nobles (including bishops, a major source of royal troops in medieval Germany) and used to man border fortresses and for mobile operations in the field.

milites casati Used in tenth-century France to denote soldiers (knights) who were maintained in a lord's household by means of cash payment ('stipend') rather than by a grant of land.

mine Tunnel dug under the walls of a fortress by besiegers; when the supporting wooden props were burned, the tunnel collapsed, thus creating a breach in the wall above.

motte-and-bailey Type of castle frequently employed by Normans in England, Wales, and Ireland. The motte was a mound of earth surmounted by a tower, which was both a defence and a residence. The bailey was a linked enclosure surrounded by a ditch, an earth bank and a stockade of timber.

ost Literally 'host', used to mean service in a military expedition, therefore 'military service'.

Pale Region around Dublin heavily settled by the English after the late twelfth century, and by the fifteenth century the only region under the English king's rule. Origin of the phrase 'beyond the Pale', referring to the native Irish whom the English considered uncivilized and barbaric.

palisade A wall/stockade made from stout timber, for example, (split) tree trunks. Used particularly in wooden motte-and-bailey castles, temporary defences, and fifteenth-century anti-artillery bulwarks/boulevards (q.v.).

paria A form of protection money levied from Muslim Spain by the resurgent Christian kingdoms from the eleventh century onwards.

pavise A tall shield, usually rectangular, used to give a man complete protection from the twelfth to fifteenth centuries, especially at sieges. It was either propped up, so that a crossbowman or hand-gunner could reload behind it, or it was carried in front of assaulting troops. Richard I was shot in the shoulder (1199) when he looked around his pavise.

petrary Latin *petrariae*, a general term for any siege engines which used torsion or counter-weights to throw large stones against fortifications in sieges (see **mangonel, trebuchet**).

poleaxes A five-foot (1.5-m) long metal-bound shaft mounted with an axe-head to the front, hammer or spike to the rear, and spearhead, popular with dismounted men-at-arms in the fifteenth century. Developed to deliver crushing blows against plate armour, which could deflect swords and lances.

quarter Either, a division of a town (also ward) from which troops were raised in units, e.g. in the Flemish towns of Bruges and Ghent; or district in a town given over to foreigners, such as the Italian maritime powers in Constantinople, with certain rights of self-government.

ram A device for battering down walls or gates in a siege. A long beam suspended from a timber framework with a metal head (originally in a ram's-head form) with a pointed metal end, was swung against the defences. Rams could be covered with 'armoured roofs' or sheds to protect their wielders from the defenders' missiles.

regalia Sovereign rights reserved by kings, for example, lordship of towns, rights to mint coins, take tolls, hold markets, grant offices, and legal jurisdiction. German kings especially valued the financial advantages offered by their Italian *regalia*. Frederick I Barbarossa fought for more than twenty years to enforce his right to them from the economically advanced towns of north Italy, eventually giving them up in return for his right to *fodrum* (q.v.).

roundship A type of large, skeleton-built sailing cargo-vessel used by western powers in the Mediterranean from the mid-twelfth century, with a rounded hull (hence the name).

routiers The name used for bands of mercenary soldiers in twelfth- to fourteenth century Europe. The name seems to be derived from the Latin for route, indicating the semi-nomadic nature of the routiers who travelled to wherever there was work.

scara Frankish term for a fast-moving force, unencumbered by a baggage train, which could be raised at short notice, because often consisting of household troops which did not need to be summoned. Used especially for rapid response punishment raids against rebellious subjects in the eighth and ninth centuries.

schiltron Circular formations of infantry armed with long spears, employed in Scotland at the end of the thirteenth century in the wars of independence against the English.

shieldwall Infantry formation used by English and Vikings standing in close order, with their shields forming an unbroken front. It is a poetic term, and in practice warriors must have had room to throw spears, and to wield spears, swords, and axes. The strength of the shieldwall was its cohesion – when broken, it was doomed.

siege engine Any machine constructed to attack fortifications. Wooden siege engines were generally constructed on the spot, although they could be dismantled and carried around with an army. *See* **cat**, **mangonel**, **petrary**, **ram**, **siege tower**, **siege train**, **trebuchet**.

siege tower A tall wooden structure, often several storeys high, which could be wheeled up against a fortification. At the top level was a drawbridge which, when lowered, made it possible to cross to the walls. Also known as a 'belfry'.

siege train Siege engines, and later, gunpowder artillery, together with supporting services (wagons, forges, engineers, sappers, and raw materials) which could accompany an army on campaign in order to conduct sieges.

Sword Brothers Small monastic military order formed for the Baltic crusades. By 1230 they had conquered Livonia (approximately Latvia), but following defeat by pagan Lithuanians (1236) they were absorbed into the Teutonic Knights.

Taborites Extremist Hussites (q.v.) who built a new town in southern Bohemia named after the Biblical site of Mount Tabor. Although religious fervour made them especially ferocious fighters, their radicalism alienated moderate Hussites. They also had poor discipline and leadership, and suffered a number of defeats.

Taifa kingdoms Successor states to the Umayyad caliphate (756-1031) in Spain.

tarida (taride) Byzantine transport galley designed in the tenth century with ramps in the square stern for backing onto beaches to disembark horses; used in the Mediterranean.

Teutonic Knights A monastic military order founded in the Holy Land c.1190, invited to Poland where by 1250 it had established an independent Order state in Prussia. The papacy authorized a permanent state of crusade, augmented by visits from foreign knights to join raids against pagans, for example, the future Henry IV of England in 1391. In the fifteenth century, the Order was defeated by and lost territory to the Polish-Lithuanian state.

thegn Anglo-Saxon of noble status, of which there were different grades: a king's thegn was commended to the king, with lesser thegns as his men. Thegns could be members of the military households of kings, ealdormen, and earls, and/or landowners who could arm themselves.

tortoise A portable roofed shed used in sieges to shield besiegers from missiles dropped from the walls by the defenders; often employed to protect a ram, or sappers removing stones from the base of wall.

trebuchet A siege engine using manpower or a large weight to accelerate the throwing arm, with the missile placed in a long sling. It was used by the Muslims and was adopted in the west by c.1200. Trebuchets remained the most effective stone-throwing engines used in sieges until the first half of the fifteenth century.

Utraquists A group of moderate Hussites (q.v.) who were not as extreme in their opposition to Rome on theological grounds as other Hussites.

wagon-fort An ancient tactic used by steppe nomads who travelled in wagons, and drew them into a circle to form a defensive enclosure. During the Hussite Wars (1419-34), Jan Zizka mounted gunpowder weapons on them and created a new vogue in tactics. At the battle of the Herrings (1429), an English convoy in France was formed into a similar field fortification. In fifteenth-century Hungary, the cannon-mounting wagon-fort was used successfully against the Turks.

White Company A mercenary band in fourteenth-century Italy, famously commanded by the English *condottiere*, John Hawkwood.

Zirids A Muslim dynasty based in Tripoli and Tunisia (North Africa) from 972 to 1148.

FURTHER READING

INTRODUCTION

Chandler, D., *Atlas of Military Strategy* (London, 1980).
Cooper, J. (ed.), 'Early Medieval Warfare', *The Battle of Maldon: Fiction and Fact* (London, 1993).
Gillingham, J., *Richard Coeur de Lion: Kingship, Chivalry and War in the Twelfth Century* (London, 1994).
Howard, C., *Clausewitz* (Oxford, 1983).
Oman, M., *History of the Art of War in the Middle Ages* (revised ed. London, 1924, reprinted London, 1991).
Riley-Smith,J.(ed.), *The Atlas of the Crusades* (London, 1991).

I THE CRUCIBLE OF EUROPE

The wars of Charlemagne

France, J., 'The Military History of the Carolingian period', *Revue Belge d'Histoire militaire*, 26 (1985).
Ganshof, F.L., *Frankish Institutions under Charlemagne* (New York ed., 1970).
King, P.D., *Charlemagne: Translated Sources* (University of Lancaster, 1987).
Einhard and Notker the Stammerer. Two Lives of Charlemagne, trans. L. Thorpe (Harmondsworth, 1969).

The Vikings in the ninth century

Brooks, N.P., 'England in the Ninth Century: The Crucible of Defeat', *Transactions of the Royal Historical Society*, 5th ser., 29 (1979), pp.1-20.
Coupland, S. & Nelson, J.L., 'The Vikings on the Continent', *History Today* (December 1988), pp.12-19.
Keynes, S. & Lapidge, M.(trans.), *Alfred the Great. Asser's 'Life of King Alfred' and other Contemporary Sources* (Harmondsworth, 1983).
Nelson, J.L.(trans.), 'The Annals of St Bertin.' *Ninth-century histories*, vol.1 (Manchester, 1991).
Sawyer, P., *Kings and Vikings. Scandinavia and Europe* (London, 1982).

Tenth-century kingdoms: the growth of England, Germany, and France

England: *Anglo-Saxon Chronicle* in Whitelock, D. (ed.), *English Historical Documents vol.1, c.500-1042* (2nd ed., London, 1979), with other valuable sources.
Stenton, F.M., *Anglo-Saxon England* (3rd ed., Oxford, 1971).
Germany: Leyser, K., 'The Battle at the Lech, 955. A Study in Tenth-century Warfare', and 'Henry I and the Beginnings of the Saxon Empire', both reprinted in *Medieval Germany and its Neighbours 950-1200* (London, 1982).
Reuter, T., *Germany in the Early Middle Ages c.800-1056* (London, 1991).
France: France, J., 'La guerre dans lla France féodale a la fin du IXe siècle et au Xe siècle', *Revue Belge d'Histoire Militaire* (1979), pp.177-98.
Dunbabin, J., *France in the Making 843-1180* (Oxford, 1985).

The Danish Conquest of England 980-1016

Lawson, M.K., *Cnut* (London, 1993).
Scragg, D. (ed.), *The Battle of Maldon AD 991*(Oxford, 1991).
Anglo-Saxon Chronicle in Whitelock, D.(ed.), *English Historical Documents, vol.1, c.500-1042* (2nd ed. London, 1979), with other valuable sources.

II WESTERN EUROPE IN THE ELEVENTH TO THE THIRTEENTH CENTURIES

The Norman conquest of England

Brown, R.A., 'The Battle of Hastings', reprinted in Strickland, M., *Anglo-Norman Warfare. Studies in late Anglo-Saxon and Anglo-Norman Military Organisation and Warfare* (Woodbridge, 1992), pp.161-93.
Douglas, D.C., *William the Conqueror. The Norman Impact upon England* (London, 1964).
Gillingham, J.B., 'William the Bastard at War', reprinted in Strickland, M., *Anglo-Norman Warfare. Studies in late Anglo-Saxon and Anglo-Norman Military Organisation and Warfare* (Woodbridge, 1992), pp.143-160.
Morillo, S., *Warfare under the Anglo-Norman Kings* (Woodbridge, 1994).
Morillo, S., *The Battle of Hastings: Sources and Interpretations* (Ipswich, 1995) appeared too late to be used in this volume.

The Angevin empire 1154-1217

Gillingham, J.B., *Richard Coeur de Lion: Kingship, Chivalry and War in the Twelfth Century* (London, 1994) contains 'The Angevin empire' and 'Richard I and the Science of War in the Middle Ages'.
Gillingham, J.B., *Richard the Lionheart* (2nd ed., London, 1989).
Prestwick, J.O., 'Richard Coeur de Lion: Rex Bellicosus', in Nelson, J.L. (ed.), *Richard Coeur de Lion in History and Myth* (London, 1992).
Warren, W.L., *Henry II* (London, 1973).
Warren, W.L., *King John* (London, 1961).

The German empire under Frederick Barbarossa 1152-1190

Christiansen, E., *The Northern Crusades: The Baltic and the Catholic Frontier 1100-1525* (London, 1980).
Freising, Bishop Otto of, *The Deeds of Frederick Barbarossa*, trans. C.C. Mierow & C. Emery (Toronto, 1994).
Munz, P., *Frederick Barbarossa* (London, 1969).

Thirteenth-century eastern Europe and the Mongols

Morgan, D., *The Mongols* (Oxford, 1986).
Christiansen, E., *The Northern Crusades: The Baltic and the Catholic Frontier 1100-1525* (London, 1980).

Thirteenth-century English civil wars

Carpenter, D., *The Minority of Henry III* (London, 1990).
Carpenter, D., *The Battles of Lewes and Evesham 1264-65* (Keele, 1987).
Gillingham, J.B., 'War and Chivalry in the "History of William the Marshal"', reprinted in *Richard Coeur de Lion: Kingship, Chivalry and War in the Twelfth Century* (London, 1994).
Holt, J., *The Northerners. A Study in the Reign of King John* (Oxford, 1961).

England and the Celtic fringe: colonial warfare

Barrow, G.W.S., *Robert Bruce and the Community of the Realm of Scotland* (London, 1965).
Bartlett, R., *The Making of Europe. Conquest, Colonization and Cultural Change 950-1350* (Harmondsworth, 1993).
Kightly, C., *A Mirror of Medieval Wales. Gerald of Wales and his Journey of 1188* (Cadw: Welsh Historical Monuments, 1988).
Prestwich, M., *Edward I* (London, 1988).
Prestwich, M., *The Three Edwards. War and State in England 1272-1377* (London, 1980).
Strickland, M., 'Securing the North: Invasion and the Strategy of Defence in Twelfth-Century Anglo-Scottish Warfare', reprinted in Strickland, M., *Anglo-Norman Warfare. Studies in late Anglo-Saxon and Anglo-Norman Military Organisation and Warfare* (Woodbridge, 1992), pp.208-29.
Simms, K., *From Kings to Warlords* (Woodbridge, 1987).

III EXPANDING EUROPE: THE CRUSADES

The Reconquista and the Normans in the Mediterranean c.1050-1150

Matthew, D., *The Norman Kingdom of Sicily* (Cambridge, 1992).
Fletcher, R., *The Quest for El Cid* (New York, 1990).
MacKay, A., *Spain in the Middle Ages: From Frontier to Empire, 1000-1500* (London, 1987).

The First Crusade

France, J., *Victory in the East: A Military History of the First Crusade* (Cambridge, 1994).
Peters, E., ed., *The First Crusade. The Chronicle of Fulcher of Chartres and other Source Materials* (Philadelphia, 1971).
Riley-Smith, J.R. (ed.), *The Atlas of the Crusades* (London, 1991). Also useful for all other crusading chapters.

The Latin states in the Holy Land

Smail, R.C., *Crusading Warfare 1097-1193* (reprinted Oxford, 1994).
Rogers, R., *Latin Siege Warfare in the Twelfth Century* (Oxford, 1992).
Pryor, J.H., *Geography, Technology and War: Studies in the Maritime History of the Mediterranean 649-1571* (Cambridge, 1988).

The resurgence of Islam and the Third Crusade

Gillingham, J., *Richard the Lionheart* (London, 1989).
Gillingham, J., *Richard Coeur de Lion: Kingship, Chivalry and War in the Twelfth Century* (London, 1994), contains 'The Angevin Empire' and 'Richard I and the Science of War in the Middle Ages'.
Lyons, M.C. & Jackson, D.E.P., *Saladin: The Politics of Holy War* (Cambridge, 1982).

The Latin conquest of Constantinople 1202-1311

Queller, D., *The Fourth Crusade* (Leicester, 1978).
Bartusis, M.C., *The Late Byzantine Army* (Pennsylvania, 1992).
Villehardouin, Geoffrey de, *The Conquest of Constantinople*, trans. Shaw, M.R.B., Joinville and Villehardouin, *Chronicles of the Crusades* (Harmondsworth, 1963).
Goodenough, Lady, *The Chronicle of Muntaner*, 2 vols. (London, 1920-21).

The Spanish Reconquista and the Albigensian crusades

Burns, R.I., *The Crusader Kingdom of Valencia: Reconstruction of a Thirteenth-Century Frontier*, 2 vols. (Cambridge, Mass., 1967).
MacKay, A., *Spain in the Middle Ages: From Frontier to Empire, 1000-1500* (London, 1987).
Sumption, J., *The Albigensian Crusade* (London, 1978).

The crusade in Africa in the thirteenth century

Marshall, C., *Warfare in the Latin East 1192-1291* (Cambridge, 1992).
Powell, J.M., *The Anatomy of a Crusade 1213-21* (Pennsylvania, 1986).
Joinville, Jean de, *The Life of St Louis*, trans. Shaw, M.R.B., Joinville and Villehardouin, *Chronicles of the Crusades* (Harmondsworth, 1963).

IV EUROPE DIVIDED: THE FOURTEENTH AND FIFTEENTH CENTURIES

The Hundred Years' War 1337-1396

Curry, A., & Hughes, M.(eds.), *Arms, Armies and Fortifications in the Hundred Years War* (Woodbridge, 1994).
Hewitt, H.J., *The Black Prince's Expedition of 1355-57* (Manchester, 1958).
Hewitt, H.J., *The Organization of War under Edward III* (Manchester, 1966).
Prestwich, M., *The Three Edwards. War and State in England 1272-1377* (London, 1980).

Italy and the Mediterranean arena c.1350-1480

Mallett, M., *Mercenaries and their Masters: Warfare in Renaissance Italy* (London, 1974).
Waley, D., *The Italian City Republics* (London, 1969).

The Hundred Years' War: the fifteenth century

Allmand, C., *Henry V* (London, 1992).
Bennett, M., *Agincourt, 1415: Triumph against the Odds* (London, 1991).
Burne, A.H., *The Agincourt War* (London, 1956).
Curry, A., & Hughes, M.(eds.), *Arms, Armies and Fortifications in the Hundred Years War* (Woodbridge, 1994).
Pollard, A.J., *John Talbot and the War in France 1427-1453* (London, 1983).

The Hussite Wars and later crusades

Atiya, A.S., *The Crusade of Nicopolis* (London, 1934).
Heymann, F.G., *John Zizka and the Hussite Revolution* (Princeton, 1955).
Housley, N., *The Later Crusades 1274–1580: From Lyons to Alcazar* (Oxford, 1995).

The Wars of the Roses 1452–1487

Gillingham, J.B., *The Wars of the Roses* (London, 1981).
Goodman, A., *The Wars of the Roses. Military Activity and English Society, 1452-97* (London, 1981).

The army and campaigns of Charles the Bold of Burgundy c.1465–1477

Vaughan, R., *Charles the Bold* (London, 1973).

A military revolution?

Parker, G., *The Military Revolution. Military Innovation and the Rise of the West, 1500-1800* (Cambridge, 1988).
Parrot, D., 'The Military Revolution in early modern Europe', *History Today* (December 1992), pp.21-7.
Rogers, C.J., 'The Military Revolutions of the Hundred Years' War', *Journal of Military History*, 57 (1993), pp.241-78.
Vale, M.G.A., *War & Chivalry. Warfare and Aristocratic Culture in England, France and Burgundy at the End of the Middle Ages* (London, 1981).

THEORY AND PRACTICE OF MEDIEVAL WARFARE

General

Contamine, P., *War in the Middle Ages* (trans. of 1980 edition, Oxford, 1984).
Verbruggen, J.F., *The Art of Warfare in Western Europe in the Middle Ages* [from the eighth Century to 1340] (trans. of 1954 edition, Amsterdam, 1976).

Cavalry, chivalry and chevauchée

Strickland, M.(ed.), *Anglo-Norman Warfare* (Woodbridge, 1992). Contains reprints of Bennett, M., 'La Règle du Temple as a Military Manual, or How to Deliver a Cavalry Charge', Gillingham, J.B., on William I, Richard I and William the Marshal. For the latter, see also Crouch, D., *William Marshal. Court, Career and Chivalry in the Angevin Empire 1147-1219* (London, 1990). For later developments, Vale, M.G.A., *War & Chivalry. Warfare and Aristocratic Culture in England, France and Burgundy at the End of the Middle Ages* (London, 1981), especially chapter 4.
Keen, M., *Chivalry* (London, 1984).
Barber, R., & Barker, J., *Tournaments* (Woodbridge, 1989).

Infantry

Rogers, C.J., 'The Military Revolutions of the Hundred Years' War', *Journal of Military History*, 57 (1993), pp.241-78.

Mercenaries

Boussard, J., 'Les mercenaires au XIIe siècle. Henri Plantagenêt et les origines de l'armée de métier',

Bibliothèque de l'Ecole des Chartes, 106 (1946), pp.189-224.
Brown, S.D.B., 'Military Service and Monetary Reward in the Eleventh and Twelfth centuries', *History*, 74 (1989), pp.20-38.
Razso, G., 'The Mercenary Army of Matthias Corvinus', *From Hunyadi to Ráckózi: War and Society in late Medieval and Early Modern Hungary*, eds. J.K. Bak and B.K. Kíraly (USA, 1982), pp. 125-40.

Armour and Weapons

Bradbury, J., *The Medieval Archer* (Woodbridge, 1985).
Coupland, S., 'Carolingian Arms and Armour in the Ninth Century', *Viator*, 21 (1990), pp.29-50.
Nicolle, D.C., *Arms and Armour of the Crusading Era 1050-1350* (New York, 1988).
Peirce, I., 'The Knight, his Arms and Armour in the Eleventh and Twelfth Centuries', *The Ideals and Practice of Medieval Knighthood*, eds. Harper-Bill, C. & Harvey, R. (Woodbridge, 1986); 'The Development of the Medieval Sword, c.850-1300', *The Ideals and Practice of Medieval Knighthood*, III, eds. C. Harper-Bill & R. Harvey (Woodbridge, 1990).
Vale, M.G.A., *War & Chivalry. Warfare and Aristocratic Culture in England, France and Burgundy at the End of the Middle Ages* (London, 1981).

The impact of gunpowder on war and fortifications

De Vries, K., *Medieval Military Technology* (Peterborough, Ontario, 1992).
Rogers, C.J., 'The Military Revolutions of the Hundred Years' War', *Journal of Military History*, 57 (1993), pp.241-78.
Vale, M.G.A., *War & Chivalry. Warfare and Aristocratic Culture in England, France and Burgundy at the End of the Middle Ages* (London, 1981).

Siege techniques and fortresses

Bradbury, J., *The Medieval Siege* (Woodbridge, 1992).
Brown, R.A.(ed.), *Castles. A History and Guide* (Poole, 1980).
Rogers, R., *Latin Siege Warfare in the Twelfth Century* (Oxford, 1992).
Pryor, J.H., *Geography, Technology and War: Studies in the Maritime History of the Mediterranean 649-1571* (Cambridge, 1988).

Shipping and amphibious warfare

Gardiner, R.(ed.), *Cogs, Caravels and Galleons: The Sailing Ship 1000-1650* (London, 1994).
Gardiner, R.(ed.), *The Age of the Galley: Mediterranean Oared Vessels since Pre-Classical Times* [to c.1700] (London, 1995).
Pryor, J.H., *Geography, Technology and War: Studies in the Maritime History of the Mediterranean 649-1571* (Cambridge, 1988).

Military manuals and the laws of war

Bachrach, B.S., 'The Practical Use of Vegetius' De Re Militari during the early Middle Ages', *The Historian*, 47 (1985), pp.239-55.
Coopland, G.W., *The Tree of Battles of Honoré Bonet* (also Bovet), (Cambridge, Mass. 1949).

Keen, M.H., *The Laws of War in the late Middle Ages* (London, 1965).

Milner, N.P., *Vegetius: Epitome of Military Science* (Liverpool, 1993).

Upton-Ward, J.M., *The Rule of the Templars* (Woodbridge, 1992).

The reality of war

Contamine, P., *War in the Middle Ages* (trans. of 1980 edition, Oxford, 1984).

Thordeman, B., *Armour from the Battle of Wisby 1361* (Stockholm, 2 vols., 1939).

CHRONOLOGY

THIS TABLE REFLECTS the periods of warfare analysed in this volume. It is not intended to be comprehensive, and chronological gaps do not indicate lack of military activity. In most areas of western Europe low-level raiding was continuous, and there are also long-drawn out periods of conflict which have not been covered here.

FRANCE & BRITAIN	GERMANY, NORTH ITALY, SCANDINAVIA, EASTERN EUROPE	THE MEDITERRANEAN, SPAIN, SOUTH ITALY & CRUSADES
		711 Arab conquest of Spain begins
		717-18 Muslim siege of Constantinople
732/3 Franks defeat Arabs at Poitiers		
768 Charlemagne king of the Franks; conquest of Aquitaine	772 Charlemagne's first Saxon campaign	
	773-4 Charlemagne conquers Lombardy	
	776-85 Frankish conquest of Saxony	
		777 Frankish invasion of Spain
		778 Charlemagne's army defeated at Roncesvalles
		780 Charlemagne campaigns in Italy
		787 Charlemagne suppresses duke of Benevento
	788 Frankish takeover of Bavaria	
	789 Frankish campaign against Avars	
790s-840s Vikings active in Ireland and Irish Sea	795 Franks destroy Avar kingdom	
	800 Charlemagne crowned emperor in Rome	801 Frankish conquest of Barcelona
	804 final submission of Saxony to Charlemagne	
	808-10 Frankish conflict with Danes	
814 death of Charlemagne		c.813-c.915 period of serious Arab naval raids on coast of Tyrrhenian and Adriatic seas
		827 Arab conquest of Sicily begins
830-34 civil wars in Frankia		
835 Viking raids on Frankia begin		
840-3 civil wars in Frankia	841 Viking force granted base at mouth of Rhine	
843 division of Frankish empire	843 division of Frankish empire	
843-65 Viking attacks concentrate on West Frankish kingdom		844 first Viking raid on Spain; Seville sacked
	845 Vikings sack Hamburg	
		846 Arab pirates sack Rome
850-51 first Viking wintering in Britain		

FRANCE & BRITAIN		GERMANY, NORTH ITALY, SCANDINAVIA, EASTERN EUROPE		THE MEDITERRANEAN, SPAIN, SOUTH ITALY & CRUSADES	
				859	Vikings raid south-west Spain
866	Viking 'Great Army' in England	862	Magyar raid into Frankish Ostmark	866	Alfonso III king of Asturias; reigns to 910 and advances Christian border to the Douro.
871-99	Alfred king of Wessex	c.870	Iceland discovered by Vikings		
877	death of Charles the Bald			875	Byzantines capture Bari from the Muslims
879-92	Viking 'Great Army' in north Frankia; Alfred reorganizes West Saxon defences and militia	879-92	Viking 'Great Army' in north Frankia (France and Germany)	880	Byzantines recapture Taranto
885-86	Viking siege of Paris; Alfred captures London	891	Vikings defeated on the Dyle	885	Byzantines established in Calabria
892-96	Viking 'Great Army' returns to England, defeated by Alfred			894	Arnulf of Bavaria invades Italy
				896	Arnulf crowned emperor
899	Alfred succeeded by Edward			899	first Magyar invasion of Italy
				902	Muslims complete conquest of Sicily from Byzantines
				903	Muslims conquer Balearic Islands
		906	Magyars destroy Moravia		
		907	Magyars defeat Bavarians at Pressburg		
		908	Magyars defeat Franks and Thuringians		
911	beginning of Viking settlement in northern France (Normandy)	910	Magyars defeat East Franks at Augsburg	910	García, king of Asturias, transfers capital to León
914-20	West Saxon/Mercian conquest of Viking East Mercia	913	Swabians and Bavarians defeat Magyars		
		919	Henry of Saxony elected king of Germany		
924-39	Athelstan king of greater Wessex	924	Magyars invade Saxony	924	Magyars sack Pavia (capital of kingdom of Italy)
				925	Abd-al-Raman III transfers capital to Córdoba; Umayyads dominant in Spain
		928-29	Henry campaigns against Slavs		
		933	Henry defeats Magyars at Riade	934	Ramiro II of León defeats Umayyads at Simancas
		936	Otto I king of Germany		
		938-39	Magyar invasion, revolts against Otto in Bavaria and Saxony; Otto wins battles at Birten and Andernach	939	Ramiro II defeats Umayyads at Zamora
				942	Magyar raid on Constantinople bought off
				951	Otto I first invades Italy
954	Magyar invasion reaches France; West Saxon control of York/Northumbria completed	955	Otto I defeats Magyars at Lechfeld, Slavs at Recknitz		
		957-58	Saxon campaigns against Elbe Slavs		
				961-65	Otto I invades Italy again
				962	Otto I, king of Italy and emperor
				969	Fatimid conquest of Egypt
				966-72	Otto I's third invasion of Italy; defeats Muslims and Byzantines

FRANCE & BRITAIN	GERMANY, NORTH ITALY, SCANDINAVIA, EASTERN EUROPE	THE MEDITERRANEAN, SPAIN, SOUTH ITALY & CRUSADES
		969-72 Byzantine emperor John Zmisces at war with Prince Sviatoslav of Kiev
		970 Byzantine victory at Arcadiopolis
		971 Byzantine victory at Dorostalon
980 Viking raids on W. and S. England		981-2 Otto II campaigns in south Italy; defeated by Arabs at Cap Colonna
	982-83 Slavs and Danes rebel against German overlordship	982 failed Byzantine invasion of Sicily
987 end of Carolingian dynasty		
991-1006 Viking fleets plunder S. and S.E. England		
991-1016 renewed Viking attacks on England		
1009-12 Thorkell the Tall's army in southern England		1009-18 first use of Norman mercenaries in south Italy
1013-16 conquest of England by Swein and Cnut		
1016 final Danish victory at battle of Ashingdon	1026 Danish naval victory over Swedes at Stangebjerg	
	1028 Danish naval victory over Swedes and Norwegians at Helgeaa	
	1030 Olaf Haraldsson killed at battle of Stiklestad	
	1045 Magnus, king of Norway repels Slav invasion at Lysborg. Harald Hardrada, king of Norway, invades England and is killed at Stamford Bridge	1038-41 George Maniakes leads Byzantine invasion of Italy
1053-54 French-Angevin invasion of Normandy		1053 Normans of south Italy defeat Papal/German army at battle of Civitate
1057 second French-Angevin invasion of Normandy		1061 Normans begin conquest of Sicily
		1064 crusade against Barbastro, beginnings of Aragonese reconquest along Mediterranean coast of Spain
1066-71 Norman conquest of England		
1066 battles of Stamford Bridge and Hastings		
1069-70 Danish fleet in England; English revolts against Norman rule	1071-75 civil war in Germany	1071 Turks defeat Byzantine emperor at Manzikert (eastern Turkey)
	1077 excommunication of Henry IV by Pope Gregory VII starts century of strife in Germany and north Italy, between princes and kings	1081 Robert Guiscard invades Byzantine empire
	1081-85 Henry IV invades Italy	
		1082 Normans take Damascus
	1083 Henry IV captures Rome	
	1084 Pope Gregory VII captures Rome with support of Robert Guiscard	
1087 death of William of England and Normandy		1085 Christians capture Toledo; advance frontier in Spain to Tagus
		1090 Normans capture Malta and Gozo
		1091 Normans complete conquest of Sicily
		1094 El Cid captures Valencia, Spain
1095 Pope Urban II preaches the crusade at Clermont		1097 First Crusade reaches Constantinople
		1097-98 crusaders besiege Antioch

FRANCE & BRITAIN		GERMANY, NORTH ITALY, SCANDINAVIA, EASTERN EUROPE		THE MEDITERRANEAN, SPAIN, SOUTH ITALY & CRUSADES	
				1099	crusaders capture Jerusalem; defeat Egyptians at battle of Ascalon; Latin kingdom established
1106	Henry I of England defeats his brother Robert at Tinchebrai, conquers Normandy	1106	Henry V emperor		
		1107-10	Henry V campaigns successfully in Bohemia		
		1108	Henry V's failed invasion of Hungary		
		1109	Henry V's failed invasion of Poland		
1135-54	disputed succession and civil war in England				
1138	Scots defeated by English at battle of the Standard (Northallerton)				
1144	Geoffrey of Anjou conquers Normandy during civil war			1144	Muslims capture Edessa, first crusader principality to fall
		1146-48	Conrad III king of Germany participates in Second Crusade, north Germans & Scandinavians campaign against Slavs	1147-48	Second Crusade fails to capture Damascus
					French king Louis VII participates in Second Crusade
		1152	Frederick I 'Barbarossa' king of Germany		
		1153	Frederick invades Italy to secure royal resources; start of 30 year conflict		
1154	Geoffrey of Anjou's son becomes king Henry II of England				
		1155	Frederick I crowned emperor		
1169	English invade Ireland			1169	Saladin vizier of Egypt
1173-74	revolt by Henry II's sons accompanied by France, Flanders, and Scotland			1174	Saladin takes Damascus, encircling the crusader states
				1176	Turks defeat Byzantines at Myriocephalon
		1176	Frederick I defeated by Lombard League at Legnano	1179-85	Saladin brings Muslim Syria and Mosul under his control
		1180	Frederick I removes duke of Saxony		
		1183	compromise peace between Frederick I and Lombard cities	1187	Saladin defeats Latin army at Hattin; captures Jerusalem
1188-89	revolt by Henry II's sons supported by Philip II of France	1189	Frederick I goes on Third Crusade	1189	King Guy begins siege of Acre
		1190	Frederick I drowns in Asia Minor		
		1190-98	Henry VI attempts conquest of Sicily		
				1191	Philip of France and Richard I arrive in Outremer; Richard I captures Cyprus en route; capture of Acre; Philip II quits crusade
1192-94	Philip II captures Norman border fortresses while Richard I still on crusade			1191-92	Richard I makes two attempts on Jerusalem; rebuilds Christian fortresses destroyed by Saladin
1194-98	Richard I regains many fortresses in Normandy, Anjou/Berry, and Aquitaine				
1196-99	construction of Château Gaillard				
		1198	civil war in Germany		
1199	death of Richard I while suppressing revolt in Aquitaine				

FRANCE & BRITAIN		GERMANY, NORTH ITALY, SCANDINAVIA, EASTERN EUROPE		THE MEDITERRANEAN, SPAIN, SOUTH ITALY & CRUSADES	
1202	John surprises and captures Poitevin rebels at Mirebeau			1202-4	Fourth Crusade; 1204 crusaders capture Constantinople; establish Latin ('Frankish') Empire
1203-04	John loses Normandy, Maine and Anjou			1205	Bulgarians defeat Franks at Adrianople
1210	John in Ireland				
1210-26	Albigensian crusade				
1211	Simon de Montfort defeats Raymond count of Toulouse at St Martin-la-Lande			1212	Spanish Christian victory over Muslim Almohads at Las Navas de Tolosa
1213	battle of Muret: Albigensian crusaders defeat count of Toulouse and king of Aragon				
1214	Philip II defeats German/English army at battle of Bouvines; John fails to regain Normandy	1214	German-English army defeated by French at Bouvines		
1215	Toulouse surrenders to the French dauphin Louis				
1215-17	civil war in England				
				1217-21	Fifth Crusade; capture then loss of Damietta (Egypt)
				1220-22	first Mongol incursions
				1224	Byzantines drive Franks out of Asia Minor and Thessalonica
1226	crusade of Louis VIII completes the conquest of the south	1226-83	Teutonic Knights conquer Prussia		
				1228-29	Emperor Frederick II's crusade, Jerusalem restored to Christians
				1236	Castilians capture Córdoba
		1237-40	Mongols conquer southern Russia		
		1241	Mongol invasion reaches Hungary and Adriatic, German army destroyed at battle of Liegnitz; Mongols withdraw following death of Ögedei		
1242	Louis VIII of France defeats Henry III of England at Saintes and seizes most of Aquitaine	1242	Teutonic Knights defeated by Alexander Nevsky in the 'battle on the Ice' at Lake Chud		
		1244	Duke Swantopelk of Pomerania defeats Teutonic knights at Rensen	1244	Muslims capture Jerusalem
		1245	Swantopolk defeats the knights at Krücken		
				1248-50	crusade of Louis IX of France
				1250	Mamluks takes control in Egypt
		1254	Ottocar II (the Great) of Bohemia founds Königsberg	1255-60	Mongols campaign in Middle East
				1258	Mongols capture Baghdad
				1259	Byzantines of Nicaea defeat Latins of Constantinople at Pelagonia
		1260	Ottocar II defeats Bela IV of Hungary at Kressenbrunn Teutonic knights at Dilrben	1260	Mongols defeated by Mamluks at Ain Jalut; end of Mongol westward expansion
				1261	Byzantines recapture Constantinople from Latins
1264-5	civil war in England; 1264 battle of Lewes; 1265 battle of Evesham			1265-8	Jaffa, Beirut and Antioch taken by Mamluks

FRANCE & BRITAIN	GERMANY, NORTH ITALY, SCANDINAVIA, EASTERN EUROPE	THE MEDITERRANEAN, SPAIN, SOUTH ITALY & CRUSADES
		1266-8 Charles of Anjou conquers Sicily
		1270 Louis IX dies on crusade at Tunis
1277 Edward I's first Welsh campaign		
	1278 Rudolph I defeats and kills Ottocar II of Bohemia at the battle of the Marchfield	
1282-3 Edward I's conquest of Wales		**1282** Sicilian Vespers, Aragonese conquest of Sicily
1294-8 war between England and France over Gascony; 1294-95 Welsh revolt		**1291** Mamluks capture Acre, last crusader city in Outremer
1296-1304 Edward I's conquest of Scotland		
1302 Flemings defeat French at battle of Courtrai		**1303** Catalan Company employed by Byzantines
1305 Robert Bruce rebels against Edward I, start of Scottish civil war		**1305** Catalan Company conquers Thrace
1314 Edward II defeated by Scots at battle of Bannockburn		**1311** Catalan Company takes over Athens
1315 Scots attack English in Ireland	**1315** Swiss defeat Leopold duke of Austria at Mortgarten	
1324-26 war between England and France over Gascony		
1327 English recognize Scottish independence		
1333 Edward III defeats Scots at Halidon Hill (Berwick)		**1333** Byzantines pay tribute to Ottoman Turks
1337 war between England and France over Gascony – outbreak of the 'Hundred Years' War'	**1339** Swiss defeat a Burgundian invasion at Laupen	
1346 English victory over French at Crécy; Scottish invasion of England defeated; Henry of Lancaster campaigns successfully from Bordeaux		
1347 English capture Calais, gain bridgehead in France		
1347-50 Black Death	**1347-50** first wave of the Black Death sweeps Europe, eventually killing up to one-third of population	
	c.1353-75 mercenary Great Companies active in Italy	**1350** struggle between Venice and Genoa for predominance in Mediterranean regions
1356 Anglo-Gascon force defeats French near Poitiers; French king captured		**1354** Turks capture Gallipoli, first European conquest
1360 Treaty of Brétigny between England and France		
1369 renewal of Hundred Years' War		**1367** Anglo-French conflict renewed in Castile, English-backed Pedro defeats French-backed Henry at battle of Nájera
1369-81 French restrict English in France to Calais, Bordeaux, and Bayonne		**1369** Henry restored to Castilian throne; Castilian galley fleet aids French in Biscay and Channel
1372 English fleet destroyed by Franco-Castilian fleet off La Rochelle		

FRANCE & BRITAIN	GERMANY, NORTH ITALY, SCANDINAVIA, EASTERN EUROPE	THE MEDITERRANEAN, SPAIN, SOUTH ITALY & CRUSADES
		1371 Turks defeat Serbs at battle of river Marica
		1376-78 War of the Eight Saints between Papacy and Florence
1377-80 Franco-Castilian fleet raids south coast of England		
	1386 Swiss defeat Leopold III of Swabia at Sempach	1387 Ottomans capture Thessalonica, second city of the Byzantine empire, after 3-year siege
	1388 Swiss end their war against the Habsburgs with victory at Näfels	1389 Ottomans defeat Serbs at battle of Kosovo
1394 Richard II's first Irish campaign		1396 Burgundian-led crusade crushed at Nicopolis
1396 Truce of Leulinghen ends second phase of Hundred Years' War		
1399 Richard II's second Irish campaign		
1400-09 Welsh war of independence led by Owain Glendwr		
1412 English expedition intervenes in French civil war	1410 Polish-Lithuanian forces defeat the Teutonic knights at Tannenberg	1402 Ottomans defeated by Mongol Timur-lenk (Tamerlane)
1415 Henry V captures Harfleur and defeats French at Agincourt		1416 Venetian fleet defeats Ottomans of Gallipoli
1417-19 Henry V's conquest of Normandy		
1419-24 Scottish forces provide bulk of Charles VII's field army	1419-36 Hussite wars in Bohemia	
1420 Treaty of Troyes makes Henry V heir to French throne		
1421-22 Henry V campaigns around Paris		
1422 death of Henry V		
1424 Anglo-Burgundian army destroys Franco-Scottish army at Verneuil	1423 outbreak of thirty years' war between Milan and Florence	1424-26 Mamluk invasions of Cyprus end in failure
1429 Joan of Arc inspires French recovery; Charles VII crowned at Reims	1427 Hussite armies threaten to invade Germany	
1435 Burgundy defects from English alliance	1434 Hussite extremists defeated at battle of Lipany	
1440 Charles VII defeats nobles		
1442 French expedition to Gascony		1442-44 Mamluk attacks on Rhodes repulsed by the Hospitallers
1444 Anglo-French Truce of Tours	1444 Swiss attack French at St Jakob-de-Birs and are destroyed	1444 Ottomans defeat crusade of Varna
1448 French occupy Maine	1448 second battle of Kosovo, Turkish victory over Hunyadi of Hungary	
1449-50 English break truce; renewal of war leading to French conquest of Normandy		
1451 first French recovery of Gascony		
1451-53 war between city of Ghent and duke of Burgundy		
1453 final French recovery of Gascony; end of the 'Hundred Years' War'		1453 Ottomans capture Constantinople

FRANCE & BRITAIN	GERMANY, NORTH ITALY, SCANDINAVIA, EASTERN EUROPE	THE MEDITERRANEAN, SPAIN, SOUTH ITALY & CRUSADES
1455 first battle of St Albans		
1459-61 first period of 'Wars of the Roses'		
1465 War of the Common Weal, noble rebellion against French king		1460 Ottomans complete control of Peloponnese
1469-71 second period of 'Wars of the Roses'		
1471 battles of Barnet and Tewkesbury	1471 Swedes defeat Danes at battle of Brunkeberge in Norway	
	1474-75 Charles of Burgundy besieges Neuss	
1475 English invasion bought off by French; English let down by Burgundy	1475-77 Charles of Burgundy attempts conquest of Lorraine	
	1476 Swiss defeat Charles of Burgundy at Grandson and Murten	
	1477 Charles killed by Swiss at Nancy	
	1479 Maximilian Habsburg defeats Louis IX of France at Guinegate	1479 union of crowns of Aragon and Castile
		1480 Ottomans capture Otranto; siege of Rhodes fails
		1481 Spanish war against Muslim Granada begins
1483-87 third period in 'Wars of the Roses'		
1485 battle of Bosworth		
	1486 the Landsknechts created by Maximilian, based on Swiss infantry	
1492 English invasion of France bought off		1492 Christian conquest of Granada completed; end of Muslim rule in Spain

INDEX

ACKNOWLEDGEMENTS

Every effort has been made to obtain permission to use the copyright material listed below; the publishers apologise for any errors or omissions and would welcome these being brought to their attention.

The following abbreviations have been used:
AKG Lon: Archiv für Kunst und Geschichte, London
BL: British Library, London
BM: British Museum, London
Bridgeman: Bridgeman Art Library, London
ETA: E.T.Archive, London
AA&A: Ancient Art & Architecture, London
MB: Matthew Bennett
Mary Evans: Mary Evans Picture Library
NH: Nick Hooper
Royal Armouries: The Board of Trustees of the Royal Armouries, London
Wallace: The Trustees of the Wallace Collection, London (a national museum, admission free)

Half-title page Wallace; **title page** Wallace; **contents page** Wallace; **10-11** Stiftsbibliothek St Gallen; **12** *top* Musée Dauphinois de Grenoble; **12** *bottom* Stiftsbibliothek St Gallen/ETA; **16** Stiftsbibliothek St Gallen; **18** AA&A; **25** *top* Bridgeman; **25** *bottom* NH; **26** *top* NH; **26** *bottom* BL; **30** State Library Gottingen; **33** MB; **36** *bottom:* Aerofilms; **40-41** Tapisserie de Bayeux; **42** *top* Tapisserie de Bayeux; **42** *bottom* Tapisserie de Bayeux; **45** Tapisserie de Bayeux; **48** Aerofilms; **50** BL; **52** Mary Evans; **54** National Monuments Record, copyright Crown; **56** Biblioteca Apostolica Vaticana; **59** BL; **60** AKG Lon; **64** BL; **67** Skyscan Balloon Photography; **68** BL; **70** *top* ETA; **70** *bottom* Skyscan Balloon Photography; **72** Public Record Office; **79** ETA; **80-81** copyright Sonia Halliday; **82** NH; **86** BL; **88** copyright Sonia Halliday and Laura Lushington; **92** ETA; **96** *top* Bridgeman; **96** *bottom* Bridgeman; **102** Biblioteca Apostolica Vaticana; **106** Oronjoz; **110** copyright Sonia Halliday, photo by Jane Taylor; **116** ETA; **119** BL; **124** ETA; **126** Scala; **128** *top* BL; **128** *bottom* Royal Collection Enterprises; **133** graph based on statistics prepared by Anne Curry; graph designed by S.Brock; **140** BL; **147** BL; **155** Wallace; **158** NH; **159** *bottom left* copyright A. F. Kersting; **159** *top right* Royal Armouries; **160** *bottom left* Royal Armouries; **160** *top right* Wallace; **161** Wallace; **162** BL; **163** BL; **165** ETA; **166** BL; **167** *top* BL; **167** *bottom* BL.